# Quality Software Management

## Volume 4
## Anticipating Change

# Also Available from DORSET HOUSE PUBLISHING CO.

*Complete Systems Analysis: The Workbook, the Textbook, the Answers*
by James and Suzanne Robertson   foreword by Tom DeMarco
ISBN: 0-932633-25-0   Copyright ©1994   592 pages, 2 volumes, hardcover

*Exploring Requirements: Quality Before Design*
by Donald C. Gause and Gerald M. Weinberg
ISBN: 0-932633-13-7   Copyright ©1989   320 pages, hardcover

*Handbook of Walkthroughs, Inspections, and Technical Reviews*
by Daniel P. Freedman and Gerald M. Weinberg
ISBN: 0-932633-19-6   Copyright ©1990   464 pages, hardcover

*Managing Expectations: Working with People Who Want More, Better, Faster, Sooner, NOW!*   by Naomi Karten   foreword by Gerald M. Weinberg
ISBN: 0-932633-27-7   Copyright ©1994   240 pages, softcover

*Measuring and Managing Performance in Organizations*
by Robert D. Austin   foreword by Tom DeMarco and Timothy Lister
ISBN: 0-932633-36-6   Copyright ©1996   240 pages, softcover

*Peopleware: Productive Projects and Teams*   by Tom DeMarco and Timothy Lister
ISBN: 0-932633-05-6   Copyright ©1987   200 pages, softcover

*To Satisfy & Delight Your Customer: How to Manage for Customer Value*
by William J. Pardee   ISBN: 0-932633-35-8   Copyright ©1996   280 pages, hardcover

*Quality Software Management Series*   by Gerald M. Weinberg
> *Vol. 1: Systems Thinking*
> ISBN: 0-932633-22-6   Copyright ©1992   336 pages, hardcover
>
> *Vol. 2: First-Order Measurement*
> ISBN: 0-932633-24-2   Copyright ©1993   360 pages, hardcover
>
> *Vol. 3: Congruent Action*
> ISBN: 0-932633-28-5   Copyright ©1994   328 pages, hardcover

*Why Does Software Cost So Much? And Other Puzzles of the Information Age*
by Tom DeMarco   ISBN: 0-932633-34-X   Copyright ©1995   248 pages, softcover

## Find Out More about These and Other DH Books:

Contact us to request a Book & Video Catalog and a free issue of *The Dorset House Quarterly,* or to confirm price and shipping information.

DORSET HOUSE PUBLISHING CO., INC.
353 West 12th Street   New York, NY 10014   USA
1-800-DH-BOOKS   (1-800-342-6657)   212-620-4053   fax: 212-727-1044
e-mail: dhpubco@aol.com or dorsethouse@compuserve.com
http://www.dorsethouse.com

# Gerald M. Weinberg

# Quality Software Management

## Volume 4
## Anticipating Change

Dorset House Publishing
353 West 12th Street
New York, New York 10014

**Library of Congress Cataloging in Publication Data**
(Revised for volume 4)

Weinberg, Gerald M.
    Quality software management.

    Includes bibliographical references and indexes.
    Contents: v. 1. Systems thinking -- v. 2. First-
order measurement -- v. 3. Congruent action -- v. 4.
Anticipating change.
    1. Computer software--Development--Management.
2. Computer software--Quality control. I. Title.
QA76.76.D47W45  1991      005.1'068      91-18061
ISBN 0-932633-22-6 (v. 1)
ISBN 0-932633-24-2 (v. 2)
ISBN 0-932633-28-5 (v. 3)
ISBN 0-932633-32-3 (v. 4)

**Visit the Author on the World Wide Web: www.geraldmweinberg.com**

Cover Design: Dennis Stillwell, IMEX Exchange

Distributed in the English language in Singapore, the Philippines, and
Southeast Asia by Toppan Co., Ltd., Singapore and in the English language in
Japan by Toppan Co., Ltd., Tokyo, Japan.

Printed in the United States of America

Library of Congress Catalog Number: 91-18061

ISBN: 0-932633-32-3                    12  11  10  9  8  7  6  5  4  3  2

*At times, while reading this book, you may notice my
prejudice against* bad *managers.  I feel so strongly about
bad managers because I have seen the wonders that
good managers can accomplish.  Therefore, I think it
only appropriate to dedicate* Volume 4 *to my
Software Engineering Management Development Groups,
for teaching me so much about the management of
software engineering as it is truly practiced, and practiced well.*

# Acknowledgments

I'd like to acknowledge the important contributions of dozens of people to the improvement of this book, through reviews, discussions, demonstrations, experiments, and examples. Those who made specific contributions are acknowledged by name throughout the book, though I've disguised all people and clients from whom I've obtained confidential information. To give you some idea of who contributed, I offer these brief descriptions.

Wayne Bailey is a student of life who sometimes forgets that fact. He is also a process expert, and is considered an "essential resource" by his employer.

Richard Cohen is a self-employed consultant interested in helping software development teams work better. He is also a sysop in the CASE forum on CompuServe® where such issues are discussed regularly.

Michael Dedolph is a member of the technical staff at the Software Engineering Institute (SEI) who designs organizational evaluation methods and consults with organizations in the areas of software risk management and software process improvement. Prior to working at the SEI, Michael taught software engineering in the U.S. Air Force and worked on the development of large inventory management and real-time satellite communications systems for the Air Force.

Dale Emery lives in Maine and is a consultant on human and humane software process.

Phil Fuhrer is a distinguished architect and reviewer of communication systems.

Payson Hall is a California-based consulting systems engineer who divides his time between technical consulting on the design and architecture of client server software systems and working with clients to implement more effective technical project management methods. He also plays poker, but always breaks even.

Jim Highsmith, a principal of Knowledge Structures, Inc., teaches, consults, and learns in the areas of software quality process improvement, project management, and accelerated development techniques—when he's not in the Utah backcountry exploring canyons, skiing mountains, or climbing rock cliffs.

John Horne is a noted organizational consultant from Tempe, Arizona.

Naomi Karten, author of *Managing Expectations*,[1] has presented keynotes and seminars to more than 100,000 people in the U.S. and abroad on how to deliver superior service and build win-win relationships.

Norm Kerth is a consultant who has been helping companies change their software engineering practice for decades. He helps them apply the material in this book to do the hard stuff—introducing methodologies so they are used, objects so they are understood, quality assurance efforts so they are appreciated, and management practices so they are both humane and effective.

Izumi Kimura is a professor of computer science at the Tokyo Institute of Technology, and the translator of a number of my books.

Fredric Laurentine has worked on change at Sun Microsystems for ten years and has changed himself in the process.

Leonard Medal is an engineer and software developer for regional health-care institutions and a specialist in project requirements and team effectiveness.

Lynne Nix is the founder and president of Knowledge Structures, Inc., a firm dedicated to working with organizations to improve the competitiveness, quality, and timeliness of the software development process and to shorten the total product delivery cycle.

Judy Noe works with business people to help them build thoughtful business solutions that meet business needs and that foster healthy relationships at all levels of an organization.

Sue Petersen is an anthropologist-turned-programmer who lives in Oregon with her husband, two sons, and a whole passel of dogs, cats, horses, and various other wildlife. Although she giggles at the image of herself as a "cowgirl coder," she has learned the painful way to leave the cowboy stuff at the barn. She thinks discussion of database issues and debates about management and software analysis and design make scintillating dinner-party conversation.

Barbara Purchia has more than twenty years' experience developing high-quality software systems. She also has a solid background in software development and software development management, and four-plus years implementing successful corporate software process improvement programs. She currently is director of software engineering operations at Kronos, Inc.

James Robertson is a consultant, trainer, and coauthor of the outstanding book *Complete Systems Analysis.*[2]

David Robinson is a systems designer, project manager, and a terrific hiking buddy (not just because he teaches mountain rescue).

Dan Starr is a biker who supports his Harley habit by fooling around with, and sometimes even learning something about, the architecture, design, and people issues of telecommunications.

Eileen Strider is an outstanding consultant with heart, one of the most skillful executives I know, and someone who is always looking for ways to make organizations more human.

Wayne Strider is a powerful consultant and a masterful facilitator; he is superb at empowering individuals to change themselves and to create more fully human teams and organizations.

Dani Weinberg is a partner in Weinberg & Weinberg, an anthropologist, and a world authority on dogs and their managers.

Janice Wormington until recently was editor extraordinaire at Dorset House, and is the principal reason my books can be understood by normal human beings.

Gus Zimmerman is an extraordinary manager, creator of processes that improve the quality and cost of engineered products.

Other contributions—some necessarily anonymous—have come from change artists and others in my client organizations, as well as numerous participants in the Problem-Solving Leadership seminars, the Organizational Change Shop, the Quality Software Management seminars, the Software Engineering Management Development Group, and various CompuServe forums.

# Permissions
# Acknowledgments

# Contents

# Preface

*We do not know at this point if these [software process improvement] results are typical. We think the best way of interpreting these results is to view them as indicators of what is possible, given a supportive environment.*[1]

— J. Herbsleb *et al.*

This book is about creating a supportive environment for software engineering—an environment in which your organization can realize the impressive gains in quality and productivity reported by some clients of the Software Engineering Institute (SEI) and other process improvement organizations.

This is the fourth volume of a series. The earlier volumes tell what must be done, and this one describes how to create the environment in which to accomplish the necessary changes. If you haven't already read the other three volumes, reading this one should motivate you to read them. You may read in any order, but this volume ought to be read last, even if for a second time.[2]

The history of software engineering is riddled with failed attempts to realize gains in quality and productivity without first creating a supportive environment. To improve bad situations, many managers spend their money on CASE tools, CAST tools, CAD tools, methodologies, outsourcing, training, application packages, and what have you, but they rarely spend anything to improve or to remove the management that made those situations in the first place.

We have always been a would-be profession, and we will remain a would-be profession until we outgrow our obsession with quick fixes that don't involve fixing the managers themselves. Some of this obsession comes from those managers who simply see each job as a stepping-stone to a higher job.  Admiral Hyman Rickover talked about what's wrong with that type of manager or worker:

> When doing a job—any job—one must feel that he owns it, and act as though he will remain in that job forever.  He must look after his work just as conscientiously, as though it were his own business and his own money. . . . Too many spend their entire working lives looking for the next job.  When one feels he owns his present job and acts that way, he need have no concern about his next job.[3]

As managers, we accept the need to grow and develop—both ourselves as people as well as our organizations.  Don't be discouraged:  I know that we can grow and develop because I've seen hundreds of managers do just that.  Once they start to grow and develop, I've seen them succeed at the wonderful software engineering activities outlined in this book, just as you can.

What are those activities?  The first three volumes of this four-volume series deal with three fundamental abilities we need to do a quality job of managing software engineering:

1.  the ability to understand complex situations so we can plan a project and then observe and act so as to keep the project going according to plan, or modify the plan

2.  the ability to observe what's happening and to understand the significance of our observations in terms of effective adaptive actions

3.  the ability to act appropriately in difficult interpersonal situations, even though we may be confused, or angry, or so afraid we want to run away and hide

*Volume 4* treats the question of organizational change: how we can manage—using all the tools of the first three volumes—so as to transform our organization into an organization that not only understands and practices the concepts of good engineering now, but also that will understand and practice them in the future.  We call such an organization "Anticipating."

All organizations change, but the Anticipating organization is the one that makes organizational change an explicit and universal function.  An Anticipating culture has four characteristics that distinguish it from the Steering (Pattern 3) culture that precedes it:

1.  It has effective *models* that help it understand both organizational and personal change, intellectually and emotionally.

2.  A substantial percentage of its employees (not just its managers) are skilled *change artists,* who are supported by organizational practices in their efforts to lubricate the wheels of change.

3.   It routinely looks ahead and *plans* for organizational change, and it knows how to *follow through* on its plans with the aid of its change artists.

4.   It makes its planned changes on top of a *stable base* of sound software engineering practices that allow it to measure and predict.

The four Parts of this book cover each of these four characteristics of the Anticipating organization and how you can achieve them.

Capers Jones, the software author and researcher, tells us that the larger the project, the greater the chance of failure.[4] His observation applies to software projects, but changing your organization's quality culture is certainly a much bigger job than any software project your organization has ever attempted. That's why I've given the subject of organizational change a volume all its own. And that's why it's the last volume in the series, because if you are to succeed, you'll need to start with all the learnings from the first three.

To lead the change of your organization's culture, you'll need to become an outstanding software engineering manager, and nobody can do this simply by reading four volumes on the subject. Most chapters in these volumes recommend further reading, and you should follow these recommendations. Also, most chapters end with a Practice section, with suggestions for testing your learning in the heat of battle.

All told, you may find yourself reading at least forty volumes (not all at once!), to which these four may be considered a guide, and spending thousands of hours in practicing your learning. Still, this load doesn't seem unreasonable when you consider how many books you read and how many hours you practiced to become an outstanding software engineer. If you could do that, you should certainly be able to attain your new goal: to become no less than an outstanding software engineering manager, capable of leading the transformation of an entire organization.

*Bon voyage!*

# Part I
# Modeling How Change
# Really Happens

*It ain't what we know that gets us in trouble;*
*it's what we know that ain't so.*
                                                            — Will Rogers

*You'll never clear the water until you get the hogs out of the creek.*
                                                            — Mountain saying

When I speak of getting the hogs out of the creek, I'm not referring to bad *people*. I'm referring, instead, to bad *ideas*. As my friend Bunny Duhl, a family therapist, says to clients who complain about their upbringing, "Your parents weren't bad; they were just wrong."

Bringing up children is a dreadful time to have wrong ideas, but bringing up software can be even worse. Children are born with an inherent capacity for recovering from (some) mistakes in upbringing, but software is not so forgiving. Perhaps that's why some organizations spend more than 90 percent of their budgets on therapy (testing, fixing, and remedial maintenance).

Software managers don't just manage the upbringing of software. They also manage the upbringing of their software *organizations*. And bringing up a software *organization* often makes bringing up software seem effortless.

Ideas about software are frequently inaccurate; ideas about changing organizations are usually downright false and, even worse, misleading. Therefore, our first step at changing the water is to remove the hogs of fallacious reasoning about change itself.

1

# 1

# Some Familiar Change Models

*It is the business of the future to be dangerous. . . . The major advances in civilization are processes that all but wreck the societies in which they occur.*
— Alfred North Whitehead

As Whitehead suggests, change is inherently dangerous. Moreover, change becomes even more dangerous when we don't know what we're doing. Attempts to change software organizations commonly fail because of inadequate understanding of change dynamics—the same reason the organizations got into crisis in the first place. This chapter considers some of the commonly held models of change and how they affect our chances of successfully changing our organizations:

- the Diffusion Model, which says that change more or less happens
- the Hole-in-the-Floor Model, which says change is dropped on changees by planners upstairs
- the Newtonian Model, which introduces the concept of external motivation to change
- the Learning Curve Model, which considers the time needed to adapt to something new

## 1.1 The Diffusion Model

The simplest of all the change models is based on the belief that change just happens—it diffuses into the organization like dye diffuses into solution (Figure 1-1). This model is often held by Routine (Pattern 2) managers who don't understand or don't accept their responsibility for what happens.[1]

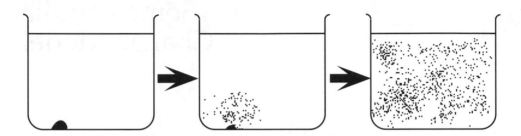

Figure 1-1.          The Diffusion Model of change is based on a chemical metaphor, as when a lump of dye dissolves in a beaker of water. Over time, the forces of nature distribute the dye more or less evenly throughout the entire beaker.

Like all the change models, the Diffusion Model contains some truth. In many instances, a change *seems* to appear throughout an organization without any specific management action. Perhaps the most striking instance of this effect in a software engineering organization is the diffusion of games and puzzles. One day everyone is playing the latest solitaire, then, as if by magic, a month later everyone is playing the latest adventure quest. Many managers envy the efficacy of games as self-propagated change, and wish they knew how to add this quality to, say, software tools or processes.

If diffusion is studied more closely, however, we find that it does have structure. A diagram of the organization will show that the diffusion follows lines of social contact (Figure 1-2), not just the official organization chart, but who talks to whom. An examination of which items diffuse and which don't will show, for example, that the design of the human interface has a great deal to do with the success of a software product's diffusion. High perceived value (of something) may provide pressure for diffusion through an organization, as if there is a flow in the beaker. Such pressure may increase the rate of diffusion in one direction or another. For instance, an examination of management policies will show why the diffusion of some changes is favored over others. A good example is the billing system for development work.

Suppose that the billing system says that building software tools is billable to customers, but working on software process development is not. In that case, managers will favor the diffusion of improved software tools and neglect the diffusion of improved processes. They'll only do this if they know about how the billing system treats this, and care about the company's financial results. Frequently, managers know these things and programmers don't, which creates hidden conflicts. The managers, if they are aware, have a variety of mechanisms to address this conflict—such as explaining the billing system or tying bonuses to billings—thus subtly influencing the diffusion.

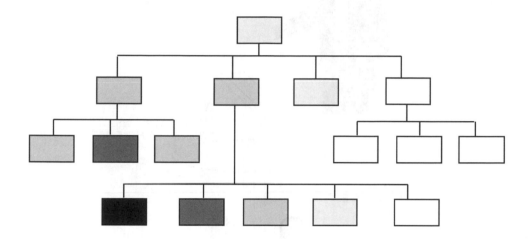

Figure 1-2.        Applied to an organization, the Diffusion Model shows gradual spreading of a rumor, an idea, a tool, or a process from one source. In practice, however, the spreading is not random, nor does it necessarily reach every part of the organization.

The same kind of favoring is built into the infrastructure. Diffusion is more likely among people in close geographic proximity, those working the same shift or project or van pool, or those using the same e-mail system. Thus, diffusion can be managed by controlling such variables.

Still, there are practical limits to the control we can exert over diffusion processes. For one thing, the diffusing object (or process) tends to change in unpredictable ways as it diffuses, degenerating like a message in the telephone game or improving through adaptations. For another, the rate of diffusion may be too slow for parts of the organization and too fast for others. And some more isolated parts of the organization may not ever be reached by diffusion.

In sum, the strength of the Diffusion Model is its attention to *change as a process*. The weakness of the model is the abdication of control over that process to passive, mysterious, "forces of nature."

## 1.2 The Hole-in-the-Floor Model

The Hole-in-the-Floor, or Engineering, Model has three steps, as shown in Figure 1-3.

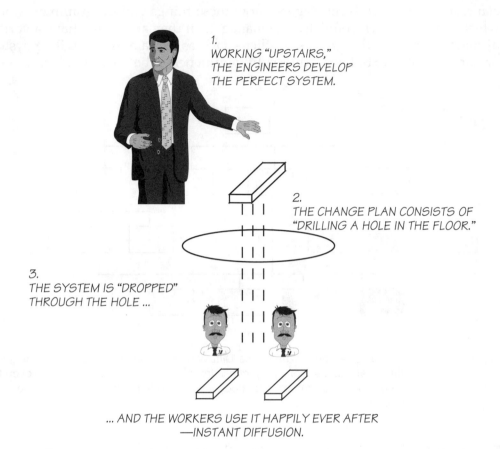

1.
WORKING "UPSTAIRS,"
THE ENGINEERS DEVELOP
THE PERFECT SYSTEM.

2.
THE CHANGE PLAN CONSISTS OF
"DRILLING A HOLE IN THE FLOOR."

3.
THE SYSTEM IS "DROPPED"
THROUGH THE HOLE ...

... AND THE WORKERS USE IT HAPPILY EVER AFTER
—INSTANT DIFFUSION.

Figure 1-3.          The Hole-in-the-Floor Model:  In the sophisticated version, the hole contains classes to teach the "targets" about the change, as if the only thing that could possibly obstruct the change plans was lack of understanding.

The Hole-in-the-Floor Model attempts to correct the weakness of the Diffusion Model by adding control of the change process.  This simplest of all the planned change models is based on the belief (or hope) that change just happens—which is similar to the Diffusion Model.  But in this model, change happens if and only if all preparations are right.  This model is often held by engineers, who believe that systems behave logically—meaning that everyone will undoubtedly recognize the beauty of their proposal and immediately accept the proposed change with great admiration for their genius.  Thus, the change will diffuse in an instant.  Usually, people who hold this model have never really thought about a change model, let alone observed many actual changes.

The Hole-in-the-Floor Model is implicitly based on several critical, and not very appealing, assumptions:

1. There are superior people and inferior people.

2. All design comes from above, that is, from the superior people.

3. There is no possibility of useful feedback from the inferior people.

4. No change is dropped through the hole until it is perfect.

5. There is no human contact needed between developer and user.

6. Sophistication in change means "carefully drilled holes," such as position papers, lecture presentations, documentation, course materials, help systems, and methodologies.

If asked directly, people who use this model may be unaware that they hold these assumptions. When trying to make changes, however, they act as if these false assumptions are true. Little wonder that their plans rarely succeed.

Nevertheless, if many people hold fast to a model, it's always a good idea to take a closer look at what might have confirmed it in their minds. For instance, the Hole-in-the-Floor Model can fit the data very neatly, if you look from a high enough level and sample at infrequent intervals. Figure 1-4, for example, shows how neatly it fits two data points: before and after.

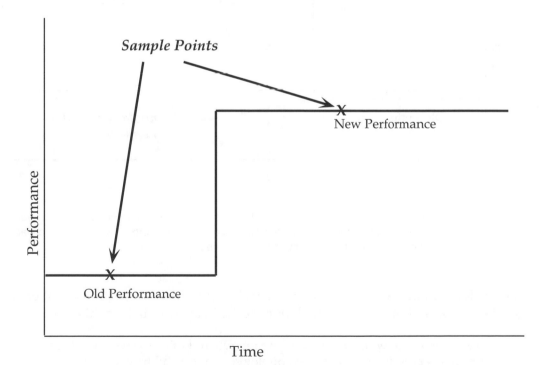

Figure 1-4.     The Hole-in-the-Floor Model fits the data well if you look from a high enough level and sample at infrequent intervals.

Who has such a high-level, infrequent view? One group is high-level executives. Another is people in a different department. A third is consultants. Tom Peters drops in and gives the troops a $50,000 pep talk. Two years later, Tom Peters drops in and checks up on how the troops are doing. Sure enough, performance has increased, and the model fits (the two points) perfectly.

To those who hold this model, the visit by Tom Peters (James Martin, Tom DeMarco, Jerry Weinberg, or whomever) is the *change intervention*. If the consultant is sufficiently technical, this act is called *technology transfer*. The people on the receiving end of the talk are called the *targets*. If the intervention is on target, the change takes place instantly. Presumably, nine hundred people stand up, leave the auditorium, return to their desks, and start producing at a new level of performance (Figure 1-5).

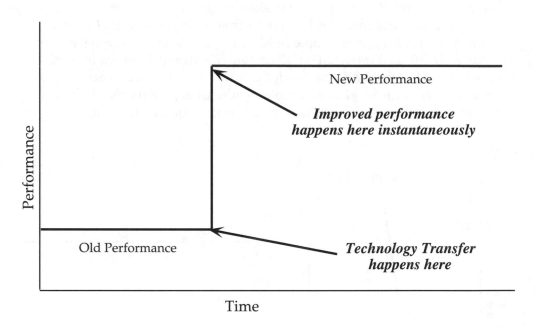

Figure 1-5.        The Hole-in-the-Floor Model implies that change is instantaneous and immediately reaches the ultimate performance level. Performance could be on any dimension, such as quality, speed, or cost.

Naomi Karten, an expert in customer service, provided me with a number of good examples of the Hole-in-the-Floor Model in action, such as this one:

> It reminds me of when a certain company where I once worked purchased its first systems development methodology. We were all trotted off to classes, and that was the extent of the change management. Thereafter, everyone was enormously creative in coming up with reasons why *their* project was an exception and they could bypass the process or skip some key steps.

Also interesting, . . . the customers (internal users) weren't informed of the purpose and impact of this new methodology, even though they were to be significantly affected by its use. One day we simply started showing up with additional forms that needed to be filled out and that seemed to them like just another harebrained scheme of IS designed to make their lives difficult. Who could blame them?

Sad thing is, management really thought they *were* managing change in this effort. That's even worse than being clueless.

Once people are given example after example like this, why in the world do they continue to believe in such an outrageous model? Well, once in a great while, changes do happen that way—if everything has been prepared in advance. There are a few instances when change *must* happen as close to this model as possible. Some years ago, for example, the Swedes changed their driving side of the road from left to right. The joke was that they should do it gradually over several weeks. Even with the most careful planning, there were some drivers who didn't make the change overnight, producing tragic consequences.

In software engineering, too, there will be times when we have to change the side of the road, though not nearly as many as some managers would have us believe. One example is changing the operating system on a mainframe. Obviously, it would be best if that could be done by just pulling the plug on the old system one night, but even in this case, it never works exactly like that. The old system is invariably kept around for those jobs that somehow don't work with the new. Over time—sometimes a very long time—the old system is phased out, not really matching the Hole-in-the-Floor Model.

Even when the model fails, the model's assumptions tend to shield true believers from feedback that might tell them what really happened. And, if some feedback happens to leak through, it's obviously coming from the "inferior people" (the targets). Thus, if the change does not work well, it's not because of the designers, but the inadequacies of the targets. If it does work well, of course, it's because of the brilliant designers.

To summarize, what's good in the Hole-in-the-Floor Model is the emphasis on *planning*. What's weak in the model, however, is that the planning leaves out so many essential factors, most notably, the most important factor: the *human* factor.

## 1.3 The Newtonian Model

One simple-minded way to introduce the human factor to the hole-in-the-floor types is by using the Motivational Model—which we could also call the Newtonian Model. The Newtonian Model is named after Isaac Newton's famous laws of motion, the first of which says that

Force = Mass x Acceleration

By a little algebra, we get

$$\text{Acceleration} = \frac{\text{Force}}{\text{Mass}}$$

Acceleration is the rate at which things change position, and mass measures the size of an object. Thus, we can rewrite the formula:

$$\text{Rate of Change} = \frac{\text{Force}}{\text{Size}}$$

Since *force* is defined as "how hard we try to change something," this formula can be pictured as in Figure 1-6, or written in plain language as

**The bigger the system you want to change, the harder you must push.**

**The faster the change you want, the harder you must push.**

Also, force and acceleration are vectors, which means they have *direction* as well as magnitude. Therefore, the model implies that

**To change in a certain direction, you must push in that direction.**

For example, if we want people to finish a project faster, we push them by paying them for working overtime. This might work, but it might boomerang. People may become tired and less productive. They may make more mistakes, which cost more time to remove. Thus, pushing in the direction of more work in a shorter time may produce exactly the opposite of the desired change.[2]

In short, the Newtonians believe that what is missing in the Hole-in-the-Floor Model is the push. In this respect, the Newtonian Model does recognize that people have a choice in what they do, and that their choice can be influenced (by pushing them) as part of the change process. Typical pushes include offering bonuses, threatening loss of jobs, or rewarding with challenging assignments.

People espousing this model frequently ignore another lesson from Newton:

**Push works both ways.**

The force in Newton's equation is "the sum of *unbalanced* forces." Many changes are set up to fail because the forces pushing for them are overbalanced by other forces that push against them.

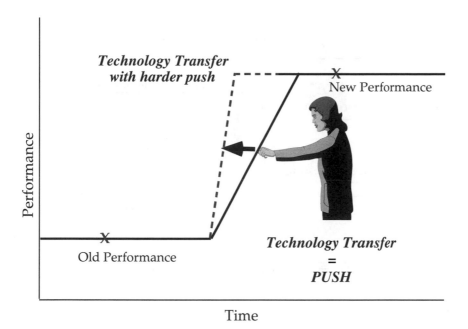

Figure 1-6.        The Newtonian Model predicts that change happens faster when you push
                   harder. Like the Hole-in-the-Floor Model, it fits the few data points available to
                   executives and consultants.

By taking unbalanced forces into account, we can produce an improvement of
the simple Newtonian Model, or what social psychologists call *force field analysis*,
a widely used method of change planning invented by the social psychologist Kurt Lewin. Lewin's method is based on listing all forces for change on
one side of a diagram, and against change on the other, then looking for ways
of shifting the balance. Figure 1-7 shows such a diagram developed for an
attempt to change to a more automated testing system, with forces on the left
tending to favor the change, and forces on the right tending to maintain the
status quo.

The force field analysis suggests several strategies for shifting the balance
of forces:

-   Enlist the service desk people in converting databases, as they will
    reap many of the benefits of the change.
-   Subsidize the new tools out of a separate budget, so as not to penalize those who had invested in tools previously.
-   Relieve schedules for projects taking place during the switch.
-   Allow an increase in the training budget for testers.

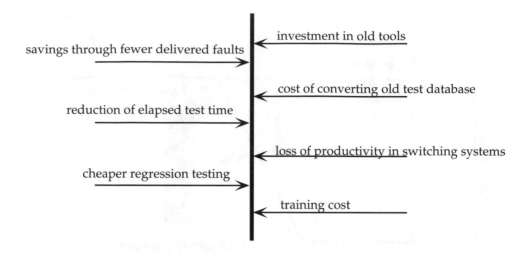

Figure 1-7.        A force field analysis diagram showing the balance of forces in an attempt to change a system of testing.

Unfortunately for the Newtonians, people are not nearly as simple as the Newtonian Model implies. If you observe real people reacting to various pushes, you'll see all sorts of reactions:

- When you push in one direction, people may move in the opposite direction.
- When you push harder, people may move less easily.
- When you push in one direction, people may move in a totally unexpected direction.
- When you push less, people may move more easily.
- When you push too fast, they may shatter—like glass when it is struck, rather than pushed.

It's not surprising that managers who try to control change using a Newtonian Model are often rewarded with a boomerang in the back.

To summarize, the strength of the Newtonian Model is the explicit introduction of the human element in the form of motivation. What's weak about it is the totally inadequate model of humanity that's used: that people can be pushed around like billiard balls.

## 1.4  The Learning Curve Model

Psychologists added sophistication to the Newtonian Model by observing that when change is first introduced, people aren't usually able to respond like a billiard ball with instant efficiency. Moreover, once they do respond, it takes time to learn to respond as well as the planners would hope, and thus to realize the intended benefits of the change. Thus, response to change takes place along a characteristic curve shown in Figure 1-8.

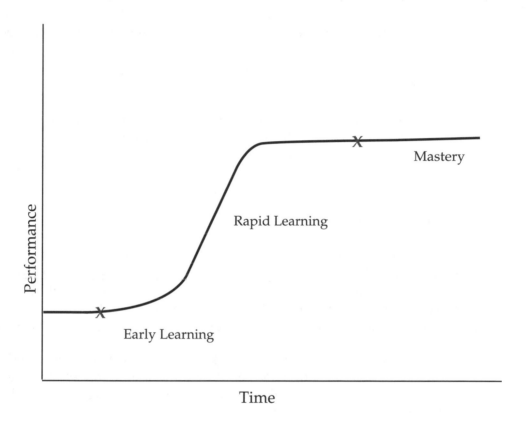

Figure 1-8.    The Learning Curve Model predicts that change happens along a curve characteristic of the people making the change. The curve is obtained by averaging performance over many individuals, and thus may smooth out significant individual variations.

A curve of this shape is often called a *learning curve*, and the model says that all change follows some sort of learning curve. Moreover, the actual values of the curve are affected by a number of psychological factors, such as relevant skill, motivation, and aptitude. This suggests the possibility of influencing the course of the change by personnel selection and training, which certainly represents a step up in realism from the Newtonian Model.

The Learning Curve Model is quite useful for predicting the time scale of large-scale change, but it doesn't go far enough as a practical tool for managing change person-by-person in a real organization. The shortcomings of this model probably arise from its derivation. The typical learning curve is not, in fact, a picture of how an individual person learns. Nor is it an example of how an organization learns. Instead, it is an average picture of the learning of many individuals, usually college freshmen taking a psychology class.

Even so, wouldn't such an average picture be useful in organizational work, where large numbers of people are involved? Can't such an average be useful in planning? An average can be useful—if all the people are doing the same simple task. Unfortunately, in changing the way an entire software culture operates, there are many tasks—not all the same, and definitely not all simple.

In sum, the strength of the Learning Curve Model is its *incorporation of the adaptive human element* in change. The weakness is the averaging out of details of individual human beings. To control change more effectively, we will need a model that knows more about how real, individual human beings respond to possible changes. That's the topic of Chapter 2.

## 1.5 Helpful Hints and Suggestions

1.   You can perform a more sophisticated version of force field analysis by using diagrams of effects.[3] Using this technique, you can surpass the simple linearities implied by force field analysis and notice both positive and negative feedback loops—loops that often produce counterintuitive systemic responses to attempts to change a system.

2.   Wayne Bailey points out: Systems thinking is not always the most efficient way to address a change problem. Usually, simple models are okay in suitably simple situations. For example, linear thinking may be adequate if both

   a.   the time span is short, and
   b.   the number of steps involved is few.

   However, if you start to plan a change with a linear model and then notice that either

   a.   the time span is growing beyond what you planned, or
   b.   the number of steps involved is increasing beyond what you planned,

   then you'd better revisit your assumptions.

3. Michael Dedolph suggests: Many variants of these models exist. Here are a few that are taught at the SEI in the Managing Technological Change course:

   1. Add a desired state to the Newtonian Model or Hole-in-the-Floor Model, as a line on the graph. For example, you now have 10 lines of code (LOC) per day during coding, and the new tool is supposed to give 20 LOC (the goal). After implementation, you have only 14 LOC. The desired state line shows that improvements often fall short of (or potentially exceed) goals.

   2. To the Newtonian Model, add a state where productivity decreases immediately after introduction of the change—which says it is normal to step backward before making progress.

   3. Add descriptions of the people to the Learning Curve Model—for example, pioneers, early adapters, late adapters. This shows that change corresponds to technology life cycles and also points out that different people may be at different points in adaptation to something new, so strategies have to accommodate these differences.

Each of these variants is incorporated in the Satir Change Model, which I discuss in Chapter 2. The existence of so many variants, often patched on to the fundamental model, shows that the models are under some strain from the reality of the situation, but they also show how hard people are trying to understand change.

## 1.6 Summary

✔ Attempts to change software organizations commonly fail because of inadequate models of change dynamics.

✔ The Diffusion Model is the simplest of all the change models and is based on the belief that change just happens by diffusing into the organization like dye diffuses into solution.

✔ A slightly more sophisticated view of the Diffusion Model recognizes that the diffusion of a change does have structure. If we control the variables in this structure, we can manage diffusion to a limited extent.

✔ The strength of the Diffusion Model is its attention to *change as a process*. The weakness is the abdication of control over that process to forces of nature.

✔ The Hole-in-the-Floor, or Engineering, Model attempts to correct the weakness of the Diffusion Model by adding control of the change process. This control involves three steps:

1. Working upstairs, the engineers develop the perfect system.

2. The change plan consists of drilling a hole in the floor.

3. The system is dropped through the hole, and the workers use it happily ever after: instant diffusion.

✔ The Hole-in-the-Floor Model is based on a number of false assumptions about the nature of people, but often fits the data on change if viewed from a sufficiently high level. Those few times when we must change the side of the road, we need to try to make change approximate the Hole-in-the-Floor Model as closely as possible.

✔ The strength of the Hole-in-the-Floor Model is the emphasis on *planning*. What's weak in the model is that the planning leaves out so many essential factors, most notably the *human* factor.

✔ The Newtonian Model (or Motivational Model) introduces the concept of external motivation to change, and says

• The bigger the system you want to change, the harder you must push.
• The faster the change you want, the harder you must push.
• To change in a certain direction, you must push in that direction.

✔ The Newtonian Model does recognize that people have a choice in what they do, and that their choice can be influenced by pushing them as part of the change process. It fails to recognize that people are not nearly as simple as the Newtonian Model implies, so that pushing often produces a boomerang effect.

✔ One useful refinement of the simple Newtonian Model is what social psychologists call force field analysis, a method that is based on listing all forces for change on one side of a diagram and against change on the other, then looking for ways of shifting the balance.

✔ The strength of the Newtonian Model is the explicit introduction of the human element in the form of motivation. Its weakness is the totally inadequate model of humanity that's used: that people can be pushed around like billiard balls.

✔   The Learning Curve Model recognizes that people aren't billiard balls, and that people are usually unable to respond to change attempts like a billiard ball with instant efficiency. Moreover, it takes time to learn to respond as well as the planners would hope.

✔   The Learning Curve Model suggests the possibility of influencing the course of the change by personnel selection and training, and it is quite useful for large-scale planning. However, it fails as a practical tool for managing cultural change person-by-person in a real organization.

✔   The strength of the Learning Curve Model is its *incorporation of the adaptive human element* in change. The weakness is the averaging out of details of individual human beings.

### 1.7 Practice

1.  Give at least one example from your experience of each of the following:

    •   Management pushes in one direction; workers move in the opposite direction.
    •   Management pushes harder; workers move less easily.
    •   Management pushes in one direction; workers move in a totally unexpected direction.
    •   Management pushes less; workers move more easily.
    •   Management pushes too quickly; workers shatter.

2.  Norm Kerth suggests: Think of a successful change you have witnessed. How did the actual change differ from the process described by each of these models? Hint: Think about how specific individuals reacted to the change.

3.  Sue Petersen contributes: Think of an actual change you are planning or are in the midst of implementing. What model is closest to the one you are following? Why? What changes can you make to *yourself* that might help the change go faster, easier, and/or more successfully?

4.  As suggested by Janice Wormington and Gus Zimmerman: Think of an unsuccessful change that you've either experienced personally or heard about from a colleague. What was the underlying change model used in attempting this change? To paraphrase Whitehead, how did it all but wreck the "society" in which it occurred? In hindsight, what could have been done differently?

5.    Eileen Strider asks:  What can a high-level executive do to protect herself from the dangers of too distant and infrequent views of the actual process of change?

6.    Phil Fuhrer suggests:  In force field analysis, it is important that the forces are considered with their viewpoint.  In the example given in this chapter, do the field support people value fewer errors and hence less work? What are some of the other viewpoints involved?

# 2

# The Satir Change Model

*If your heart is a volcano,*
*how shall you expect*
*flowers to bloom*
*in your hands?*
— Kahlil Gibran

The Learning Curve Model is an *averaging* model. If you ask people to describe major changes they've experienced, they will tell you many things that simply don't appear in the Learning Curve Model. They may sketch a learning curve like Figure 1-8, but most of their attention and energies will be concerned with their emotional reactions to the change. Time after time, it's these emotional reactions that seem to confound the change planners, because they lack a place for them in all of their models discussed in Chapter 1. To manage change effectively, you must understand precisely those emotional reactions that the other change models exclude, because human systems do not change unless the individuals change, one at a time.

## 2.1 Overview of the Model

One of the cornerstones of the family therapist Virginia Satir's work was her model of how change takes place.[1] The Satir Change Model is a very general model that applies to individuals as well as systems of individuals. The model describes four major stages of change, the transitions between stages, as well as "meta-change" (changing the way change takes place). It describes how each stage of change feels, how it affects thought processes and bodily functions. It also suggests what kinds of interventions are appropriate in each stage, a subject which runs through this entire book, starting in Chapter 3.

I have found the insights from this model essential to the successful transformation of software organizations to cultures that are capable of producing higher-quality software, cheaper and faster. I take what is useful from all the other models, but the Satir Change Model is, for me, by far the most useful. I find that my clients can relate directly to the model, and they are able to use it to analyze contemplated courses of action.

The Satir Change Model says that change takes place in four major stages, called

1.    Late Status Quo (or Old Status Quo, as it is called when it is *very* late)

2.    Chaos

3.    Integration and Practice (or sometimes just Integration, for short)

4.    New Status Quo

The model also describes a higher level of change, or meta-change, which involves changing the way we change. It describes what kinds of interventions are helpful, and which are harmful, in each stage. The model also describes how different personalities, or temperaments, respond to the various stages, and to change in general. It accounts for different kinds of information feedback during change processes, as well as different levels of performance (Figure 2-1).

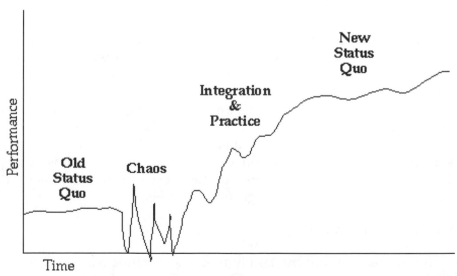

Figure 2-1.      The Satir Change Model shows how performance changes in four different stages of change.

Let's start examining the Satir Change Model by sketching the four stages. Because the model says that change is an unending series of cycles, we can start anywhere. We'll begin with the stage in which everything seems all right: Late Status Quo.

## 2.2 Stage 1: Late Status Quo

In this stage, the system (either an individual or a group) has developed a set of predictions and expectations. Indeed, Late Status Quo represents a kind of success; it is the logical outcome of a series of attempts to get all the outputs of the system under control.

In Late Status Quo, everything is familiar and in balance, but as Figure 2-2 suggests, that balance may require various parts of the system to have an unequal role in maintaining that balance. The question to ask during Late Status Quo is, "What is each part paying to keep up this state of affairs?"

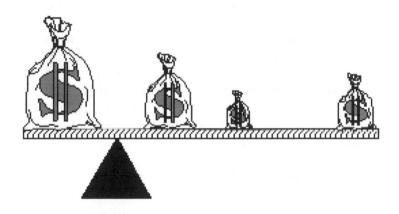

Figure 2-2.      The Late Status Quo stage of the Satir Change Model is characterized by a balance, but a balance in which the various parts are paying different prices to maintain it.

In Late Status Quo, the cost each part is paying is demonstrated by the symptoms that part is displaying in its state of unhealth. Recognizing the Late Status Quo stage is important in software quality dynamics because it always precedes the so-called crisis. The Satir Change Model recognizes that the crisis is not a sudden event, but merely the sudden realization that things have been very unhealthy for a long time.

There are many familiar examples of Late Status Quo, both in everyday life and in software projects. Here are a few:

- ❏ An individual has a bad heart and smokes two packs a day, but plays racquetball intensively once a week to compensate.
- ❏ A family has an alcoholic father who abuses his wife and children, but when sober he is super-loving and buys them expensive gifts.
- ❏ A software company has outgrown its obsolete building that would be expensive to replace, though the environment is lowering productivity.
- ❏ A software development team supports three low-performing members by everyone else doing a bit extra and nobody saying anything about it.
- ❏ A twelve-year-old inventory system is under extensive and growing maintenance, but nobody thinks about it.
- ❏ A software product development team has evolved over a period of eight years, and really can no longer produce anything innovative.

You can recognize the Late Status Quo stage by both personal and organizational symptoms. People may be experiencing anxiety, generalized nervousness, and gastrointestinal problems. Constipation is a perfect metaphor for the over-control that characterizes Late Status Quo.

In the constipated organization, it seems impossible to get anything new accomplished. There is no sense of creativity, no sense of innovation. Absenteeism creeps up for no apparent reason. People don't feel good, but have a difficult time locating any specific cause for their ailments. The most important sign that the system is in Late Status Quo is denial: the inability or unwillingness to recognize all the other symptoms, or to attach enough significance to them to warrant doing anything.

### 2.2.1 Upsetting the Balance: The Foreign Element

Systems stay in Late Status Quo until something happens that the people in the system can no longer deny. Satir calls this "something" the *foreign element*. The new element may be from inside or outside the organization, but it is always outside in the sense that it is part of the randomness that is always outside the scope of the system's controller and upsets the balance (Figure 2-3). I'll never forget one manager on a desperately troubled project who got the news that a key employee had quit, gotten married, and left the country. He stared disbelievingly for a long moment, then muttered, "She *can't* do that. It's not part of my plan." That was a foreign element.

The system cannot simply ignore the foreign element, though it may try. The system usually tries to expel the foreign element and return to Late Status Quo, because, as Satir says,

**Familiarity is always more powerful than comfort.**

All too often, the system succeeds in getting back to the old, uncomfortable stage, and remains in Late Status Quo until another foreign element arrives.[2]

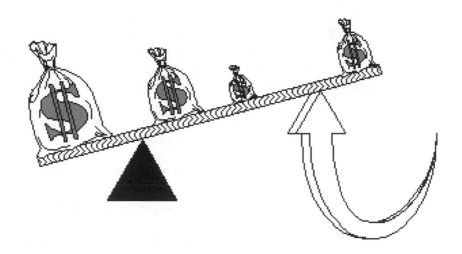

Figure 2-3.        The foreign element comes from outside and upsets the balance of the Late
                   Status Quo stage.

Here are a few examples of foreign elements:

❑    The individual has chest pains when playing racquetball.
❑    The alcoholic father crashes the car and kills two pedestrians.
❑    Rats get into the software company's obsolete building and chew on
     the removable disks that store the entire library archive.
❑    A critical team member on the software development team resigns or
     is promoted, leaving an inadequate team to perform all the work.
❑    An audit reveals that there are $23 million in parts missing from the
     twelve-year-old inventory system.
❑    A competitor announces an innovative software product, and the
     software product development team has no idea how to respond.

You can recognize the foreign element by the way people become protective
and defensive. They look and feel tight, which can be seen in their tight and
shallow breathing. Their senses tend to be diminished, so they don't see or
hear things they usually notice.

At the organizational level, the foreign element may be the only thing that
arouses any kind of new activity. If you examine the content of the activity,
however, you'll see that most of it is simply an attempt to expel the foreign element. One approach is to tighten internal controls: Issue lots of memos about
locking doors and filling out forms correctly; hold oppressive meetings about
getting to work on time or reducing expenses; mandate more frequent and
detailed status reporting.

Another approach to expelling the foreign element is to waste a great deal of time and emotional energy doing studies to figure out "How did we get here?" rather than "Where are we? What next?" Yet another is to attack the outside world, which is seen as the source of the trouble: Appeal for government assistance, or sue somebody. The one thing you *never* hear is, "Oh, my, that's a clear indication we'll have to change something about the way we do our daily business."

Many of the foreign elements experienced by parts of an organization are introduced by misguided management actions, such as

- The development manager adds another project to a group that is already overloaded.
- Upper management takes away a critical resource but refuses to extend a schedule.
- In order to help an exhausted team catch up, managers increase the length of the required work week.

To complicate a difficult management problem even when managers are making a sensible attempt to change the Late Status Quo organization, their interventions are frequently seen by workers as foreign elements. These workers genuinely feel that such management moves are a threat to the continued existence of the organization, and that they must deny or defer or deflect them in order to ensure the safety of the organization. Such interventions from on high, these people believe, show that management doesn't really understand what it takes to run this organization *as it has always run.* Sometimes, however, what management wants to do is run a *different* organization, so naturally the interventions will be seen as a threat to the Old Status Quo.

## 2.3 Stage 2: Chaos

Sometimes, management, after experiencing these denials or deferrals or deflections, simply gives up trying to intervene. Eventually, however, some foreign element cannot be denied, deferred, or deflected, and someone acknowledges that the emperor is naked. With this recognition, the system (individual or group) becomes disarranged and the system goes into Stage 2: Chaos (Figure 2-4).

In Chaos, old predictions no longer work. Old expectations are not fulfilled. As feared, the Old Status Quo system has been disrupted. People try random behavior, or try reverting to even earlier behavior patterns, perhaps from childhood. They desperately seek sweeping, magical solutions, because they are operating with reduced sensing and thinking ability.

**Chaos is definitely not the time to make long-term decisions.**

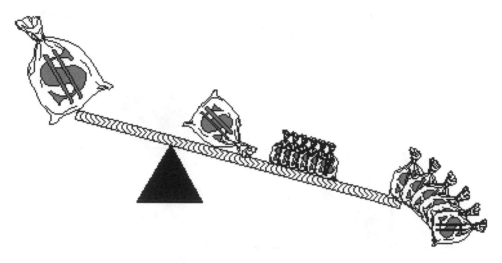

Figure 2-4.        In the Chaos stage, the old balance is gone, and nothing works the way it
                   used to.

It may not be easy for people in Chaos to acknowledge it's happening to them, but it's easy to spot examples of Chaos in *other* people (Figure 2-5):

❏    The individual starts playing racquetball left-handed, and only with certain opponents.

❏    Mother breaks down into sobbing fits.  Junior, age 9, starts sucking his thumb and wetting his bed.

❏    People start losing their office keys, jamming the vending machines, spilling copier toner, and generally not functioning.

❏    The software team surges into violent conflicts, followed by sudden and total withdrawal.

❏    Everyone bypasses the inventory system, going directly to the parts bins to take what they need.

❏    The old reliable software product starts crashing and producing bizarre responses after minor maintenance.  People don't show up at meetings or answer messages.

People in Chaos may be shaky, dizzy, or off balance, and they generally suffer problems of the central nervous system, such as tics, nail-biting, and mysterious rashes.  Back, head, and neck problems are common.

(If you want to experience a very mild, but very clear, form of Chaos, clasp your hands with your fingers interlaced.  Notice how comfortable that feels, and whether the right or left thumb is underneath.  Then reclasp your hands with the thumbs reversed.  The tiny odd feeling you experience is an example of Chaos.  Now imagine this magnified by a thousand or a million, and you will have some idea of what it feels like when, for example, somebody hears that his or her job is being eliminated.)

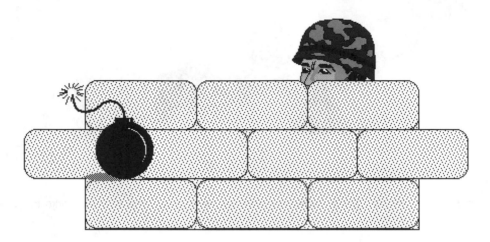

Figure 2-5.        People in a system that's in Chaos feel crazy. They are afraid and vulnerable. Their old survival fears are aroused, and they become extremely defensive and alienated.

In the chaotic organization, awareness and effectiveness may oscillate between high and practically zero. People encounter people they've never seen before, and functions they never knew existed. Some startling new ideas may emerge, but if they work at all, they only work for a short time.

### 2.4  Stage 3:  Integration and Practice

Eventually, one of these new ideas seems to rise above the noise of Chaos and people see the beginning of a new possibility. This is the *transforming idea*—the "Aha!" that can change everything and, with sufficient practice, can lead toward a new integration. Just as the foreign element marks the beginning of the Chaos stage, the transforming idea marks the beginning of its end.

The transforming idea often arrives with the feeling described in the biblical phrase "the scales fell from my eyes," or the relief that arrives when the chiropractor realigns your spine. It is often seen as a new birth or a honeymoon. Chaotic feelings disappear, and in moments of apparently clear vision, everything looks like it's going to be solved, perhaps by turning old ways upside down (Figure 2-6).

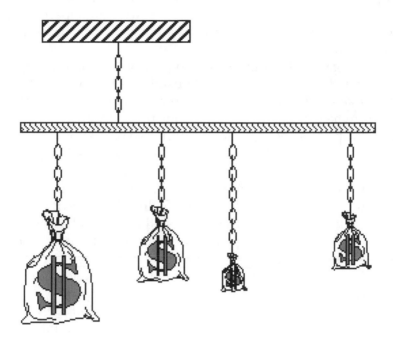

Figure 2-6.        In the Integration stage, everything feels like it will be solved, often by turning
                   old ways upside down (as this diagram shows by inverting the balanced beam
                   from resting on a fulcrum to hanging from the ceiling).

However, the moments of clarity are often replaced by old feelings of doubt, as
feelings swing back and forth, albeit much more slowly and smoothly than
during Chaos.  For example,

❑      The individual with the bad heart gives up smoking and racquetball
       and starts walking four miles a day.
❑      The alcoholic father completes one dry week at the treatment center.
❑      A new building is announced, and planning sessions begin.
❑      A new, popular leader takes over the software development team.
❑      A design team visualizes an entirely different design approach for
       the inventory system, which starts by rearranging the stock layout.
❑      The company purchases a new software tool to assist in software
       development, the first such tool ever purchased from outside the
       company.  It also purchases training to go with the new tool, and
       actually provides time for people to attend.

Some people describe the Integration stage as one in which they "feel like schoolchildren." They feel young, and giddy with anticipation, but they also experience a slight feeling of background anxiety, as if the good feeling will go away as mysteriously as it came.

People feel good, although unable to control the good feeling. To regain a sense of control, they often try to create fixed points to which they can anchor the feelings, like making a committee into a permanent team. They are easily disappointed when things don't work out perfectly the first time, and they need much support, although they may not seek it explicitly. Absenteeism diminishes, as nobody wants to miss a day because something new might happen.

A major component of the good feeling is the "Aha!" rush that often comes with the transforming idea. This feeling is so terrific, it's no wonder many people believe that *this* is the change—that all you have to do is have the right idea and the change takes place automatically. But this Hole-in-the-Floor Model belief cannot be correct, because the rush often accompanies other ideas: ideas that don't work out. If they don't work out, you go right back into Chaos, perhaps more discouraged than before.

The memory of this rush is so strong, however, that the work of *integrating* the transforming idea is often forgotten. Yet it's in the integration that we have the most control over the success or failure of the change process. Here is where we can create an environment that encourages *practice*—the opportunity to perfect a good idea, or to reject one that turns out to be bad—rather than demand immediate perfection as if we hold to the Hole-in-the-Floor Model. Or, if we hold to some form of the Newtonian Model, this is where we will push, rather than support. The Learning Curve Model, on the other hand, supports the proper kind of activity in this stage: appropriate training plus time and safety to enhance the application of learning.

## 2.5 Stage 4: New Status Quo

Successful Integration and Practice eventually leads to a New Status Quo stage. Unfamiliar things become familiar, and a new set of expectations and predictions evolves (Figure 2-7).

In general, things are getting a little better every day, as we can see by these examples:

❑ The individual with the bad heart discovers how much he enjoys walking, and how many creative ideas he gets about work problems while he walks through the neighborhood.

❑ The alcoholic father returns to work at a new job, and the mother joins a volunteer group that gets her out of the house four days a week.

- ❏  The new building is well into its shakedown period, and people have posted new signs and pictures in their offices.
- ❏  All members of the software development team have found ways to contribute, and appreciate one another.
- ❏  The new inventory system has located most of the missing parts, and has solved other problems that people weren't even aware they had.
- ❏  Everyone is using the new design tool. Almost weekly, someone discovers a new way to use a feature and shares it with other designers.

As the transformation is integrated and the New Status Quo stage develops, people are calm, their posture and breathing improve, and their senses are alert so that they notice little things. They feel balanced and have a sense of accomplishment. They may feel a bit awkward, but rather enjoy the feeling because it is part of their new consciousness and deepening awareness of themselves and their surroundings.

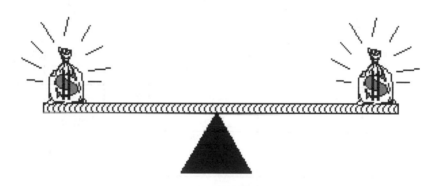

Figure 2-7.    As the integrating proceeds, a new balance—a New Status Quo—begins to emerge, which is much more efficient and more sparkling than the Old Status Quo stage.

The organization itself is seen as less of an obstacle and more of an opportunity. People may even decide that management is not completely stupid. But, unless we take charge of the change process, the newness of the status quo wears off, and we drift toward another Old Status Quo stage.

## 2.6  Helpful Hints and Suggestions

1.  Colleagues have suggested a relationship between the four stages of the Satir Change Model and four kinds of competence, or skillfulness. Table 2-1 shows one possibility, courtesy of my colleagues Norm Kerth, Fredric

Laurentine, Lynne Nix, and Gus Zimmerman, although they don't all agree on the precise mapping between the two models:

Table 2-1.
A Popular Model of Consciousness and Competence
Fitted to the Satir Change Model.

| Stage in the Change Model | Consciousness/ Competence | Description | Example |
|---|---|---|---|
| Late Status Quo | Unconsciously Incompetent | You don't know that you are making mistakes, but think you know what you're doing. | Ask five-year-olds if they can drive a car. They'll say yes. |
| Chaos | Consciously Incompetent | You're very aware that you don't know what you're doing, and you're bothered by that knowledge. | What happens when you're first learning to drive and your instructor tells you to tap the brake lightly. |
| Practice and Integration | Unconsciously Competent | You know what you're doing, but still think you're incompetent because you're very aware of small mistakes. | Driving your first car and not having any problems. How long did it take before driving became secondary to the travel? |
| New Status Quo | Consciously Competent | You know, and are aware of what you know. | You know you are a good driver, and you notice what you're doing that prevents accidents. |
| Transition from New to Old Status Quo | Unconsciously Competent | You are still competent, but no longer do things with awareness. You thus become vulnerable to incompetence if the environment should change—because you won't notice. | You don't notice that you're growing older and your reaction times have changed. You now have anti-lock brakes, but you still pump them. |

This model suggests why the Routine (Pattern 2) culture tends to be unstable.[3] When things become routine, people start to lose awareness: "That's just the way we do things around here." They are on their way to an Old Status Quo, from which they are vulnerable to any environmental change. Anticipating (Pattern 4) cultures avoid this trap; Steering (Pattern 3) cultures may or may not avoid it.

2.   Fredric Laurentine explains how he uses this model to help him manage new employees:

> I explain that aptitude with the model will get them through the steps faster.  For example, not only am I conscious of the fact that I am an incompetent software developer, but I have learned to infer that I make mistakes that I am unaware of.  While learning software programs, I make a rapid progression through the four steps.
>
> I also explain that by providing feedback, I will move them out of unconscious incompetence rapidly, and this will aid their learning process.  For example, one of my new managers—being unfamiliar with local norms (when to leave voice mail versus when to make contact)—had ticked off a fellow manager.  I explained that he was causing a problem and didn't know it, but that was to be expected of a new manager. Now, however, he needed to learn.

3.   Dale Emery writes about how the Satir Change Model is related to the standard plot model that shows up in almost every Hollywood movie:

> First, the protagonist and the setting are introduced.  In a two-hour movie, this lasts for about thirty minutes.  The introduction includes a description of a flaw in the protagonist.  Then "Plot Point 1" happens.  Something happens to throw the protagonist's world into Chaos.  For about an hour, the protagonist tries one thing after another to overcome the flaw, but fails to deal with the problem.  The protagonist nearly gives up.  Then "Plot Point 2" happens (at ninety minutes into the film).  This is when the protagonist either corrects the flaw or finds a way to turn it into a strength.  The protagonist tries something new, and it works, and everyone lives happily ever after and gets an Oscar.
>
> I noticed today that this fits Virginia Satir's Change Model, with one pretty important difference.  Plot Point 1 is the foreign element.  Before that is the Old Status Quo, and after that is Chaos.  Plot Point 2 is the transforming idea. The last three minutes of the movie (and everything that happens after we leave the theater) is the New Status Quo.
>
> The difference is that the movies leave out the Integration and Practice phase of the change model.  In the movies, the protagonist gets the transforming idea, tries it once, and it works! That's cheating, isn't it?

Perhaps the reason people don't pay enough attention to the need for practice is that we've been exposed to too many movies.

4.   Sue Petersen notes: "It is probably impossible to maintain conscious competence in *every* part of your life, though it still strikes me, a perfectionist,

as something that I *should* be striving for. When I'm having trouble in one area (work, family, or hobby), I focus on that trouble spot and become unconsciously competent (or worse) in the rest of life. There is no such thing as 'perfect balance'—there is always going to be waver in the system. As I get better at balance, the waver becomes smaller—but it never disappears. It remains to cushion me against the truly unexpected event from the environment."

5.    As pointed out by Payson Hall: One of the reasons that changing a culture is so difficult is that everything is connected to everything else. Thus, a transforming idea in one area can easily become a foreign element to another. For instance, if the architects introduce a new design method, the project managers find that their previous estimating parameters no longer correctly predict how long a project will remain in various stages, and the software testing group is surprised to discover a different distribution of faults.

## 2.7 Summary

✔  To manage change effectively, you must understand emotional reactions. Virginia Satir's model of how change takes place applies to individuals as well as to systems of individuals, and definitely incorporates the emotional factor.

✔  The Satir Change Model says that change takes place in four major stages, called

1.    Late Status Quo (or Old Status Quo, as it is called when it is *very* late)

2.    Chaos

3.    Integration and Practice (or sometimes just Integration, for short)

4.    New Status Quo

The model also describes a higher level of change, or meta-change, which involves changing the way we change.

✔  The Late Status Quo stage occurs as the logical outcome of a series of attempts to get all the outputs of the system under control. Everything is familiar and in balance, but various parts of the system have an unequal role in maintaining that balance.

✔  The Late Status Quo stage is a state of unhealth that always precedes the
    so-called crisis.  The Satir Change Model recognizes that the crisis is not a
    sudden event, but merely the sudden realization that things have been
    very unhealthy for a long time.

✔  In Late Status Quo, people may be experiencing anxiety, generalized ner-
    vousness, and gastrointestinal problems.  Constipation is a perfect
    metaphor for the over-control that characterizes Late Status Quo, where
    there is no sense of creativity, of innovation.  The most important sign that
    the system is in Late Status Quo is denial: the inability or unwillingness to
    recognize all the other symptoms, or to attach enough significance to
    them to warrant doing anything.

✔  Systems stay in Late Status Quo until something happens that the people
    in the systems can no longer deny, a condition Satir calls the *foreign ele-
    ment*.  The system usually tries—often successfully—to expel the foreign
    element and to return to Late Status Quo because familiarity is always
    more powerful than comfort.

✔  When a foreign element arrives, people become protective and defensive.
    Still, the foreign element may be the only thing that arouses any kind of
    new activity, but most of that is simply trying to expel the foreign ele-
    ment.

✔  Eventually, some foreign element cannot be denied or deferred or deflect-
    ed, and the system goes into Chaos, where old predictions no longer
    work.  The Old Status Quo system has been disrupted.

✔  People try random behavior and desperately seek sweeping, magical
    solutions in order to restore the Old Status Quo.  It may not be easy for
    people in Chaos to acknowledge it's happening to them.  They feel
    crazy, afraid, and vulnerable; and they become extremely defensive and
    alienated.

✔  When in Chaos, people encounter people they've never seen before, and
    functions they never knew existed.  Some startling new ideas may
    emerge, but if they work at all, they only work for a short time.

✔  Eventually, one of these new ideas seems a real possibility.  This is the
    transforming idea—the "Aha!" that starts the Integration and Practice
    phase.  Chaotic feelings disappear, and during moments of apparent clari-
    ty, everything looks like it will be solved.  However, the moments of clari-
    ty are often replaced by old feelings of doubt, as feelings swing back and
    forth.

✔  During Integration and Practice, people feel good, but feel unable to control the good feeling. They are easily disappointed when things don't work out perfectly the first time, and need much support, although they may not seek it explicitly.

✔  A major component of the good feeling is the "Aha!" rush that often comes with the transforming idea. The memory of this rush is so strong, however, that the practice needed to integrate the transforming idea is often forgotten.

✔  Successful practice eventually leads to a New Status Quo stage. Unfamiliar things become familiar, and a new set of expectations and predictions evolves. People are calm, balanced, and have a sense of accomplishment. But, unless they take charge of the change process, the newness of the New Status Quo wears off, and they drift into another Old Status Quo stage.

## 2.8 Practice

1.  Norm Kerth suggests: Think about your experience learning to ride a bicycle (or learning a similar skill). Can you identify each of the four stages? the foreign element? the transforming idea? Remember that you might go through the change model several times.

2.  An exercise recommended by a CASE tool buyer is to critique the typical sequential process for implementing CASE in light of the Satir Change Model:

    •  Identify the optimum methodology for system development.
    •  Identify the techniques needed to accomplish the steps in this methodology.
    •  Identify an integrated CASE tool that supports these techniques.
    •  Choose a pilot project.
    •  Educate your managers so they will understand what it will take to achieve the results you are planning.
    •  Train the team members of your pilot project.
    •  Run the pilot project, measuring the appropriate variables.
    •  Conduct a review of the pilot project to refine the CASE process.
    •  Break up the pilot team and put one member into each new CASE project.
    •  Repeat these steps for subsequent CASE projects.

3.   Show how the Satir Change Model actually subsumes all the models of
     Chapter 1 as special cases.  Give an example of a set of conditions under
     which the Satir Change Model will look like the Diffusion Model, the
     Hole-in-the-Floor Model, the Newtonian Model, or the Learning Curve
     Model.  Discuss the emotional reactions in each stage and how they will
     be manifest in each model's stages.

4.   Michael Dedolph points out that there are many individual signs that
     could tell us which stage of change we are experiencing.  For instance, he
     says,

     > For me, the indicator that I'm in Chaos from a foreign element is my
     > response to routine things.  When I am under schedule pressure, I am
     > likely to be ultrasensitive to noise and clutter, and less conscious of
     > time—which is a thing I should be paying attention to.  I have also
     > spent hours on details such as meeting minutes and travel vouchers
     > rather than the late task.

     Work with a group of coworkers and discuss the signs by which each of
     you can know what stage the others are in.  Discuss how you can use this
     information to help each other.

5.   As suggested by Jim Highsmith:  If Chaos is definitely not the time to
     make long-term decisions, when is? Look at the four stages and discuss
     when the optimal time to make long-term decisions might be.

6.   Lynne Nix and others recommend:  Recall a paradigm shift in your own
     professional career—for example, changing

     *   to a new operating system
     *   from tape storage systems to disk storage systems
     *   from mainframe to distributed PCs
     *   to a new programming language
     *   from a procedural language to an object-oriented one
     *   from undocumented systems to documented systems
     *   from a hierarchical database to a relational database
     *   from developer to tester (or vice versa)
     *   from team member to team leader
     *   from team leader to manager
     *   from undocumented requirements to documented requirements
     *   from saying "Yes" to everything to saying "Here's what it will cost
         you"

     Report on your experiences in each of the stages of the Satir Change
     Model.  Consider yourself, your colleagues, and people you regarded as

external to the change, such as customers, documenters, and quality assurance people.

7.   Gus Zimmerman suggests:  Make your own mapping between the Satir Change Model and the Competence/Consciousness Model (see Table 2-1). How well does it agree with the one given above?  Make your own mapping between the Satir Change Model and some other change model you know, such as the Kübler-Ross Model of death and dying, or the Piaget Model of childhood development.

# 3

# Responses to Change

*So at any given moment you're only
the sum of your life up to then.
There are no big moments you can reach
unless you've a pile of smaller moments to
stand on.  That big hour of decision,
the turning point in your life, the someday
you've counted on when you'd suddenly
wipe out your past mistakes, do the work
you'd never done, think the way you'd never
thought, have what you'd never had—
it just doesn't come suddenly.  You've trained
yourself for it while you waited—
or you've let it all run past you and
frittered yourself away.*[1]
— Lillian Hellman, *The Autumn Garden*

*Change happens one person at a time.*[2]
— Virginia Satir

According to the Satir Change Model, change happens one person at a time, and each person or organization has many choice points—many points at which several responses are possible.  The cumulative effect of these choice points creates the change, which—in spite of appearances—doesn't come suddenly.  These are the points of great interest, because they are the points at which the change process can be managed.  This chapter will examine some of the factors that influence the choice of response.

## 3.1 Choice Points

Figure 3-1 is an overall diagram of the Satir Change Model, emphasizing choice points (in rounded rectangles):

- The foreign element can be rejected, or not rejected.

- The foreign element can be accommodated into the old model of reality.
- The old model can be transformed to receive the foreign element.
- The transformation can be integrated or not integrated into the model.
- The transformed model can be mastered or not mastered through practice.
- In addition, there is the choice of how much time should pass before the explicit introduction of a new foreign element, though some foreign elements don't give us that choice.

Let's work through examples of each, using the attempted introduction of object-oriented technology as the foreign element in question.

### 3.1.1  Rejecting the foreign element

When management announces that a project will use an object-oriented methodology, the managers want to ensure that this approach is accepted. Developers, however, may perceive it as a foreign element, and many of them may attempt to reject it by such actions as

- not seeing the announcement memo in their e-mail.
- proving that an object-oriented approach cannot be used on their module.
- proving that an object-oriented system would be hopelessly inefficient.
- proving that changing approaches would take too long.
- forgetting to attend required classes.
- making halfhearted attempts, then becoming discouraged when they don't work, saying "It was a stupid idea anyway."
- producing a working version the old way, then rationalizing, "We might as well use it."

Some of these actions are simply passive-aggressive, while others contain potentially valid arguments. Although arguments don't have to be valid to be used in an attempt to reject a foreign element, the possibility that they are valid makes them harder to counter. Fortunately, the job of management is not to counter arguments, but to get the job done, so the first step toward success is to stop arguing and realize that opposition to a foreign element is perfectly natural, and not a personal attack.

Once managers understand it's not personal, they'll be in a position to listen to the sense of each argument and, more importantly, to the emotional "music" behind it. By responding to the emotions, managers will generally be more successful than trying to counter the arguments. Of course, if "object-oriented" is just a disguised symbolic battleground for "who's in charge," then they have a different situation entirely—and the attacks may very well be personal.

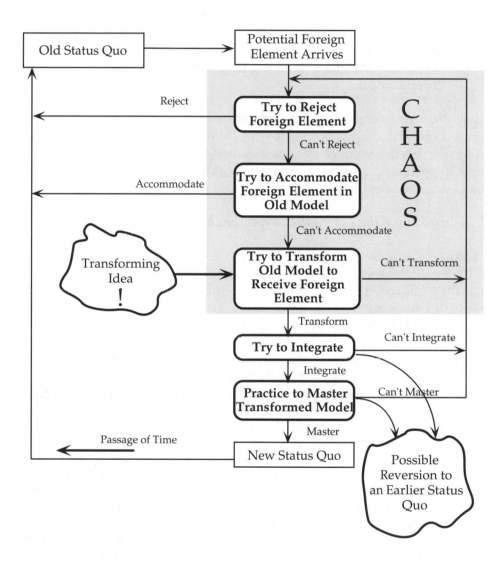

Figure 3-1.     According to the Satir Change Model, there are many choice points that can undermine or support the change process.

### 3.1.2  *Accommodating the foreign element into the old model*

If these attempts to reject the new methodology don't succeed, a developer may resort to accommodating the foreign element into the old model by such actions as

- claiming that the COBOL code is "actually object-oriented, more or less"
- doing everything the same old way, but adding a step at the end to translate code into something that will be compiled by the object-oriented compiler

Because the foreign element is accommodated into the old model, the developers truly believe they are doing object-oriented development, so it's never a good idea to accuse them of passive-aggression. Instead, a good strategy is to have an experienced and tactful person work with them "to improve their use of object-oriented development."

### 3.1.3  *Transforming the old model to receive the foreign element*

The tactics of rejection or accommodation to the old model may actually be tried by the developers, or they may simply be tried in their heads. In either case, if they fail to get rid of the foreign element and go back to the Old Status Quo, the developers may then try to transform their old models.

At this stage, the purveyors of change make one of their most common and devastating mistakes. Instead of helping the developers see ways in which an object-oriented approach resembles what they already know, they emphasize how everything is entirely new and different. One developer told me of her experience in an introductory object-oriented programming course:

> On the first morning of the first day, the instructor, who wore a suit and tie (which no developer in our company ever wears) and looked about seventeen years old, stood up in front of the class and declared, "The first thing you must do is forget everything you ever thought you knew about programming. I will not answer questions about how object-oriented programming is like anything else, because it is not like anything else, so please don't waste my time." He then told us his name.
>
> I completely tuned out, and the only other thing I clearly remember was when he said he was the principal consultant to our company on the change to object-oriented programming, so he would be working with us in the coming weeks to make it a reality. I remember laughing to myself and thinking, "Fat chance!" I don't know if anyone else had the same reaction I did, because nobody ever talked about the course, the instructor, or object-oriented programming. I do recall seeing him in the corridors once or twice, but then he was gone, and I hadn't thought about him again until just now.

From a distance, it's easy to recognize that this brash young instructor probably didn't *know* anything about any other approach to programming, and so had to protect himself by prohibiting questions. The new messiah should have had the knowledge and inclination to show people that they really had a vast amount of knowledge about programming, and that object orientation was only a small, logical increment to that knowledge base. For example, a good way to do this is for the instructor to encourage the developers to rethink some of the tough problems they have previously solved, but use the new paradigm as an added tool.

### 3.1.4  *Integrating the transformation*

The introduction of object-oriented methods often fails at the point where the new way must be integrated into practice. Some people just don't get it, but many get it in class and then lose it when they try to create examples. That's why workshop classes are more effective when they use real examples.

Few workshop instructors take the trouble to generate *real* examples, which is not the same as spending hours formatting and polishing an artificial example that would be easy to understand. Quite often, the problem here is a kind of Newtonian rush—pressure to get it not just correct, but fast. This is the typical classroom mentality, where students are ridiculed because they didn't complete an assignment in the allocated thirty minutes, especially if it's a schoolbook example that the instructor has worked out in advance. The effective instructor establishes a no-ridicule environment, and is willing to work privately with each student until they've all had a taste of personal success to start them on the way to Integration.

Even when the instructor does a good job, the same pressure for speed is seen when the novice is expected to return from a class and immediately use the new approach on an ongoing project—with an increase in productivity, and certainly no loss, an expectation that flies in the face of the temporary loss predicted by the Satir Change Model. A better management approach is to have the novice sit alongside an experienced person, watching a real example unfold, then try parts of an example while being observed by the experienced person. If no experienced person is available, you'll have to plan a lot of extra time and variability for learning, so find an experienced person.

In either case, the pressure to go quickly in an unsafe environment often leads sincerely dedicated people to fail to integrate the new idea, and they return to Chaos, thus aborting the change effort. A change of this magnitude requires a vast approach, with much more than dipping the sheep in a class or two. If instead, we get a half-vast approach, people fail to integrate the new way. Worse than that, the next half-vast approach to introduce object-oriented methods is met by the rejection, "We tried that already, and it didn't work."

### 3.1.5 *Mastering the transformed model*

Once the change has been integrated into a few working examples and the system enters the New Status Quo stage, a return to Chaos becomes far less likely—but still possible if conditions are bad enough. Though the transforming idea may be monumental, lots of minor adjustments are required to make it work in practice. If managers lack patience with details or, worse, denigrate those who implement those details, the monument may crack on the first try, like the Liberty Bell.

A second common shortcoming in the New Status Quo stage is the failure to allow for scaling-up from small examples. Object-oriented techniques are an archetypical example of this dereliction. With a change this large, I like to move my clients gradually from half-hour classroom examples to two-hour applications, followed by one-day applications, then one-week applications, before doing a significant pilot project of a month or longer. This expenditure of time may render the Hole-in-the-Floor gang despondent, but if the change doesn't justify the expense, perhaps you shouldn't be doing it in the first place.

### 3.1.6 *Timing*

Perhaps the most common cause of failing to change is the question of timing—as seen in the interference from other changes. Changes do not come in isolation. Often, we are hit by a second change long before we have reached New Status Quo on the previous one. Or, changes may be few and far between, with long gray periods resting in Old Status Quo. In any case, managers who wish to introduce change will want to know how often they can reasonably introduce foreign elements. For guidance, they can use the Zone Theory.

### 3.2  Timing Change Interventions with McLyman's Zone Theory

To deal with the timing of change, Lynda McLyman of Progress Associates marked out four zones in the Satir Change Model, as shown in Figure 3-2. According to this model, we receive change opportunities differently, depending upon the zone in which we find ourselves.[3]

### 3.2.1 *The Red Zone*

The Red Zone is the time before a previous foreign element is transformed, accommodated, or rejected. When a new foreign element arrives while the system is in the Red Zone, chaos from both foreign elements increases. Moreover, the chance of ever finding a transformation for either foreign element decreases, and the likelihood of rejection or accommodation increases.

In short, the change that might have been stimulated by the foreign element is much less likely to take hold. If a number of Red Zone cycles occur in quick succession, the system may get stuck in Chaos and become totally non-productive. Multiple foreign elements in the Red Zone *could* also lead to concurrent changes and synergy, where the transforming idea accommodated multiple concurrent changes. This is the kind of "holy grail" idea that makes people sit around immobilized waiting for Sir Lancelot to arrive on a white stallion. They shouldn't hold their breath! After a while, they'll start getting dizzy and seeing illusions—making Hatchet Man look like Sir Lancelot.

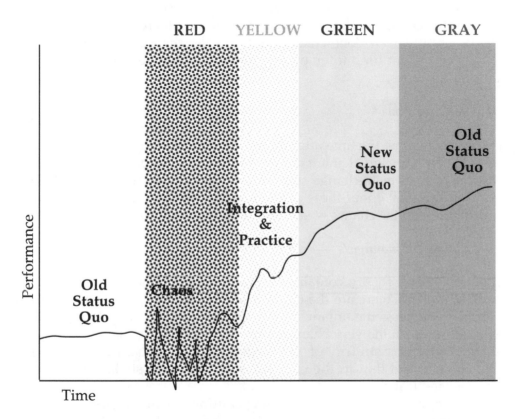

Figure 3-2.        McLyman's Zone Theory predicts that responses to a new foreign element will differ according to where the system or individual is in the current change cycle.

### 3.2.2 *The Yellow Zone*

The Yellow Zone is the time interval when a previous transformation is still being integrated. When a new foreign element arrives while the system is in the Yellow Zone, chances of successful change are reduced, but not as seriously as with Red Zone foreign elements. The system may lose its grip on the original transforming idea and be thrown back into Chaos.

More important is the effect over time. With successive Yellow Zone foreign elements, the system builds an *energy debt:* Successful change becomes less and less likely, and productivity drags. After four or five Yellow Zone foreign elements, the system loses all chance of successful change and slips into Chaos. After that, further attempts to change will create Red Zone effects, and breakdown is close at hand.

### 3.2.3 The Green Zone

The Green Zone is the time between late Integration and early New Status Quo. When a foreign element arrives in the Green Zone, the system's chances of successful change are maximized. Not only is there no energy debt, but each successful Green Zone change increases the chances for the next. There has been sufficient time to enjoy the successful change and to recharge the emotional batteries.

### 3.2.4 The Gray Zone

The Gray Zone is all the time after the system has been in Late Status Quo for a while. When a foreign element arrives in the Gray Zone, people have already lost some of their meta-change skills, for old learnings about change have lost their usefulness. Without these meta-change skills, change is once again slow and difficult, and the chance of successful change declines.

### 3.2.5 Lessons for managers

McLyman's Zone Theory contains several lessons for those who would manage change. First, there are the obvious lessons of timing. Managers who are in a hurry and press the organization with too many changes too quickly will merely slow down the very changes they are trying to accelerate. Similarly, if managers adopt the strategy of "hit them with a lot of changes, and some will stick," they'll find that in the end, none of them will stick. Or, worse, the wrong ones will stick.

The Yellow Zone holds particular caution for managers who attempt these strategies. A few hits in the Yellow Zone may happen to succeed, thus encouraging a manager to keep piling on foreign elements, much like a gambler who happens to win the first few bets.

Most managers are aware of the Gray Zone and try to stimulate the organization with frequent changes. What they may fail to notice, however, is that parts of the organization are not touched by these changes, and are deep in the Gray Zone in an otherwise Green Zone organization.

### 3.2.6 One person at a time

Perhaps the most important lesson of the Zone Theory is that not all parts of the system are in the same zone at the same time. This is true at every level of the organization, right down to the individual. Foreign elements don't segregate according to parts of our lives. Regardless of their origin, they all add together. Thus, in a department that is generally in the Green Zone, there may be one individual who has been experiencing a large number of personal foreign elements, and may be deeply in the Red Zone.

In the same Green Zone department, a few individuals may be largely untouched by the changes all around. These people may be in their personal Gray Zone, and simply not know how to cope with change when their turn arrives.

Most books and courses on change management emphasize the need for strategic planning. The Zone Theory reminds us that although change must be managed at a high level, we must never ignore the impact on individuals. As Satir said, "Change happens one person at a time."

## 3.3  Patterns of Information Flow

Obviously, managers need a continuing flow of information to make successful interventions in change. Unfortunately, change tends to disrupt information flow. The Satir Change Model helps us to understand what each stage does to information feedback mechanisms. It also shows us that during change, the most reliable information is the *emotional signals from the people experiencing the change*. You can use these signals, for instance, to determine the appropriate zone strategy, or what kind of information you need to supply.

### 3.3.1  Old Status Quo

During an aging Status Quo stage, old feedback mechanisms are eroding slowly. Information is not getting through. As the system starts breaking down, behavior becomes less predictable, and to make it more predictable, people often ignore what information does get through. For example, as the number of trouble incidents from the field grows, managers may compare them to the previous week. That way, the increase may be lost in the noise or labeled not so bad.

In the Old Status Quo stage, interventions should be designed to get people to recognize what is, rather than what they've grown accustomed to seeing. To evaluate the current number of trouble incidents, managers should compare them to the average performance in the past, so as to reveal—rather than conceal—any long-term upward trend.

### 3.3.2  Foreign element

When the foreign element arrives, the old feedback mechanisms may fail completely. Very often, the arrival of the foreign element is merely a breaking through of the illusions created by the old feedback mechanisms. The best interventions here are to help people stay with the information and believe it, even though believing it will send them into Chaos. For example, the Public Project Progress Poster (PPPP) places information about schedule slippage right out in front, where everyone can see what it is, and if it's being manipulated.[4]

It's especially important not to let the system punish those who bring the new information. The PPPP gives this type of protection by making schedule updates a routine matter, not subject to choice and thus not subject to intimidation.

### 3.3.3 Chaos

In Chaos, the old feedback mechanisms are shattered. The system runs wild, and people are unable to reconnect with any model of what's happening to them. People desire stability so greatly that they may attach themselves to any source that appears to know what's happening, from tea leaf readers to con artists to methodology vendors. What's needed here is persistent, compassionate offers of reliable information about what's really happening, not the often brutal, so-called facts that will destroy, but also not the kind of placating that will allow temporary return to the status quo: "We're losing nine customers per month . . . but that's not *too* bad. We could be losing ten per month."

Continued cycles of group discussions and individual experimentation will help ensure that people are listening. The only schedules that should be maintained are schedules driven by the need for learning, such as getting people to sources of new information on time.

### 3.3.4 Integration and Practice

During Integration, new arrangements of feedback mechanisms begin to appear. As they are tested in Practice, some order evolves. At times, because the new mechanisms are not well developed, feedback is slower than needed and this causes the system to oscillate wildly. At this point, people can be helped with specific techniques for getting information, such as how to read their emotional state more quickly and reliably. Managers must try to create a climate in which it's okay even for senior technical leaders not to know things, and to ask questions about those things. Because the goal is merely to get control of the learning process, schedules should contain lots of slack. The payoff in speedy performance will come later, when the New Status Quo is reached.

### 3.3.5 New Status Quo

As the system moves into the New Status Quo, new mechanisms are in place and working rather well. Practice brings improvement, but appropriate information flows freely to and from the system. In this stage, what people need most is the permission to make mistakes—to be honest so that they can explore and learn about their newly mastered professional skills. People cannot optimize their performance if they are not allowed to make mistakes.

### 3.4 Meta-change

For major changes, the system may go through the Change Model many times. For instance, in learning to ride a bicycle, you may have one stage of learning to ride with training wheels, another of riding without the training wheels, and yet another of riding no-hands. For me, I was stuck in an Old Status Quo stage of riding with hands on the handlebars for about thirty years. Then, once I learned to ride no-hands style, a foreign element arrived in the form of a pothole. I went through another change in which I learned to keep at least one hand on the handlebars at all times.

Going through repeated changes can make us excessively anxious, but there is a mitigating factor, called *meta-change*. Not only do systems and individuals learn during the change cycle, but after several complete change cycles, they learn *how to learn*—and learn about the *importance of learning in a change process* as well. At that point, the introduction of the foreign element produces almost total excitement and almost zero anxiety (see Figure 3-3).

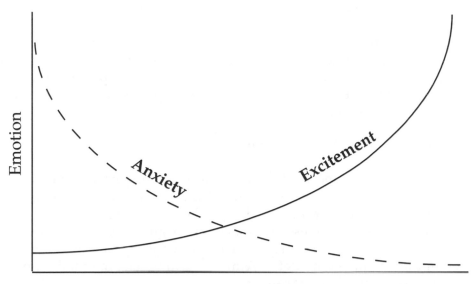

Time
(Number of conscious experiences of the Change Model)

Figure 3-3.    After many complete change cycles, systems and individuals learn to learn, and the introduction of the foreign element produces almost total excitement and almost zero anxiety.

Examples of meta-change include

❏ The individual with the bad heart takes up swimming, and figures out how to do his job in a less stressful way.
❏ Mother goes back to school, and Junior graduates. Father gets laid off, but finds a better position.
❏ The building layout is remodeled, and people are moved, under a comprehensive moving plan developed by a team consisting of management, workers, architects, and building support personnel.
❏ The software development team regularly promotes old members and brings in trainees to replace them.
❏ Further changes are introduced to the inventory system, based on suggestions from the users.
❏ The company adds a fifth new software design tool to its tool kit, appointing a special team to facilitate the introduction.

Much of this meta-change takes the form of mastering the choice points in the Satir Change Model (Figure 3-1). People recognize when they are trying to reject or accommodate the foreign element. They learn to be patient when seeking escape from Chaos through the transforming idea. They appreciate the need for Practice, both in themselves and others. By knowing where they are and what's happening to them, they improve their sense of timing, and their attitudes about change are transformed.

By the third or fourth similar cycle, people begin to feel luscious excitement at the prospect of a new cycle of growth. They feel alive, healthy, and creative. Some people around them may be frightened or put off, but experienced change artists are able to deal in a truly helpful way with those to whom the prospect of change is a threat.

## 3.5 Change in the Anticipating Organization

The state of excitement and readiness that derives from meta-change is why I call the Pattern 4 culture the *Anticipating* culture.[5] What participants in such a culture are anticipating is the next challenge, the next change.

Anticipation can be a blessing or a curse. A great deal of the trouble we have in experiencing change comes from a false set of expectations engendered by oversimplified change models. A more accurate change model helps by making our expectations more realistic.

In organizational life, for example, we are often expected to do business as usual while a change is taking place. In reality, the relationship between performance and change is what we saw in Figure 2-1: not very smooth at all. The smooth performance of the Learning Curve Model, by contrast, is obtained by averaging many Satir Change Model's performance curves, which smooths out all the jagged oscillations (Figure 1-8). Such a smoothed model may be fine for gross, overall planning, but it totally misleads the working manager who has to deal with the oscillations day to day. If your model says that good change is smooth and emotionless, you can easily get upset by every small deviation from plans, and then you can get upset about being upset. As a consequence, you'll be even less able to manage your own changes.

If you can take account of these oscillations in your plans, change becomes less stressful. That's one reason change becomes easier with each new cycle: Your model is more realistic, so you don't make change harder by defeating yourself with romantic expectations. Moreover, as meta-change occurs, the performance curve for each individual actually becomes smoother. In an Anticipating (Pattern 4) organization, the Satir Change Model and the Learning Curve Model converge to some extent, making planning by averages more reasonable.

Historically, in software engineering organizations, most strategic change plans haven't worked out. Tools are purchased but sit on the shelf. Methodologies are worked at for years, but never take hold. Training programs are introduced with a bang but die with a whimper. Then, as Naomi Karten says, there are the fads:

> People buy into the latest-and-greatest fad and plunge full speed ahead to implement it without seeing that the change people must go through is so great that the odds of it working are slim. Reengineering is a good (that is, bad) example. Suddenly, the great gurus of reengineering are conceding that they underestimated the minor matter of the human element.

In some of these cases, there was no plan at all. Even when there was a plan, however, there was no attention to the individual response to change. That's why the Anticipating (Pattern 4) organization needs both change planners and change doers, or change artists, which will be discussed in the following chapters.

### 3.6 Helpful Hints and Suggestions

1. My colleague Fredric Laurentine relates the Competence/Consciousness Model to McLyman's Zone Theory:

   > When people are on a fast track, they never hit conscious competence (CC) because they are transferred before they reach full understanding of their job/effectiveness. Without reaching CC a few times in your career, you are apt to be insecure in your own ability—although the people around you may be seeing your competence.
   >
   > My own experience as a consultant gave me a CC experience that really anchored my self-esteem. And recent experience growing a job up our company hierarchy over a few years has done the same.

2.  Norm Kerth comments: "I have had great success by tying the Change Model to the development cycle—keeping a team in the Green Zone. At the end of every project, we do a retrospective review and ask, 'What do we do differently next time?' The team selects their own foreign element. We combat postpartum depression—while the next project is ramping up—by initiating a program to work through Chaos and Integration and Practice.

    "For example, we know object-orientation is in our future, so let's get a C++ compiler. But let's just use it as a 'better-C' to get acquainted with it as a tool. Let's try objects in just one small area. Let's see what we can learn if we treat everything over the network as an object."

3.  Change requires patience. John Stevens tells this story from the martial arts:

    > Once, a young man petitioned a great swordsman to admit him as a disciple. "I'll act as your live-in servant and train ceaselessly. How long will it take me to learn everything?"
    > "At least ten years," the master replied.
    > "That's too long," the young man protested. "Suppose I work twice as hard as everyone else. Then how long will it take?"
    > "Thirty years," the master shot back.
    > "What do you mean?" the anguished student exclaimed. "I'll do anything to master swordsmanship as quickly as possible!"
    > "In that case," the master said sharply, "you will need fifty years. A person in such a hurry will be a poor student."[4]

    We can understand this story in terms of the Change Model, particularly the Zone Theory. A student in this much hurry to change will stay perpetually in the Red Zone, and never advance. Indeed, the harder he works, the slower the change.

4.  Jim Highsmith observes: "I like the Satir model, especially the choice points shown in the figure. [See Figure 3-1.] Most writers on change management sometimes make it seem that everything is/should always be changing, and that all change is good. The figure has another side that should be discussed: about how a person or organization rejects 'bad' changes. The 'escapes' from the process—Can't Transform, Reject, and so on—can be positive ways of rejecting changes that really shouldn't be made. Just as reviews should accommodate an outcome that says to halt the project, a change model ought to reject ill-conceived changes—and this model works both ways."

## 3.7 Summary

✔ According to the Satir Change Model, the change process contains many choice points—points at which the individual or organization can respond in one of several ways:

- The foreign element can be rejected, or not rejected.
- The foreign element can be accommodated into the old model of reality.
- The old model can be transformed to receive the foreign element.
- The transformation can be integrated or not integrated into the model.
- The transformed model can be mastered or not mastered through practice.
- In addition, there is the choice of how much time should pass before the explicit introduction of a new foreign element.

✔ When management announces a change, many employees will perceive the announcement as a foreign element and attempt to reject it. The first step in dealing with these attempts at rejection is to realize that opposition to a foreign element is perfectly natural, and not a personal attack. Then, listen to the sense of each argument and, more importantly, to the emotional "music" behind it. Responding to the emotions will generally be more successful than trying to counter the arguments.

✔ Other people may resort to accommodating the foreign element into their old model, and truly believe they are doing the change. A good strategy here is to be tactful yet explicit in what needs to be done to accomplish the change.

✔ A good strategy when introducing change is to emphasize how the changed state resembles the current state. Instead, some people introducing change emphasize how everything is entirely new and different. To be successful at change, you need to show people that they really have a vast amount of knowledge so that the change is only a small, logical increment to their knowledge base.

✔ The introduction of a change often fails at the point where the new way must be integrated into practice. In training, real examples give the most effective practice, especially if the environment makes it safe for you to make mistakes and to go at whatever speed is needed to integrate the new material. Practice doesn't end when classes end; the introduction of new ideas to the actual job needs lots of safety and support from experienced people.

✔   Once the change has been integrated into a few working examples, a return to Chaos becomes far less likely, but still possible if conditions are bad enough. Many petty adjustments are required to make any real change work in practice, and much time must be allowed for scaling-up from small examples.

✔   Perhaps the most common cause of failing to change is timing—the interference from other changes. Changes do not come in isolation, and McLyman's Zone Theory is an excellent guide to timing the introduction of new foreign elements, based on zones.

✔   The Red Zone is the interval of time before a previous foreign element is transformed, accommodated, or rejected. When a new foreign element arrives while the system is in the Red Zone, Chaos from both foreign elements increases. Moreover, the chance of ever finding a transformation for either foreign element decreases, and the likelihood of rejection or accommodation increases.

✔   The Yellow Zone is the period during which a previous transformation is still being integrated. When a new foreign element arrives while the system is in the Yellow Zone, chances of successful change are reduced, but not as seriously as with Red Zone foreign elements. With successive Yellow Zone foreign elements, however, the system builds an energy debt. Successful change becomes progressively less likely, and productivity drags.

✔   The Green Zone is the time between late Integration and early New Status Quo. When a foreign element arrives in the Green Zone, the system's chances of successful change are maximized. Not only is there no energy debt, but each successful Green Zone change increases the chances for the next.

✔   The Gray Zone is all the time after a system has been in Late Status Quo for a while. When a foreign element arrives in the Gray Zone, people have lost some of their meta-change skills, for old learnings about change have lost their usefulness. Without these meta-change skills, change is once again slow and difficult, and the chance of successful change declines.

✔   Managers who are in a hurry and press the organization with too many changes too quickly will merely slow down the very changes they are trying to accelerate. Similarly, if managers adopt the strategy of "hit them with a lot of changes, and some will stick," they'll find that in the end, none of them will stick.

✔ Not all parts of the system are in the same zone at the same time. This is true at every level of the organization, right down to the individual. Although change must be managed at a high level, we must never ignore the impact on individuals.

✔ Change tends to disrupt the information flow needed to manage change. The most reliable information is the *emotional signals from the people experiencing the change.* Use these signals to determine the appropriate zone strategy, or what kind of information you need to supply.

✔ During an aging Status Quo stage, old feedback mechanisms are eroding slowly. Information is not getting through. Behavior is less predictable, and to make it more predictable, people often ignore what information does get through. Interventions here should be in the direction of getting people to recognize what is, rather than what it is supposed to be.

✔ For major changes, the system may go through the Change Model many times. Not only do systems and individuals learn during the change cycle, but after several complete change cycles, they "learn to learn"—and they also learn about the importance of learning in a change process. Experienced change artists feel such high self-worth and unlimited coping ability that they are able to deal in a truly helpful way with those to whom the prospect of change is a threat.

## 3.8 Practice

1. Norm Kerth's retrospective approach ensures that

   **Every project is also an experiment in improving the process.**

   This experimental approach is typical of the Anticipating (Pattern 4) organization. Hold a retrospective for your next project (or project stage) completion, and decide what to change for the next project. Make a plan and follow through, noting the reaction to a self-induced foreign element.

2. Sue Petersen asks: The place in the Satir Change Model for a healthy organization is New Status Quo, but is the best we can hope for an oscillation between New Status Quo and Chaos? Chaos seems frightening, and it is this fear that keeps an organization denying foreign elements, until its members finally go into a *huge* and undeniable Chaos. Create a diagram of effects showing this dynamic, and where the choice points are for management.

3. Sue Petersen adds, "I like the descriptions of the change process, but they're very N. As an S, it helps me to anchor these descriptions to an

actual project, with actual events and the responses that various people gave. I'd suggest that other S's reading the book would like to do this as an exercise, with a change project they know personally." Do this, and share your observations (if possible) with a mixed S/N group. Observe what the two groups notice and omit from their descriptions.[7]

4.    Now here's a similar exercise from an N personality type, Naomi Karten (with an example to help the S's):

> I have found it helpful to look within at my own personal voyages through the change cycle. It's instructive to identify things that are foreign elements for me, to observe how it feels when I'm in Chaos, and to reflect on what kinds of things serve as transforming ideas and how it feels to emerge from the Chaos. This awareness makes the entire process less stressful and makes it easier to believe that the Chaos really will come to an end.
>
> For example, when I'm asked to give a presentation that's significantly different in some way from what I've done before, it's sometimes a major foreign element. I'm sometimes thrown into total Chaos, unable to concentrate or organize my thoughts. Eventually, a transforming idea appears. For a presentation I'm preparing now, the transforming idea came via a conference call with the event sponsor to help me understand the industry and its service issues. Suddenly, ideas flowed. I'll slip back into Chaos a few times before I'm through preparing this talk. But the difference now from days of old is that I now have the Satir Change Model to provide a framework for what I'm experiencing. So I recognize the pattern and simply accept it as the way I react to this type of foreign element. I know I'm in a sort of Chaos, but I also know it won't last forever. And I know what sorts of things may be sources of transforming ideas.
>
> So, stated as a Practice item, it would be something like: Think about situations in which you have experienced the change process, and reflect on what the foreign elements have been, how the Chaos felt, and where the transforming ideas came from. How can this awareness help you at a meta-change level?

To which I would only add, Share these experiences with some friends to see what you can learn by comparing notes.

5.    Lynne Nix comments: Since change happens one person at a time, we also have to consider the effects on each person of seeing other people in different stages of the Satir Change Model. What is the effect on others of the early adapters? What is the effect on others of the late adapters? What steps can a manager take to diminish the harmful effects and accentuate the helpful ones?

6.    Janice Wormington suggests: Discuss how an organization remains in the Green Zone. Brainstorm as many tactics and strategies as you can.

# Part II
# Change Artistry in the Anticipating Organization

*Facilitating the change process is like sculpting a block of wood. Although we who envision the change may have images of the results we want, we do not have control; there is interplay with the wood. Our primary task as change agents is to "raise the grain" of the material we're working with, to uncover the ideas and symbols that will contribute to the change strategy.*

*In this process, I have come to rely heavily on listening and questioning. As a listener, I try to give people a chance to explore an issue openly; I focus on the aspects that are unresolved or painful to them, and on their hopes and visions of how the situation could be different. This allows ideas to emerge that can become the seeds of strategy.*[1]

— F. Peavey *et al.*

Change artists are the lubricant that makes change plans work—not always running smoothly because people aren't machines, but not grinding to a rough halt either. To develop change artistry, you need theoretical learning (as from these volumes) and experiential training (as from workshops), but the Satir Change Model says you also need practice and experience.

Over the years, through the training of thousands of change artists, Dani Weinberg and I—with the help of a number of colleagues—have developed a number of practical experiments to put theoretical change artistry to the test. We call these experiments *challenges*, and we challenge you to put your theoretical learnings to the test by accepting the challenges in the following chapters.

The challenges should be done in order, mastering each before proceeding to the next. We suggest you use no less than one week for each challenge, and repeat a challenge if you feel you still need practice. The best environment for the challenges is in a group of three or more colleagues who are attempting the same challenges at the same time, then getting together to share learnings. We strongly recommend you find such a supportive group, even if you have to go outside your own organization.

# 4

# Change Artistry

*The CEO has to introduce the change process
and be eternally vigilant in support of it, but
ultimately change needs lots of practitioners.
You're looking for recruits in every department
or division.  The broader the base,
the faster you can change.*[1]
— John F. Welch
CEO of General Electric

*Save all the pieces.*
— Aldo Leopold's First Rule of
Intelligent Tinkering

*Leave no bodies.*
— Virginia Satir, *on changing systems*

*Change always comes from below.  Nobody
with four aces asks for a new deal.*
— Anonymous

The Satir Change Model is an effective guide to cultural change because it addresses both the individual and organizational levels—the tactical and the strategic—and because it addresses both the intellectual and emotional responses to change.  But understanding the Satir Change Model is not the same as having the artistry to use it effectively.  Moreover, managers sometimes change organizations without knowing the Satir Change Model at all, using only the more common strategic, intellectual models of Chapter 1.  How can this be?

Whenever we look into organizations that have accomplished cultural changes, we find a large number of people whom we call *change artists*.  Moreover, we find these change artists at all levels of an organization and in all units, because for cultural change to occur, it must occur at all levels and in all units.  When these change artists are present—whether recognized or not—

they deal with the individual emotional responses to change, and thus increase the chances for success of any change plan.

This chapter shows how the Satir Change Model and other models guide people in becoming change artists, and offers some examples of how change artists function in an organization.

## 4.1  Personal Responses to Change

The Satir model does not say that change will *always* follow the four stages. As the flow of Figure 3-1 shows, the change process can be short-circuited by choices at any stage. Thus, if an organization wants to help change happen, someone may have to make explicit interventions to keep things on track. In the Steering (Pattern 3) organization, some people have become change artists—ready, willing, and at the right place at the right time to facilitate change. In the Anticipating (Pattern 4) organization, to some degree *everybody* has become a change artist. Thus, the devotion to developing change artistry is one of the distinguishing marks of this cultural pattern, and one of the dominant practical themes of this book.

### 4.1.1  The person of the change artist

The Satir Change Model is a model of how individual people in a system affect, and are affected by, change. Thus, the primary tool for change is neither things nor procedures, but *people.*

Change artistry consists of knowing how to facilitate change, knowing what to change, when to change it, where in the organization the change should be introduced, and who should take what roles in carrying it out. Even more, it consists of the ability to take congruent action when under great stress, and when surrounded by people under stress.

The change artist who wishes to be helpful must personally be able to work in the following ways:

- listen actively
- respond honestly and clearly
- set clear boundaries between himself or herself and others
- allow others to struggle with their own chaos
- interact with love and respect
- activate possibilities in each person

There is no single way to be a change artist, and different approaches are needed for different jobs (Figure 4-1). The key point is to have a change artist in the right place at the right time to facilitate each little piece of the grand plan.

Figure 4-1.      There are different styles and degrees of change artistry, and each may be sufficient for certain types of jobs.

### 4.1.2 Types of interventions at each stage

As part of their activities, change artists have to intervene in the change process. Each stage of change is different, and each stage requires different types of intervention. Fully matured change artists are able to operate well, making appropriate interventions in all phases:

- Systems in Old Status Quo need to be provoked by a foreign element. Change artists supply ideas or measurements, or arrange contact with those people who can supply them. Although change artists know how to be supportive, they do *not* support Status Quo systems that continue doing the same old thing.
- When a foreign element arrives, change artists provide support in the form of persistence to overcome avoidance and denial. Change artists do *not* provide support for a return to the Old Status Quo.
- Change artists help individuals and systems in Chaos to avoid making any long-term decisions. They dissuade people from attempting to short-circuit the change process with magic. Change artists may supply ideas that might transform, but these ideas are merely floated in the air, not pushed. Change artists give people in Chaos time to think, opportunities to talk, and the safety to do both.

- During Integration and Practice, change artists provide support, hand-holding, and sometimes a small amount of teaching of new coping techniques. They offer people safe opportunities to practice and explore, and perhaps they contribute small ideas to work out the bugs in the new way of doing things.
- As the system moves into the New Status Quo, change artists continue to provide opportunities to practice in a safe environment, but their interventions grow smaller and smaller. They give people space to practice on their own, without inflicting overbearing help. Change artists also assist the system to develop ways of communicating its new learnings to newcomers.

### 4.1.3  Change and temperament

Some change artists can do all these things, and do each at the right time. Others, however, are primarily effective at only one stage, simply because it happens to match their skills and personalities. These change artists shouldn't intervene in other stages until they understand their own tendencies—that way, they can do what the client requires, rather than what comes out of their own needs. For instance, each of the four temperaments identified by Keirsey and Bates tends to react in characteristic ways to change situations.[2]

The *Visionary* (NT) likes working with ideas. NT Visionaries are most interested in designing, rather than implementing, change. They are concerned that change be both optimal and fair, but they expect it to be completed without much ado. They think their ideas should catch on and be put to work immediately, so they tend to lose interest and grow impatient with the process as soon as Integration starts. They like to provoke with ideas, even during Chaos when such provocation is inappropriate and may cause much pain and confusion.

The *Catalyst* (NF) likes working with people to help them grow, but is concerned that people should not suffer from change. NF Catalysts are needed to keep people working together through the rough spots of the change process, and to support individuals going though tough emotional times. NF Catalysts can be teachers, so they are very useful once Integration is under way. On the other hand, they have a tendency not to let people experience their own pain, so they may short-circuit Integration by trying to be helpful. They are such team players that they may want everyone to do the same thing, even if their personalities are different. Also, they may want everyone to do something at the same time, even if people are at different stages of the change process.

The *Organizer* (SJ) likes order and system. The important thing to SJ Organizers is not just doing it, but doing it *right*. They are thus concerned that change can become messy and inefficient. They are best at carrying the transformation into actual practice, long after the NT Visionaries have gotten bored. Without the SJ Organizers, no change would ever be completed. Although SJ Organizers tend to fear quick change, they may push for quick closure, like getting firm commitments during Chaos when it is inappropriate. They may also stifle all change by requiring that success be provable in advance. As one correspondent said:

> This reminds me of a locally famous quote from one of our upper managers (delivered in front of an audience of a couple hundred, and meant as a compliment): "I really respect people who take risks and win!" Everybody just silently nodded—we all know what this guy thinks of people who take risks and lose.

The *Troubleshooter* (SP) likes getting the job done. SP Troubleshooters want quick fixes, not elaborate plans. They are the least likely to deny the foreign element, because they see it as an opportunity to swing into action. Their early recognition of problems does not ingratiate them with the others, especially the SJ Organizers, who like the appearance of calm order. For the SP Troubleshooters, change should be fast, so they don't get stuck with something that's boring. As a result, they are impatient with planning, and may provoke change for its own sake, piling one change on another, even during Chaos. Impatient with Integration and Practice, they may drop out if change seems too slow.

These temperaments, of course, are merely tendencies—what you may do instinctively when you act without thinking. As you develop as a change artist, you learn to recognize your tendencies, honor them for their strength, note their weaknesses, and learn to set them aside if they are inappropriate for the current situation. Awareness is the first step; lots of practice is the second.

## 4.2 Case Study: Changing Geography

Change is a long-term process, but a living organization lives in the immediate present. Thus, without careful management, long-term change is invariably sacrificed to short-term expedience. And short-term expedience is taking place all the time, everywhere in the organization, essentially out of the view of high-level management. That's why change artists have to be in every nook and cranny, as the following case illustrates.

DeMarco and Lister have given us much useful information on the effects of geography on software development effectiveness.[3] One manager, Ruben, reading *Peopleware*, was inspired to change the seating geography to improve customer relations. His semiannual customer satisfaction survey had given the developers very low marks on communication.  So, instead of seating people for efficient performance of today's work, he wanted to seat them to encourage communication, by putting eight developers in the customers' offices. However, when he surveyed customers six months later, Ruben found a large decline in their satisfaction with communication, precisely in those offices into which he had moved a developer.

What had typically happened was this.  The developer would move to the customer's office and set up shop.  Communication improved, but the first time there was a software emergency, the developer would rush back "home" to get the problem solved.  Emergencies were rather frequent, and soon the developer would find it expedient to establish a "temporary" office in the developer area.  After a while, the temporary office was occupied 99 percent of the time.  In terms of the Satir Change Model, the foreign element—Ruben's move—had been rejected.  Even worse, the customers were left staring at an empty office they were paying for, which reminded them of how hard it was to communicate with developers.

Ruben noticed, however, that in one customer's office, satisfaction increased.  In that office, the scenario had been different.  Polly, a customer and change artist, sat in the office next door to Lyle, the developer, and noticed how often he was missing.  She listened to comments made by other customers, and then she took action.  Interviewing Lyle, she discovered that there were two main reasons why he kept leaving to solve problems:

- The PCs in the customer's office had less capacity than the ones in the developers' office, and that capacity was needed to run debugging tools effectively.
- There were two other developers Lyle needed to consult on most of these problems, and they still resided in the developers' office.

Polly knew these were typical problems of the Integration phase of the Satir Change Model, so she simply arranged to have Customer Service upgrade Lyle's PC.  She then explained the benefits of having the two developers come to the customer's office, which was, after all, only two floors away.  They were only too glad to come, and took no small pleasure in being able to show the customer how much work it was to fix "simple" problems in software.

With Polly as Lyle's neighbor, Ruben's strategic concept was implemented.  Without using his survey to connect the strategic and the tactical, he would never have learned that it was possible to make the new geography work, and the success would have been limited to Lyle's area.  Polly was sent around to the other developers who had moved, and she managed to get five out of seven working smoothly by similarly upgrading their PCs and encouraging developers to solve problems close to where they occurred.

Polly also had the skill to recognize that the remaining two departments were having deeper problems with information systems, problems that wouldn't be solved by upgrading PCs or encouraging proximity. Indeed, she saw that proximity was only making matters worse because the people were unskilled in handling interpersonal conflict. Thus, instead of blindly applying the same solution to everyone, she suggested to the managers that certain people could benefit from training in teamwork skills.

## 4.3 Case Study: Patching

The most common sacrificial scenario in software engineering is that something must be "fixed" in a hurry, so a patch is hacked in and comes back to haunt the organization for many years. Even if the patch is a successful one, the act of patching violates standard process, and so encourages further process violations over time. So, although the patch maintains stability in one area, it is a foreign element in several others.

Here's how the change artists in one Anticipating (Pattern 4) organization evolved a process to resolve this conflict between short-term product and long-term process: Whenever there is a product problem that needs to be fixed quickly, or a tool that needs to be repaired to get development back on line, a QUEST team is formed. A QUEST (Quick, Usable, Extendable Solution Team) consists of three people: a hacker, a guardian, and a healer (each of whom wears badges and other symbols of the role):

- The *hacker* is responsible for solving the immediate problem, constrained by the guardian and the healer.
- The *guardian* is responsible for seeing that no harm comes to the product (aided by the hacker) or process (aided by the healer) as a side effect of the hacking or the healing.
- The *healer* is responsible for amending the process to prevent further occurrences, or to be prepared to handle them better, constrained by the guardian and the hacker.

For instance, while on a visit, I witnessed a QUEST team that was formed to handle a failure of the source code maintenance tool. The hacker developed a clever work-around, the guardian assembled a review team to ensure that the work-around had no unforeseen side effects, and the healer contacted the vendor for a fix to the product. When the fix had been installed, the guardian assembled a review and test group to ensure that the problem was truly fixed with no side effects, and the healer implemented a plan to go back and undo all the work-arounds, of which she had been maintaining a careful list.

Because you never know when someone is going to go into Chaos over which foreign element, one other component is needed to make the QUEST approach work. Change artists must be widely distributed throughout the organization, and all must know the QUEST approach, so that no Chaos triggered by a high-priority problem is likely to escape their attention. When

Chaos is detected, a team is assembled, roles are assigned, and the problem is disposed of with no harm to the present product and usually with improvements to the future process.

### 4.4  Case Study: Knowing What to Leave Alone

I don't want to give the impression that change artists rush around organizations inflicting help on everyone.  Perhaps the toughest skill for a change artist to learn is the skill of knowing what people and what situations to leave alone.

For instance, there's a Vietnamese proverb that says, "While it is notable to assist a stricken elephant in rising, it is foolhardy to catch one that is falling down."  Change artists need to learn how to recognize whether specific people or departments are willing to help themselves rise.

For instance, change artists should have lots of potentially transforming ideas on hand.  Most of these ideas are on the process level—that is, processes for finding ideas.  Such processes might include

- reaching out to other organizations, departments, professional societies, libraries, consultants, or classes
- facilitating brainstorming processes
- keeping an inventory of sample problems, toy exercises, and simulations for right-brain exploration and left-brain investigation
- conducting focus groups, and knowing how to recognize when the group lacks the necessary knowledge (just as a lens doesn't focus anything if there's no ray of light)
- changing the mixture of people to obtain more diversity and knowledge
- combining ideas from several sources to produce new ideas

A good example of combining ideas is the process of connecting what the individuals want with what the organization or the change artist wants.  If the change artist thinks the elephant might be falling down, she might make her presence (what they want) conditional on their participation (what she wants).  Or, if management wants the group to take a risk, the change artist might negotiate some kind of insurance to give the group safety, such as extra time in the schedule, relaxed specifications, suspension of the usual measurements, or a guarantee to get their old jobs back if the project flops.

Here's an example of this kind of negotiation.  In an organization producing electronic equipment with embedded software, top management threw in a foreign element by mandating certain process improvements.  Some of the more traditional managers were highly technical engineers, and claimed that the other managers, being service engineers, weren't sufficiently technical to do process improvement.  Thelma, a change artist, was supposed to facilitate the entire group of managers working on the improvements, but she faced a problem: Who should have the job, given that the technical managers weren't doing it, and the service managers wanted to do it?

Thelma applied several change artist principles:

- *Always find the energy for change and go with it.* In this case, the service managers wanted to work on change, and the technical managers didn't.

- *Don't get hooked into negative energy.* The technical managers knew dozens of reasons why these changes could not be made.

- *Talk in their terms and find out what the issues really are.* It turned out that the technical managers were overloaded with assignments just getting products out the door. The service managers were overloaded, too, but they felt that their overload was due to service requests arising from faulty technical processes. They were willing to invest their time to reduce their future load.

- *Once you're prepared, go to the source.* Having assembled all these facts, Thelma made a recommendation to upper management that the service managers be given the process improvement responsibility, and that the technical managers no longer be required to attend process improvement meetings. In return, the technical managers promised their full cooperation on an as-needed basis. Upper management was happy to accept her solidly based recommendation.

- *It's perfectly all right to do nothing for a time.* Dormancy periods in seeds and hibernation in animals are adaptive strategies in an environment with fluctuating opportunities for growth. In human organizations, the Zone Theory says that it sometimes makes good sense just to lie low during periods of rapid change. Knowing that Chaos is contagious, Thelma wisely decided to leave the technical managers alone. Their time would come.

## 4.5 Helpful Hints and Suggestions

1. One short chapter can only touch on the key role of the change artist. That's why the rest of the book will be sprinkled with tips on change artistry, and one chapter is totally devoted to practice exercises for change artists. These tips and exercises should suffice to convince you of the power of change artistry and, I hope, of the necessity for learning even more. Learning to be a change artist is learning that never stops, not in one lifetime at least.

   There are many places you can go to deepen your change artist skills. Much of what a change artist needs to know is contained in workshops that I and others have been giving for a number of years.[4] Many books have captured this workshop material, particularly the MOI Model,[5] the Satir Change Model,[6] the diagram of effects,[7] the Satir Interaction Model,[8] the Myers-Briggs Type Indicator (MBTI),[9] models of stability,[10] models of conflict,[11] and models of diversity.[12] Any would-be change artist can benefit from such workshops and/or a library of such books.

2.    One particularly handy trade-off used by change artists is based on *Copeland's Law of Discontinuity:*

      **A discontinuity is an opportunity to stop doing old things and start doing new things.**[13]

      Copeland's Law is particularly useful for stopping things. A change artist, dealing with a group in Chaos from an overload of foreign elements, might propose they simply stop doing some old reports to management. This relieves some of the pressure, and it's about the only time you can ever get any bureaucratic nonsense stopped.

3.    Effective change artists do a lot of teaching, although not necessarily formal classroom teaching. It's no surprise, then, that these change artists have the characteristics of effective teachers:[14]

      • They act approvingly, acceptingly, and supportively toward their clients.
      • They have an intellectual grasp of what they're trying to convey.
      • They make use of ideas and opinions expressed by their clients.
      • They are enthusiastic about what they're trying to accomplish.

4.    Michael Dedolph says calling anything an "art" risks having techies look down upon it, and some people do use the term "change agent" in their models. But lots of people look down on the term "agent" as well—it sounds like the operative of some secret government agency, or a tool of management. Besides, "agent" is more of a title than a description. An artist has to be able to produce works of art, but you can be an agent and have no skill whatsoever.

### 4.6 Summary

✔    Whenever we look into organizations that have accomplished cultural changes, we find a large number of people whom we call *change artists*. Moreover, we find these change artists at all levels of an organization and in all units, because for cultural change to occur, it must occur at all levels and in all units. When these change artists are present, they deal with the individual emotional responses to change, and thus increase the chances for success of any change plan.

✔ In the Anticipating (Pattern 4) organization, to some degree *everybody* has become a change artist. Thus, the devotion to developing change artistry is one of the distinguishing marks of this cultural pattern, and the primary tool for change is neither things nor procedures, but *people.*

✔ Change artistry consists of knowing how to facilitate change, knowing what to change, when to change it, where in the organization the change should be introduced, and who should take what roles in carrying it out. Even more, it consists of the ability to take congruent action when under great stress, and when surrounded by people under stress.

✔ There is no single way to be a change artist, and different approaches are needed for different jobs. The important thing is to have a change artist in the right place at the right time to facilitate each little piece of the grand plan.

✔ Each stage of change is different, and each stage requires different types of intervention. Fully matured change artists are able to operate well in all phases: Old Status Quo, Chaos, Integration and Practice, and New Status Quo. Some change artists, however, are primarily effective at only one stage, simply because it happens to match their skills and personalities.

✔ The NT Visionary likes working with ideas and is most interested in designing, rather than implementing, change. The NF Catalyst enjoys working with people to help them grow, and is best at keeping people working together through the rough spots of the change process. The SJ Organizer, who likes order and system, is best at carrying the transformation into actual practice, long after the visionaries have gotten bored. The SP Troubleshooter likes getting the job done and is least likely to deny the foreign element, because it offers an opportunity to swing into action.

✔ The temperaments are merely tendencies: what we may do instinctively when we act without thinking. More fully developed change artists recognize their tendencies, honor them for their strengths, note their weaknesses, and set them aside if they are inappropriate for the current situation.

✔ Without careful management, long-term change is invariably sacrificed to short-term expedience. Such expedience takes place all the time, everywhere in the organization, essentially out of the view of the high-level management. That's why change artists have to be in every nook and cranny of an organization.

✔ The act of patching violates standard process, and so encourages further process violations over time. Though the patch maintains stability in one area, it is a foreign element in several others. Change artists in Anticipating (Pattern 4) organizations evolve a process to resolve this conflict, such as a QUEST team consisting of a hacker responsible for solving the immediate problem, a guardian responsible for seeing that no harm comes to the product, and a healer responsible for amending the process to prevent further occurrences, or to be prepared to handle them better.

✔ Perhaps the toughest skill for a change artist to learn is the skill of knowing what people and what situations to leave alone. Change artists need to learn how to recognize whether specific people or departments are willing to help themselves rise, and to connect what the individuals want with what the organization or the change artist wants.

✔ Among the important principles of change artistry are these:

- Always find the energy for change and go with it.
- Don't get hooked into negative energy.
- Talk in their terms and find out what the issues really are.
- Once you're prepared, go to the source.
- It's perfectly all right to do nothing for a time.

## 4.7 Practice

1. Which Myers-Briggs types or Keirsey-Bates temperaments do you think would best match the hacker, the healer, and the guardian? How would different types and temperaments approach these different tasks?

2. Discuss the following idea of Michael Walsh, CEO of Tenneco, about where to get change artists:

   The best workers are volunteers. You can't order people to perform at peak levels. They have to be motivated. A leader can create an encouraging environment, but there has to be something inside the people as well. You've got to pick those people with a burning desire for change. They're often buried down in the organization.[15]

3. Norm Kerth suggests: Given your temperament,

   - identify your strengths in each stage of the Satir Change Model
   - identify your weaknesses in each stage of the Satir Change Model

   For each weakness, identify ways to

- isolate the system you're working with from the weakness
- compensate for the weakness with one of your strengths
- grow beyond the weakness
- transform the weakness into a strength

4. From Michael Dedolph: Using Thelma's list in Section 4.4 to prime the pump, start collecting all the change artist principles you can gather— from reading this book and others, from observing your organization's attempt to change, and from taking the challenges in Chapter 6.

5. Michael Dedolph further suggests: Think of change efforts in which some principle or principles you have gathered were ignored by would-be change artists. What happened? How could application of the principles have avoided this situation?

6. Payson Hall offers another variation: Think of someone you've known whom you would characterize as an effective change artist.

- What were that person's strengths?
- In what circumstances was he or she most capable?
- What were that person's weaknesses?
- In what circumstances was that person least effective?
- What might he or she have done differently to perform more effectively under unfavorable conditions?

Now answer the same list of questions for yourself.

7. Michael Dedolph points out another approach: There are, of course, many other models of how people work, besides the Myers-Briggs types and Keirsey-Bates temperaments. If you have been trained in one of these other models, apply your results to the domain of change artistry. What does the model tell you about the challenges you may face in order to be effective in each particular phase of change?

# 5

# Keeping Most Things the Same

*. . . it is readily believed that organized effort is normally successful, that failure of organization is abnormal. . . . But, in fact, successful cooperation in or by formal organizations is the abnormal, not the normal, condition. What are observed from day to day are the successful survivors among innumerable failures.*[1]
— Chester I. Barnard

*Recognition of the distinction between a stable system and an unstable one is vital for management. The responsibility for improvement of a stable system rests totally on the management. A stable system is one whose performance is predictable. It is reached by removal, one by one, of special causes of trouble. . . .*[2]
— W. Edwards Deming

These two great management theorists agree that as a manager, you are the guardian of the longer-term, wider-scope knowledge of the organization. When you concentrate on the process of change, it's easy to forget that most of the time, you don't want to change *most* things in your organization. So, a change artist's first and foremost responsibility is to use that longer-term, wider-scope knowledge to keep most things the same—even in the face of innumerable failures. Until you know how to *maintain* an organization, you will not know how to *change* one.

## 5.1  What Are You Maintaining?

In a world full of threats, long-term survival of a complex system is not an accident, but rather a carefully orchestrated system of mechanisms to ensure that survival. Indeed, most of the effort in a living system is expended on survival, and large organizations certainly resemble living systems in this regard. Thus, you can discover what is being maintained by examining the mechanisms. As the great biologist Walter Cannon points out:

> Another of my articles of belief, which seems so self-evident that it hardly needs stating, is that structure and function are inseparably related. This implies that peculiarities of structure are associated with corresponding peculiarities of function. Where structure is complicated, function is likewise complicated.[3]

Both change artists and managers charged with maintaining a system need to know why things don't change. Cannon's principle shows them how to investigate just what these elaborate mechanisms are maintaining, which is not always what the organizations *say* they are maintaining.

### 5.1.1 *Management power, perquisites, and prestige*

All organizations, regardless of their culture, need mechanisms to maintain themselves. My colleague Dan Starr gave me a marvelous application of Cannon's principle,[4] identifying some of the mechanisms needed to maintain a Variable (Pattern 1) culture:

> In *Volume 1* of *Quality Software Management,* the Variable culture is shown as having no feedback control mechanism and no observation of outputs.[5] I don't think that's true, at least not in a large Variable organization. I see a very well-developed feedback control mechanism making observations and taking actions based on process models just like in the Steering (Pattern 3) culture.
>
> The difference is in what's measured and what the process models concern. In the Steering culture, the controller is able to observe/measure X, the desired product of the process. In the large Variable culture, the controller isn't able to take reliable measurements of X, because the projects aren't measurable. But the controller is able to take pretty good measurements of some of the other outputs, notably the level of ritual displays of commitment and dedication, such as
>
> * willingness to commit to clearly impossible goals and schedules
> * large amounts of overtime, particularly weekends
> * acceptance of arbitrary reductions in resources
>
> Further, the controllers take actions suggesting that displays of commitment and dedication are the desired output of the system:
>
> * encouraging and publicizing "stretch" goals, meaning schedule reductions that nobody has any idea how to achieve

- calling favorable attention (for example, in the company newspaper) to the fact that a team worked overtime or weekends to achieve some goal
- stressing the importance (at personnel review time) of being seen as a "willing worker"

In other words, most of the control mechanisms in these Variable (Pattern 1) cultures are devoted to the survival of a system of management power, perquisites, and prestige—or perhaps to preserving the *appearance* of management power. Such a culture is not ready for a trip to an Anticipating (Pattern 4) culture, so do not expect to get respect for a well-planned, well-managed change project. The typical perception will be, "You had the easy part, or else you were lucky."

### 5.1.2  Failure orientation

Another reader, who prefers to remain anonymous, supplied me with a different application of Cannon's principle. She observed her own organization's set of measurements and management response to those measurements:

1.  Management puts great store in quick response time to problems. The management response is to watch the techies and administrators as they try to fix (or at least Band-Aid™) the problems, and keep the pressure on.

2.  The organization also measures response time of the system (and crashes and related problems) so they can identify whether they really get improvements when new hardware arrives—and whether that improvement stays around, or the capacity gets eaten up in a week.

3.  They use few peer reviews, and not enough testing—until after systems go over the wall to the users. The measurements are the problem reports, and the number of things that get through that we should have caught. The response has been convincing the money people to pay for more testing for the next release.

4.  Style and consistency are measured in major off-site walkthroughs after each release goes out.

Rich Cohen offers a valuable clue to just what this organization is actually maintaining by observing that the indicators mentioned are "lagging," rather than "leading," indicators.[6] That is, they report trouble after it has happened. Such use of lagging indicators is a good way to recognize failure-oriented organizations, ones that *assume* they will fail. Instead of working to prevent failure, they are working to keep the failure level low enough to elude attention.

They're also working to establish evidence they can use to point blame at someone else.

Using failure indicators is like steering a car blindfolded, using the jolts of bumping into things. In biological systems, the leading senses (sight, sound, and smell) were developed later than the lagging ones (touch and taste). Because they anticipate, the leading indicators may not be as accurate; they need mental effort to be interpreted properly. But because they give early warning, they are a lot more useful. When you actually feel the lion's teeth on your throat, you don't have a lot of good options left to correct the situation.

In failure-oriented organizations, failure becomes institutionalized. Author Naomi Karten offers this story to illustrate how this happens:

> One company used to have production failures regularly. Its managers knew they had a problem, and they came up with a solution. To eliminate the need for reruns? No. Their solution was to institutionalize the problem. Thus emerged the official position of Rerun Manager, filled by Aaron, who had the key responsibility to arrange reruns and to coordinate the scheduling of all related production runs. This was more than ten years ago. The company has since undergone successive reorganizations, cutbacks, and downsizings, and most of the people I used to know there have left or been laid off. Recently, right after another round of layoffs, I ran into Aaron. "How are things?" I asked, not sure if he still worked there. "Great," he told me, "I'm the Rerun Manager. I'll always have a job."

### 5.1.3 *Technology mentality versus accounting mentality*

Another way to understand what a culture values, and what it is trying to maintain, is to examine what it measures. Two of the most common cultures are characterized by the measurement of consumption and the measurement of production.

Accounting managers measure by *consumption*. They know, as Oscar Wilde said, the "price of everything, and the value of nothing." Routine (Pattern 2) organizations are run by those with an accounting mentality—not surprisingly, many of these Pattern 2 organizations originated as computing divisions within Accounting departments, and may still report there.

Technology managers measure by *production*. They know the value of everything, but sometimes are careless with cost. They tend to be in charge of Variable (Pattern 1) and Steering (Pattern 3) organizations.

Neither an accounting mentality nor a technology mentality is adequate to the job of software engineering in an Anticipating (Pattern 4) culture, first, because neither consumption nor production alone is a sufficient measure and, second, because both together are inadequate to explain the organization's ability to survive in the future.

## 5.2  Exposing the Theory in Use

In organizations, it's not always possible to look at structures and determine their purpose.  Some structures acquire purposes for which they were not designed, and these purposes could be either consistent or inconsistent with the organization's espoused goals.  In dysfunctional organizations, many structures are created precisely to mislead employees, customers, or higher management.  Other structures actually mislead the very people who seem to espouse the opposite of what they produce.

These systems of maintaining cultures of failure and/or management power are examples of what Chris Argyris calls *espoused theory* versus *theory-in-use*.[7]  The espoused theory behind so-called stretch goals is employee achievement; but the theory-in-use is, Keep the employees under (my) control.  The espoused theory behind the failure measurements is quality; but the theory-in-use is, Quality is not really achievable.

A common example of structures that can mislead, either consciously or unconsciously, are project reviews.  Although the ostensible purpose of project reviews is to provide accurate information, in many organizations they are used to put a stamp of approval on less-than-secure projects—and thus produce purported information that is anything but reliable.

In order to achieve an Anticipating (Pattern 4) culture, someone needs to expose these hidden purposes.  Otherwise, they'll block the path of process improvement.  One way to determine the real purpose of a project review is to offer measurements in advance for judgment:

1.    Fill out $N$ summary reports in advance for $N$ possible action outcomes of the review,  plus the names of proposed reviewers.

2.    Present one of the $N$ reports to the manager who will receive the actual report and ask, "What will you do if you get this report?"  Repeat the question for all $N$ possibilities.

3.    If the manager isn't prepared, say, to accept a "Discontinue" decision, then you know the purpose of the review is not really to discontinue unsound projects.  The same is true for the other decisions.  Sometimes a manager isn't prepared to go ahead with an "Accept" decision either, the true agenda being to kill the project or to embarrass the project manager.

What if the manager simply lies?  Naturally, managers with hidden purposes may not tell you directly what they would actually do, but you can always tell by their nonverbal reaction.[8]  Or they will usually give it away with their words, such as, "Well, of course I would discontinue the project if that's what the review board recommended, but no sensible reviewer could possibly make that recommendation, knowing the political situation."  In these cases, find a way to avoid wasting your time doing the project review. If a mock review has to be conducted to cover these lies, arrange to be out of town. Association with sham events cannot possibly help your career as a manager or a change artist.

## 5.3 Deterioration

Although maintaining an organization may not sound as thrilling as changing one, maintenance is a busy job. It's not sufficient to set up a process and then expect it will go on forever. Without constant tending, any process will deteriorate, and deterioration of the process invariably leads to deterioration of the product.[9]

In an article in *Software Maintenance News*, Irv Wendel relates an instructive case of an IS department that first renewed itself, and then was allowed to deteriorate:

> Procedures within the department changed. Phased implementation brought with it tight schedules that, in actuality, prevented formal walk-throughs; this had been where project standards were enforced. Instead, we held informal one-on-one walkthroughs as time permitted.[10]

The as-time-permitted dynamic for technical reviews, of course, means that those programs that most need reviewing never get reviewed. Even when such programs do get reviewed, the degenerated process means that the reviews are not very effective. Wendel's article continues:

> While reviewing changes made to the master file update program made by another programmer, I noted that the changes were of a different style than the rest of the program. I asked the programmer why she had deviated from the program's standardized style. She replied that was how her instructor taught her to write structured code. I pointed out that there were many styles in COBOL that could be considered structured programming. I also delineated the benefits of consistency. She was not swayed. . . .
>
> Despite my disapproval, her modifications went into production unchanged. This incident (and a few others, such as the elimination of our tech writer) indicated that the quality of the system was eroding and would probably erode further, with management's de facto approval.

Erosion of the product leads to further erosion of the process—one instance of which was given in the conclusion of Wendel's story:

> Shortly thereafter, I decided that my time had come and I obtained a contract with a different division within the bank.

When the process goes sour, good people go south.

## 5.4 Design Maintenance Debt

Around 1980, a few Cassandras started crying out about the coming millennium, when all the two-digit date fields would destroy databases and the software that accessed them.[11]  It's not always easy to predict the future of an information system, but it was relatively easy to predict that the year after 1999 would be the year 2000.  If people had started converting their date fields in 1980, they could have done an incremental change, one-twentieth each year.  If they started ten years later, they'd have to have done one-tenth each year.  It was within the power of software engineering managers to make this a relatively minor problem, or to make it a crisis.  Most made it a crisis.

### 5.4.1 Design deterioration

Thousands of other more obscure problems of *exactly* the same nature lurk in old systems.  Money fields, for instance, have been subject to inflation.  I recall several cases of insurance companies that had systems with two digits for hospital daily room rates (which seems incredible now).  They all waited until the systems wouldn't work before they did anything, even though they could see the rates growing for years.  Then, in crisis mode, they did a poor, patchy job.

These are examples of *design deterioration*—design decisions that didn't age well.  Other examples that come to mind are faulty design assumptions about the future relative speed of storage devices, lost wagers on the size/cost trade-off in memory, dependence on minor languages or operating systems that run out of maintenance, and hard-coded mappings to human interface devices.  Each such shortsighted design decision adds a little to the *design debt* carried by the existing software inventory.

Perhaps none of these design deteriorations seems sufficiently large or exciting to make an issue over.  But as the Scotsman said, "Many a mickle macks a muckle."  After a couple of decades of such decisions and little effort to correct them, many an IS organization is in an enormous muckle of Late Status Quo.  Nothing will happen until a foreign element is introduced, like the new manager in this story told by Naomi Karten:

> At the RST company, I was in charge of a billing system with space for amounts up to $999.99.  When it became apparent that amounts were exceeding that and would do so increasingly, we prepared plans for a system-wide modification.  Every time we proposed it, it was shot down.  Instead, we were told to identify bill totals that would exceed $1,000 and produce a report identifying them so the users could pull those bills and reproduce them manually (and correctly).  The system was finally modified (after I left), but not until a new high-level manager took over who heard about the problem and said, "Fix it!"

### 5.4.2 Maintenance deterioration

A second form of software deterioration, called *maintenance deterioration*, is more difficult to isolate than design deterioration—not that design deterioration is easy to isolate. Maintenance deterioration comes from patching programs in a way that does not entirely preserve their designs. A first-class design endures years of hastily considered patches and finally turns to trash. Perhaps that was why the managers at the RST company introduced an increasingly burdensome manual system; they were afraid of what one more change might do to their deteriorated system.

When deterioration continues for a time without abatement, a debt accumulates. Design debt accrues when designs deteriorate; maintenance debt accrues from ongoing maintenance deterioration. The sum of design debt and maintenance debt is *design maintenance debt*. Design maintenance debt—not the "size" of the modification in function points or lines of code—is the major determining factor in the cost of making a modification to an existing system. This debt is often a major cost and complicating factor in changing a software engineering culture (Figure 5-1).

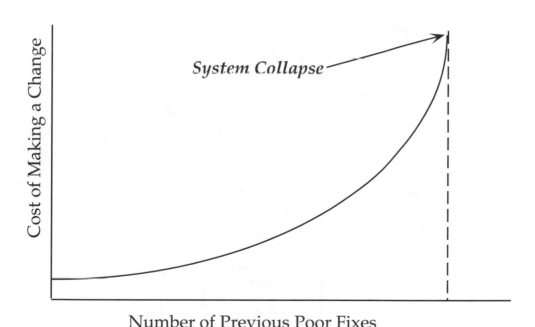

Figure 5-1.    Design maintenance debt plays a major role in determining the apparent size of a change, and eventually produces system collapse by preventing further change at any reasonable cost.

We in the IS industry have not been paying our way. We have been accumulating a massive design maintenance debt that will be paid by our successors, one way or another. Reducing this debt is one of the major tasks of software engineering managers if they intend to meet their large-scope, long-term responsibilities.

## 5.5 Change Artistry Debt

Design maintenance debt is not the only kind of debt an organization incurs when it doesn't pay the ongoing costs of maintenance. In many software engineering organizations, yet another enormous debt stands squarely in the way of eradicating the hidden debts in mountains of code. For years, these organizations have stagnated in the Gray Zone, neglecting to maintain the organization's ability to change. Some of these organizations have *actively* attacked their change artistry with such activities as covert communications, promotion by buddy system, rumors used to tarnish reputations, punishment of risk-takers, and acceptance of special favors from vendors.

What makes up this change artistry debt? The MOI Model says that in order to change, we need motivation, organization, and information (Figure 5-2).[12]

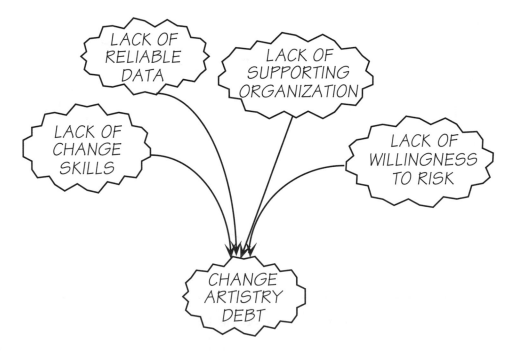

Figure 5-2.     To change, people must have the requisite motivation (willingness to risk), organization (supporting structures), and information (skills plus reliable data). Lack of any one of these items creates a change artistry debt.

For change, motivation may come from many sources, but any motivation to change can be killed by a fear of taking risks.

Organization consists of a variety of forms, such as good strategic planning, a reliable infrastructure (such as e-mail, phone system, and meeting facilities), sensible budgets, and a consistent culture. Covert communications, old-boy networks, and special favors quickly destroy the logic of any organization.

Information for change is needed at two levels. The first kind—contained in the various change artist skills—is of little use without the second—reliable data on the organization's current product and process. Obviously, covert communications and rumor-mongering corrupt useful information.

## 5.6 Destroying Change Artistry

How does an organization incur a change artistry debt? Here is a story told to me by a project manager and would-be change artist in an IS organization:

> In the past five years, I have served on no less than six special teams. Three were called "focus groups," two were "task forces," and one was an "emergency team." Three of them produced reports on how to improve our software process. Two of them were disbanded when management changed. One just faded away. I think the sponsoring manager got bored with it. Each of the reports was put on the shelf.
>
> In two cases, very specific recommendations were directly contradicted by the managers who had set the process in motion. The managers wanted us to recommend large purchases of tools from a particular vendor. We concluded that there were organizational issues that would prevent the tools from being used effectively, mostly on the basis that we've never used tools successfully. Our outside consultants supported us fully. The managers bought the tools anyway. In one case, six managers went on a week-long junket to a resort in Arizona, paid for by this vendor, and came back and signed an order for $450,000 worth of hardware and software. None of it was used for long, and it certainly didn't do us any good.
>
> Unless asked directly, I never admit that I was on any of these teams, because it hurts your reputation around here. You just hope it doesn't come up on your review, and you'd certainly never list it. And you can be sure that I never volunteer for these teams. If forced to join another one, I'll serve my time in a minimal way. And I'm not the only one—but others may not even be willing to talk about it, even with you.

This organization displays a culture fraught with what Deming calls "deadly diseases" and "obstacles" to quality:[13]

- lack of constancy of purpose
- mobility of management
- performance reviews
- neglect of long-range planning in favor of "emergencies"

- blaming the work force for problems
- false starts, or fad of the month
- belief in the magic of computers
- protection from foreign elements from the outside (as expressed in the phrase, "Anyone that comes to try to help us must understand all about our business.")

Figure 5-3 illustrates the addition of these obstacles to the core diagram of effects of Figure 5-2, and shows how effective this management was at creating change artistry debt. What is omitted from this diagram is any acknowledgement that change artistry debt feeds back into some of these destructive management behaviors. For instance, because of the lack of change artistry skills, the organization becomes much more emergency-driven. Other feedback effects are left as practice for the reader, because this web is already tangled enough to show how management can destroy an organization's ability to change.

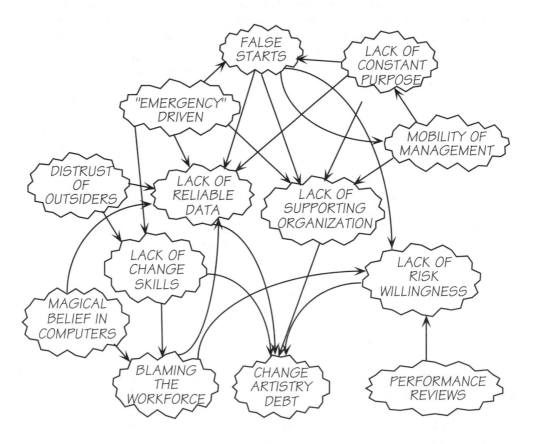

Figure 5-3.      The various components of change artistry are intertwined with management behavior, so that certain behaviors over time create an enormous deficit in an organization's change skills.

## 5.7 Simple Rules for Managers

Without management attention, every organization or part of an organization slips into Late Status Quo. Deming offers an excellent guide to building and maintaining change artistry in an organization. Though some of his points don't translate directly from his manufacturing setting to a software engineering environment, everything he writes about management translates very well indeed. For instance, Deming always emphasizes simplicity, which is one of the primary strategies to prevent the deterioration of change artistry.

In political systems, for example, we recognize a need for simple, clear rules to avoid corruption. "One person, one vote" sounds rather simple-minded until you examine the history of abuse of other "superior" systems. "No censorship" certainly seems overly simple, considering all the things each of us would like to see eradicated, until you examine the history of censorship.

In the same way, managers need simple rules to govern their behavior if they are to conserve what's good in the present organization while promoting change to an Anticipating (Pattern 4) organization. Here are several rules (some derived from Deming and some from my own experience) that create a climate in which change artistry can survive and even grow:

- Don't blame. Give and receive information.
- Don't placate. Take no job that you don't believe in.
- Cut out the superreasonable slogans and exhortations.
- No tricks. Means *are* ends.
- Trust, and merit trust.
- Never stop training yourself in change skills.
- Never stop seeking improvements right around you.
- Remember that you were born little, just like everybody else. Just because you have a title, you haven't ceased to be a human being.

Perhaps all these rules could be summed up into one big rule:

- **Be an example of what you want others to be.**

## 5.8 Helpful Hints and Suggestions

1.  Population and social organizations generally survive for a long time not by reproduction but by a more or less gradual replacement of parts in various roles. For a very critical role (for example, that of the Pope or the queen bee), elaborate procedures are necessary to ensure continued survival. In human organizations, these procedures themselves evolve to be taken as symbolic of the importance of the person protected by them, so that procedures are adopted not to protect, but to show importance when there is really nothing to protect. The Pope, after all, is replaced from time

to time, and very few large corporations fail to survive the sudden death of a CEO. Thus, an accumulation of symbolic status mechanisms surrounding the executives is a possible sign of a change-indebted organization.

2.    Segregation (as in distributed systems) protects a system against variation in its environment. In highly segregated systems, change is usually triggered from the inside, when one of the segments changes. In such organizations, much of the change artistry must be devoted to triggering change by creating foreign elements in one place, not everywhere at once.

3.    Centralization protects a system against *internal* variations. In highly centralized systems, change is usually triggered from the outside, when something happens for which the standard internal structure is not designed. In such systems, change artistry must be devoted to overcoming the system's great skill at rejecting internally generated foreign elements.

4.    Sue Petersen observes: When you're trying to change an organization's control systems from lagging to leading indicators, you risk being labeled "negative." Because the leading indicators aren't as accurate, an organization that wants to use them effectively must accept some false alarms *without* blaming the messenger. This is one more reason why *blaming* cultures cannot become Anticipating (Pattern 4) cultures.[14]

## 5.9 Summary

✔    A change artist's first and foremost responsibility is to use longer-term, wider-scope knowledge to keep most things the same even in the face of innumerable failures. Until you know how to *maintain* an organization, you will not know how to *change* one.

✔    All organizations, regardless of their culture, need mechanisms to maintain themselves. You can discover what is being maintained by examining the mechanisms that maintain them. Cannon's principle shows you how to investigate just what these elaborate mechanisms are maintaining, which may not be what the organizations *say* they are maintaining.

✔    Some Variable (Pattern 1) cultures are devoted to survival of a system of management power, perquisites, and prestige. Such a culture is not a good candidate for a well-planned, well-managed change project.

✔    Observing *how* an organization measures is a good way to apply Cannon's principle. For example, the use of lagging indicators is a good way to recognize failure-oriented organizations, ones that *assume* they will fail. Instead of working to prevent failure, they are working to keep the failure level low enough to elude attention. They're also working to establish evidence they can use to point blame at someone else.

✔ Another way to understand what a culture values, and what it is trying to maintain, is to examine *what* it measures. Two of the most common cultures are characterized by the measurement of *consumption* and the measurement of *production*. Accounting managers typically measure by consumption. Technology managers typically measure by production.

✔ Neither the accounting mentality nor the technology mentality is adequate to the job of software engineering in an Anticipating (Pattern 4) culture—first, because neither consumption nor production alone is a sufficient measure and, second, because both together are inadequate to explain the organization's ability to survive in the future.

✔ These systems of maintaining cultures of failure and/or management power are examples of what Argyris calls espoused theory versus theory-in-use. To achieve an Anticipating (Pattern 4) culture, you need to lay bare these hidden purposes.

✔ It's not sufficient to set up a process and then expect it to go on forever. Without constant tending, any process will deteriorate, and deterioration of the process invariably leads to deterioration of the product.

✔ Design deterioration is the result of a set of design decisions that didn't age well. Each such shortsighted design decision adds a little to the design debt carried by the existing software inventory. Although no single design deterioration seems sufficiently large or exciting to fuss about, after a couple of decades of such decisions—and little effort to correct them—many an IS organization finds itself in Late Status Quo.

✔ Maintenance deterioration comes from patching programs in a way that does not entirely preserve their designs. A first-class design endures years of hastily considered patches and finally turns to trash.

✔ The sum of design debt and maintenance debt is *design maintenance debt*. This debt—not the "size" of the modification in function points or lines of code—is the major determining factor in the cost of making a modification to an existing system. It is often a major cost and complication factor in changing a software engineering culture.

✔ In many software engineering organizations, change artistry debt stands squarely in the way of eradicating the hidden debts in mountains of code. Some organizations have *actively* attacked their change artistry with covert communications, promotion by buddy system, rumors used to tarnish reputations, punishment of risk-takers, and acceptance of special favors from vendors.

✔  The MOI Model says that in order to change, we need motivation, organization, and information. For change, motivation may come from many sources, but any motivation to change is killed by a fear of taking risks. Organization consists of a variety of forms, such as good strategic planning, a reliable infrastructure (such as e-mail, phone system, and meeting facilities), sensible budgets, and a consistent culture.

✔  Information for change is needed at two levels. The first kind—the various change artist skills—is of little use without the second—reliable data on the organization's current product and process.

✔  The various components of change artistry are intertwined with management behavior, so that certain behaviors over time create an enormous deficit in an organization's change skills. To overcome this debt, an organization needs management attention. Managers need simple rules to govern their behavior if they are to conserve what's good in the present organization while promoting change to an Anticipating (Pattern 4) organization.

✔  Some of the more effective management rules for conserving what's good during change are these:

- Don't blame. Give and receive information.
- Don't placate. Take no job that you don't believe in.
- Cut out the superreasonable slogans and exhortations.
- No tricks. Means *are* ends.
- Trust, and merit trust.
- Never stop training yourself in change skills.
- Never stop seeking improvements right around you.
- Remember that you were born little, just like everybody else. Just because you have a title, you haven't ceased to be a human being.
- Be an example of what you want others to be.

## 5.10 Practice

1. Sketch the process of reviewing those parts of a system for which time permits. Consider which parts will be latest, and which parts will have the most quality troubles.

2. Add some other effects to Figure 5-3 from your own experience in organizations.

3.  Michael Dedolph suggests: In organizations with maintenance responsibilities, any significant design maintenance debt can contribute directly to the change artist debt. Construct a diagram of effects to show why this might be true.

4.  By this time it should be clear that change without preservation is a disaster, but preservation means different things to different people. A park ranger, a zoo keeper, and a taxidermist are all concerned with preserving rare species, but their goals are different. Which type of preservationist are you?

5.  Jim Highsmith observes: Careful articulation of the motivating factors can be a big factor in whether an organization gets through a change, especially an organization in Chaos. Maybe Variable (Pattern 1) and Routine (Pattern 2) organizations change only when the "pain" is that of failure: They can't break old habits by just wanting to be better organizations. Anticipating (Pattern 4) cultures, on the other hand, change when they anticipate failure (or, more positively, see an opportunity). An Anticipating (Pattern 4) culture doesn't have to actually fail in order to change. Some organizations just can't survive even one failure, so they either become Anticipating or they don't survive at all. If the failure to change is because of motivation, then perhaps you can create a situation in which a single large failure is simply unacceptable. Discuss how to do this without creating such a climate of fear that the organization is paralyzed.

6.  Michael Dedolph further suggests: Consider how design debt and maintenance debt contribute to the overall design maintenance debt. Extend this reasoning by analogy to an "organizational change debt" by first realizing that most organizations are *designed* and that the formal design structure is *maintained*. (Hint: If the design does not facilitate communication, the organization will lack reliable data; and if the organizational structure has deteriorated, the organizational infrastructure for supporting change will be absent. What needs to be in place to support building change skills and willingness to take risks?)

# 6

# Practicing to Become a Change Artist

*Things do not change;*
*we change.*
— Henry David Thoreau

The purpose of this chapter is to give you an idea of what change artists specifically do, and how they might be trained to do it. If you want to try these challenges yourself, who's to stop you?

## 6.1 Going to Work

*Nobody makes a greater mistake than he who did*
*nothing because he could only do a little.*
— Edmund Burke

Your first challenge is to undertake a change project of your own, of a very specific nature. The purpose is to have you experience the Satir Change Model and some of its emotional consequences.

*The Challenge*

Your challenge is to go to work tomorrow in a different way.

*Experiences*

The first experience of this assignment is what goes on in your head and heart when you first read it. Here are a few typical examples from people I've worked with:

✔   I immediately experienced panic (Chaos). What if I was late to work? I've already found the optimal way to work, because I've been driving it for four years. Suddenly, I understood exactly how it felt being in the Late Status Quo, and I knew that I would have more consideration for the people whose work I was trying to change.

✔   My first thought was, "Impossible!" I simply could not think of a single alternative to the well-developed route I took to work. After all, there was only one bridge across the river. What was I supposed to do, swim? I decided I simply wasn't going to do it, which allowed me to relax. Then I realized that the assignment said "in a different way," not "by a different route." I hadn't even understood the foreign element, and I had rejected it.

Now consider some of the comments I received after the assignment was completed:

✔   I decided to go to work wearing a tie, which I've never done before. The reaction of other people was totally unexpected, both the number of people and their intensity. I learned how easy it is to be a foreign element, and that you can't change just one thing.

✔   I went to work with a different attitude—more positive. The whole day was entirely different. It's a much better place to work than it was last week.

✔   In driving by a different route, I got lost and discovered a part of the city I'd never seen before. I was late to work, but it was fun. I decided to go a different way each day, and I've been doing it now for six months. I like it.

✔   I always go to work in a different way every day, so I wasn't going to do the assignment. Then I realized that a different way for me would be to go the same way. So I drove the same way every day for a week and learned a couple of things. First of all, the same way isn't the same way, if I pay attention. Second, I'm not the same every day. Some days I can't tolerate waiting for the light at 35th Street, but other days I welcome the time to reflect about things. I used this learning to reintroduce a proposal that had been rejected last month. This time, they loved it.

## 6.2  Making One Small Change

> *I report a conversation with a colleague who was*
> *complaining that he had the same damn stuff in*
> *his lunch sack day after day.*
>
> *"So who makes your lunch?" I asked.*
>
> *"I do," says he.*[1]
>
> —R. Fulghum

Your next challenge is to undertake a change project of your own, but this time to seek support in making this change. The purpose is to launch your career as a change artist by experiencing in the "real world" some of the theoretical learnings, but in as small and safe a way as possible.

### The Challenge

Choose one *small* thing *about yourself* you want to change. Novice change artists tend to be too eager for their own good. If you want to eat a whole elephant, start with a single bite. If you finish one change, you are free to do another, and another—so don't worry that it's too small.

Find an interested change artist (or associate, or some willing person), meet with him or her, and explain the change you want to make. Contract with that person for the kind of support you think you need to accomplish your change. Check with your supporter periodically to update him or her on your progress.

### Experiences

Since readers of a book can't easily exchange observations about experiences, let's examine a few instructive experiences of other change artists accepting this challenge to make one small change.

✔  When I have a hot idea in a meeting, instead of blurting it out, I write a little note to myself and wait a couple of minutes. I noticed that about 60 percent of the time, somebody else comes up with essentially the same idea. Then, when I support the innovator, the idea has a very great chance of being adopted.

I've increased the number of my ideas that get adopted, but I'm not getting credit for them—at least not directly. But several people have told me that I've really become a leader in meetings. This was a surprise, because I thought they would consider me a leader when I had the most ideas—and they didn't. My supporter explained that I seemed more "statesmanlike," more calm and more respectful of others.

✔ I take a break every hour when I'm alone, but when I'm in meetings, I find this is really hard to do. I don't want to interrupt anyone, but my supporter gave me some good suggestions about how to "test the waters" before doing it in a meeting. To my surprise, most people welcomed the breaks, most of the time. I learned that people (including me) often don't say what they want, and this has transferred to the practice of polling groups more often to find out how they feel about what's going on in meetings.

✔ I posted hours when I would be uninterruptable, and hours when I would always be available for interruptions. At first, people didn't respect these hours, as they didn't believe I would really do it. I couldn't say no to any-one, so my supporter actually came into my office from four to five o'clock one day (the busiest time) and coached me on how to dispatch people to the posted schedule.

   This worked pretty well for me, but it was a strain for some of them. I then realized that four to five would be a good time for drop-in time, so I changed the schedule. After two more schedule adjustments, the thing seems to be working. I've learned that it's impossible to plan anything perfectly if it involves other people—you have to try it out, then be pre-pared to adjust a couple of times.

✔ I keep my wallet in a different pocket. The first time I reached for my wallet, I was in an absolute panic—I was sure I had lost it. My supporter pointed out to me that this may be the way people feel when I change things in the system and don't tell them—or even if I do tell them, because they have the habit of finding things in certain places.

✔ I made a healthier lunch for myself. I learned that I don't like "healthy" food. My supporter told me that I'm too health conscious anyway, and that the kind of lunch I made was rather fanatic. I guess she's right. It made me aware that I'm a perfectionist, but that it's not in the nature of human beings to be perfect. Even if I eat a pickle now and then, or a cookie, the world won't come to an end. Also, even if my teammates make a mistake in their code from time to time, or don't design something perfectly, we'll survive.

## 6.3 Changing Nothing

*Of course I am idle, but I am not idle by nature;*
*I simply haven't yet discovered what I can do*
*here. . . .*
                                        —Sophie Tolstoy

The purpose of the next challenge is to find out what's driving you to change things, and what happens if you don't respond to that drive in the usual way.

### The Challenge

Next time you're part of a team or group effort, sit back, listen, and observe. Your job is to try not to change *anything*. Take particular notice of your urges to change things, and what happens when you don't do anything about those urges.

### Experiences

Here are a few experiences of other change artists who accepted this challenge to do nothing at all.

✔   Wow! I couldn't do it! I lasted almost three whole minutes. I resisted the temptation to open the window, or to ask someone to do it. I resisted the temptation to move the flipchart so everyone could see it. I resisted the temptation to move over one seat to make room for a latecomer. But when Jack stood up and grabbed the marker pen (AGAIN), I couldn't resist suggesting that someone else should take a turn. It was out of my mouth before I knew it! But I just HAD to say it!

After my first miserable failure, I decided to try again, the next day. I got through the mechanics a lot more easily—the window and the flipchart and the chairs—and with somewhat more difficulty, I let Jack grab the pen again. I was on a roll, and I managed to keep it up for almost fifteen minutes. When I finally did say something about the direction the meeting was taking, the other people reacted as if I was the President of the United States. They gave me their full attention, let me finish everything I had to say, and then did exactly what I proposed. I think there's a clue there for me. I'm working on it, and I'm going to try this again.

✔   I didn't think this would be very hard for me. I would just sit in the meeting and do what I usually do—keep my mouth shut and observe. I was doing a good job of this when all of a sudden I realized that I was changing things *in my mind* about one every thirty seconds. Then I said nothing about any of them, and I found myself getting angry that nobody else was doing anything about them. Aha! Were they doing exactly what I was doing?

Armed with my new insight, I worked out a plan for the next meeting. I sat in my usual way, quietly fanning my smoldering anger and frustration. When I got to the proper amount of emotional heat—not so much that I wouldn't be able to control it—I said a sentence that I had written down and practiced: "Is there anything about this meeting anyone would like changed?" The reaction was instantaneous, and the changes poured out. The rest of the meeting went very differently from our usual meetings, though I didn't say another thing.

✔ This was a pretty boring exercise for me, so I had to do something to occupy my mind. I decided to try to observe emotional reactions, because I had always thought our meetings were rather flat and unemotional, but our consultant told me they weren't. I noticed lots of things that I never saw before. For instance, two of our folks were really suffering—I didn't know from what, so I asked them about it after the meeting. Was that a violation of the assignment? If it was, I don't care, because I learned some things I had never even suspected before, and my relationships with two members of the team have gone up several notches.

## 6.4 Changing a Relationship

*Conflict is the gadfly of thought. It stirs us to observation and memory. It instigates to invention. It shocks us out of sheeplike passivity, and sets us at noting and contriving. . . .*
—John Dewey

Your next challenge is to undertake changing a *relationship*. The purpose is to apply some of your learnings about congruence and conflict.

### The Challenge

Choose one *relationship* you have with another person that's not all you would like it to be. It could be a good friend with whom there's one thing that annoys you but you've suppressed it, or something you like that you'd like more of. It could be a work associate with whom you're not on the terms you'd like to be. Again, don't start by tackling the most difficult relationship you have. If you finish changing one relationship, you are free to do another, and another, so don't worry that it's too small.

As before, find an interested change artist, or associate, or some willing person, meet with the person, and explain the change you want to make. Seek assistance in planning how to go about changing this relationship—assistance with ideas, in checking your ideas, and possibly in practicing in a role play. Then carry out your plan with the actual person.

This challenge will especially give you a chance to confront the difficulties you have in the presence of strong (or potentially strong) emotions in others. After all, you won't know in advance how the other person will respond to your attempt to change the relationship. A person might cry, or go into Chaos, or get involved in a conflict with you over it, or become incongruent in a variety of ways. How will you handle yourself in those situations? Will you fail to take a risk because you anticipate one of these reactions?

*Experiences*

✔ I decided to get to know my boss better as a person, and not just as a "boss." I asked her to lunch. She was a bit taken aback, but once we agreed it would be Dutch treat, she was okay with it. We found out that we both have a passion for softball, but play in different leagues. That gave us a lot to talk about, and since then I've given her the benefit of the doubt when she comes out with some edict I don't understand.

✔ I'm responsible for upgrading all the Mac software for my department, and one of the users has been a pain in the derriere for me ever since I got this job. I decided to sit down with him and ask him how he felt about the service he'd been getting. He said that people seemed to avoid him when he had problems, and he was pleased that I'd take the time to sit down with him. I was able to show him a few things that prevented trouble, and cured some things he hadn't even bothered to complain about. He's still a pain, but just in the neck, and I can deal with it. At least it's a little higher up. [smiles]

✔ I have an employee who drinks excessively. I had been avoiding the topic because I didn't really know what to do. I paid a visit to our employee assistance program, and the staff there gave me some booklets and some coaching. Next time he came to work drunk, I knew what to do, and didn't pretend it wasn't happening. He had to confront the impact he's having on his job, and he's now working with employee assistance. He may not solve his drinking problem, but if not, I can handle it.

✔ I did this a little backward. I decided to change a relationship *back* to what it was before. Grace and I worked together for a couple of years, and were very good friends. Then I took a transfer to a different project and moved to another building. I guess I was feeling guilty, like I deserted her—which isn't the way a good friend should behave—so I avoided seeing her or even calling her. I decided just to go over and pay her a visit, like we used to do when we were in neighboring cubes. She wondered where I'd been, and we're back to being great friends. All "her" feelings about me "leaving" were in my imagination.

✔ I'd been playing golf with our hardware salesman for a couple of years— he'd take me to his country club almost every Saturday. I never felt good about it, like it was somewhat unethical. So I told him I couldn't play with him anymore unless I paid my way. He objected, saying it wasn't costing him anything, since his company was paying for it. I told him that was the point. He said okay. Now we still play golf, but I feel a lot better about it.

✔ I'd been locked in a struggle with Harmon for almost a year over which CASE tool we should use in the organization. I decided to approach him from the point of view that our conflict was only helping those reprobates who didn't want to use *any* CASE tool. We made a pact that we would join forces to get *some* CASE tool going, somewhere. We actually flipped a coin to see who would help whom. I lost, so I swallowed my pride and helped him sell his team on using the tool he liked. Once we joined forces, they were a pushover. He was going to help me sell my team on the tool I liked, but by this time I like his tool just as well—actually a little better.

## 6.5  Being the Catalyst

*Look abroad thro' Nature's range.*
*Nature's mighty law is change.*
　　　　　　　　—Robert Burns

Although change artists often work as prime movers, they more often work through understanding natural forces and creating slight perturbations of Nature. In this challenge, you will practice facilitating the change projects of others, using various ways of empowering from the position of *catalyst*.

In chemistry, a catalyst is a substance that added to a reaction accelerates that reaction by its presence, without itself being changed by the reaction. A human catalyst is someone that rouses the mind or spirits or incites others to activity with a minimum of self-involvement—in other words, by empowering others. For people to be empowered to change their organization, the MOI Model tells us that the following ingredients are required:

### Motivation

- self-esteem
- a value system and a vision held in common
- a sense of difference between perceived and desired

### Organization

- mutuality of support, based on personal uniqueness
- a plan for reducing the perceived/desired difference
- a diversity of resources relevant to the plan

### Information

- a systems understanding of what keeps things from changing
- an understanding of empowerment versus powerlessness
- continuing education appropriate to the tasks

Often, only a single ingredient is missing, but the person who doesn't know which one it is can feel completely disempowered. The recipe suggests which ingredient might be missing. A change artist who supplies that missing ingredient can catalyze change with minimal effort.

## The Challenge

Your challenge is to facilitate other people's change projects, approximately one per week, for at least two weeks. You should attempt to be a *catalyst* for change, not the prime mover for change. To be a catalyst, you should involve yourself

- as effectively as possible
- in the smallest possible way
- without depleting your capacity to catalyze other changes

If possible, use each ingredient of this recipe for empowerment at least once. Keep notes in your journal and be prepared to share learnings with the group you are catalyzing.

## Experiences

✔ A group in the shipping department asked me to help them run their planning meetings. I said I would do it if they enrolled two people in our facilitation class, and that after taking the class, they would work alongside me. After one meeting, they are now facilitating their own.

✔ I led a technical review of the design of a very controversial project, and apparently I did a good job because I got three other invitations to lead difficult reviews. I did lead two of them, but I decided to try being a catalyst on the third. I told them I wouldn't lead the meeting, but I would play shadow to a leader of their choice and we would switch roles if their leader got in trouble. She didn't.

✔ One of my groups wasn't using—or even attempting to use—the new configuration control system. Ordinarily, I would have *ordered* them to use it, with threats of reprisals. I thought about the minimum thing I could do—with no force and no blaming—to get them moving. I decided to call them in for a meeting and give them the problem of how to get them moving.

They told me they just didn't have time to switch their partially developed project to the new system. I asked them how much time they would need. They huddled and came up with a two-week extension to their schedule. (I had been afraid they would say two *months*.) Since they were off the critical path, I said they could have the two weeks, but only if they switched to the new system. They actually did the job in one week, and in the end, they made up four days of that—partly, at least, because of using the better tool.

I've now used this consultation method several more times. "What would you need to give me what I need?" turns out to be a great catalyst, and I like being a catalyst much more than being a dictator.

## 6.6 Being Fully Present

*It always seems to me that so few people live—*
*they just seem to exist—and I don't see any rea-*
*son why we shouldn't LIVE always. . . .*
                    —Georgia O'Keefe

In order to be a successful catalyst for change, you must learn the art of being fully present. To be fully present, you must

- Pay full attention to the speaker.
- Put aside any preconceived ideas of what the speaker is going to say.
- Interpret descriptively and not judgmentally.
- Be alert for confusions and ask questions to get clarity.
- Let the speaker know that he or she has been heard, and what has been communicated.[2]

Here are a number of common hindrances to being fully present:

- *Ignoring:* lack of attention (looking elsewhere, fidgeting), boredom, disinterest, pretending to listen
- *Selective listening:* hearing only parts
- *Sidetracking:* changing the subject (without proper transition); telling your own story; making light of, with inappropriate humor
- *Evaluative listening:* agreeing or disagreeing before the explanation is finished

- *Probing:* asking too many questions (from your frame of reference) with little sense of the person
- *Interpretative listening:* explaining what's going on based on your own motives and behavior
- *Advice giving:* offering solutions; focusing too much on content

### The Challenge

Your challenge is to pick one habit that keeps you from being fully present, and focus on reshaping that habit in all your interactions.

### Experiences

✔ I decided to try going through a meeting without telling any jokes. I didn't actually make it all the way, but they seemed to appreciate my joke more, when I finally told it.

✔ I didn't really know what to do, as I thought I was a good listener. I got a support person who told me that I should stop reading my mail during meetings. That really surprised me, because I thought myself so good a listener that I could read mail and listen at the same time. Besides, it kept me from interrupting.

My supporter told me that even though I might be hearing everything that was said, my reading made it look like I wasn't paying attention, or at least didn't care what was being said.

✔ I'd read about not giving solutions during review meetings, but I was strongly opposed to the idea. It just didn't make sense to me. But, since I had to do this assignment, I decided to try doing one review without offering any solutions. I did have two solutions to offer, but the author came up with one of them a few minutes later, before I said anything about it. Actually, I guess it was pretty obvious, and if I'd said it, he probably would have thought I considered him stupid. I saved the other until after the meeting, and it was really appreciated. It seemed to be a pretty good review, actually one of the better ones I've ever attended.

✔ I have to tell you that I'm known around here for being the person who can get anything out of anybody with my penetrating questions. I decided to try a new tactic. Whenever I found myself thinking of a neat question, I caught myself and asked, instead, "What else do you want to tell me?" I got just as much information as I ever get, so maybe I'm not such a great questioner as I thought. Or maybe I'm greater—I can do it with just one question!

✔   I looked at whoever was speaking.  Every time.  I had been missing a lot, not seeing facial expressions and posture.  I think I'll do it again.

## 6.7  Being Fully Absent

> *Whoever is in a hurry shows that the thing he is*
> *about is too big for him.*
> —Lord Chesterfield

During the Great Plague of 1666, Isaac Newton was forced to go home for a holiday when schools closed in London.  While idling under a tree, he got the basic idea for his Theory of Universal Gravitation.

During the heyday of telephone exploitation circa 1877, Alexander Graham Bell got married and took a year-long honeymoon in Europe.  While there, he had his grand vision—not for the telephone, but for the telephone system.

So much for not being able to leave a project for vacation!  As your powers as a change artist grow, it's easy to get the grandiose idea that the world can't change without you.  This challenge is a challenge to that idea.  It's also a way to trick you into taking care of yourself.

### The Challenge

Your challenge is to take a week away from work, and when you get back, notice what changed without you being there.  You must not do anything about your change artist work for a whole week, but notice what thoughts come into your head, or what apples fall on it.

Do you think you can't do this?  Then you have a different assignment, suggested by Wayne Bailey: "If you're going on a week-long vacation and feel the project cannot do without you, then take a two-week vacation."

### Experiences

✔   We took two weeks and went to Hawaii.  It was our first vacation in seven years—really since our honeymoon.  I'd always dreamed of a Pacific island paradise, and we found it.  The first few days, Shanna and I drove all over the Big Island like tourists.  It was interesting, but it wasn't the vacation of my dreams.  Then we just started frolicking on the beach, eating, lying about in the shade, eating, really talking to each other, eating, swimming, and eating.

After about seven days of this bliss, I woke up early one morning and realized that although I hadn't consciously thought about work at all, I suddenly had a complete vision of how our process improvement program had to be restructured. Shanna was still asleep (it was *real* early), so I slipped out for a walk on the beach. When I got back about two hours later, I had the entire thing worked out in my mind. I didn't even have to write it down—it was so clear that I knew I couldn't forget it.

Then I put it out of my mind and enjoyed the last three days of our vacation in paradise. When I got back to work, I had a new and revitalized organization. More important, I had a new and revitalized marriage.

✔  I decided to spend a week hiking a segment of the Appalachian Trail. I hadn't done any backpacking for a couple of years, so I had to take out all my equipment, replace some of it, and reconsider everything. While doing that, I realized that I needed to do the same thing at work. I was so eager to get started that a little voice inside me said to forget the hike and get back to work. But I resisted. I was able to use the hike—even though it rained most of the time—as a metaphor for the changes I had to make at work. Come to think of it, that was probably *because* it rained all the time.

✔  I stayed home and played solitaire, did jigsaw puzzles, and cleaned the house. I also rearranged my thoughts. Thank you for this assignment.

✔  I went to Spain, where I could refresh my school Spanish. I spent a week in Madrid and a week in Barcelona, with a few side trips into the country. Perhaps it was living in another language for two weeks, but I didn't think of work at all. When I came back, I discovered that they had gotten along very well without me, and were eager to show me some of the nifty things they'd accomplished. At first I was depressed, thinking I wasn't as essential as I had thought. Then I was elated when I realized that I had done a good job of preparing them to keep improving things when I wasn't there. I guess that's really the change artist's job, isn't it?

## 6.8 Applying the Principle of Addition

> *The peculiar vanity of man, who wants to believe*
> *and who wants other people to believe that he is*
> *seeking after truth, when in fact it is love that he*
> *is asking this world to give him.*
> —Albert Camus

Satir's Principle of Addition says that people change behavior by adding new behaviors, rather than getting rid of old ones. The behaviors that are reinforced are done more often, leaving less and less time for behaviors that are not reinforced.

## The Challenge

Your challenge is to practice giving affirmations for behaviors you wish to increase. This can be in the form of an e-mail note, a card, a phone call, a brief office visit, a comment in the corridor. It must be done, however, directly to the person, not through some third party.

**Each and every day, give one affirmation to one person.**

## Experiences

✔ This challenge forced me to pay attention to what people were doing.

✔ This was really hard! Something deep inside me got caught in my throat when I started to form an affirmation of someone. It's a good thing I had a support group to help me figure out where that came from. I'm still not very good at it, but I can get the words out.

✔ I thought I was already doing this, so it would be a really easy assignment. It turned out that nobody recognized when I was giving an affirmation, because I always cut the corners off it by some little joke, or discount.

✔ I'm pretty good at this, in person, so I decided to start sending little cards to people who had done something that helped one of my change projects. Boy, was I surprised at how delighted they were! Something about a card made them really sit up and take notice; maybe it showed that I was thinking of them when they weren't present, and I took that little extra time to do this in a way that wasn't the easiest, such as e-mail. Maybe that made it seem extra important.

✔ I made a list of people I ought to affirm, and made five copies, one for each day. I would check each one off the day's list so I would have a measure of how well I was doing. My goal was to be able to do everybody in one day by the end of the week. There were 14 people on the list, and my scores for the five days were 4, 7, 6, 11, 14. I was very proud of myself, and on Saturday I showed the list to my husband, Will, and explained the assignment. He read over the list and told me I had forgotten someone. I was devastated: What good was a perfect score if it wasn't the whole list?

But I couldn't for the life of me figure out who was left off. On Sunday, in church, I was still thinking about it and not really listening to the sermon. Will leaned over and whispered in my ear: "You."

At our church, some of us stay after the service for a discussion of the sermon. God must have been watching over me when He sent the sermon that day because the subject was "Love thy neighbor as thyself." I understood that if I didn't love myself very much, loving my neighbor as myself didn't mean very much. I'd say I had a religious experience because of this exercise.

## 6.9  Organizing the Grand Tour

*When you stop learning, stop listening, stop looking and asking questions, always new questions, then it's time to die. . . .*
                                            —Lillian Smith

One of the most important sources of ideas for change is ideas that have already worked in a similar organization. Moreover, one of the most supportive acts you can perform is to ask someone to teach someone else what they do well. When people teach other people about what they are doing, it forces them to become aware of their own processes.

### The Challenge

Your challenge is to organize a tour of your workplace for other change artists. Have the people in your workplace teach the change artists "what we do well that others might want to imitate."

### Experiences

✔  I thought this was a silly assignment—until it paid off with a savings of about $40,000 a year in our printing operation. One of the programmers on the tour had never seen an actual printer in operation. Once she understood the way things worked, she easily changed one of our major applications so that weekly printing was significantly faster.

✔  We found that another team's performance analyzer did things that we never imagined. We felt a bit foolish using the crude tool we had concocted, but I was proud that we didn't defend it in the face of an obviously superior product (change artist training helped with that). With more than a little help from their team, we switched tools—and, as a side benefit, no longer had to maintain our homemade kludge.

✔  The effect on my group was fantastic, and that really surprised me. First, they grumbled about all the trouble it would be to prepare for the tour, but then they started cleaning house. It was like when my mother comes to visit—I clean the toilets and put away things that have been laying out for months.  The group did the same thing with their code and their supporting documentation.  I don't know if the visitors got anything out of their visit, but they sure saw a clean operation.  And—this is the best thing—it stayed clean.

Actually, I do think they got something out of it, because we've been asked to give four more tours to groups where someone wants to clean house.

✔   Well, we didn't learn much, and they didn't learn much, except that we do things pretty much the same way.  I guess that's confirming.  And I learned that they're nice people.  Perhaps in the future we'll be able to help each other, and that feels good even if we don't have any specific current benefits to show.

## 6.10  Learning from History

*The liberation of a tree is not the freedom from its roots.*
                    —Rabindranath Tagore

The Grand Tour shows you what's going on now, but perhaps more interesting to a change artist is how things got the way they are.

### The Challenge

Your challenge is to discover the history of some practice that you consider nonproductive.

### Experiences

✔   Darn you!  This assignment almost got me fired.  I started questioning why we chose our LAN software, and then it came out that my boss was the one who made the study that led to the decision.  We got into a BIG argument over what I considered a *dumb* choice that was really hurting communication around here.  He gave me a copy of his original study (actually, he practically shoved it down my throat) and I grudgingly read it.  I was halfway into it when I realized that they really had chosen the best that was available at that time.  The system I was favoring didn't even exist then.  I don't think the company that makes it even existed then.  I didn't know that; I didn't even *think* of that.

Well, I learned a couple of things:

*   Don't argue with the boss until you have all your facts straight.  (I suppose I knew this, but needed reinforcing.)
*   Everybody really is doing the best they can, with what they have, at the time they do it.

- I'm likely to make the same mistake (if it really is a mistake) of not seeing far enough into the future.
- An apology actually works with my boss, and doesn't kill me (though it embarrasses me).

✔ While studying how we used consultants in the past, I learned that we have a pattern of paying them a lot, putting in a lot of work with them, and then putting their reports on the shelf. I don't know what I'm going to do about this, but obviously something has to change. Perhaps we won't hire consultants anymore, or we'll hire different ones, or we'll work with them differently. Maybe we're expecting too much from a report.

✔ I found out why we put quarters in the bowl at meetings when somebody interrupts someone else. That started before I came to this group. Now we give that money to charity, but originally it was used for beer after the meeting. I've reinstituted the beer-sharing—we really needed some kind of team-building or team-repairing like that. Don't worry, though. We still give the quarters to charity, and just take turns buying the beer.

✔ I wanted to find out what really happened to the previous two process groups. I did. I'm going to make a few changes, right away.

✔ Well, I couldn't do this assignment. I wanted to study the history of our weekly status meetings, but I couldn't find anyone who remembered how they got started. I couldn't find anyone who remembered *why* they got started. I couldn't even find anybody who knew why we were still doing them. So we're not doing them anymore. But I didn't do the assignment.

### 6.11 Putting Theory into Practice

> *There's nothing more practical than a good theory.*
> —Kenneth Boulding

Reading a book is one thing. Applying what you learn is quite another. If you don't apply it soon, it simply fades away. The same is true of any educational experience. If you come back from a class and don't start using some of the material, you may as well not have gone in the first place.

### *The Challenge*

Your challenge is to review the chapters in any of the four *Quality Software Management* volumes concerning specifics of the Anticipating (Pattern 4) organization and to consider each idea in terms of the artistry that you can use to introduce it to your organization. Try to create at least one specific action item that will advance the transformation to that way of doing things.

*Experiences*

✔  I started a brown bag special-interest group on our new CASE tool as a place for people who were using it to share learnings, and as a low-risk place for those who weren't using it to find out about it. The hardest part for me—and the real challenge—was to be the first speaker. I haven't been a person who enjoys speaking in front of groups, but I got some support and made myself do it.

  The group now runs on its own—with little nudges from me once in a while—and there's no trouble getting speakers. It has tripled in size as our use of the tool has grown, and people think that without the group the tool would have died in the original group, or at least not spread.

✔  I set out to measure something that would be useful to upper management and to the people whose work was being measured. After a few false starts, I hit upon measuring resolution time for failures found in test. I set up a system to capture this data from our bug database and to plot it automatically week by week.

  One of the surprising things it showed was the way the new configuration management system actually slowed down resolution time. Since I was advocating the new system, I was rather disappointed, but I resisted the temptation to fudge the figures. Management wanted to throw the system out, but I invoked the Satir Change Model to get a few weeks' grace period. With the help of some investigation into the causes of Chaos, the graph improved. In about three weeks, the resolution time was back to what it was before the tool, and after six weeks, the time was cut by 32 percent. This was the first time anyone had ever demonstrated the value of a new tool in our organization.

✔  My challenge to myself was to open up information in my organization. To do this, I decided to be the model by using Public Project Progress Posters for the three projects I'm managing. I was surprised by the emotional reactions—mine and others'. I was apprehensive and defensive, yet proud of my courage. One of the other managers came into my office, shut the door, and started screaming obscenities at me for embarrassing him (because he wasn't going to post *his* progress).

  The people in the projects were generally accepting, although I spent a lot of time in the next two weeks explaining how to read the posters, what certain slippages meant, and what I was going to do about them. It was a lot more trouble than I anticipated, but now that things have settled down, it seems to be worth it.

## 6.12  Developing Yourself

> *A book can give you only what the author has to tell.  But the learning that comes through self-knowledge has no limit, because to learn through your own self-knowledge is to know how to listen, how to observe, and therefore you learn from everything: from music, from what people say and the way they say it, from anger, greed, ambition.*
>
> —Jiddu Krishnamurti

The biggest benefit from change artistry comes when you start teaching other people to be change artists.

### The Challenge

Your challenge is to make up a change artistry challenge of your own, one that will give you practice in an area you need most.  Accept your own challenge and offer it to others.

# Part III
# Planning for the
# Future Organization

*Recognition of the distinction between a stable system and an unstable
one is vital for management.  The responsibility for improvement of a stable system rests totally on the management.  A stable system is one whose
performance is predictable.  It is reached by removal, one by one, of special
causes of trouble. . . .*[1]

— W. Edwards Deming

There are many ways to categorize software organizations.  In this series, I use
the concept of *software cultural patterns*,[2] based on the work of Philip Crosby.[3]
The focus of this book is on creating an Anticipating (Pattern 4) culture, assuming that you already have a Steering (Pattern 3) culture.  Every culture changes,
of course, but the Anticipating culture is a continuously changing culture that
*plans* its changes to shape the organization it wants.  Thus, it is concerned with
both the process of fostering change and the process of maintaining stability in
the face of change.

Most writers on improving software engineering emphasize the essential
changes, but neglect the subject of *how* these changes are to be brought about.
These writers seem to assume that all that's required is *telling* people what to
change.  This is the Routine (Pattern 2) paradigm.

The Pattern 4 paradigm emphasizes process before product, and this
emphasis carries over to the process of changing the organization itself.  Until
you know *how* to plan for change, you will continue to be frustrated, knowing
*which* things to change, but never seeming able to accomplish them.  If you
hope to transform your software engineering organization to Pattern 4, you
must master the art of planning for change, and that is the subject of Part III.

# 7

# Meta-planning, Part I: Information

*Climate is what you expect.*
*Weather is what you get.*
— Anonymous

*The winds and waves are*
*always on the side of the*
*ablest navigators.*
— Edward Gibbon

Change artists practice their skills on three levels, involving three different time scales and three different sets of skills. Sailing provides a nice metaphor for these three levels. Change artistry "in-the-small" deals with people and problems face-to-face and day-to-day: a spinnaker ripping, a crew member getting seasick, or someone dropping the charts overboard. This level is what we change artists call *tactics*.

Tactics don't always involve reactions to unexpected events; many are planned in advance. Change artistry "in-the-middle" is what we call *tactical planning:* noticing the cloud formations to anticipate a shift in the winds and the sails that will be needed, laying out the watch rotation so that crew members will be fresh, and keeping a spare set of charts in the captain's locker.

Change artistry "in-the-large" is what we call *strategic planning:* deciding on a destination; describing the kind of ship, sails, and crew needed to reach that destination; and buying or creating the charts to cover the entire voyage.

Strategic planning creates the climate that we hope puts the wind and weather generally on the side of those artists who must navigate the changes.  To be able navigators, managers must be able to cope with weather while on their way to the climate they are trying to create.

If we are berthed in some lesser port, but our destination is the Port of Anticipation (Pattern 4), then change is our voyage.  To make this voyage of change, we must practice change artistry at the very top, in the form of strategic planning for change.  For years, I thought that *everyone* understood strategic planning, but it slowly dawned on me that all everyone knew were the kind of generalities that landlubberly armchair sailors knew.  Therefore, this and the following chapters switch to an explicit, action-oriented format, giving the problem, the cause, and the action needed to prepare your organization for a variety of planning situations.  If you're already an able navigator, please forgive me and sail ahead.

## 7.1  Start by Meta-planning

Figure 7-1 gives an overview of strategic planning as practiced by many effective software engineering organizations.  The strategic plan addresses two broad questions for a time interval that is typically three to five years long:

- What products/services will we supply?
- What processes/resources/culture will we need in order to supply them?

These two visions are, of course, interrelated, so the strategic planning process will have to be able to estimate the feasibility of some of the visions, asking

- Can we build these products with the processes/resources/culture we now have?

If the answer is yes, then the process vision is one of maintaining and perfecting the present process.  If the answer is no, then the planners must decide whether to reduce their ambitions or to raise their process vision.

The reason we create these visions of product and process is so they can become inputs to a tactical planning process.  Some organizations, however, lose sight of this purpose, and the actual strategic planning process more closely resembles Figure 7-2, which was drawn for me by one of my clients.  In this so-called strategic process, planning becomes an end in itself, unconnected with the rest of the organization and producing lots of filed paper but no action.

Looked at cynically, the process of Figure 7-2 is what you get when some of the big shots are given the chance to play at being "executives."  A more realistic interpretation is that these are scared folks, just like you and me, who have been forced by their management to carry out a process for which they

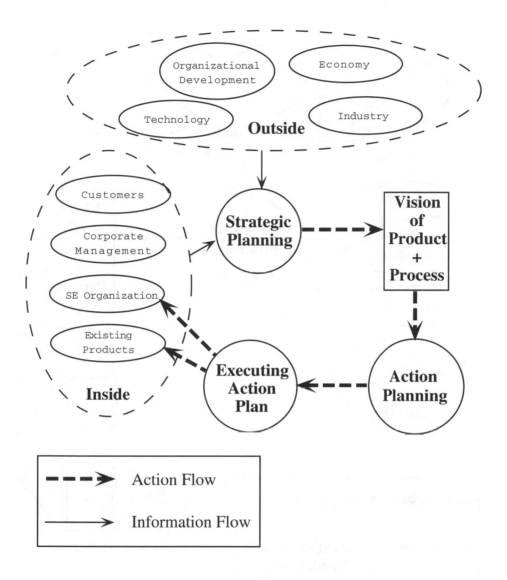

Figure 7-1.    The strategic planning process uses both internal and external information to generate visions of both product and process. These visions, in turn, drive the action planning process.

have no experience, aptitude, training, or skill. Managers who do not know how to get good feedback about business information feel out of control. The only things they have any sense of control over are time and money—hence, the popularity of budget and deadline restrictions. No wonder so much drinking goes on. Perhaps the organization is fortunate that their product goes into the files, never to be seen again.

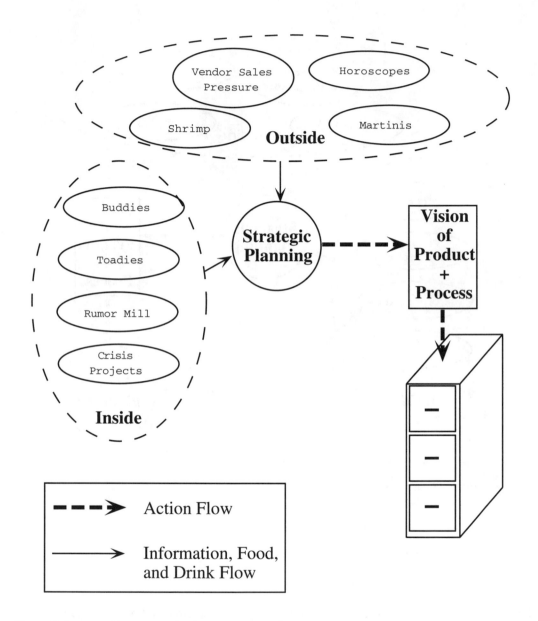

Figure 7-2.          How strategic planning is actually practiced in some organizations.

When done well, however, the entire process of strategic planning for change can be regarded as having three major components carried on iteratively to produce successive versions of the plan:

- *information gathering,* including both observing and ignoring information from the entire organization and all parts of its environment

- *problem solving,* including systems thinking, negotiating, and translating into action-generating principles
- *mechanics,* including knowing when, where, and how the planning is done, as well as who is involved, and understanding the difference between tactics and strategy

In Variable (Pattern 1) and Routine (Pattern 2) organizations, strategic planning attempts are almost always a fruitless exercise. Until problems in all three components are cleared up, the essentials needed for a fruitful change strategy plan are simply not available. In these circumstances, you need to bootstrap the plan process. You must restrict the output of your first planning sessions to *meta-plans*—plans that need to be carried out for the planning process itself before you can do effective planning on the rest of the organization (Figure 7-3).

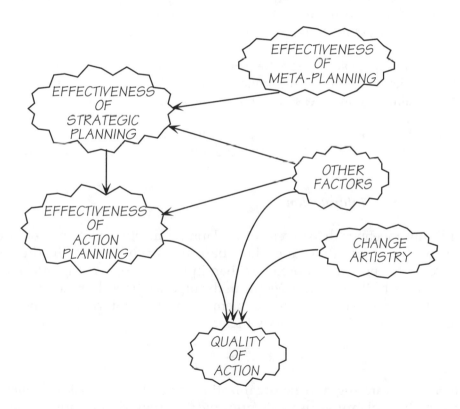

Figure 7-3.          The effectiveness of meta-planning has a major impact on the quality and effectiveness of every stage of the organizational change process.

Some of these meta-plans will concern the quality and quantity of information, and that's mostly a matter of skill at communicating with people. For instance, one of the most powerful meta-plans is a blueprint for training to raise the communication skill level of the planners. Some of the meta-plans will deal with mechanics, such as steps leading to the use of a skilled facilitator. And some of the steps will deal with problem solving, such as learning to think about risks and trade-offs.

The sections of this and the next chapter consider each of these components from the point of view of how they can be managed or mismanaged. These chapters provide a checklist of dangers you need to watch for, and they suggest meta-plan actions to initiate when any dangers are perceived.

## 7.2 Information Gathering

The information for making strategic decisions needs to come from both inside and outside the organization. The quality of the planning will be supported by the quality of the information. Three types of problems plague the quality of the information used in strategic planning:

- omission of some essential source, particularly those doing the work
- dependence upon an unreliable source
- wallowing in excessive detail, while ignoring relevant details

Let's look at each of these three types of information problems in some detail, to discover their causes and to frame meta-plan actions that might overcome them.

### 7.2.1  Omission of information

As with any meeting, the success of a planning meeting is 90 percent determined by the events that take place before everybody gets in the room. Nowhere is this principle more clear than in the case of missing information. Managers may be the smartest people in the organizations, but they're not psychic. Following are some typical problems of missing information, their causes, and suggested actions to remedy them.

*Problem:* Software engineering organizations often fail to consider customers' wishes in their planning process, arguing that they don't know what they want, or else that they want everything. Naomi Karten gives an example that would be funny if it weren't tragic:

> A company invited me to help them establish a service-level agreement. When I got out there, they explained that this effort was part of a compre-

hensive IS-wide strategic review and a revamping of their services, policies, and the like. They explained that this effort had been given the name "The Voice of the Customer," and it had been in progress for more than a year. "Oh," I said, "and to what extent have customers been involved?" "Not at all," they told me. The Voice of the Customer?

*Cause:* Though it hides behind blaming (see Appendix E), this problem is pure irrelevance. Managers hide out because they feel inadequate when actually forced to communicate and negotiate with customers. Some managers hide because they don't know how to tackle what appears to be a massive and unfamiliar undertaking in which they fear they'll have to give away the store.

*Meta-plan Action:* In the strategic meta-plan, specify that customer satisfaction will be measured regularly and systematically. Also specify that information on customer desires will be updated regularly, using such varied techniques as brainstorming, focus groups, surveys, and questionnaires.[1] Until you've executed this meta-plan, there's not much sense holding your first planning meeting.

The measurement of customer satisfaction need not be overly precise, nor imply that every customer's tiniest whim must be satisfied. It does have to be accurate, however. It also has to be made available to everybody in the development organization, so they can understand their customers and will have the information needed to make sensible decisions on all scales. As my colleague Lynne Nix points out, developers in many organizations don't even know how to use the product they're developing. How could such developers ever make sensible decisions about anything that might affect usability?

Sometimes this change to hearing "the voice of the customer" involves removing management-imposed barriers. For example, Norm Kerth observes

> One of my clients won't let his software developers meet their customers because
>
> (1)    "They would embarrass us."
> (2)    "They would make it a boondoggle."

And Phil Fuhrer adds, from his experience,

> (3)    "They might disclose product plans before they are ready."
> (4)    "They might make promises that can't be kept."

✳    ✳    ✳

*Problem:* Frequently, organizations fail to consider *potential* customers, those people who could be using their products and services but are not. One anonymous correspondent from a failing software company related the following story:

> At our peak, we had about 1,200 customers for our mainframe package. When we were down to about 600 customers, I suggested we interview some of the customers we had lost to find out what we should do differently. I was told that we didn't want to hear from people who weren't "loyal" to our company. When we got down to 300 customers, I left. Now I'd be surprised if they still had 100.

*Cause:*   Managers do not know, or are afraid to use, any processes to gather information on satisfaction of existing customers, let alone potential customers, so they deny that such information is important.

*Meta-plan Action:*   In the strategic meta-plan, specify that customer measurement must be extended beyond current customers to include former customers and potential customers.

✳   ✳   ✳

*Problem:*   Even if managers completely ignore their customers, you'd logically assume that they would not want to ignore their own executives. Thus, they would want the corporate business plans to be part of the planning information base. Yet, software engineering managers are often unable to demonstrate any relationship between their software engineering strategy and the firm's overall business strategy. Indeed, in one organization,

> Someone said we should look at the corporate strategic plan. Nobody had one at the meeting, so we took a break while we went to look for one. After thirty minutes, nobody could find a copy, so we resumed our planning session without it. The next day, somebody brought one, but by that time, most of our work was done. Besides, everybody thought it was too thick to read.

*Cause:*   Sometimes the planning process produces a report purporting to show how software engineering relates to the overall corporate strategy—but the report turns out to be a fraudulent assemblage of obfuscating verbiage. In one organization, a secretary is given the job of preparing this document, which consists of filling in arbitrary connections according to a formula. This process actually saves executive time since nobody will ever read the document anyway.

*Meta-plan Action:*   In the strategic meta-plan, specify that departmental plans must be reviewed by upper management before they become corporate plans, and that steps are taken in the planning process to ensure that this review passes.

❊    ❊    ❊

*Problem:*  Amazingly, managers at many strategic planning sessions use essentially no information of any kind from within their own organization.  A technical lead told me this story:

> I'd never been at one of the strategic off-sites, but my boss was sick so I had to take her place.  The only thing they used was an org chart, and they jockeyed back and forth, trading people and projects like the National Football League.  I was scared to say anything, so my boss lost seven of twenty-nine people who were working for her.  She was really mad at me, but I guess it didn't matter, because I was one of the seven.

*Cause:*  Quite possibly, no useful data have ever been collected.  Instead, participants simply give their opinions of how things *should* be.  They don't have any measures of the productive capacity of their organization, nor do they have a clue about the magnitude of the design maintenance debt of existing products that they plan to modify.

*Meta-plan Action:*  In the strategic meta-plan, specify that staff along with the managers—not the managers alone—establish a system of measurement to provide the measures needed for future strategic planning.[2]

❊    ❊    ❊

*Problem:*  When it comes to outside sources of information, the track record of these organizations is no better.

*Cause:*  Frequently, managers enter the planning process with lots of technology data, but this tends to be supplied by a favored vendor or two.  Sometimes, the entire executive crew is wafted off to a vendor site for a technology briefing as preparation for the planning process.  One of the more enterprising vendors actually "facilitated" the strategic planning at a country club, with some of the major decision-making done on the golf course.

*Meta-plan Action:*  In the strategic meta-plan, specify that staff with managers establish a system of environmental search—scanning what exists in the world outside of the organization—to provide the measures needed for future strategic planning.  This search is not to be limited to technological information, for technology is only part, a small part, of the total context in which a system lives.  Moreover, the sources need to be reliable and unbiased.

❊    ❊    ❊

*Problem:*   As poorly informed about technology as the planners may be, when it comes to knowledge of organizational development possibilities, many software engineering managers are better informed about the performance characteristics of their BMWs.  At least when it comes to the state of the economy and their industry, they read *Business Week* or *Time*.  A fellow consultant told me the following story:

> I conducted a telephone survey of nine managers, one of whom had invited me to facilitate a strategic planning meeting dedicated to upgrading their development organization.  Six of them had never heard of the Software Engineering Institute.  Two of them had heard of it, but couldn't tell me what it was, or what it did.  The only one who knew something about it was the one who invited me.  I suggested they do some reading before they had the meeting.  They got themselves a different facilitator.

*Cause:*   Many software engineering executives lack training in what structures and processes are possible in organizations.  Moreover, since many have spent their careers in a single organization, their experience is limited.

*Meta-plan Action:*   In the strategic meta-plan, specify training in organizational possibilities for future planning participants.  This training should include working in a staff position for a period of time to experience the workers' realities.  Also, specify participation in planning sessions by some organizational development specialists

A radical alternative solution is to abandon strategic planning for change altogether and adopt the SEI approach whole hog.  At the very least, the planning team should be required to read and discuss the SEI's Capability Maturity Model[SM] (CMM).[3]  Although I disagree with the SEI on many points, and I believe the CMM doesn't cover half of what has to be done, this approach would save a lot of time and would produce a better plan than three fourths of the strategic change planning efforts I've witnessed.  If you can't do it better, why not reuse someone else's work—and be a model for your developers?

✳   ✳   ✳

*Problem:*   Given a lack of valid information, any sort of planning would be a sham; yet it continues to be done in this way, at great cost and disruption to the organization.  Such a sham demoralizes workers and discredits their management.  As one wag expressed the principal advantage of strategic planning in his organization, "At least it keeps them out of the office so we can get some work done."

*Cause:*   When the planning is strategic, however, the impact is so far in the future that it's easy to hide the emperor's nakedness.  When all the alleged planning is done at a luxurious executive retreat, the grunts at the office may suspect it's a sham but, like their managers, have no data to prove their theory.

*Meta-plan Action:* In those organizations that do plan effectively, strategic planning sessions are not some sort of executive perquisite, but hard, intelligent work based on meaningful data. Specify that the planners do their homework and come to the sessions informed about the critical areas that will affect their plans. Hold the sessions more openly, and conduct them in slightly more Spartan surroundings than a five-star resort. Another good idea is to require a public display and review of a substantive work product produced by the planning.

### 7.2.2 *Unreliable sources*

Unfortunately, simply working hard to gather data is not sufficient, because most of the data that are readily available are of questionable quality.

*Problem:* Internal reports are not reliable indicators of what's happening in the organization, or if they are reliable, they're irrelevant.

*Cause:* Deming's Fifth Deadly Disease is "running a company on visible figures alone." He points out that there are some good things like ecstatic customers that cannot be reduced to figures in any regular way.[4] But fear of customers and employees leads managers to hide behind their spreadsheets.

*Meta-plan Action:* Use the technique of "management by walking around" prior to planning exercises to validate those information systems that are buried several levels down from the manager. As skilled managers know, a few sample conversations will quickly indicate whether or not the information in formal reports has the meaning it appears to have. Some managers hire consultants to do this, but walking around does the same and more if the managers know how to listen.[5] If they don't know how to listen, they create great, unregulated disturbances by walking around, and they're better off hiding in their offices.

\* \* \*

*Problem:* The processes being measured are so unstable that measurements have no meaning except to show the instability, as one developer illustrated in the following case:

> Our test manager reported to the meeting that the bug file had increased from 11,392 to 12,514 since the last monthly meeting. This, he said, was an indicator of progress, because this was the first time since we started measuring that the monthly increase, at 9.8 percent, had been less than 10 percent.

*Cause:* The causes of instability are many. Systems thinking—the ability to reason about nonlinear feedback systems—is needed to root them out.[6]

*Meta-plan Action:* In the strategic meta-plan, focus on the steps necessary to stabilize any unstable process before any attempts are made to optimize it. For instance,

- What does it take for measurements to have meaning?
- How can the results of those measurements be fed back into the planning process in a stabilizing way?
- What do we have to do so we can recognize commitments to customers?
- How do we know when projects are finished, rather than just delivered?

✳     ✳     ✳

*Problem:* Organizations need strategies based on data, not opinion, no matter how the information is gathered. One correspondent offered me the "proof" that his management had given that their process improvement efforts were right on track:

> We pay (about $150,000) for an annual survey conducted by an outside consulting firm. This year, the survey showed that the managers thought our software development effort had improved from an average of 3.4 (out of 5) to 3.9.

*Cause:* People lose sight of the difference between data and opinions about data. A large number of managers thinking that an organization is on track doesn't make it on track.

*Meta-plan Action:* In the strategic meta-plan, call for measurement systems that can be replicated and validated, independent of opinion. For instance, projects can be tracked with Public Project Progress Posters (PPPPs) so that the open air will cleanse the opinion from the data.[7] PPPPs apply to organizational change projects just as well as they do to software development projects—if they are properly planned.

### 7.2.3 Wrong level of detail

Even when the available information is reliable, planning sessions get into trouble by working at the wrong level of detail.

✳     ✳     ✳

*Problem:* The planning group spends too much time on irrelevant details. How to determine if the details are irrelevant? It's usually as obvious as one correspondent reported to me:

I once watched in awe as a group of managers spent more than three hours of their two-day off-site planning meeting designing a new logo for their process improvement campaign.

*Cause:* A planning group wallowing in irrelevant details is usually a symptom of something else that's wrong. It may be that the group lacks a sense of the planning process or is poorly facilitated. It may be that the group has run out of real issues, or has no real data on real issues. Frequently, there is some hidden issue that the group is dancing around.

*Meta-plan Action:* When you become aware that a group you're in is wallowing in details, comment on the situation. For example, you might say, "I notice we have spent a lot of time on what seem to me to be details. Am I missing the issue here?"

A good process should help eliminate this problem. If you have a good process, the question might be, "Are we following our process now?" or "Where are we in our process right now?"

If the process isn't so good, the question might be, "Is our process working for us right now?" or "Do we need some different process to keep us on track?"

✳   ✳   ✳

*Problem:* Data from different sources are not of comparable detail. Here are three lines from a spreadsheet labeled "Strategic Plan":

> Early line: Estimated workload increase: 30 percent
> Middle line: Average line of code, labor: 48 minutes, 37.2 seconds
> Bottom line: Needed increase in person days: 2,397.874

*Cause:* The most frequent source of this problem is when historical data are compared with predictions of the future.

*Meta-plan Action:* The planning team insists that data be supplied with estimates of variance. For illustration, notice the difference between each pair:

- Development cost per function point = $700 \pm $500 vs. $700 \pm $50
- Predicted market share = $17 \pm 7\%$ vs. $17 \pm 1\%$
- Cost of process improvement per developer = $1375 \pm $900 vs. $1375 \pm $90

The large variance on predictions will limit the detail used from other sources. In the strategic meta-plan, specify this estimation of variance for all future measurements.

✳   ✳   ✳

*Problem:* Either every issue is worked to death, or important issues are treated superficially. My correspondent reported that in the same meeting that devoted three hours to a logo, the question of training was dismissed with the comment, "Oh, the training department knows their job."

*Cause:* Before the planning session, either no system of priorities exists, or if there is one, it consists of bogus statements such as "all issues are Priority One."

*Meta-plan Action:* In the strategic meta-plan, specify that future issues will come to the planning session with priorities, or use a prioritizing process that becomes a front end to the whole planning process.
    Such a process should be based on *The Law of Limiting Factors*:

> **When a number of conditions are necessary to a process,
> its rate is controlled by the least favorable of these conditions.**[8]

Concentrate on the area that is limiting, not on the one for which there happens to be the most data. Frequently, there will be the least, or the least reliable, data for the limiting area—that's why it has become limiting.

✳   ✳   ✳

*Problem:* Planning sessions are swept along by the latest software engineering fad, and the root problems at home are ignored. In a discussion on a CompuServe software engineering forum, one of the correspondents noted, "Of course technical reviews are a good idea, but we do embedded real-time systems using object-oriented analysis, so we don't need them."

*Cause:* Planners are easily swayed off course when they're not sure of their planning process or their data. When they are under pressure for quick solutions to entrenched problems and their self-esteem is low, they are suckers for any patent medicine huckster who rolls into town. If vendors are actually present in planning sessions, the temptation to placate them becomes irresistible to some. Others can't resist attacking them. Neither approach contributes much to successful planning.

*Meta-plan Action:* Most importantly, keep vendors out of your own organization's planning sessions. To accomplish this purification, you need a process specified in the strategic plan by which vendor information can be gathered in advance and appropriately evaluated and summarized. The planning output sets the parameters to guide any necessary vendor negotiations. Of course, this advice flies in the face of strategic partnerships. In that case, your partners must be consulted and kept informed, but you do not need to allow them to put their hands in your purse by involving them in your own organization's strategy sessions—at least until you become a Congruent (Pattern 5) organization.

Remember what Bertrand Russell said: "All movements go too far." Don't get sucked in by appeals to your vanity, such as, "You can be the first, the world leader." Use your own organization's culture and business needs as the key to what you can and should do. For instance, if you haven't reached the point where you can keep track of what each project costs and how long it takes, don't even consider using some fancy estimating software. Guesses-in will always produce fantasies-out.

## 7.3 Mechanics

I won't discuss the mechanics of running strategic planning sessions here, but that's not because the mechanics are unimportant. On the contrary, the subject is well-explored, well-documented, and very important, and you can easily obtain books on it. Here are a few suggestions:

1.   Start with Doyle and Strauss, *How to Make Meetings Work: The New Interaction Method.*[9] This book lays out the fundamentals of conducting any meeting, as well as a method that can be adapted rather well to planning meetings.

2.   Spencer's *Winning Through Participation* documents a carefully developed general method for conducting planning meetings.[10] This method was created for use in international situations, and has since been adopted for use in much less demanding circumstances.

3.   Peña's *Problem Seeking: An Architectural Programming Primer* describes the *problem seeking method* used by these world-famous architects for initial planning of large projects.[11] Several of my clients have adapted this method for both software engineering projects and organizational change projects.

4.   Gause and Weinberg's *Exploring Requirements: Quality Before Design* has also been used by many of my clients as a guide to strategic planning meetings.[12]

Each of the above approaches does a reasonable job of gathering information and creating a list of possible strategic actions, but I've watched each of them break down when it came time to negotiate priorities among the potential actions. I've come to understand that negotiating skills are in short supply among managers, and even those who possess them often fail to use them congruently. The most frequent problem is placating—saying yes to conflicting priorities or saying yes to more than the organization can possibly do.

Some books I've recommended in these situations are Laborde's *Influencing with Integrity: Management Skills for Communication and Negotiation*,[13] which takes a Neurolinguistic Programming (NLP) approach, and Karass's *Give and Take: The Complete Guide to Negotiating Strategies and Tactics*,[14] which takes more of an old-fashioned business approach. Finally, there is the classic from the Harvard Negotiation Project, *Getting to Yes*.[15]

In the end, though, the problem with mechanics is confounding cause and effect. Organizations that are capable of responding rapidly and effectively tend to have a common set of values, a vision, and a strategic plan. The common misconception is that if your executives put these things into place, your organization will be successful, too. The mechanics are necessary, but they're far from sufficient, as we'll see in succeeding chapters.

## 7.4 Helpful Hints and Suggestions

1.  Of all the temperaments, the NT Visionaries are the best planners, but they're also the most likely to believe they can conduct successful planning meetings without information. The NF Catalysts easily fall in with NTs' fantasies if they think that good people are involved. Yet, in most software engineering organizations, the upper management and planning staff are almost all NTs, with a sprinkling of NFs. To improve your planning, search for some SJ Organizers and SP Troubleshooters to add to the process—and listen to their pleas for data.

2.  Phil Fuhrer observes: Technical reviews are one corrective action that applies to all of the shortcomings of strategic planning. Reviewers should be drawn from the people who are expected to implement or track the plan, including software developers, testers, technical support staff, quality assurance people, and researchers. The plan is not done until it is reviewed by its users.

3.  Lynne Nix comments: If strategic plans are not to become fileware, they must eventually be translated into tactical plans that lead to action. If the tactical plans don't fit with the strategic plans, however, the strategic plans are meaningless. One way to maintain this alignment is to establish a culture of including "parent" documents with every action plan. This is a simple way to create a linked list that can be used to trace any action back to the strategic plan, or to discover that the two are unrelated.

4.  Michael Dedolph notes: Although we need strategies based on data, not opinion, data *about* opinions usually need to be taken into account. Opinions can suggest reality, and group or individual opinions can be self-fulfilling. For example, in risk assessment, it's often useful to work

on the basis of what people *think* is the highest risk because that's the risk that will influence their actions the most.

Many organizational assessment techniques measure opinions, supported to varying extent by other mechanisms. Although useful, opinion surveys have a potential drawback in that managers with extensive marketing backgrounds may try to change the opinions rather than address the sources of the problems. Advertising may induce people to try a new product, but it will rarely get people to try a counterfeit product twice.

5.   Training is another general strategy that creates an adaptable organization capable of overcoming planning errors. Many organizations make the mistake of overplanning their training, becoming preoccupied with cost-effectiveness (pronounced "cost") and goal-oriented training. Although training should be applied to whatever skill goals are clearly identified, other training is needed to cover those areas that cannot be recognized from the top.

An adaptable way to plan training is at a meta-level. For example, management can specify training to meet the planned needs, but in addition, each employee gets a guaranteed time and money budget for personally chosen training. Employees can pool their budgets to bring in particular persons, events, or resources. Other employees can then participate, but they have to pay their share out of their own budget. Over the year, each employee's budget has to be spent, or the employee's manager is in hefty trouble.

## 7.5 Summary

✔   Change artists practice their skills on three levels, each involving three different time scales and three different sets of skills. Change artistry "in-the-small" deals with people and problems face-to-face and day-to-day—this level is what we change artists call *tactics*.

✔   Tactics are not all reactions to unexpected events. Change artistry "in-the-middle" is what we call *tactical planning:* looking ahead to be ready to handle such events.

✔   Change artistry "in-the-large" is what we call *strategic planning:* setting the climate in which tactical planning takes place. The strategic plan addresses two broad questions for a time interval that is typically three to five years in length:

  •   What products/services will we supply?
  •   What processes/resources/culture will we need in order to supply them?

✔ The strategic planning process has to be able to estimate the feasibility of some of the visions by asking: Can we build these products with the processes/resources/culture we now have? If the answer is yes, then the process vision is one of maintaining and perfecting the present process. If the answer is no, then the planners must decide whether to reduce their ambitions or to raise their process vision.

✔ When done well, the entire process of strategic planning for change can be regarded as having three major components:

- *information gathering,* including observing and ignoring
- *problem solving,* including systems thinking, negotiating, and translating into action-generating principles
- *mechanics,* including knowing when, where, and how the planning is done, as well as who is involved, and understanding the difference between tactics and strategy

✔ The information for making strategic decisions needs to come from both inside and outside the organization. Three types of problems plague the quality of the information used in strategic planning:

- omission of some essential source
- dependence upon an unreliable source
- wallowing in excessive detail, while ignoring relevant details

✔ The information for sensible change planning is simply not available until all three types of problems are cleared up. Until they are, you need to restrict the output of the plan to *meta-plans:* plans that need to be carried out concerning the planning process before you can do effective planning on the rest of the organization. Most of these meta-plans will concern the quality and quantity of information.

✔ There are a number of typical problems of missing information:

- failing to consider customers' wishes in the planning process
- failing to consider potential customers
- inability to demonstrate any relationship between the software engineering strategy and the firm's overall business strategy
- failing to use information of any kind from within the organization
- failing to use outside sources of information
- lack of knowledge of organizational development possibilities
- sham planning that costs a lot and disrupts the organization

✔ There are a number of typical problems of using information from unreliable sources:

- using internal reports that are irrelevant or are not reliable indicators of what's happening in the organization
- measuring processes that are so unstable that measurements have no meaning, except to show the instability
- creating strategies based on opinion, not data

✔ Even when the available information is reliable, planning sessions get into trouble by working at the wrong level of detail:

- spending too much time on irrelevant details
- using data from different sources that are not of comparable detail
- working everything to death, while treating important issues super-ficially
- being swept along by the latest software engineering fad, ignoring the root problems at home

## 7.6 Practice

1. Phil Fuhrer asks: "When is a plan done?" Phil's answer is, "when people no longer use it." What does he mean? Can you improve his answer?

2. Phil Fuhrer adds: Planning requires information and other prerequisites. In other words, the plan needs to be planned! Write a plan for a plan, including

   (1) who wants it
   (2) who is affected
   (3) how will the results be measured
   (4) under what conditions will the plan be completed, abandoned, obso-lete

3. Michael Dedolph offers: Do the following steps at home, but only if you're willing to accept an element of risk. This exercise can have surpris-ing and long-lasting results:

   - Start by setting strategic goals for yourself, by yourself.
   - Next, hold a family meeting and establish a strategic plan for the family.
   - Then, check your own strategic goals.
   - Check to see how much the family's (organizational) goals support your individual goals, and vice versa.
   - Compare the levels of detail in your goals and in the family plans.

This exercise may tell you something about your style as a planner. For example, Did your goals change to totally reflect the family goals? Are your goals and the family's totally or partially disconnected?

If you can't complete the family planning process—if there are major spats, communication failures, or everyone's goals are totally disparate—you may want to consider engaging an organizational consultant. Now think about any parallels at work.

4.  Lynne Nix suggests: Find your organization's latest strategic plan. (How long did that take?) Review what projects are currently under way. What is their relationship to the strategic plan? What does it take to determine this?

5.  Janice Wormington inquires: If you've ever participated in strategic planning for your own organization, was it closer to Figure 7-1 or 7-2? Why? How could it be improved?

6.  Michael Dedolph asks: How good are your listening skills? One way to tell is by having someone observe you "walk around." How can they tell whether your walking around is doing harm or good? This may be an excellent (if painful) chance to assess your listening skills, but only if you can listen to your observer.

7.  Payson Hall points out: Managers whose work history has been exclusively with one organization tend to have difficulty being effective planners. This is because

    •  they are too close to see what's going on—they lack perspective
    •  for better or worse, they helped get the organization where it is, and it's hard to recognize errors when you were involved in making them
    •  in the career-path progression from college to programmer to analyst to senior analyst to manager, it's easy to believe that something magic happens that teaches you about working with human beings, effective interpersonal communications, negotiations, project management, leadership, and understanding your own behavior

    Brainstorm some meta-plans to deal with this problem of ingrown management.

# 8

# Meta-planning, Part II: Systems Thinking

*Every kind of peaceful cooperation among men is primarily based on mutual trust and only secondarily on institutions such as courts and police.*
— Albert Einstein

Now let's switch our metaphor from navigating to cooking; they are, after all, not so different. Superb ingredients are the first half of a recipe—necessary, but not sufficient, to create a culinary masterpiece. The second half is the skill of the chef. Without a skillful chef, all you get is a mess of fine ingredients.

In the same way, the right information—at the right level, using the right process—guarantees nothing about the success of change planning. As an organization grows and matures, the problems grow from baking a cupcake to creating a wedding cake. All these ingredients must be assembled with the master touch, and that is provided by clear systems thinking, perhaps a luxury when the organization is small, but an absolute necessity as it grows.

This chapter will examine some of the more common systems thinking challenges that arise in strategic planning for software engineering organizations, particularly as the organization grows and matures. It will suggest the sources of these challenges, and offer some approaches available to the planning team.

## 8.1 Problem Solving

There are many problem-solving approaches, ranging from individuals' styles to elaborate processes described in books (such as those listed in Section 7.3) or sold as high-priced proprietary systems by consulting firms. But, as they say, too many cooks spoil the broth. One approach is all you need—no more, no less. Your first challenge is *deciding* which one. If you can't meet that challenge, how can you imagine you could plan for an entire organization?

### 8.1.1 The Big Game

*Problem:* Planning sessions degenerate into arguments over whose problem-solving approach to use. The key word here is "degenerate," since a reasonable amount of discussion is necessary and appropriate. You'll know a session has degenerated when it becomes unreasonable:

> One of my clients delayed strategic planning for more than three years while two senior vice presidents battled over whose captive consultant would lead the sessions.

*Cause:* This has nothing to do with problem solving, but with the Big Game— who gets to tell whom what to do.

*Meta-plan Action:* Comment on the situation. For instance, "It seems to me that we have a conflict over whose approach to use. I believe we're lucky to have more than one approach available. If we are intelligent enough to do strategic planning, we are intelligent enough to get the best out of any of these approaches." Then stop talking and wait. Repeat as necessary.

### 8.1.2 No systematic approach for decision making

*Problem:* Planning sessions may move smoothly through data sharing and setting priorities, but bog down when it comes time to decide on actions.

*Cause:* Many planning approaches focus excessively on data gathering, and lack any systematic process for actually solving problems, or even defining them.

*Meta-plan Action:* Apply a four-step approach that I use for the problem-solving phase of strategic planning:

1.  Define a problem in terms of a difference between what is perceived and what is desired, and when.[1] For instance, we perceive that we are spending $5.5 million a year reworking our products after they are shipped. We desire to spend no more than $1 million within three years.

2.  Develop a diagram of effects relating the perceived/desired variables to other variables.[2] In the example, this diagram would show what variables influence the cost of rework after shipping, such as the number of faults shipped, the design debt, the software engineering aptitude of the involved organizations, and the effectiveness of the process for dealing with customer problems (Figure 8-1).

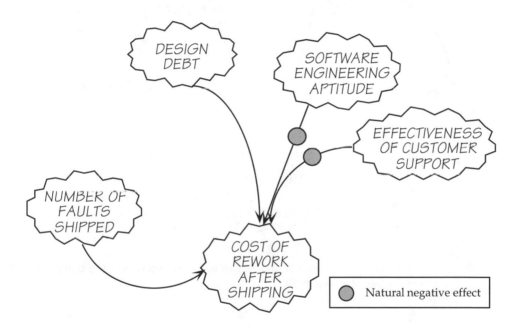

Figure 8-1.    A diagram of effects can be used to relate the perceived or desired variables to other variables. In this instance, the number of faults shipped and the design debt tend to increase the cost of rework after shipping. The software engineering aptitude and the effectiveness of customer support tend to decrease it (as indicated by the gray dots).

3.  Examine the diagram of effects to discover the dynamic that is holding the perceived situation in place. If you can't discover that dynamic, then discover what is preventing you from discovering it. For instance, design

debt makes rework more costly, but costly rework leads to shortcuts, which in turn lead to more design debt (Figure 8-2). Moreover, design debt leads to more errors shipped, which raises the cost of rework, which increases design debt. A third loop describes one company's practice of using the best people from product support to do the rework, thus reducing the effectiveness of customer support, thus increasing the rework. These three loops tend to raise the cost of rework, even when we try to lower it directly.

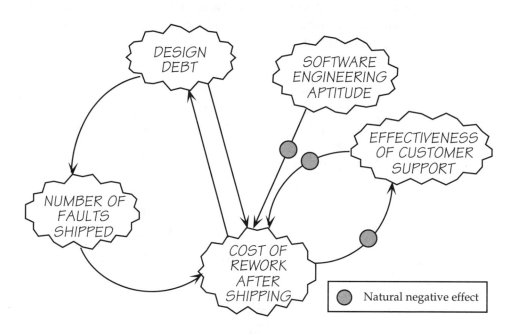

Figure 8-2.        An elaborated diagram of effects can be used to discover the dynamics locking the perceived variable in place.

4.    Once you understand the dynamic, identify choice points where you can break the stability control of the perceived values. These define your strategic actions. For instance, you may determine that the practice of assigning customer support people to rework is counterproductive, and may thus plan to add good people to customer support when demands for rework start to increase. Or you could develop a different plan that somehow decouples customer support from the rework cost.

If you don't understand the dynamic, identify actions that will obtain the information that will allow you to discover the dynamic. In this case, these data-gathering actions become part of your strategic plan. If, for instance, you don't know *why* rework costs are so high, set in place a measurement team to model the influences on rework costs. For an organization that doesn't already have the appropriate measurements in place, this new measurement process is the starting point for modeling the problem in the next planning exercise.

## 8.2 Growth and Size

Development seems always correlated in nature with growth. That is, the shape of a thing is the result of the relationship among the growth rates of its various parts. This is in contrast to organizational changes (or change attempts) that are supposed to take place just by writing them down in a strategic plan. In nature, the elaboration of the same form to a larger size eventually doesn't work at all; an insect the size of a dog could not oxygenate its tissues, and a blade of grass the size of a redwood would merely bend over and serve as mulch on the forest floor. For similar reasons, planners often discover trouble with their planning approach when the system grows larger, or faster, and the different parts are no longer in sensible proportions.

### 8.2.1 Growth produces bigness

*Problem:* As quality improves, the business improves, then grows. But growth produces bigness, which often has negative effects on quality.

*Cause:* Figure 8-3 is similar to Deming's chain reaction, but has two feedback loops. In software organizations, economies of scale aren't as strong as in manufacturing, so the loop through "Cost Efficiency" is weaker. On the other hand, as a software business grows, systems grow and quality becomes harder to maintain, so eventually this feedback loop becomes self-limiting.

*Meta-plan Action:* As Figure 8-3 indicates, the translation of market appeal into growth rate is a management choice. It's merely a cop-out to say that "we must grow at the fastest possible rate." The strategic planning team must make decisions on what growth rate can be handled, and what explicit actions will be taken to control the quality level as the organization grows.

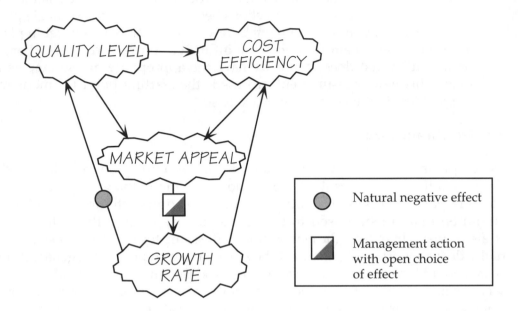

Figure 8-3.          Based on Deming's chain reaction but with feedback added, this effects diagram shows how quality can lead to growth, which can lead to limits on quality. As the left-hand loop (bigness can destroy quality) comes to dominate the power of the right-hand loop (economies of scale), it becomes counterproductive for the system to grow larger.

### 8.2.2 Complexity restricts development

*Problem:* As we add explicit mechanisms to control quality, the organization seems to be harder to organize further.

*Cause:* *Minot's Law,* from biology, says that the rate of growth of an organism begins a steady decline from the moment of conception (Figure 8-4):

> This suggests a general principle of organization: that once a system becomes organized, . . . it becomes progressively more difficult to reorganize the system. That is, organization inhibits reorganization. Further, organization can be strongly modified only when active processes of organization are going on, and this accounts for critical periods of development.[3]

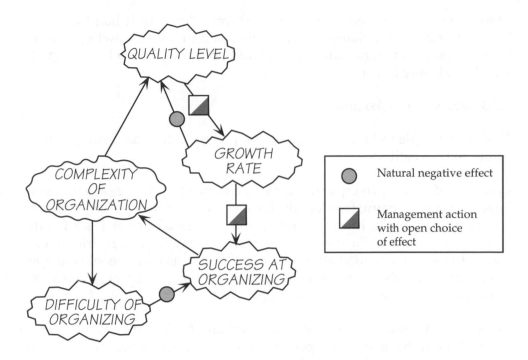

Figure 8-4.    Minot's Law, extended to organizational growth, says that management's efforts to raise quality by successful organization may succeed for a while, but may also produce a more complex organization, which becomes harder to organize for additional improvements. Thus, the current changes eventually become growth-rate-limiting structures for future changes.

*Meta-plan Action:* In the strategic plan, avoid adding complexity that doesn't contribute to the organization's goals. Applying a bias toward simplification will allow the organization to prosper longer without feeling the limiting effects of Minot's Law.

Second, understand the theory of *critical periods of development*, which says that early small decisions about the organization may have an enormous impact on the ultimate success of the organization. So, early in the organization's life, realize that strategic planning can have great positive impact, but at the cost of great danger of negative impact. Perhaps that's why new organizations rarely do strategic planning, and most of those that do fail in their attempts.

Later on, it's much harder for organizations to change, for good or bad, so strategic planning isn't as critical. Organizations have lots of capital to tide them over mistakes, capital in the broadest sense of "knowledge imposed on the physical world." But, as Boulding said, "Capital is *frozen* knowledge," so capital readily becomes one of the impediments to change, although it is often thought to foster change in some magical way: "If we only had the resources." Very few successful changes can be obtained just by throwing resources at them. To succeed, organizations must add new and flexible knowledge to that which is already frozen.

### 8.2.3 Size restricts freedom

*Problem:* People feel that because of overplanning, they are losing their opportunity to be creative.

*Cause:* Of course, overplanning can happen in any size organization, but beyond a certain point, freedom diminishes as numbers increase within a finite space. For example, in heavy traffic, the individual driver loses freedom of choice. To reduce traffic density, however, we may have to restrict freedom of choice to be on the road at all. Or, closer to home, as more people are updating the source code library, we have to restrict the types of usage, or else we have to restrict use to specially trained people.

*Meta-plan Action:* These effects have nothing to do with planning, but with scale—unless the planning is poorly done. You must make the trade-offs, but then make them public so people will understand what they are getting for the price they are paying.

Be careful of the tendency to make changes of wider scope than they really have to be. Examine your motives: This tendency can be a power game and, if it isn't, it often looks like one to the people down below. When planning some standard or constraint, ask, "What is the narrowest scope that we can use to accomplish our goal?"

Increased depth creates the same effect as increased scope, so don't succumb to the temptation to micro-plan. If, for example, you plan to the level of five-person teams, rather than the level of the individual, you reduce the effective size of the plan by a factor of five or so. If you plan to the level of fifty-person departments, you reduce the effective size by a factor of fifty. Such macro-planning requires trust in your teams and department managers, and, more important, it *demonstrates* trust.

### 8.2.4 Tools influence thought

*Problem:* Planning projections don't seem to work as well as they used to. As one frustrated manager told me, waving a five-pound sheaf of spreadsheets in my face,

> Five years ago, I was all in favor of introducing spreadsheet models into our planning. Now, however, we have a three-person department that does nothing but create seven-decimal-place spreadsheets between planning ses-

sions. If I could put a bug in all our spreadsheet programs so they'd all stop working, I'd do it without hesitation.

*Cause:* Planning tools may be the problem, because they don't scale up as the system size grows. Spreadsheets, for example, are most easily used as linear projection tools, and usually produce bogus results when the system goes non-linear—and growth is always nonlinear.

More sophisticated modeling tools use more complex models, but because of this complexity, they tend to become black boxes to their users.

*Meta-plan Action:* Examine your planning tools. View spreadsheet projects with particular suspicion. Open your modeling tools and study the assumptions upon which they were based. Update them, or discard them.

### 8.2.5  Big isn't the same as small

*Problem:* To illustrate the problem of growing organizations, here's a quote taken from an e-mail message from a potential client:

> I can't figure out what's happening around here. We've been a successful small company, but now nothing seems to be working right. Meetings take longer, but critical people are often absent so that parts of the meeting have to be repeated. People argue more for their own area of responsibility and don't listen to each other. Key data can't be found, or everybody has their own incompatible version. Suboptimization seems to be the default solution to everything.

*Cause:* Centuries ago, Galileo described *The Principle of Similitude:*

- With increased size, the ratio of surface to volume decreases.
- Different growing shapes will have different balance points of surface and volumetric effects.

Galileo's Principle of Similitude applies well to the growing organization. "Volume" is the internal part of the organization. "Surface" is the interface between the organization and its outside. As the organization grows, its relationship with the outside is strained as it tries to maintain its internal viability.

This principle applies to the entire organization and its relationships to customers and vendors, but it also applies to the internal parts of the organization. Communication among parts becomes strained. Each part tends to become a feudal domain that seems surrounded by high, thick walls, but is actually just concentrating on its internal problems. Sometimes, creating and protecting a feudal group is an effective strategy, as when creating islands of excellence, or at least islands of competence, that will eventually outlive the larger organization. More often, though, upper management is unconsciously encouraging this trend by dispensing rewards to individual groups with no coherent strategy and no attention to the systemic ill effects.

*Meta-plan Action:* Within the organization, keep groups as small as possible, and plan activities that regularly cross groups, such as requiring one outsider in each technical or project review. Communication with the outside must be given as a sole responsibility to people trained for the job and measured by their communication success.

Do not attempt to counter the Principle of Similitude with posters, slogans, and pep talks. The forces of nature will always overcome words, and the words will backfire and produce contempt and ridicule for management. Set rewards based on organizational performance, not on the performance of individual groups.

### 8.3 Risk and Reward

Strategic planners need to think in terms of risk and reward trade-offs. One of the most common trade-off decisions in strategic planning is between added value and certainty of success (Figure 8-5). By taking a chance on a new technology, for example, you may get a great increase in value or a decrease in costs. But new technologies are risky and, if you fail, your payoff may be nothing at all, or actually negative.

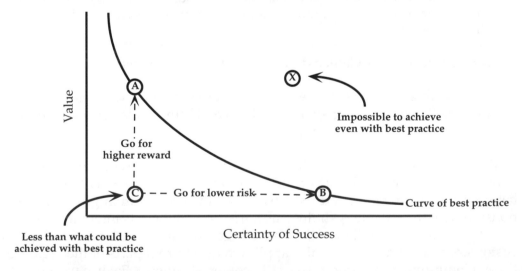

Figure 8-5.        In choosing a way to go about engineering a certain product, first you need to consider the trade-off between risk and reward. Points on the curve represent the combination of risks and rewards for the best ways of doing things. We may not do this well, but we can't do any better. (Point X is just one point in the area above the curve that's impossible to reach. A plan that specifies point X is an impossible plan.) It is up to the management to choose the point on which it wishes to operate—A or B or somewhere else—and then to plan and act consistently with that choice.

Still, the choice of position on the curve of Figure 8-5 depends on the organization's situation, which is a good example of why your planners need to know the organization's financial position, the engineering competence level, and how both stand with respect to the rest of the industry.

### 8.3.1  Always be first

*Problem:*  A start-up software company has much to lose if its leaders don't do something spectacular, and fast.

*Cause:*   They may need to take a high risk in order to get a high enough reward to stay in existence.  Even if the organization doesn't *need* such a high reward, the owners of the company may not be interested in simply surviving in a small niche, with a product that's just a little different from everyone else's.

*Meta-plan Action:*  They will take actions that establish a gospel of high risk, high reward, and those actions, if effective, will create the culture that fits these goals.  For instance, they may plan to

- pay employees low salaries, but with high stock options
- set ambitious schedules to beat competitors to the market (but if the schedules are unreasonable, they guarantee failure to deliver)
- promise outrageous levels of functionality to dominate every competitor (but if the levels are so outrageous that they can't deliver, they disappoint everybody, and perhaps become a laughing stock)
- approve only the newest, most innovative tools and processes, even though they are untried (which increases their chance of failing because of tool failure)

The problem with such a strategy is to keep it aggressive but reasonable. Anyone can sell anything, as long as they don't have to deliver it.

### 8.3.2   Always be second

*Problem:*  The high-level managers of a large, established software provider have much to lose if they make high-risk plans.

*Cause:*   Someone once said that IBM's secret motto is, "Always be second," and that's the way IBM's planners look from the outside.  But from the inside, they make perfect sense:  Don't stick your neck out, but once someone else has taken the big risk and succeeded, be ready to move in a swift, sure-footed way.

*Meta-plan Action:*  A planning group in a large, established company might create a contrasting set of cultural decisions:

- Pay competitive starting salaries with great benefits, but offer no stock options.
- Set modest schedules, but block competitors with elaborate pre-announcements (if you don't mind being unethical).
- Dominate competitors with vague promises of "We know what's best."
- Approve only those tools and processes that have stood the test of time.

One side effect of this strategy, though, is that good people may find it stifling or ethically unacceptable. Over a long period of time—extended by the large pool of capital—the organization's advantage may erode, and only be noticed when it's too late to do anything about it. Thus, one additional strategy should be added:

- Invest a small but protected percentage of your income in activities that explore—in a safe way—the newest and the most spectacular. Various forms for this investment include an Advanced Technology Group, a Software Engineering Process Group,[4] or a Research Group. At the very least, this strategy will give you a group of people who are ready to move quickly when one of the new approaches proves sound.

### 8.3.3 Don't risk

*Problem:*   Each culture encourages some risks and discourages others. In a risk-averse culture, following the dictates of the strategic plan may seem a greater risk to people than violating them.

*Cause:*   Almost every problem can be traced to the solution to some previous problem. Creating special groups for taking risks may give the rest of the organization the message that other groups are not allowed to take any risks.

Another source of this problem is the attitude about risk that is shaped by reward and punishment systems. Variable (Pattern 1) and Routine (Pattern 2) cultures tend to punish for errors but reward for successful process violations. So, deviating from the strategic plan becomes identified with heroic individualism.

*Meta-plan Action:*   Never prohibit any group from attempting small process improvements in their own bailiwick. Indeed, bring improvements into the system by budgeting for them, allocating slack time and money that is to be used in cooperation with the special risk groups like Advanced Technology. Measure managers on their willingness to use these resources in the intended way.

Study the reward and punishment systems and take steps to reverse them, if necessary. For example, how do you deal with an error in a tool, such as a compiler or configuration manager?

- Variable (Pattern 1) culture rewards hacking the product.
- Routine (Pattern 2) culture rewards hacking the tool and punishes hacking the product.
- Steering (Pattern 3) culture rewards hacking the tool and the product if done openly when other means have failed.
- Anticipating (Pattern 4) culture creates a different process to deal with the primary process that isn't working, and rewards using that different process (for example, the QUEST process described in Chapter 4).

### 8.3.4 Don't even talk about risk

*Problem:* The analysis of risks gives managers a chance to steer more effectively, but such improvement is possible only in a culture where risks can be discussed freely and openly. In some organizations, however, risk is not considered a proper subject of discussion. According to SEI staff member Michael Dedolph, SEI's Risk Program has found that the single biggest barrier to implementing risk management is that management is unwilling even to talk about risk. If anyone brings up the possibility that a planned action may fail, that person is accused of being a "nattering nabob of negativity"—instead of the pragmatic predictor of peril the organization requires to improve itself.

*Cause:* The unwillingness to discuss risk in a rational manner is a symptom of low self-esteem. It may seem that the unwillingness arises from a lack of skill, but ultimately the lack of skill arises from an unwillingness to study risk and learn about it. A culture of blame contributes to the problem by increasing the risk in bringing up the subject. Individuals on the strategic planning team may blame others for raising the subject of risk, or they may attempt to distract attention from the subject by acting irrelevantly.

*Meta-plan Action:* Deal with incongruent coping behaviors before making any further attempts to plan,[5] and don't allow the strategic planning team to make any decision based on risk factors that cannot be discussed. In the strategic plan, create a strategic action item calling for a culture in which risk can be discussed freely and openly—that is, a culture where the Five Freedoms are practiced. As described by Virginia Satir,[6] these are:

- the freedom to see and hear what is here, instead of what should be, was, or will be

- the freedom to say what one feels and thinks instead of what one should
- the freedom to feel what one feels, instead of what one ought
- the freedom to ask for what one wants, instead of always waiting for permission
- the freedom to take risks on one's own behalf, instead of choosing to be only "secure" and not rocking the boat

## 8.4 Trust

We've seen how stability is essential to an improving organization. If for no other reason, unstable systems are harder to think about, to plan for. Upper management has the responsibility for assuring there are stable systems at all levels—certainly a strategic question.

To achieve stability you can manage intellectually, you need to build an organization in trustable —*tru-stable*—units. Each unit has a job, and you can manage each unit through its input and output only, as if it were a black box. This approach greatly reduces the need for communication among units, as well as between the bottom and top. As we have seen, this approach also reduces the complexity of planning.

One part of trust is knowing that you can count on others to share the same knowledge base and values. To see how common knowledge replaces communication, try the following exercise: Two isolated people are told to write a number from 0 to 100 on a piece of paper, and if the sum is 100 or less, each gets the number they wrote in cents. If, however, the sum is greater than 100, each gets zero.

In most cases, though they can't communicate, they both write 50. This little trial illustrates how a common body of knowledge and values can replace a certain amount of information. Thus, when the system changes so that the old body of knowledge is no longer valid, the information load increases as people have to confirm they're on the same wavelength.

### 8.4.1 You go first

*Problem:* Lower-level people don't trust management, and will adopt a you-go-first attitude toward implementing actions of the strategic plan.

*Cause:* They know from the past that the strategic plan will be undermined, and volunteers will be left holding the bag. Experience tells them that their managers will cancel most of these strategic actions at the slightest excuse. For example, as a first response to a little budget pressure, the organization may have been quick to cancel training programs valued by the staff. This is one way managers destroy trust.

*Meta-plan Action:* In the strategic plan, ensure that programs that require resources are funded in an untouchable way for sufficient time to prove their worth, and also ensure that measures of that worth are established up front and maintained. For instance, managers should not be rewarded for saving their training budget to offset increased rework costs.

Action items that can be funded out of discretionary budgets are an even better way to get risky programs started. In any case, the planning should include slack for each new program's budget. Change artists distributed throughout the organization are another kind of slack that protects against action items dying for lack of skilled human resource.

### 8.4.2 Management swooping

*Problem:* Management keeps swooping down to correct actions at lower levels, which demotivates people from attempting anything. A popular format is too-frequent status reports, or even "emergency" status reports, like being called before a midnight tribunal.

*Cause:* There's an old Russian proverb:

> *When the cranes are flying, don't look up.*
> *If you must look up, close your mouth.*

Of course, you don't know the cranes are flying unless you peek, and that's what people do when their managers are "swooping cranes." People know they're up there, waiting to swoop if they stumble, or to drop something nasty if they should open their mouths or put something deemed to be incriminating in a status report.

*Meta-plan Action:* Create plans to train your managers, to conduct sessions between managers and workers on the subject of swooping, and to measure managers on their ability to develop employees and processes they can trust. Also, schedule review points and trigger criteria up front to ease anxiety and assure time for mastery.

The interval between management interventions is a measure of trust, and so is the depth of intervention. These measures can change over time, and part of the planning job is to see that they do. A short interval means less trust, but too long exposes you to risk. Too short prevents learning that will allow you to make the intervals longer. The same is true for too deep.

### 8.5 Moving Off a Dead Stop

Sometimes, even in what seems to be a hospitable climate for change, great ideas just don't seem to get off the ground.

### 8.5.1 Critical mass

*Problem:* The new approach seems sure to work, but doesn't quite achieve a critical mass of participants.

*Cause:* Directory systems, such as e-mail or telephone systems, require a minimum number of subscribers before the system becomes attractive to the new subscriber. Each potential subscriber is waiting for the other to sign up.

Utility systems require a minimum number of subscribers before the system becomes attractive to the sponsor. For example, why pay for a high-cost tool out of your meager tool budget until you are sure you can spread the cost over lots of people who are going to use it?

*Meta-plan Action:* In these situations, try a subsidy approach to get started. An example of an indirect subsidy would be to put something attractive on the e-mail system that would get people signed on every day, or several times a day. One manager primed the system by putting job postings only on e-mail. Another company used a more direct subsidy: It held a free-lunch lottery every day, and the only ticket holders were those who had signed on e-mail that day. Within a month, 90 percent of employees were signing on every day, checking their mail.

Another way to subsidize is to provide figurative insurance. Projects trying a new tool are given a 20 percent longer schedule, in contrast to those organizations that expect them to be done 20 percent faster because they're using a new tool for the first time.

### 8.5.2 Chicken-and-egg syndrome

*Problem:* C-maven Tom Plum says,

**Everyone wants to be first to try a time-tested idea.**

When introducing a new process or technology, we often get a chicken-and-egg syndrome. Nobody will use it until it's tested by someone.

*Cause:* The heavy front-end investment implies that we need to be shown first, which is actually quite reasonable.

*Meta-plan Action:* Don't be seduced by vendors' or evangelists' suggestions of how clever your organization is to be first. Wherever possible, get someone else's firm to time-test the idea. Then pay the users, if necessary, to show you the pitfalls. It usually won't be necessary to pay, because they'll be so proud of themselves they'll simply want to show off.

When you can't get someone else to do it first and teach you how, build up in an escalating series of small successes. The first trial should be zero risk, with payoff not a consideration.  One hour or one day is long enough.  As the projects escalate, do everything to alleviate stress.  Gradually increase the payoff, but maintain low risk in any case

Of course, the first time you use a new process or do a new thing is not going to be typical of how you use it later, when you are very experienced.  Therefore, trying it out, even in stages, will not be a completely accurate way of judging an unfamiliar process.  There will always be risk, and eventually you will have to commit significant resources.  When that happens, you will reduce your risk if you remain skeptical and watchful for those things that never happened in small-scale tryouts.

In particular, the first people to use a new idea are never typical of the ultimate users.  Therefore, the process they use is not a model of the ultimate process of penetrating the entire population.  For that reason, pause after a few successes and design a special process.

### 8.5.3 Wrong cultural prescriptions

*Problem:*  Letting others try ideas for you has its limits.  Prescriptions for one culture sound meaningless or backward for another cultural pattern.  For example, managers from a Routine (Pattern 2) organization would be shocked and befuddled to see how little time is spent on machine testing by an Anticipating (Pattern 4) organization.  Struggling as they are with massive test efforts to eradicate swarms of bugs, they wouldn't even perceive the amount of effort that the Anticipating organization puts into prevention and testing throughout its entire process.

*Cause:*   Each strength becomes a weakness when it comes to change:

- An Oblivious (Pattern 0) organization gets its strength from the close relation between the work and the person doing the work.  The weakness of this closeness is the way it closes the worker/user to foreign elements from the outside.
- A Variable (Pattern 1) organization gets its strength from individuality and variability, but these make it difficult to disperse good ideas.
- A Routine (Pattern 2) organization gets its strength from sticking to its routine, but that routine makes it hard to change quickly in response to events in the life of a project.
- A Steering (Pattern 3) organization is rather conservative about changing the process, such as by adopting new tools, because of its preoccupation with keeping things stable.
- An Anticipating (Pattern 4) organization overcomes Pattern 3's preoccupation with stability in all things, but is so hung up on planned optimal use that it often misses small unplanned increments that could really be helpful.

- A Congruent (Pattern 5) organization picks up these small things and good ideas from any source, and propagates them through product and process. What the weakness in this pattern might be, we don't know, because we haven't seen any weaknesses.

*Meta-plan Action:* Modify the basic system for handling change in each unique organizational situation. That means the planning team must tailor its plans to the cultural strengths and weaknesses of its own organization. For instance, to introduce self-correcting processes into Routine organizations, the plan might call for efforts that would build up self-esteem, create safety, and provide interpersonal skill training for managers. These would be largely redundant efforts in a Steering organization.

### 8.5.4 Hooked by resisters

*Problem:* Excessive planning energy is devoted to overcoming the objections of a few people with loud, strident voices.

*Cause:* A manager can easily get hooked by a group of people who will never change when that manager has a rule that says,

**I have to please everybody all the time.**

*Meta-plan Action:* If possible, transform your rule into a guide.[7] This rule, for example, could become "I can sometimes please everybody, but only when they are reasonable and their desires are not contradictory about everything."

In any case, think of all the *other* people who won't be pleased if improvements aren't made. Just remember that the violent objectors are not feeling *safe*, so you need to find a way to give them safety. Listen for what valid information is in their objections, no matter how obnoxiously they are presented. Correct what you can, then say, "I know from the Satir Change Model that people go through a change at different rates. Not everybody is going to be ready to try this immediately. I'll understand if you wait in the background to see how it comes out for other people."

### 8.6 Helpful Hints and Suggestions

1. When reading this chapter, Wayne Bailey was hoping to hear the following optimistic message:

    There's a natural vicious cycle in which an organization's growth and maturity give rise to its own destruction. With the right skills and proper planning, however, you can transform this vicious cycle into a virtuous one, one in which maturity is an asset and handling growth becomes easier as the organization gets bigger.

I, too, wish that I could say it becomes easier, but it doesn't. The actual message of this chapter is neither optimistic nor pessimistic, but as close to real experience as I can make it:

> With the right skills, proper planning, constant attention, and congruent action, you can handle growth by consciously changing the culture as the organization gets bigger. It doesn't get easier—you always have to work at it—but if you keep learning, it need not get harder either.

2.   Even if we choose the right problem to work on, it still is only one of many problems. Once it is solved, there will be other problems. For example, we keep automating one part of the process, but this keeps leaving unsolved problems in the nonautomated parts.

 This observation puts a limit on the planning horizon. At any moment, there is at most one place that will give a 50 percent or more improvement. This may determine that planning has to take place in stages, because something that is important at stage 4 may not have even been noticed at stage 3, or earlier.

3.   Sue Petersen notes: Those of you who happen to be in a family business will recognize another twist to the Big Game: "If you really loved me, you'd . . ." And, if you're not lucky enough to be in a family business, you may find the same game being played as, "If you were really a loyal employee, you'd . . ."

4.   With regard to the statement that "the first people to use a new idea are never typical of the ultimate users," Naomi Karten comments: Even worse, there seems to be an inclination among many people to conduct a pilot with "our best users," ignoring the fact that the results obtained can't be used as a model for full-scale implementation. Such results can be used in another way, however. If you can't succeed with a scaled-down pilot tried out on your most receptive users, then you can forget about scaling up and including everybody.

5.   Jim Highsmith, who works with many project teams, offers this useful overview that seems to capture the essence of risk management problems. Use it as a handy checklist when assessing risk. He says it's based in part on principles in *Volumes 1* through *3:*

> **We don't know what we don't know.** Ignorance of risk areas may really hurt the project/organization. These can be external (competitor does something) or internal (we don't understand that we don't really know anything about developing this new client/server stuff).

*We don't see what we do know.*  Knowing most of the risks in the projects, but ignoring them, or thinking that management wants to ignore them.

*We don't act on what we do know.*  Being afraid to act.

6.     Sue Petersen points out:  Sometimes, planning sessions bog down when it's time to decide on actions because some people have hidden agendas. As long as plans are expressed in vague concepts, it's possible to hide the real agendas in the shadow of generalities.  Then, when someone tries to get specific, the ones with the hidden agendas have to object or lose their secret desire.  When nothing gets decided, that's a good time to look for hidden agendas.

## 8.7  Summary

✔    Problem solving presents a variety of difficulties at the level of action planning.  For example,

- Planning sessions degenerate into arguments over whose problem-solving approach to use.
- Planning sessions may move smoothly through data sharing and setting priorities, but bog down when it comes time to decide on actions.

✔    The planning group needs to agree on an approach, which need not be complex, but must be common to all the planners.  One simple four-step approach is as follows:

1.     Define a problem in terms of a difference between what is perceived and what is desired, and when it is desired.

2.     Develop a diagram of effects relating the perceived/desired variables to other variables.

3.     Examine the diagram of effects to discover the dynamic that is holding the perceived situation in place.  If you can't discover that dynamic, then find out what is preventing you from discovering it.

4.     If you understand the dynamic, identify choice points where you can break the stability control of the perceived values. These define your strategic actions.  If you don't understand the dynamic, identify actions that will obtain the information to allow you to discover the dynamic.

✔ Development seems always correlated in nature with growth. This is in contrast to organizational changes (or change attempts), which are supposed to take place just by writing them down in a strategic plan. Here are some characteristic planning problems in a developing organization:

- As quality improves, the business improves, then grows. But growth produces bigness, which then destroys its quality.
- Complexity restricts development. As explicit mechanisms to control quality are added, the organization seems to be harder to organize further.
- Size restricts freedom. People feel that because of overplanning, they are losing their opportunity to be creative.
- Planning projections don't seem to work as well as they used to because tools don't scale up as the system size grows, and growth is always nonlinear.
- Big isn't the same as small. As the organization grows, its relationship with the outside is strained as it tries to maintain its internal viability.

✔ Strategic planners need to think in terms of risk and reward trade-offs. One of the most common trade-off decisions in strategic planning is between added value and certainty of success. By taking a chance on a new technology, you may get a great increase in value or a great decrease in costs. But new technologies are risky, and if you fail, your payoff may be nothing at all.

✔ Different organizations make different choices of trade-offs, and those choices influence their culture:

- A start-up software company has much to lose if its leaders don't do something spectacular, and fast. They may need to take a high risk in order to get a high enough reward to stay in existence.
- The high-level managers of a large established software provider have much to lose if they make high-risk plans. They don't stick their necks out, but once the big risk is gone, they're ready to move in a swift, sure-footed way.
- Each culture encourages some risks and discourages others. In a risk-averse culture, following the dictates of the strategic plan may seem a greater risk to people than violating them.
- The analysis of risks gives managers a chance to steer more effectively, but such improvement is possible only in a culture where risks can be discussed freely and openly. In some organizations, however, risk is not considered a proper subject of discussion.

✔  Incongruent coping behaviors must be dealt with before anyone makes any further attempts to plan. The strategic team should refrain from making any decision based on risk factors that cannot be discussed. The team should create a strategic action item calling for a culture in which risk can be discussed freely and openly—that is, a culture where Satir's Five Freedoms are practiced:

- the freedom to see and hear what is here, instead of what should be, was, or will be
- the freedom to say what one feels and thinks instead of what one should
- the freedom to feel what one feels, instead of what one ought
- the freedom to ask for what one wants, instead of always waiting for permission
- the freedom to take risks on one's own behalf, instead of choosing to be only "secure" and not rocking the boat

✔  Unstable systems are harder to think about—that is, to plan for. Upper management has the responsibility for assuring that there are stable systems at all levels.

✔  To achieve stability that you can manage intellectually, you need to build an organization in trustable—*tru-stable*—units. Each unit has a job, and each unit can be managed through input and output only, as a black box. This approach greatly reduces the need for communication among units, as well as between bottom and top. It also reduces the complexity of planning.

✔  Lack of trust produces a number of characteristic problems for planners:

- Lower-level people don't trust management, and will adopt a you-go-first attitude toward implementing actions of the strategic plan.
- Management keeps swooping down to correct actions at lower levels, which demotivates people from attempting anything.

✔  Sometimes, even in what seems to be a hospitable climate for change, great ideas just don't seem to get off the ground. There are four possibilities:

- The new approach seems sure to work, but doesn't quite achieve a critical mass of participants.
- When introducing a new process or technology, we often get a chicken-and-egg syndrome. Nobody will use it until it's tested by someone.

- Letting others try ideas for you has its limits. Prescriptions for one culture sound meaningless or backward for another cultural pattern.
- Excessive planning energy is devoted to overcoming the objections of a few people with loud, strident voices.

## 8.8 Practice

1. Try the hundred-pennies exercise with some of your friends. Particularly notice their emotional reactions, and the arguments they use to try to figure out what the other person will do.

2. Phil Fuhrer suggests: Discuss what would happen if you raise the ante of the hundred-pennies exercise to one million dollars. How does this affect the choices? Why? Suppose you do the exercise with four or five people. How does this affect the choices? Why? Change the rules so that each player is measured not by achieving the most revenue, but by how much that player beats the other players. How does this affect the choices? Why? Which set of rules most resembles your business and/or your management's choice of strategy?

3. Naomi Karten asks: Can the subsidy approach work in the reverse situation companies are now facing: people spending all their time surfing the Net instead of doing their job? Discuss the pros and cons of a subsidy approach for *not* doing certain things.

4. Janice Wormington raises the question: According to Minot's Law, success at organizing leads to increased complexity of organization (which increases the difficulty of organizing, which, in turn, decreases the success at organizing), but does increasing complexity always increase quality? Why? Create a diagram of effects showing your reasoning.

5. James Robertson recommends: Consider the models of change described in Chapter 1. If planners hold one of these models, how does it affect their approaches to solving the problems raised in these chapters? How do their solution ideas compare with those generated from the Satir Change Model?

6. Michael Dedolph notes: One thing missing from Figure 8-5 is the idea of "extending best possible practice." That would involve actually moving the curve upward in some fashion—a research function not to be undertaken lightly by typical software development organizations. Discuss under what conditions an organization should attempt to extend best possible practice in the profession. Under what conditions must they not? What are the risks, either way?

# 9
# Tactical Change Planning

*In its very nature, successful economic development has to be open-ended rather than goal-oriented, and has to make itself up expediently and empirically as it goes along. For one thing, unforeseeable problems arise. . . . Economic development [is] a process of continually improvising in a context that makes injecting improvisations into everyday life feasible.*[1]
— Jane Jacobs

What could be more demoralizing to an organization than investing time and resources into creating a strategic plan that is never used? Yet that's the fate of most of them. In observing hundreds of strategic planning sessions, I've seen two major mistakes that contribute to otherwise good plans falling into the trash:

1. The planners create tactical plans instead of strategic plans, giving too much how and not enough what or why.

2. The planners create strategic plans that couldn't possibly be translated into action, or are so ambiguous that they could justify almost any action.

Both of these problems are reduced when the strategic planners are well-versed in tactical planning. It's the change artistry of the organization that allows the strategic plan to be translated into tactical plans, and then facilitates putting those plans into action. There is a third problem, though, even when the planners are well-versed in their trade:

3. Software organizations often have difficulty with strategic and tactical planning when the project is not primarily software.

Change projects are not software projects. There are resemblances, to be sure, but that sometimes makes it harder for the experienced software planner to notice the differences. In this and the following chapter, I'll offer some tips to help you make the translation.[2]

## 9.1 What Is Tactical Change Planning?

A change plan is a design. It's the design of a set of actions that we hope will take a system from point A (a perceived state) to point B (a desired state). Points A and B are supplied by a strategic plan, explicit or implicit. Such a change can be accomplished by actions to affect

- the perceptions of A
- the desires for B
- the realities of A or B

Tactical planning is a way of increasing your chances that the design will get you from A to B—that is, your chances of getting what you think you want. Planning is considering possible actions and their outcomes in advance, and arranging them in a way that maximizes your chance of success. When you are planning something that you understand well, you probably plan by breaking the jump from A to B into smaller jumps, as A to Q, then Q to B, as shown in Figure 9-1.

Figure 9-1.    The jump from A (perceived) to B (desired) is usually planned in terms of inter-mediate states, such as Q, and the actions between states.

In Figure 9-1, the arrows represent actions of the form

If you are at A, and you take action #1, then you will arrive at Q.
If you are at Q, and you take action #2, then you will arrive at B.

I call these "If . . . action . . . arrive" statements *intervention models.*

Most formalized planning processes and tools assume that perceptions and desires remain fixed throughout the entire process, so that we only plan on the realities. These assumptions may work well when the plan involves changing the way you make a product ("assemble a car out of car parts"). They are not as useful when planning organizational change, though, because—like the economic development that Jane Jacobs discusses—most organizational change projects involve working on all three levels: perceptions, desires, and realities.

## 9.2  Open-Ended Change Planning

The process I am describing will act as your guide to the process of planning for organizational change, or any change, for that matter, where perceptions, desires, and realities might be changing over the life of the plan. If you evaluate a change plan in the light of the Satir Change Model, you can see that as soon as people react to action #1, everything goes into the cloud of Chaos. From this Chaos, there are several unpredictable outcomes, only one of which is Q.

I should warn you that the concept of open-ended rather than goal-oriented planning runs counter to many people's notion of how planning should work, which is sequential and cause/effect based. This more simplified linear view of planning assumes that the rules stay fixed throughout the change, so that action #1 applied to A always produces Q.

I am not opposed to cause/effect planning. I use it all the time in designing computer programs. But when intervention models involve human beings, their outcomes cannot be single-valued, so cause/effect planning simply doesn't work. For a plan to be valid for more than one step, it would have to look something like this:

> If you are at A, and you take action #1, then you will arrive at Q,
>     or R, or S, or T, or . . .
> If you arrive at Q, and you take action #2, then you will arrive at B.
> If you arrive at R, and you take action #3, then you will arrive at B.
> If you arrive at S, and you take action #4, then you will arrive at B.
> If you arrive at T, and you take action #5, then you will arrive at B.
>     . . .

A programmed cause/effect plan such as this assumes that you can accurately predict every single outcome of action #1 starting at A, which in the case of complex organizations, competitors, and market complexity, is quite unlikely. Even if you could list all possible outcomes, you would quickly create an elaborately branching tree that you couldn't manage.

Planning for change projects in the real world is much more like Jane Jacobs' view of economic development than the simplified linear planning process. It has to be "open-ended rather than goal-oriented, and has to make itself up expediently and empirically as it goes along." Thus, there are three major parts to such planning:

(1)  Use the most current information about goals and capabilities to create a plausible plan to an appropriate level of detail.

(2)  Start to execute the plan, gathering information on

-  where you actually go, as opposed to where you planned to go
-  how the organization actually acts, as opposed to how you thought it would act
-  what the emotional reactions are of people who are affected by the plan, including yourself

(3)  In the light of the information from (2), check whether you want to stop. If not, set new goals and repeat (1).

This approach is not so different from the spiral model of software development,[3] except that most spiral planners totally ignore emotional information: the basis for successful change planning.

### 9.3  Plans Are Made Backward

Inexperienced planners tend to be confused when they notice that planning tends to proceed backward, from desired results back through interventions to preconditions. They think it's cheating, but if so, then cheating is the key to formulating plans. For example, once you feel you know what point B is, start sketching a plan for getting from A to B (Figure 9-2).

Figure 9-2.     The initial sketch of a plan for moving from A to B.

Work backward from B to A, identifying a point Q from which B would be feasible to reach (Figure 9-3).

Figure 9-3.     The plan for moving from A to B, with a feasible intermediate point, Q.

Then move to a point X from which Q would be feasible to reach (Figure 9-4).

Figure 9-4.          The plan for moving from A to B, with two feasible intermediate points, X and Q.

The test at each step is to ask yourself,

**"Do I know how to move from this point to that point?"**

If not, you must break the trip down into smaller steps.  At each step, make a series of checks to tell whether the plan is adequate for that step.

### 9.3.1  Test:  Is it clear?

- Can you draw a diagram?  The only test here is actually drawing it. Diagrams drawn in the air with moving hands are not sufficiently clear, so watch for waving hands.
- Can people who didn't participate in drawing the diagram understand it?  Test them by asking questions about it.

### 9.3.2  Test:  Is it specific?

During the planning, the plan diagram may be sketched, leaving out details as in Figure 9-4.  But before the planning is finished, many specifics must be filled in, either on the diagram or pointed to by the diagram, so you can easily answer these questions:

- Does the final diagram show what is to be done?  One way to do this is to diagram each action as a standard task unit, showing prerequisites, action, and a review for termination.
- Does the diagram show *why* it is being done, or does it point to that information?  You'll need to know why things were done so you can change the plan when desires or perceptions change.
- Does the diagram indicate by whom and with whom?
- Does the diagram indicate where and when it is to be done?
- What do you think it will cost?  On what is this estimate based?
- What resources are committed?  Are they truly committed?  How do you know?

### 9.3.3 Test: Is each component accountable and dependable?

A plan is not a plan unless and until all the people who are part of the plan are *committed* to the plan. Commitment comes not from someone dropping the plan on them, or ordering them to do what it says, but from a process of negotiation. If there has been no negotiation process, you can be sure that you don't have a real plan, but only a fantasy plan.

How to do the task should be left to the people doing the task, but if you don't feel that you can leave it to them, that's a sign that you haven't reached the stopping point, and thus you must continue decomposing the steps into more detail.

People who have tasks in the plan should commit to those tasks willingly. If they don't, the plan needs to be revised or clarified. If you're surprised by unwillingness, then perhaps you've paid insufficient attention to gaining rapport with the people on whom the plan rests.

Commitment should be realistic. People who have committed to tasks have not committed to do them unconditionally. Instead, you want them to commit to do one of the following:

- Do what the plan says.
- Say clearly and in a timely manner, "I haven't done it yet, and here's when I will do it."
- Say clearly and in a timely manner, "I'm not capable of doing it," and, if possible, why not. For example, "I don't understand how to do it," or "I'm lacking the following resources."
- Say clearly and in a timely manner, "I won't do it," and why not. For example, "I believe the rationale is changed."

You must also take into account the culture that makes people accountable. To what extent is it really in their total control? For instance, do you also need to negotiate with their managers for their time? Are their commitments likely to change due to outside factors or new management priorities?

## 9.4 Choosing a New, Realistic Goal

For almost any real project, planning won't proceed in a simple sequence. Typically, you'll have a sketch of a plan, not all parts of which can be validated because the planned sequence passes through Chaos too many times to be that predictable. Suppose the plan is to move from A to X to Q to B, but you don't know if A to X is feasible. Consider choosing a shorter goal with a structure of A to W to X to Q to B (Figure 9-5).

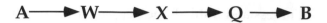

Figure 9-5.        The  plan for moving from A to B, with three feasible intermediate points, W, X, and Q.

Then stop planning, try to achieve W, and notice what you learn from the attempt.  In the real world of organizational change, one thing you'll learn is that you won't be exactly where you thought you'd be—at W—but at W* (Figure 9-6).  This deviation is okay, because the point of the open-ended planning process is to learn from the attempt.

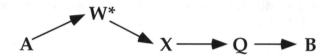

Figure 9-6.        The  plan for moving from A to B has been distorted, for in an attempt to reach W, the organization actually reached W*.  In the process, though, you learned some important things to use in the next version of the plan.

While achieving W*, you also learned how the organization reacts to change. For instance, you may have gotten the answers to such questions as these:

- Was the organization eager to change, or reluctant?
- Did certain people come to the fore as change artists?
- Were certain departments more threatened than you predicted?
- Did the budgetary processes slow down the plan?
- Did you gain or lose support for your goals and methods?

This kind of information about the organization's dynamics helps you know what is realistic for this organization.  Since W and W* are different and your knowledge of the organization is different, your plan for going from A through W to B may no longer look as reasonable as it did before.  Generally, you will want to replan.  Such replanning is not a failure, but a success.

The organization is now at state W*, you have a new plan, and you also have a new understanding of the dynamics.  This new state of affairs can be called A*, to suggest that the past is past, and you're starting with a new plan (Figure 9-7).

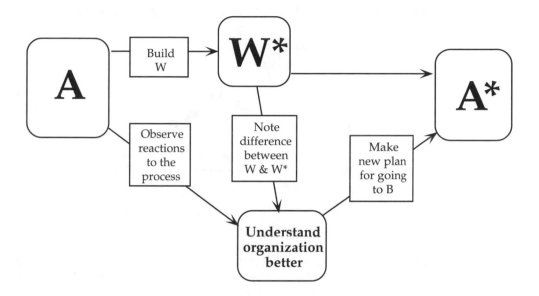

Figure 9-7.     A better plan uses information obtained from early stages to replan later stages. (States are in rounded boxes; actions are in rectangles.)

Other things will have changed while you were going from A to W*. Most important, you need to determine if the customers still really want to go to B. Your customers may now want to go to B*, which may resemble B, but is not exactly the same (Figure 9–8). If you find your customers want to go to C, which is totally different from B, you should abandon this plan and start the planning process for a new project from square one. Failure to do this is one of the major causes of disastrous projects.

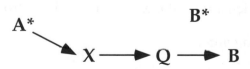

Figure 9-8.     By the time you get to W*, the plan for moving from A* to B may no longer look attractive to your customers, who now want to move to B*.

With a new starting point (A*) and a new goal (B*), you now revise the plan. Though you'll want to remember the old A-to-B plan for learning and for project review purposes (Figure 9–9), you need to let go of your emotional attachment to it.

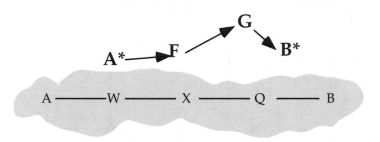

Figure 9-9.     By the time you have a revised plan to go from A* to B*, the original plan to go from A to B may be only a foggy memory. Keep records so everyone will be able to learn to plan the next project better.

If you structure the definition of your change project this way, you will find the actual changing quite easy because you will have anticipated change and not considered it a failure. Or, if changing the plan isn't so easy, you'll have a pretty good idea why not. That way, you'll be able to make the next one easier.

## 9.5 Congruence from Start to Finish

To the inexperienced, open-ended change planning seems like a lot of work. According to Satir's description of meta-change, however, change becomes easier over time when the people involved remain congruent, maintaining a balance among the Self, Other, and Context.[4] If one of these factors ever slips out of sight of the change planning, the plan itself goes out of balance and the results become even less predictable. Thus, during each planning cycle, you must monitor each participant for the balance of all three, from start to finish.

### 9.5.1 Self: Where are you now?

Change planning starts by taking a good look at all aspects of point A: not just the physical or logical aspects, but even more important, the *emotional* aspects. Perhaps the most common mistake made by change artists is losing track of themselves in the midst of their efforts to change others. If you do not take care of yourself, you will easily become discouraged by the effort it takes even to *define* a change project. Instead, think of the definition work as accompanying every step in the change process.

The definition process is often harder and more rewarding than any other part of the process. By the time you have a good definition, the project will be well on the way to completion, so prepare yourself psychologically for numerous refinements, some of which may happen very close to the project's completion.

### 9.5.2 Other: Who will be affected?

You, of course, are not the only person involved in the change you're planning. To plan each step, remind yourself that different people will react differently to the same intervention. You must know who will be involved in the change, or you cannot predict anything. I consider as an "other" *anyone* who will be affected by the change—for better or for worse, intentionally or unintentionally.

Therefore, one of the first tasks of the change artist is deciding *whose* desires for change are to be satisfied, because these are the customers. Then decide who else will be affected, even if you feel they don't have to be satisfied, and even if they don't want to be. People who are left out of change planning invariably turn up late in a change project to haunt you.[5] Ask yourself, "Who else will affect or be affected by the change or, in some way, have a stake in its success or in its failure?"

### 9.5.3 Context: What should be preserved?

Once you have established who the others are, you must ask them, "Before you consider changing things, what things do you want to keep?" Point A is the initial context of the change. Context includes the culture of the organization, which tends to be invisible to the organization's members. It's very easy to take point A for granted, then find that in achieving some minor change, you've destroyed the very thing the customers wanted most.[6] Also, be sure that your perception of the starting state is the same as your customers', or at least not incompatible.

## 9.6 Selecting and Testing a Goal

Actually, the opposition of "goal-oriented" and "open-ended" planning is a false one. Just because planning is open-ended doesn't mean it won't involve goals. Once you have established a congruent starting point (A), you need to establish a goal, or point B. Ideally, you'll receive such a goal from a strategic plan, but you'll generally need to refine it. In effect, you must ask, "What do we want that's different?"—even though you don't always get a clear answer, or even find out by asking directly.[7] You must, therefore, work with desires statements until you have a clear goal. You continue to test and revise the goal statement until it becomes an acceptable goal statement, or until you discard it. Here are some tests you can perform.

### 9.6.1 Use a positive format

Work with the desires statements until they are in terms of what is wanted, not in terms of what is not wanted. Such negative statements focus energy on the wrong things. Consider this statement:

*a.*     No software development project will run over budget.

You could achieve this goal simply by not having any software development projects, or by not having any budgets, or by declaring software development projects complete when they have used up their budget. What you probably want is closer to

*b.*     We will have at least ten software development projects completed in the next fiscal year. Each software development project will have a budget and a set of requirements that are agreed upon by general management and project management before the project begins. Each project will be completed (will satisfy its set of requirements) within the agreed budget.

There is still work to be done, but statement *b* gives a much better idea of what is desired, rather than what is not desired.

### 9.6.2 Be sure it's achievable

Frame the desires in ways that are achievable by the customers themselves. Avoid statements that involve other people changing. For instance, a manager's goal might be drafted as

*a.*     All programmers will be using the new workstation by January 1.

You may be able to restate this goal as

*b.*     I will be satisfied with the progress toward use of the new workstation by January 1.

With statement *a*, the goal might be achieved and the manager still not satisfied. Statement *b* points you in the direction of work to be done. You must next find out, "What will satisfy me?"

### 9.6.3 Be sure it's observable

Ask the question, "How will my customers know when we have accomplished the change?" This will take some digging, because most people aren't used to stating their true desires. Some people's statements tend to be too high-level and vague, such as

*a.*    I want to increase productivity and quality.

This is not really a goal, but a vision. It is the type of statement that everyone can agree with (who would be against quality?), until you actually start doing something. Then you'll find that people have very different ideas about the meaning of abstract words such as "productivity" and "quality." A clearer statement might be

*b.*    I want to increase productivity and quality, and this is what I mean by those words:

   •    productivity is observed when . . .
   •    quality is observed when . . .

### 9.6.4 Make it specific

To be usable, the goal statement must specify what observations will confirm or deny that the goal has been reached. Check your goal statements with the question, "What will I see, hear, or feel that will confirm that my goal has been achieved?"

*c.*    I want to increase productivity and quality:

   •    productivity is measured by our total revenue divided by our total labor cost
   •    quality is measured by the overall score on our annual customer satisfaction survey

When you are specific in terms of concrete measurements, there won't be any arguments about whether or not you have achieved your goal. These measurements may or may not be quantitative. For instance, the measure of quality may be "when the boss says she loves it." This is concrete, though it may not be as useful in planning as something more quantitative and predictable.

Nevertheless, there won't be any arguments at the end about whether the boss loves it, because she'll tell you. There may, however, be arguments at the outset about whether that's what you really want. That's good! Better to have the arguments at the beginning of the project than at the end.

### 9.6.5  Be sure the goal is not too tight

In an effort to make it specific, people often state their goal in a way that overly constrains the project.  For example, a goal statement might be

*a.*     There will be 100 IBM workstations installed by March 15.

This might mean that clones are not permissible, even if they result in a large savings, but it might mean something much more flexible than that.  In order to find out just what it does mean, you have to perform a number of tests.

### 9.6.6  Explore variations

Although "specific" and "not too tight" may seem to contradict, you can resolve this apparent contradiction by *being specific about the amount of variation that's allowed.*  Check your goal statements by exploring the *range* of meaning of each word or number.  In the above statement, for instance,

- Does 100 mean 95-105?  Does it mean more than 50?  At least 100?
- Does IBM mean only IBM?  Does it mean new IBM?  Sold by IBM? Serviced by IBM?  Does it mean every part of the system must be IBM?
- Does workstation mean a particular configuration?  A range of configurations?  Does it include software?  What software?
- Does installed mean on the floor?  Plugged in and working?  In use? How much use?  By whom?
- Does March 15 mean before March 15?  Not before March 15? Sometime in March?  Are there circumstances under which we can delay that date?  Would earlier be better?  Would all 100 workstations arriving on March 14 be okay, or is there some preferred pattern of installation?

### 9.6.7  Eliminate solution statements

People often jump ahead a step and describe an action to achieve a goal, rather than the goal itself.  Goal statements should be in terms of the state you want, not in terms of what actions it will take to get there.  For instance, consider again the statement

*a.*     There will be 100 IBM workstations installed by March 15.

You can test this statement by asking "Why?"  The answer might be something like:  "That will give programmers the capacity they need to be using the new design tool by July 1."

In that case, the goal is clearly not getting workstations, but using the new design tool by July 1. Getting the workstations is a subgoal, which someone thinks will facilitate getting the design tool in use by July 1, a superior goal. Of course, getting the design tool in use by July 1 can also be subjected to this same test, continuing until you reach the truly fundamental goals. My wife and colleague, Dani Weinberg, applied this method when she was consulting with information systems people in the newly formed Republic of Georgia:

> They first said their goal was to get rubles. I asked them what they would do with the rubles, and they said they would buy Russian lumber. I was puzzled about why they wanted Russian lumber, since they were information systems people, so I asked. They said they would sell the lumber in the West and get U.S. dollars. And why did they want U.S. dollars? So they could buy some IBM workstations!

Once you know their *real* desire, you'll be prepared to work backward to consider various alternative subgoals that may help to achieve it.

### 9.7 What Stands in the Way of Achieving the Goal?

Once you have a specific, measurable goal, you can begin to look for what things have an effect on that goal. Look for those things that create a risk that you won't achieve what you want. These are the things you must work through to achieve your goal. This step may be called *risk assessment*, the first step in managing risks. Because so many managers are afraid to talk about risks, I tend to emphasize *stability*, the confidence that you can control the plan at every step. Stability is, in effect, the inverse of risk, because a stable plan is one that can cope with risk.

To support this effort, you might want to use a checklist of risks (or threats to stability) encountered in projects of this type. Simply listing risks, however, will provide an insufficient basis for further planning. To discover how risks are interrelated and to uncover hidden risks, develop a diagram of effects, then apply a series of tests.

#### 9.7.1 Check for obstacles

Using a checklist and diagramming the effects allows you to create a reasonably comprehensive list of what might get in the way. Many books urge you to think positively, and that advice is often interpreted to mean, "Don't think of obstacles." But if you are truly positive, you can say to yourself, "I'm not afraid to think of obstacles because I can work through anything that comes up. With me at the helm, this is a stable project." Also, considering obstacles often helps define what it is you're really trying to accomplish. Just don't fool yourself into believing that you can ever think of *every* obstacle in advance.

For example, consider who might be unhappy with a particular change. If you don't consider these people in advance and face them squarely, they'll surprise you and throw your project off balance.

Furthermore, are there any obstacles that are outside your power (or desire) to change or remove? Can you live with the risk they represent? Can you work around them? At what cost? If you can't or don't want to pay the cost, perhaps this is the time to abandon the project.

### 9.7.2  Look for stabilizing feedback loops

Stability is the ability to ward off change. Therefore, we want stability in our project, but not in the thing we're trying to change. Of all the stabilizing obstacles to change, those embedded in feedback loops are the hardest to overcome. They may actively hold the Old Status Quo in place, so search them out and look on the diagram for places to break them.[8] For example, if the strategic plan calls for improving the accuracy of status reports to management, you may have to contend with the diagram of effects in Figure 9-10. By rewarding for accurate reporting, rather than punishing for bad news, the stabilizing effect of these loops can be broken. Thus, your tactical plan will need to determine what actions could have that effect.

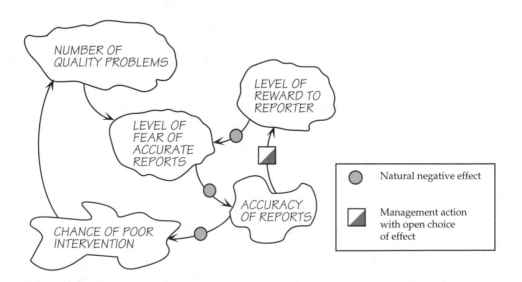

Figure 9-10.     Two feedback loops acting together or in opposition can work to stabilize the level of accuracy of reports to management. These loops act as an obstacle to raising the level of accuracy.

## 9.8 Models for Planning in the Face of Unpredictability

Risk assessment is *not* risk management, but only the first step in risk management. The second step is *risk abatement planning*—planning to get a predictable
result in spite of an unpredictable environment. Diagramming the effects creates a complete list of what can be employed to contribute to the goal of getting from A to B. Again, this may help you clarify what is really meant by the
definition.

### 9.8.1 Check risks and resources using the PLASTIC Model

To plan effectively, you must get the big steps right up front, saving the little
ones for later. This is an example of building a plan in *tru-stable* units. As a
guide in choosing the appropriate planning level, I use the acronym PLASTIC,
which stands for

**P**lan to the
**L**evel of
**A**cceptable
**S**table
**T**alent
**I**n
**C**ompleting Projects

In other words, you plan down to the level whose performance you can trust,
and no further. For example, let's follow the interactions of Pat (a manager),
Lynn (a project manager), and Chris (a technical specialist), who are planning
to introduce data security reviews into their projects.

**Chris:**   This plan looks good, except that we've never really practiced data
design around here. Until everybody can reliably produce accurate
data designs, reviewing is going to be a hit-and-miss thing. [*I don't
trust our data designing ability.*]

**Pat:**   Why can't we just work on security?

**Lynn:**   That task isn't on the critical path, so we'll simply be marking time
while avoiding the main obstacle that Chris pointed out.

In this case, Chris and Lynn are saying that data design still hasn't reached the
level of a stable talent in completing projects, meaning they don't feel they can
reliably depend on getting correct data designs from the whole organization.
Therefore, they can't plan on any level that *depends* on data design, such as
improving their security techniques. Otherwise, they take the risk that a cer-

tain security approach may turn out to be quite different once they know how to design data reliably.

**Pat:**      Well, we have *some* designers that understand good data design. Why don't we use them, and get a head start?

**Chris:**   For security, I wouldn't feel safe if only *some* people were able to review designs. [*I don't trust partial, nonstandard designing.*]

**Pat:**      I guess I'd have to agree with that. Well, at least our people have the ability to learn. [*Their ability to learn is a level I trust.*]

**Lynn:**    I agree, but I don't want to leave it to on-the-job learning. A class will help us arrive at one standard way of representing designs, at least. [*I don't trust self-teaching to give us the standardization we need.*]

To reduce their risk, they search for a level of stable talent that can be used as an intermediate step to reach the level of being able to design data. They agree that people in their organization have the ability to learn through classes, so that classes may be a way to get the stability (that is, reduce the risk) they need.

**Pat:**      Do we know of a good instructor?

**Lynn:**    I heard that Joe Bloe has a data design course.

**Pat:**      Well, then, let's go with Joe Bloe. So that takes care of it.

**Lynn:**    Not really. A course by itself isn't going to be enough unless they're given time to practice. [*I don't trust classroom learning by itself.*]

**Pat:**      So let them find the time.

**Lynn:**    Not that easy. *You've* got to insist that each project allocates time, and adjust their schedules accordingly. Otherwise, it won't happen. [*I don't trust their ability to wrest time from their immediate projects.*]

**Pat:**      All right, you've caught me at it again, trying to get something for nothing.

They've checked to see that their plans are acceptable: Do classes constitute sufficient resources to learn to do data designs? The check led them to discover that a certain amount of time is needed for practicing. Since they haven't allocated an acceptable amount of time already, they move to the level of their ability to budget and use budgeted time. Using these stable levels, they might derive the change plan in Figure 9-11.

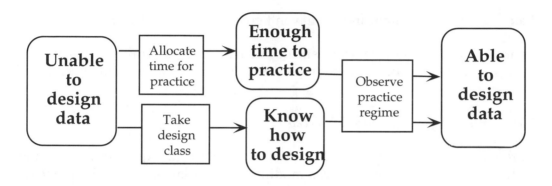

Figure 9-11.     A plan for developing the capability to do data design in projects. State A is unable to design data and state B is able to design data. The rectangular boxes will be converted to standard task units, with entry and exit criteria. This notation isn't critical; just be sure you can show actions, states, and dependencies: "If the system is in state A and we do X, then the system will be in state B."

### 9.8.2  Check resources against the MOI Model

When you have constructed a plan diagram, check against the MOI Model. Will each state really be produced by the planned interventions? For example, under what conditions will taking a class provide the motivation, organization, and information needed to learn to design data? In order for it to happen, there must be

- motivation, such as people wanting to go to the class
- organization, such as the ability to contract for and schedule the class and to handle the class materials
- information, such as an informed instructor and class materials that fit the way the organization does development

**Chris:**   Hold on! I remember Joe Bloe. He discourages students by belittling their intelligence. I don't think we want him back here. If he acts that way, it will discredit the whole idea of data design. [*Motivation is missing.*]

**Pat:**     You got any other suggestions?

**Chris:**   Nope.

**Lynn:**   Then we better put something in the plan to search for a good instructor.

**Pat:**   That takes time, and we haven't got time. [*I don't think it's acceptable.*]

**Lynn:**   I can go on-line and ask the members of the Training Forum. It shouldn't take more than a week to get some names and check them out.

**Pat:**   All right, make it so! [*I accept!*]

In this case, the MOI question led to investigation of the qualifications of the instructor, so part of the plan was modified to the plan shown in Figure 9-12. The additional steps were designed to reduce the risk of taking a class of unknown value.

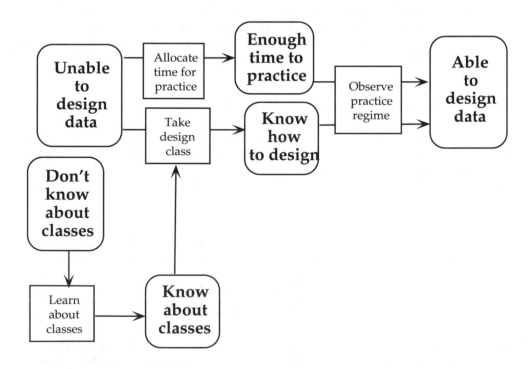

Figure 9-12.      A revision of Figure 9-11, with a new plan for reducing the risk of taking unknown classes.

### 9.8.3  Check human resources using emotional information

Planning tools may simplify the job, but it's easy to make the mistake of believing your planning charts are gospel.  People don't act like nice little boxes on planning graphs.  Don't take your human resources—your people—for granted.

For instance, your customer may say, "I want X very badly," but when you ask how much time she is willing to devote to getting X, she says, "Oh, I'm too busy to be bothered.  You just go do it and bring me back the result." This statement helps to clarify what "very badly" means, and might suggest that you don't have an adequate motivational component to make the change project successful.

This kind of checking—like the entire process of risk management— requires the change artist to learn to pay attention to emotional information. Some of it comes directly in the words people say, such as "Oh, I'm too busy to be bothered."  But much of it comes in the other channels.  For instance, suppose you need data flow diagrams for your data security project and you ask one of your systems analysts, "Do you know how to use data flow diagrams?" The answer is "Of course," but his tone of voice and his posture indicate something incongruent.  Then you must pursue the matter further.

Perhaps the analysts are *supposed* to know data flow diagrams.  Perhaps they've had a course in data flow diagrams, but they have no real experience applying them or applying them to this kind of situation.  Skilled questioning in a safe environment will enable the change artist to get more reliable information than the face value of "Of course," and this information can be used to make a more reasonable plan, thereby reducing the risk of going forward under a false assumption.  Perhaps there needs to be an additional practice step for some of the analysts to develop some real experience, or perhaps you can use a more experienced analyst at the beginning, or perhaps you can get what you need without using data flow diagrams.[9]

## 9.9  The Feedback Plan

Open-ended planning requires that the plan is revised on a more or less continuing basis, using feedback from each group of people affected by the plan. Managers who understand this principle often fail to carry it out in practice because once the plan is set into motion, they are too busy to notice what is changing, or to remember some of the people affected.  The true change artist knows this and thus knows that any real plan must contain *a plan for revising the plan*.  This plan for revising the plan is comprised of one or more negative feedback loops that stabilize the change process itself (Figure 9-13).

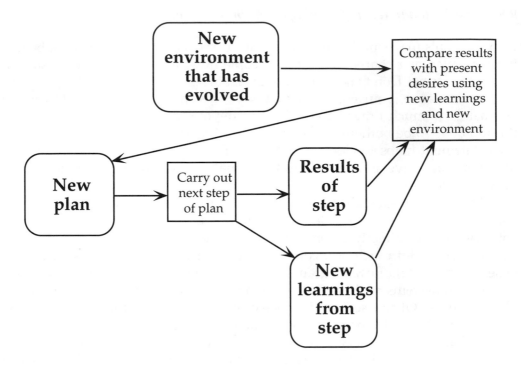

Figure 9-13.       A diagram of the generalized iterative tactical plan, containing a plan for revis-
                   ing the plan and for learning for the sake of future plans. Notice that this is
                   expressed as a loop back to *New plan*, though of course each iteration is dif-
                   ferent.

The testing and replanning must not be done so often as to disturb the execu-
tion of the plan. On the other hand, they must be done frequently enough that
the plan cannot go far out of line before someone notices. One good test is the
question: "If we find out that the plan is way off track, will we have invested
so much that we cannot afford to restart?" By "afford," we mean not only
money and time, but also emotion. Can people face reality if they have so
much invested in this plan?

Adjustments to the plan should be as small as possible, so that they do
not become significant foreign elements in themselves. The replanning cycle
should thus be based on the anticipated size of the adjustments, which will
depend on the uncertainties involved in going through Chaos.

Adjustments must be based on real information. If your goals have
passed all the tests, then this should be relatively easy. Does the plan provide
for generating real information as it goes along? If not, people will be dis-
turbed by stopping to get information, and you will more likely get fantasies
than facts. Does the plan provide for keeping a history of the plan, including a
record of why things were changed? Over time, impressions of the plan's his-

tory become inaccurate. It's best if the plan is under version control, just like software documents.

Is the feedback process a real plan? Does it pass all the tests that the rest of the plan has passed, such as being clear and specific, and having the committed authority and resources?

Is the planning process a real process? Are the planners really involved, or are they merely going through the motions? When it comes to open-ended planning, merely going through the motions will never succeed. Remember what Dwight D. Eisenhower said: "The plan is nothing; the planning is everything."

## 9.10  Helpful Hints and Suggestions

1.  This chapter is not a Bible. It's intended to help you remember some of the ways that tactical change planning differs from planning in a stable environment. You should use what's in this chapter as an addition to the considerable amount you already know about planning. If you don't already know how to plan in a stable environment, then you should study that subject to help yourself use this chapter effectively.

2.  Figure 9-13 could be seen as a description of prototyping, but many would-be prototypers don't really plan at all. Instead, they just blunder from stage to stage. The difference between true prototyping and mere hacking is that prototypers stop to breathe (reassess risks and realities, and replan accordingly) between stages.[10]

3.  Jim Highsmith comments: "When I do exercises on change, I ask the class to define what they believe to be the core constraint to change, the single obstacle that seems to be the most difficult to overcome. I then tell them that the core constraint cannot be time. This always causes a ruckus, their usual response being that time is the main culprit. My response is that lack of time is a *symptom*, not a core constraint. There is always time to do some things, those with higher priority. If the change were really important, they would find the time."

4.  Lynne Nix points out: The planned feedback is intended to see that the plan is used, but implementing the reviewing part of the plan requires *discipline* to follow through. If detailed plans are developed and never updated as circumstances change, planning becomes just an interesting exercise, perhaps revealing a few initial problems. In addition to failing to make the planned changes, the planners' credibility with implementors, with management, and with customers is greatly compromised, along with the possibility of future organizational changes.

### 9.11  Summary

✔  It's the change artistry of the organization that allows the strategic plan to be translated into tactical plans, and then facilitates putting those plans into action.  Tactical change planning is an essential part of change artist training.

✔  Three major difficulties contribute to otherwise good plans falling into the trash:

  •  The planners create tactical plans instead of strategic plans, giving too much how and not enough what or why.
  •  The planners create strategic plans that couldn't possibly be translated into action, or are so ambiguous that they could justify almost any action.
  •  Software organizations often have difficulty with strategic and tactical planning when the project is not primarily software.  Change projects are not software projects.

✔  Planned change is taking a system from point A (a perceived state) to point B (a desired state).  Points A and B are supplied by a strategic plan, explicit or implicit.  Such a change can be accomplished by working on

  •  the perceptions of A
  •  the desires for B
  •  the realities of A or B

✔  Tactical planning is considering possible actions and their outcomes in advance, and arranging them in a way that maximizes your chance of success, using intervention models.  The assumption that perceptions and desires remain fixed throughout the entire process is not very useful when planning organizational change, because most organizational change projects involve interventions on all three levels: perceptions, desires, realities.

✔  To be successful in organizational change planning, you need to use a planning method that is "open-ended rather than goal-oriented, and has to make itself up expediently and empirically as it goes along."

✔  Open-ended change planning is described by the following steps:

  (1)  Use the most current information about goals and capabilities to create a plausible plan to an appropriate level of detail.

  (2)  Start to execute the plan, gathering information on

- where you actually go, as opposed to where you planned to go
- how the organization actually acts, as opposed to how you thought it would act
- the emotional reactions of people affected by the plan, including yourself

(3)   In the light of the information from (2), check whether you want to stop. If not, set new goals and repeat (1).

✔   According to Satir's description of meta-change, change becomes easier over time when the people involved remain congruent, maintaining a balance among the Self, Other, and Context. Thus, during each planning cycle, you must monitor each participant for the balance of all three, from start to finish.

✔   Just because planning is open-ended doesn't mean it won't involve goals. Indeed, open-ended planners need to know *more* about goals, since they will have to test and revise goals on every planning cycle.

✔   Risk assessment is the first step in managing risks. Stability is, in effect, the inverse of risk, because a stable plan is one that can cope with risk. Planners must create a list of risks (threats to stability), discover how risks are interrelated, and uncover hidden risks.

✔   Risk assessment is *not* risk management, but only the first step in risk management. The second step is risk abatement planning, planning to get a predictable result in spite of an unpredictable environment. The PLAS-TIC Model, the MOI Model, and models of human emotionality can be used to plan steps that will place risks under project control, to the extent possible.

✔   Open-ended planning requires that the plan will have to be revised on a more or less continuing basis, using feedback from each group of people affected by the plan. Any real plan must contain *a plan for revising the plan*. This plan for revising the plan is comprised of one or more negative feedback loops that stabilize the change process itself.

## 9.12  Practice

1.   Janice Wormington suggests: Use a simple example from your own experience to go through each step of the tactical planning process, as summarized above. For example, develop a plan to make breakfast for your family or take a vacation somewhere. Don't skip any steps. How did your plan change as a result?

2.    Wayne Bailey recommends:  Choose a step in the planning process that seems a little fuzzy to you.  Come up with three examples from your own experience to help you understand.  If you can't come up with three examples of your own, try explaining the step to someone else, and asking them for examples.

3.    Sue Petersen comments:  "Your principle of avoiding statements that involve other people changing is so important I think you could probably write an entire book on it alone!  I think it deserves more prominence in this one!"  So, get together a small discussion group and share instances when someone else's plan dictated that *you* had to change.  How did you feel?  What did you do?  Did you change according to plan?  Did the dictate make it more or less likely that you would change?

4.    Phil Fuhrer and Michael Dedolph contribute:  A plan is a design for change.  Discuss the resemblances between the way you design software systems and the way you plan for change.  In what ways are they different?  Why?  How would the planning approach described in this chapter fit with the software development lifecycle model that you use?  What are the pitfalls of that model, and how would this type of planning address those pitfalls?

5.    If a design is a plan for change, and a design is a wager on the future, what is at stake in the wager on planned organizational change?

6.    Janice Wormington asks:  Where else might you get a goal (point B) besides the strategic plan?  How does the source of the goal affect the tactical planning process?  For example, how do implicit goals differ from explicit goals?

7.    James Robertson notes:  Deming warns us that setting measurable goals may encourage behavior we didn't intend—or what is really needed.  Show how tactical planning allows you to respond to a realization that your goals are motivating unintended  behavior—desirable or undesirable.

# 10

# Planning Like a Software Engineer

*The organization expects the leader to define and express—both in writing and, especially, through behavior— the beliefs and values of the institution.*

*The leader is responsible for lean and simple statements of policy consistent with beliefs and values, vision and strategy.*

*Equity is the special province of a leader.*

*A leader ensures that priorities are set, that they are steadfastly communicated and adhered to in practice.[1]*
*— Max DePree*

The third volume in this series, *Congruent Action,* describes some serious disadvantages carried by a technical person who chooses a career in management.[2] To add to the disadvantages, Chapter 9 of this volume explores some ways in which organizational change planning is different from software project planning. This may be discouraging, but the true engineer also brings some advantages to the change planning process.

This chapter describes how thinking like an engineer—in trade-off terms—helps the manager obtain the strategic vision needed to integrate the engineering efforts of many others, always with equity. Indeed, it's only the Anticipating (Pattern 4) and Congruent (Pattern 5) organizations that can truly be considered *engineering* organizations, because it's only in these patterns that participants consistently think like engineers.

## 10.1  What Engineering Control Means

Engineers are not simply technicians. Engineers must do much more than just understand engineering technology. What makes their work so difficult is the same thing that makes management work so difficult: They must put engineering ideas into practice in a way that's consistent with all parts of a strategic vision and equitable to all the people involved.

### 10.1.1  Dynamic models, not magic formulas

First of all, the phrase "engineering technology" suggests a misleading model. The activity called engineering can be done in many ways. Contrary to the hopes and actions of some people, engineering has no gospel, no holy book in which you can look for all the answers. As an engineer or an engineering manager, you literally write a new gospel every day—by the things that you do and the things that you say and, because you are an engineer, by the things that you build.

Effective engineering is not a set of magic formulas by which you can always get what you want. Neither is effective engineering management.

Indeed, any competent engineer knows that if you could always get what you wanted, you wouldn't need engineers, nor engineering managers. Instead of seeking magic formulas, engineers study the dynamics by which different variables are connected. Figure 10-1, for instance, shows one way an engineer thinks about quality, economy, and schedule: as a diagram of effects. Each one is connected to the others, so that we cannot get more of one without paying with one or both of the others.

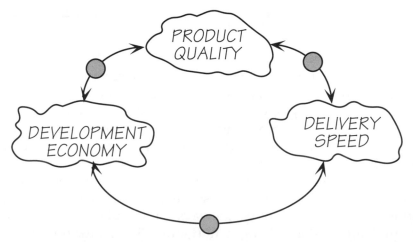

Figure 10-1.    Engineers are not trying to build perfect systems. They are trying to contend with dynamic interactions among variables—such as quality, economy, and schedule—so as to produce the most satisfaction possible under a particular set of circumstances. This diagram of effects suggests that the three variables are locked in a stabilizing feedback loop in which increasing one leads to a decrease in one or both of the others (as indicated by the circles on the effects arrows).

Contrast this view with the typical nonengineering manager who accepts the mandate that the programmers must work faster *and* more precisely, but without spending more money and without giving them any idea just how this is to be done. Real software engineers know that they can sometimes work faster and more precisely if their managers know how to spend money to improve their technology. Or they know how to work more precisely by using more time to get the job done, without their managers spending more money.

Engineering is what is done when you *can't* get everything you want, because it's the art of getting as much as you can under the circumstances. Engineering does mean you make conscious decisions about what you're *getting* for what you're *giving up*, and *why*.

### 10.1.2 Trading off

If there were anything like a gospel for engineers, it would be a diagram like Figure 10-2, a typical trade-off curve showing what you must give up to get something else. A similar trade-off curve in Chapter 8 (Figure 8-5) related risk and reward, while this particular curve is derived from the dynamic of Figure 10-1, showing how you generally have to trade off between quality and economy in order to hold to a constant schedule.

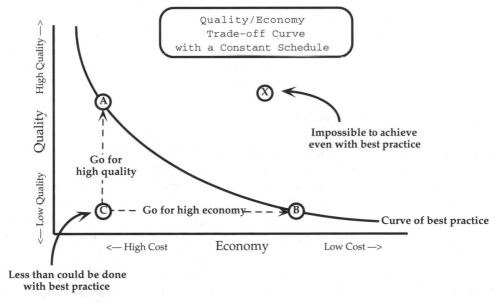

Figure 10-2.     The dynamics between a pair of variables with all other variables held constant can be seen in a trade-off curve. In this case, the curve shows quality versus economy. The leading edge curve represents today's best engineering practice. Points like C, below the curve, are less than we know how to achieve today. An organization operating at point C is not a well-managed organization, because management could move the organization to point A and achieve higher quality at the same cost, or to point B and achieve higher economy without sacrificing quality (since B and C are on the same level). Points like X, above the curve, are impossible to achieve with today's best practice, no matter how good the management may be.

(The reason I choose *economy* rather than cost in Figure 10-2 is to preserve the convention in trade-off curves that bigger is better. When you use this convention to choose your variables, all trade-off curves will resemble Figure 10-2. Wayne Bailey warns that you may be misled by this graph: Although it implies that with a very small reduction in economy you could get a very large increase in quality, which is true, the cost to obtain a small reduction in economy would be *very* large—so the additional quality is actually very expensive. It's a good idea to be skeptical of any model, because models always distort some aspect of reality to emphasize certain others.)

The curve represents the boundary between the possible and the impossible with today's best engineering practice. Points like X that are above the curve are impossible, for now at least. Points like C that are under the curve are possible today. Points like A and B that are on the curve are the best that can be done today. Notice that to the engineer, "best" is not a point, but rather a curve, a collection of points. (This is the so-called leading edge.) So if you ask an engineer to give you the best possible system, you have underspecified the task.

Engineering also means that you know how not to get *less* than you can. In terms of Figure 10-2, it means knowing what you have to do to *stay on the curve*, not slip off to some point such as C. From C, a good engineer would know how to move toward B, which gives more economy at the same quality, or toward A, which gives more quality at the same economy.

In other words, software *engineering* management is a set of *choices*, not a set of *compulsions*. Good software engineering management is the ability to stay on or near the curve of best practice at a point that represents the most appropriate trade-off among the variables.

### 10.1.3 Juggling multiple variables

Any real engineering problem, of course, has many more than two dimensions. The two-dimensional trade-off curve is a simplification of a curve, or surface, in $n$-dimensional space. We often make this simplification because most of us can't work very well in more than two dimensions at one time. Some people can handle three dimensions quite well, and for them three-dimensional graphs such as Figure 10-3 are helpful. For most of us, the best we can do is handle two-dimensional projections like Figure 10-2, which, in effect, represents a slice through the surface of Figure 10-3, a surface represented by a family of such slices. Each slice is the plane on which the schedule has a particular constant value.

Another way to represent the three-dimensional surface is by using a family of curves in two dimensions, as shown in Figure 10-4. Each curve in the family represents a slice through Figure 10-3—in other words, the quality/economy trade-off for a given schedule.

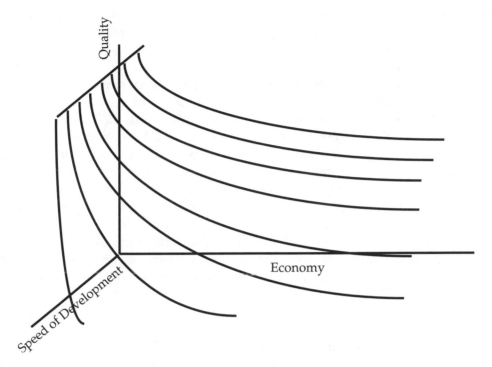

Figure 10-3.    A three-dimensional plot of the trade-offs among quality, economy, and speed of development.

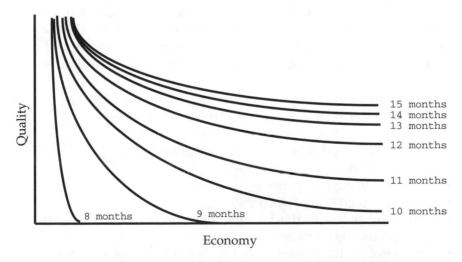

Figure 10-4.    The trade-offs among quality, economy, and speed of development can be represented as a family of curves in two dimensions. Each curve in this family represents the quality/economy trade-offs for a different schedule.

For certain engineering variables—such as capacity, access time, and cost in the design of a database—the family of curves can be given great numerical precision. When we describe an entire software project, however, we are not looking for such precision, but for the general shape and spacing of the curves. Sketching the curves gives us a basis for discussing the potential trade-offs.

Even when they are rough sketches of best opinions, such a family of curves contains a great deal of engineering information. In this case, for instance, the family suggests that extending the schedule from thirteen to fifteen months would not offer any great benefit, because the curves are so close.

On the other hand, trying to cut the schedule from ten months to eight months would make it very costly to achieve high quality. Moreover, the nine-month curve intersecting the zero quality axis means that unless you're willing to spend more money (less economy than this intersection point), it will be impossible to produce a system at all, even using best practices.

Using these families of trade-off curves, you can quickly select your preferred position, for example, how much quality, economy, and development time you want. My colleague James Robertson points out that if you have a set of such curves for your most common project trade-offs, you could do rapid back-of-the-envelope planning. Such a set of curves, of course, would characterize your culture, and you could use them to ask, "How would we like these trade-offs to be different in our organization?" From that, you could take action that produced a culture with a different set of curves.

### 10.1.4 Handling new levels of technology

Instead of the family of quality and economy curves versus schedule, we can plot the family for constant schedule and variable technology, as shown in Figure 10-5. When a new technology becomes available, an engineering manager is often faced with the choice of whether or not to leave the old curve and jump to the new. Although these two curves may make the choice seem obvious, we must remember that this is just a projection of an $n$-dimensional space of variables.

To make the new-technology decision in a truly strategic manner, the engineering manager must consider many other variables, such as

- the cost of operating during a learning period that is below both curves
- the risk to current projects
- the cost of making the change
- the probability of the technology taking hold, versus having the technology rejected
- the probability of the technology's not working as promised
- the risk to previously completed projects, which may be incompatible

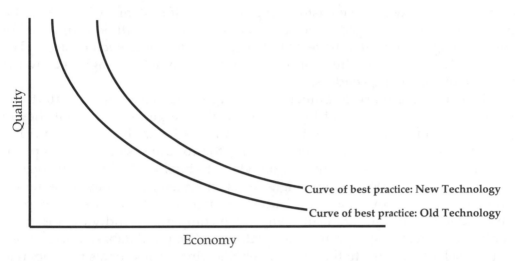

Figure 10-5.    Two trade-off curves for quality and economy, each for a different technology.

Even so, this technology decision is relatively easy compared with the one illustrated in Figure 10-6, where neither technology is clearly dominant over the other for all possible objectives. In this case, technology A is better at producing economical systems while still maintaining quality. Technology B, on the other hand, is better at producing high-quality systems more economically than A.

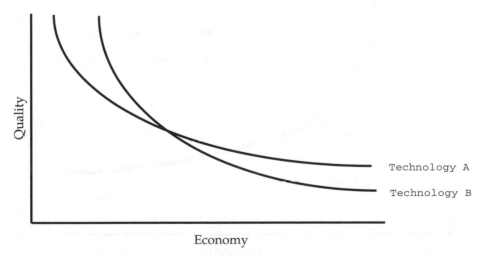

Figure 10-6.    Sometimes, the two technology curves cross. In this case, technology A is better at producing economical systems while still maintaining quality. Technology B, on the other hand, is capable of producing high-quality systems at less expense.

Technology A may involve customizing off-the-shelf systems, while technology B may be a full-fledged systems development effort. Millions of hours of software engineering time have been wasted arguing over such choices. The battles often become highly politicized, and are sometimes agitated by the presence of competing vendors.

Effective software engineering managers approach such situations remembering that they want to know what they're getting for what they're giving up, and why. The family of curves helps focus the discussion. For example, an organization that never intends to produce systems of high precision may never find itself in the region where technology B shines. If such an organization ever needs a single high-precision system, they may be better off contracting with an external organization of professional software developers. This, indeed, is the situation in many large companies. Individual departments may develop spreadsheet templates and simple database applications for themselves, yet turn to the software engineering professionals in a separate department when they need a new network to connect all the personal computers in their department.

By handling each kind of problem in a different way, we have created in effect a third, composite, technology: a mixture of A and B (Figure 10-7). But for this to be a complete technology, it takes more than just A and B. The missing ingredient is a *management decision* concerning when to use A and when to use B. Without this type of management choice, the organization does not really have software engineering, but only a collection of techniques applied more or less at random.

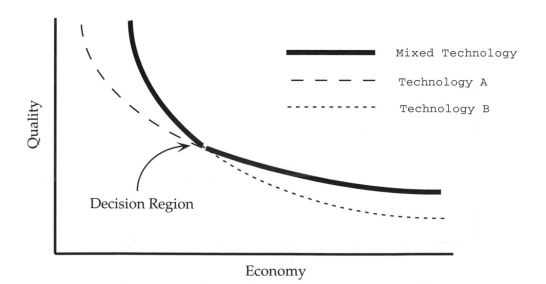

Figure 10-7.     One way to handle crossing technology curves is to create a mixed technology that combines the best of both, one on each side of the crossover. In this case, we choose technology A when we require greater economy, and technology B when we require higher quality.

## 10.2 The Fundamental Graph of Engineering Management Action

Engineering is difficult because of the complexity of choices. Everywhere I turn in analyzing software engineering management, I find choices, many of which are captured in Figure 10-8, which I like to call *the fundamental graph of engineering management action.* I give it this high-sounding name because it shows the major types of choices facing the engineering manager:

- when to make efforts to improve the use of existing technology
- how to direct the use of a technology to meet larger objectives
- what is possible with present technology
- which of two or more competing technologies to use
- when to use one technology, and when to use another
- where to invest the profits from a new technology
- whether to use the new technology as an excuse to achieve other goals

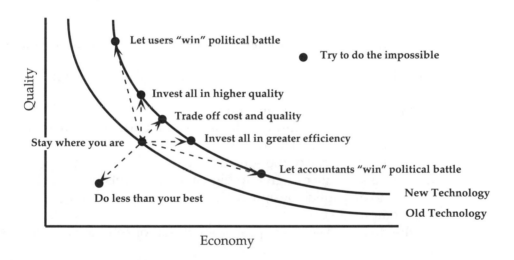

Figure 10-8.      Even after you have decided to move from an old to a new technology, there are still choices about where to invest what you gain from the technology, because you can still choose to use the new technology in different ways. You even have the choice to grind your favorite political ax: economy or quality. This is the fundamental graph of engineering management action because it shows so many of the important decisions facing an engineering manager.

The fundamental graph does not tell the manager how to make these decisions, but helps make these decisions explicit. The decision-maker must ask

- Where are we now? Are we doing as well as we can with what we already have? If not, why do we think we'll do any better with something new?

- Where do we want to be? Would our culture support us being there, or do we need to make cultural changes before trying to move?
- What technologies are possible from where we are now?
- Which ones provide possibilities closest to where we want to be?
- Precisely where do we want to be on that curve of possibilities?
- What actions take us toward this desired point? Which move us away?

Of course, people whose hidden agendas are not aligned with the explicit organizational objectives will not like this kind of questioning, but that won't bother the true engineering manager. Quite the contrary.

## 10.3  Levels of Control

When I used the term "technology" in the previous section, I was using it in a very broad sense,[3] encompassing

a.    the application of science, especially to industrial or commercial objectives

b.    the entire body of methods and materials used to achieve such objectives

Technology in this sense would include such choices as the following:

- what programming language to use
- whether to use a subroutine or a macro for a particular function
- how to organize a test laboratory
- who to put in charge of the source code
- whether to separate design into high and low levels
- whether to do explicit design at all
- what compiler to use
- whether to have a separate professional staff of software developers
- how to name a particular variable
- what sort of training program to support, and how to support it

### 10.3.1  Multilevel stability

Software engineering management is concerned with choices about technology, and those choices are made at many levels. In particular, the Feedback Control Model (or Cybernetic Model) itself is a technology, so all the trade-off curves apply to its application, and especially to multilevel control.[4] Figure 10-9 extends the simple view of a feedback controller to a multilevel feedback controller, to show that the environment of each level contains the levels above and below. Control at one level is not really possible unless the levels above and below are also in control. For instance,

- It does no good whatsoever for the director of software development to issue an order to reduce shipped errors by 50 percent without increasing cost or delivery time if the programmers don't know how to do that.
- It does no good whatsoever for a middle manager to establish a quality level to be achieved in testing if programmers can't build to a certain level in the first place, or if upper management orders the product shipped on a certain date without regard to the test results.
- It does no good whatsoever for programmers to develop a flawless piece of code if middle management has given them the wrong requirements.

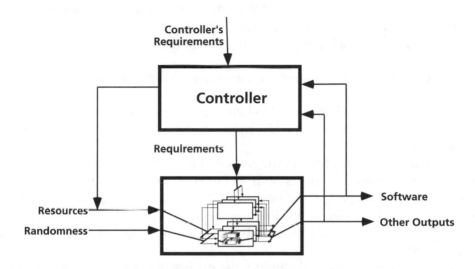

Figure 10-9.        In a system of nested feedback, control takes place at various levels.  If control is not in place at one level, it becomes more difficult to control at another because the environment of that level is formed by the levels above and below it, and that environment becomes unstable.

As Deming says,

> It is totally impossible for anybody or for any group to perform outside a stable system, below or above it.  If a system is unstable, anything can happen.  Management's job, as we have seen, is to try to stabilize systems.  An unstable system is a bad mark against management.[5]

### 10.3.2 Placing decisions at the right level

For a software engineering organization to be well managed, *all* of the levels have to be well managed.  But, in addition, they have to be coordinated with one another.  Therefore, software engineering managers have to decide on *what level* to place various control responsibilities. The rule of thumb I like to use is based on the Swiss political system:

a.   **Push every decision down to the lowest level that has the information and tools to make that decision.**

b.   **Push all tools and information to the lowest level that will take them.**

Ideally, the lowest levels should make all decisions relating to the product itself; the middle levels should manage the process by which this and other products are made; and the higher levels should concern themselves with the general cultural issues that will set the environment in which the process will function. If your organization cannot do these things consistently, you have not yet become an Anticipating (Pattern 4) organization.

### 10.3.3 *Decisions at higher levels can control decisions at lower levels*

As an African folk saying goes, "When elephants fight, the grass gets trampled." In management terms, "Decisions at higher levels act to control decisions at lower levels."

For example, if middle management has decreed a maximum module size, then a programmer's decision may be something like this: "I need a large module to meet my program's performance objectives. Management has set down rules about the size of modules, so before I design the module this way, I take the precaution of checking my design with management to avoid getting reprimanded."

Or, in a different cultural climate, the programmer may cheat the management by making a nonfunctional split of the module. Or, in a third, the programmer may think, "I'll document my choice and talk it over with a peer. I believe that a larger module is needed, but a second opinion will help. Anyway, I should document the reasons for the eventual maintainers." In an Anticipating organization, the programmer would think, "I believe this is needed, and I know we have a process for making exceptions to our guidelines. I'll follow that process, so there won't be any doubt whether I'm doing the right thing."

If management has given no clear guidelines, the programmer's decision may be a little different. "I need a large module to meet my program's performance objectives. A large module can cause trouble in testing, so I take the precaution of checking my design with a more experienced programmer to avoid getting in trouble with testing, and to avoid the ridicule of my peers when the module is reviewed."

Clearly, the different styles of the two higher-level decisions tend to foster different behaviors—and a different culture—at lower levels.

### 10.3.4 *Decisions at low levels can control decisions at higher levels*

In a feedback control system, the roles of system and controller are symmetrical. It's only our perception that determines which is controller and which is controllee, which is high and which is low. Therefore, we shouldn't be surprised to find that lower levels often act as controllers to higher levels. You can think of the CEO as controlling programmer salaries, but you can also think of programmers controlling the money that funds the salaries the CEO pays. Also, to the extent that the CEO's pay is determined by the success of the company, the programmers exert control over the CEO's pay.

This ability of lower-level decisions to control higher-level functions is one of the reasons that software development seems so hard to manage. Top management can set an objective such as portability. Middle management might translate that cultural requirement into some process decision, such as "Use only C as a programming language." But programmers can write code in C that's not portable at all. With no more process structure than "Use only C," the programmers could well develop a system that is practically impossible to port to new systems.

On the other hand, upper management may have given no directives about portability whatsoever, yet the programmers may have a culture that produces highly portable C code. When upper managers finally wake up to the need for portability, their ability to take effective action will be controlled by earlier decisions by the programmers—decisions that were invisible to the managers.

This portability example shows that the control of upper levels by lower levels could be either good or bad for the organization and, in any case, is not something we can stop. We can, however, be a bit more aware of why we put which control decision on which level.

### 10.3.5 *Amplification by position*

Stephen Covey tells a story of forcing his daughter to share her birthday presents. He concludes the story by saying:

> In an attempt to compensate for my deficiency, I *borrowed strength* from my position and authority and forced her to do what I wanted her to do.[6]

People who move to higher levels of control are often tempted, like parents, to compensate for their personal inadequacies by borrowing strength from their position. Covey goes on to explain what's wrong with such borrowing:

> But borrowing strength builds weakness. It builds weakness in the borrower because it reinforces dependence on external factors to get things done. It builds weakness in the person forced to acquiesce, stunting the development of independent reasoning, growth, and internal discipline. And finally, it builds weakness in the relationship. Fear replaces cooperation, and both people involved become more arbitrary and defensive.

Covey somewhat understates the case. Borrowing strength from position is actually much worse, because it also has a similar effect on all the other people in an organization who simply *witness* the borrowing. And, as General Vinegar Bend Stilwell put it, "The higher a monkey climbs, the more you see its behind."

High control position is like the long arm of a lever (Figure 10-10). The higher the position, the longer the arm; the longer the arm, the more any little incongruence is magnified. People in high positions are often seen as less congruent than the "ordinary" people down under. I believe they're probably about the same or even a bit more congruent, but because of this leverage, they *appear* a great deal less congruent. And, of course, their every little incongruence produces just that much more morbidity in the organization, and makes effective change just that much more difficult.

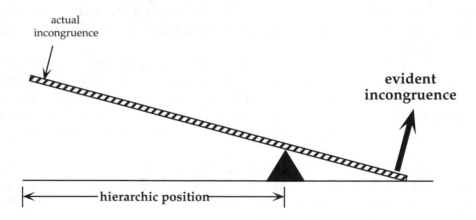

Figure 10-10.    High control positions amplify incongruence, making those in authority appear less congruent than those under them.

## 10.4  Helpful Hints and Suggestions

1.    Wayne Bailey points out that both engineers and managers plan the deliverables for a project, be it for developing a product or for changing an organization. Engineers and managers can apply the decision-making ideas of this chapter, but anything not considered a deliverable tends to be left out of the equation, as Wayne notes:

> For example, in our ISO project, managers focused on tangible deliverables like documented procedures and delivery of training on these procedures, measured by the number of pages written and percentage of people who had been trained. At the same time, they avoided planning or even thinking about what capabilities the resulting Quality System (i.e., all those documents) would provide to the company.

As in any engineering work, anything you leave out of your equations tends not to be found in the final product.

2.   The hyperbolic form of the trade-off curve emphasizes a number of things:

   a.   Some level of quality exists even for zero cost (the value of doing nothing).
   b.   No matter how much you spend, you're not likely to get infinite quality.
   c.   As cost increases, there's a diminishing return in quality.
   d.   As quality decreases, there's a diminishing return in economy.

3.   One way to determine the level at which decisions should be made is to consider the financial consequences of an erroneous decision.  Donald Norman once observed,

> In all the cases I have examined, the error correction mechanism seems to start at the lowest possible level and slowly works its way higher.[7]

Norman is talking about correcting errors in handling everyday things, like being unable to insert the car key, trying again, trying the key upside down, trying another key, wiggling the handle, trying another door, and finally realizing that it's the wrong car.

But the same way of progressing through levels is commonly found in correcting organizational faults.  If there is a $50 million programming error, the first action is to fire the programmer who last put hands on the code.  The last action is to change the upper management that designed the organization that would allow a $50 million error to slip through.  This may explain why organizational errors are so hard to correct.  In my view,

**If it's a $50 million error, then the management at the $50 million level *must* be responsible.**

4.   In multilevel organizations, the environment often becomes competitive, and the competition is carried to destructive levels.  Managers often tell me that although they don't like it, in such an environment, they must compete.  Others tell me—perhaps with greater self-understanding—that they love the competition.  Concerning competition, I have had much success following Koichi Tohei's advice:

> A person who likes contests and matches should try having one with himself.  For instance, a quick-tempered man might say, "Today I'm not going to get angry once."  If he manages to hold his temper all day, he wins; if he does not, he loses.  If we make progress without

causing anyone else trouble and without bearing ill will against anyone, we will get to the point where we are always winning. That is
real victory. If we fail to win over ourselves, even though we win over
others, we are doing nothing but satisfying our own conceit and vanity. If, on the other hand, we do win over ourselves, we have no need
to win over any other person. People will follow happily where we
lead. A relative victory is fragile, but a victory over oneself is
absolute.[8]

## 10.5 Summary

✔ Anticipating (Pattern 4) and Congruent (Pattern 5) organizations are truly engineering organizations, because people in them consistently think in engineering terms.

✔ Engineering can be done in many ways; there is no gospel, no holy book in which you can look for all the answers.

✔ Engineering is what you do when you *can't* get everything you want, because it's the art of getting as much as you can under the circumstances. Engineering *does* mean you make conscious decisions about what you're *getting* for what you're *giving up*, and *why*.

✔ A trade-off curve represents the boundary between the possible and the impossible with today's best engineering practice.

✔ Good software engineering management is the ability to stay on or near the trade-off curve of best possible practice at a point that represents the most desirable trade-off between the variables.

✔ Sketching a family of trade-off curves among critical variables gives engineering managers a basis for discussing the potential trade-offs, as among quality, economy, and schedule.

✔ Most technologies are formed from a mixture of other technologies, and they are linked by management decisions about when to use which.

✔ The fundamental graph of engineering management action shows many of the important decisions facing an engineering manager.

✔ Software engineering management is concerned with choices about technology in a broad sense of that term, and those choices are made at many levels. If control is not in place at one level, it becomes more difficult to control at another.

✔   For a software engineering organization to be well managed, *all* of the levels have to be well managed.  But, in addition, they have to be coordinated with one another.  Therefore, software engineering managers have to
decide on what level to place various control responsibilities.

✔   We know that decisions at higher levels act to control decisions at lower
levels, but decisions at low levels can also control decisions at higher levels.  We need to be aware of why we put which control decision on which
level.

## 10.6  Practice

1.   Phil Fuhrer suggests:  Discuss why the graph of Figure 10-2 is really fundamental to *all* engineering and only by extension to the *management* of
engineers.

2.   Strategic plans often mention customers, community, employees, and
stockholders, but tend to hide the trade-offs among them in vague visionary phrases.  Show trade-off curves for pairs of these constituencies, and
show how typical vision statements beg the question of how things will
be traded off.  Use specific variables such as salaries versus profits, profits
now versus profits later, or employee training versus profits now.

3.   Can you think of a decision (or nondecision) by your management that
has influenced the culture of the lower levels for the better?  For the
worse?  Analyze the dynamics of each decision.

4.   Can you think of a decision (or nondecision) by your technical staff that
has influenced the culture of the higher levels for the better?  For the
worse?  Analyze the dynamics of each decision.

5.   The U.S. Constitution outlaws "titles of nobility."  However, Americans
seem to be fascinated with titles, and although we may think that heredi-
tary titles are not okay, we strive to have titles added to our name to put
us above other people.   Here are some levels of titles from one Routine
(Pattern 2) organization, given to me by a new hire who had just studied
the ladder above him:

   *   Programming Trainee
   *   Associate Software Developer (Grade 1, Grade 2, Grade 3)
   *   Software Developer (Grade 1, Grade 2, Grade 3)
   *   Senior Software Developer
   *   Assistant Project Lead, Local Taxes
   *   Project Lead, Taxes
   *   Senior Project Lead, Payroll Systems

- Manager, Payment Systems
- Director, Financial Systems
- Assistant Vice President, Information Systems
- Vice President
- Group Vice President
- Senior Vice President
- Executive Vice President
- President
- Chief Executive Officer
- Board Vice Chairman
- Board Chairman

What effect do you think these levels have on the ability to change the software function to an Anticipating (Pattern 4) culture?

6.   Phil Fuhrer comments: The title of Philip Crosby's book *Quality Is Free* seems to deny the idea of trade-off curves.[9] Explain why quality is or isn't free based on long-term versus short-term feedback. What do you think the title really means?

7.   Phil Fuhrer suggests: Explain the software cultural patterns (Oblivious, Variable, Routine, Steering, Anticipating, Congruent) as a series of technology curves. Use these curves to illustrate how each pattern allows certain trade-offs.

8.   Phil Fuhrer adds: Explain why not all problems are best solved using the latest and greatest technology, and describe how your organization might choose to use less than its best technology.

# Part IV
# What Changes
# Have to Happen

*Nearly all men can stand adversity, but if you want to test a man's character, give him power.*

— Abraham Lincoln

If you truly understand change, and how to make it happen in an organization, you have great power. But to use that power effectively, you still need to know what kinds of changes to make, and especially what to preserve. Moreover, even with this knowledge, you will be powerless unless you are supported by a more-or-less stable organization.

Part IV applies the change processes of the earlier Parts to the processes that comprise the stable basis for an Anticipating (Pattern 4) software engineering organization. Before you can leap into Pattern 4, you'll need to ensure that these fundamental processes are in place.

# 11

# Components of Stable Software Engineering

*Cybernetics has accepted that mistakes, breakdowns, and random interferences occur in any system, and has shown how these things may be taken care of in the design of a machine.*[1]
— Stafford Beer

Software engineering managers often tell me that they tried to improve their organizations, but their improvement plans ran into some "bad luck." In response, I suggest that they use a cybernetic approach to managing change. Cybernetics is the science of steering, the science of getting a process to go the way you want it to go, even in a world that's not perfect. Indeed, you can think of cybernetics as a science that helps us make the world more perfect, if that's our goal.

Figure 11-1 is a cybernetic diagram of what it means to control any process by means of feedback and anticipation of environmental actions. The diagram, however, says nothing specific about software and could be a model for controlling any type of engineering process, such as the process of building software or the process of improving a software engineering organization.

This chapter will elaborate this diagram by addressing two key questions:

- What are the fundamental problems that make software engineering so different from other engineering?
- What are the fundamental components needed to control software engineering—to provide the stable base on which you can build an Anticipating (Pattern 4) organization?

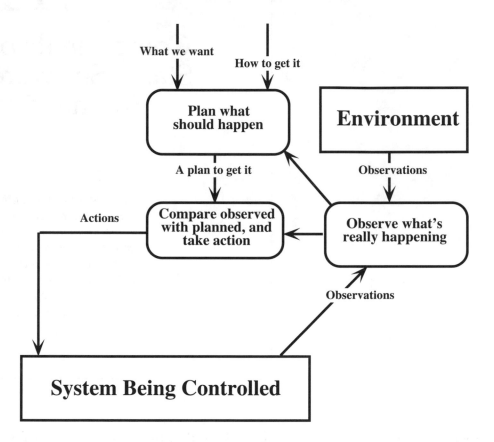

Figure 11-1.          Control of a process by feedback and by anticipation of environmental action.

## 11.1 Why Software Isn't Different

Why is software so different? One answer to this question is that it is a trick question: At first glance, software isn't so different. If engineers in other engineering disciplines worked the way software developers work, they would have the same types of problems. And, of course, they often do. People die when buildings collapse, when nuclear reactors melt down, when power fails, and when software operates incorrectly.

Do people really die from software defects? Peter Neumann of the ACM was quoted as saying that the ACM's software engineering group had monitored sixteen deaths caused by defective computer programs.[2] "This is just the tip of the iceberg," Neumann said.

Software, like every engineering discipline, has learned through costly failures.[3] We certainly don't like *any* deaths, but, as engineering failures go, sixteen known deaths in forty years is doing pretty well.[4] The nuclear engineering discipline is about the same age as the software industry, and hasn't done nearly as well in recent years. For a young industry, we've done very well, but of course nobody expects—nor desires—computers to kill *anyone*.

For an engineering discipline, though, forty years is not a very long time to mature. One difference, then, is that we're a very young engineering discipline, and maturity tends to mean reliability. In steam boiler engineering, for instance, on a capacity basis, the safety of boilers increased by a factor of $10^{13}$ in the 110 years between 1850 and 1960.[5] Put another way, if the safety of boilers had not increased by a factor of $10^{13}$, *we would all be dead*, many times over, killed in steam boiler accidents.

Of course, we would not actually all be dead, for without great increases in reliability, the boiler industry would never have grown to the enormous size it enjoys today. Even so, in the years between 1955 and 1963, twenty-nine explosions occurred, with thirty-two deaths and thirty-one injuries. Like software engineers, mechanical engineers don't think that's good enough, and many of them study successes and failures to improve their record.

## 11.2 Why Software Costs So Much

Over forty years of studying software successes and failures, the one question I am asked most frequently is, "Why does software cost so much?"[6] I don't like the way the question is framed, because it *assumes* that software costs too much, but if everyone is asking the question, there must be something of importance behind it. So, let's rephrase it into a more neutral, engineering-style question:

*What factors determine software costs?*

This is the question addressed by Barry Boehm's classic study of software engineering economics.[7] Figure 11-2 is adapted from the cover of Boehm's book and summarizes the *cost drivers* Boehm finds to be the most important determinants of the ultimate cost of software development. Guided by these drivers, we can determine which areas are potential sources of control difficulty and ought to be given management priority.

Roughly, the size of a driver is the ratio between the 90th and the 15th percentile of all the projects in Boehm's study. This means that if your project is near the bottom of all projects on a driver, the ratio is the multiplier you can expect to gain from moving to near the top. Two ratios can be combined by multiplication of categories as Boehm did, for example, by combining analyst capability (2.06) and programmer capability (2.03) to produce a new category called personnel/team capability (4.18).

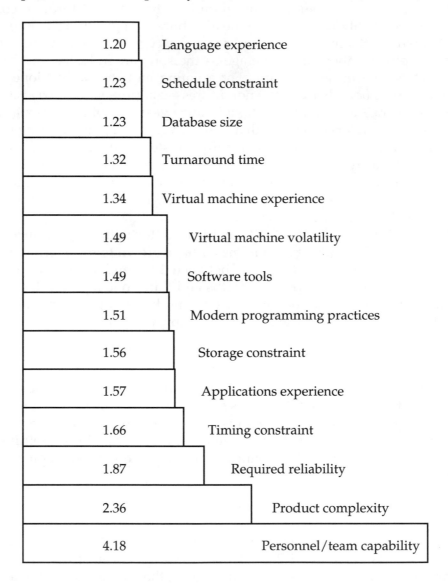

| 1.20 | Language experience |
| 1.23 | Schedule constraint |
| 1.23 | Database size |
| 1.32 | Turnaround time |
| 1.34 | Virtual machine experience |
| 1.49 | Virtual machine volatility |
| 1.49 | Software tools |
| 1.51 | Modern programming practices |
| 1.56 | Storage constraint |
| 1.57 | Applications experience |
| 1.66 | Timing constraint |
| 1.87 | Required reliability |
| 2.36 | Product complexity |
| 4.18 | Personnel/team capability |

Figure 11-2.     Boehm's chart from his studies showing which attributes drive software costs the hardest. The number is the ratio between the 90th and the 15th percentile projects on that attribute, and thus shows what the expected payoff might be from improving that factor.

### 11.2.1 System size

Because drivers can be combined by multiplying them together, we can easily create our own combinations. For instance, we can define a new category called *system size* or *complexity* (in answer to the question, How big is your problem?) as a combination of Boehm's categories:

- product complexity  (2.36)
- required reliability  (1.87)
- timing constraint  (1.66)
- storage constraint  (1.56)
- virtual machine volatility (changes in the target configuration) (1.49)
- database size  (1.23)
- schedule constraint  (1.23)

Multiplying these ratios gives an overall ratio of 25.76 for our definition of system size. In Chapter 20, you'll see why we give a great deal of emphasis to reducing system size as a tactic for getting or staying out of control trouble.

### 11.2.2  People factors

Similarly, we can combine the following ratios to produce a category called *people ratio:*

- personnel/team capability  (4.18)
- applications experience  (1.57)
- virtual machine experience (experience with target configuration) (1.34)
- language experience  (1.20)

Multiplication gives a people ratio of 10.55. Again, you'll see throughout this volume why we emphasize getting the most out of your people as a control strategy.

### 11.2.3  Tool factors

From the remaining ratios we can derive a tool ratio of 2.97. This seems impressive, but when compared to the other two ratios, it loses some of its luster as a source of control. This lower ratio might be attributable to the lack of useful tools, or perhaps most tools don't make any significant difference. Or, to put a generous interpretation on it, perhaps this small ratio is a tribute to the past effectiveness of tool-building efforts. In any case, tools are not the major source of control over software costs.

### 11.2.4  Poor management

Curiously, there is a fourth factor that Boehm didn't put on his chart. That factor is *management,* about which he says, "Poor management can increase software costs more rapidly than any other factor."[8]

After explaining why he cannot put exact numerical values on poor management, Boehm gives six "mismanagement actions" that he says have "often been responsible for *doubling* software development costs." Assuming that the six doubling factors can be applied together, we obtain an estimated management ratio of 64. I personally think this is an underestimate. There are other poor-management actions, and Boehm's study doesn't take into account totally failed projects. Nevertheless, this poor-management factor is already much bigger than any of the other factors.

## 11.3 Where Improvement Can Be Found

Figure 11-3 shows these four combined ratios on a chart. Now, suppose the elements of the chart had not been labeled, so that all you saw was a list of four impact ratios: 2.97, 10.55, 25.76, and 64.00. If you were a project manager, where would you spend most of your time seeking improvement?

Figure 11-3.     Boehm's drivers have been combined into categories to show where management might expect the best returns on investment. Boehm cites the management category as having the most influence on software costs, but he doesn't give an estimate. This estimate was taken from six actions Boehm says are often "responsible for *doubling* software development costs."

The question would be absurd except for the fact that most managers would answer in reverse order *if they were given only the names*—tools, people, system, and management. Perhaps that's why Boehm actually found the factors in this order. Perhaps the reason certain drivers are bigger than others is that *management spends so little time paying attention to them.*

Try this experiment: Read a computer trade publication such as *Software Development* or *Computerworld.* Tabulate the amount of advertising space given to tools and compare it with the space given to management. The results may suggest why software engineering managers have been driven by the vendors' claims about the wonders of tools.

You can perform a similar experiment by studying the titles and number of pages of computer books. In fact, I tabulated the quantity (quality is another matter) of each of the four factors in my own books and articles over time and found the interesting trends in Figure 11-4.

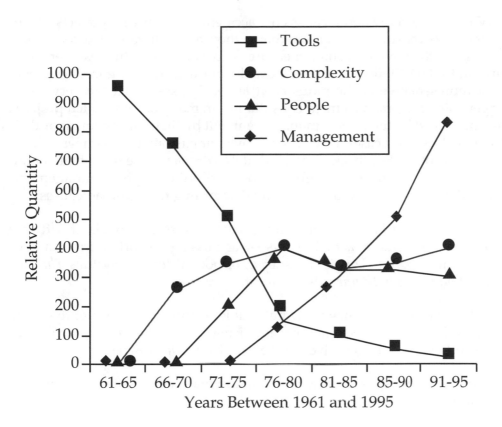

Figure 11-4.     How my own writing shows an increased emphasis on people, system size/complexity, and management versus tools over more than thirty years.

In my old age apparently, I've realized the error of my ways and have instinctively spent more of my energy on Boehm's most important factors. I'm now leaving most of the tool business to my younger colleagues and am concentrating on improving the effectiveness of the other three factors: people, system size/complexity, and management.

## 11.4 Why Software Projects Fail

In his text, Boehm explains why he doesn't have more data on poor management, and this explanation is, in effect, a seventh factor concerning poor management: *failing to collect data on their experiences, so that their future performance could be improved.*

In the light of the control model of Figure 11-1, this factor is probably more important than all of the others, because it prevents managers from getting the information they need to improve their control performance. But, if software engineering is to become a true engineering discipline, we, too, will have to study our failures and compare them with our successes. What are these managers missing when they fail to collect data on their experiences?

What do we know about causes of "accidents" in software projects? Over my career, I've consulted with more than a thousand software projects. About 90 percent of these were in some measure successful, while the rest were total failures in that they failed to deliver a usable product. These figures are probably not representative of the industry at large. I suspect that the very worst managers never use management consultants. In many of these failed projects, I was not invited by the project management, but by their management or their customers. In several cases, I was invited by their customers' attorneys.

In terms of the Feedback Control Model, *every one* of the more than a hundred failures I've studied closely can be attributed to poor management. Almost all of those failures can be classified according to two broad causes:

1.   ***Information Failures.*** Control information—such as models of software processes or data on actual results—was missing, distorted, irrelevant, or just plain wrong. This is the subject of both *Volume 1, Systems Thinking* and *Volume 2, First-Order Measurement.*

2.   ***Action Failures.*** Managers were unable to function congruently—they blamed, they placated, they became irrelevant—when taking actions as controllers. This is the subject of *Volume 3, Congruent Action.*

This volume's purpose is to show how you can make changes that will prevent those failures.

## 11.5  Information Failures

The rest of this chapter deals with information failures, which can be further classified into the following sources:

- not knowing what product is wanted
- not understanding the nature of the processes
- having no visible evidence of progress
- lacking sufficient stability for meaningful measurements
- lacking or losing design integrity

Let's take up each of these in turn.

### 11.5.1  Not knowing what product is wanted

Many projects fail because *they never know what kind of product is wanted.* Instead of precise knowledge, they have a collection of fuzzy desires. Sometimes, they deliver a product, only to find out it isn't acceptable. Sometimes, they discover the fuzziness during development and collapse under the attempt to make last-minute changes. Sometimes, the product is delivered, and goes into use, but fails to meet desires in some significant way.

### 11.5.2 *Not understanding the nature of the processes*

Other projects fail because the management doesn't understand *the nature of the processes of software development.* These projects usually break down during the development itself, though a common instance involves delivery of an untested product, in the vain hope that "we can fix it in maintenance."

### 11.5.3 *Having no visible evidence of progress*

The first two types of failure are found in any engineering discipline. Unlike most engineering disciplines, the software product is often considered invisible, so management has *no visible evidence on how the process is proceeding.* Software, however, is invisible only when we have not developed the correct engineering measurements. A hundred years ago, electricity was considered invisible. We only knew of its existence when it shocked us. And fifty years ago, radiation was invisible—until people died of cancer twenty-five years afterward.

### 11.5.4 *Lacking sufficient stability for meaningful measurements*

Sometimes, projects fail because information, though present, is meaningless. Like other immature engineering products, software often *lacks sufficient stability to make meaningful measurements.* Software projects often fail because of their maintenance debt of poorly designed or implemented code patches, confusion over different versions, and other undocumented changes. Software is so delicate that inverting a few bits can crash a mammoth project, such as putting telephone service out of operation for minutes or hours:

> Between June 10 and July 2 last summer, some twenty million telephone customers lost service for several hours in eight mysterious incidents of signaling equipment failure. . . . Common to all of [these incidents] was a software failure: one line of code among thousands in a signal transfer point (STP) contained a flaw involving only 3 bits. What should have been a binary D (1101) was instead a binary 6 (0110); in 3 bits of the character, 1's and 0's had been transposed. . . .[9]

If this kind of problem can occur under the strictest of controls, willy-nilly changes to a complex code structure will cause endless and unpredictable problems, and you won't know—and will be unable to know—from one day to the next if you are even measuring the system you thought you were.

### 11.5.5 *Lacking or losing design integrity*

Even when the product is stable and visible, its *design* may be so complex that we can't figure out how our actions will affect it. The design may have been too complex to begin with, or it may have grown complex and incurred design debt after multiple ill-considered changes. Even when the design is well done and maintained, Minot's Law predicts a tendency to lose integrity as the system grows. Thus, we often hear the software warning cry "Don't touch the code!"—that means "Don't attempt any control action that involves understanding the design." When we don't heed the warning, the software often collapses beyond the reach of any control action whatsoever.

Figures 11-5 and 11-6 summarize these failures due to managers' not getting the needed control information.

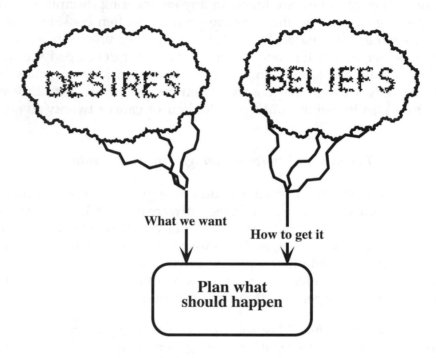

Figure  11-5.    Problems arise because we have vague desires instead of clear statements of what we really want, and we have vague beliefs, rather than robust models, about how to get it.

## 11.6  Evolving Solutions to Information Failures

Critics of software engineering may use this list of information failures to show that we are not making progress, but the picture is much more optimistic. Over the short life of software engineering, we have begun to evolve our own tools and techniques for combatting these sources of failure—gathering requirements, developing process models, observing what's going on in a process, controlling changes, and maintaining design integrity. Specific techniques and tools for doing these things are well described in the references for this chapter. This volume, on the other hand, addresses these tools and techniques in terms of how they relate to management and cultural change—*what is necessary to institute and manage such processes.*

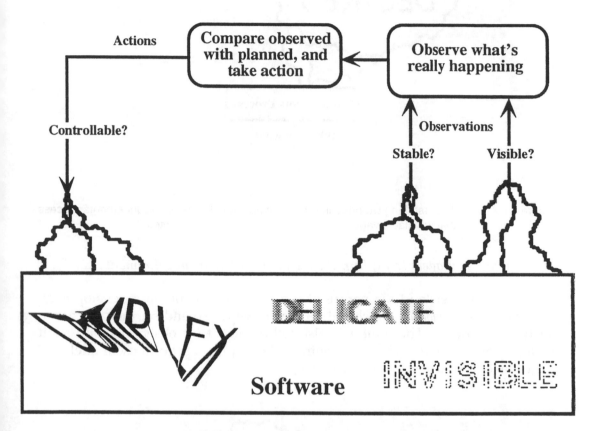

Figure 11-6.     Software engineering has additional problems because of the nature of software. When we build software in an uncontrolled manner, we are trying to work with an invisible product that is extremely delicate, so we have great difficulty observing what we have at any time without making special efforts. When the product has a complex or unknown structure, we can't apply effective feedback control actions because to do so, we would need a reasonable model of how the product would respond to various actions.[10]

### 11.6.1 A requirements process to identify what product is wanted

In order to know what kind of product is wanted, we have a *requirements process* to translate vague desires into something from which we can build a product (Figure 11-7). This process may be highly automated or done with pencil and paper, but if a project is to be successful, the requirements process must be done explicitly and with clarity.[11]

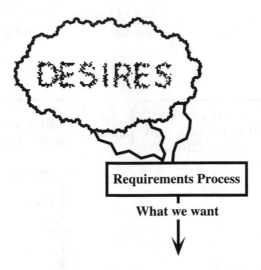

Figure 11-7.        The first thing we need in order to manage software is a requirements process
                    that translates vague desires into precisely what is wanted.

## 11.6.2  Process models to explain the nature of software development

In order to understand the nature of the processes of software development, we have *process models,* which tell us that if we do so-and-so, then thus-and-such will happen.  These models also tell us that if we observe so-and-so, it means that thus-and-such is happening.  Developing a set of these models is a major task of *Volume 1, Systems Thinking.*

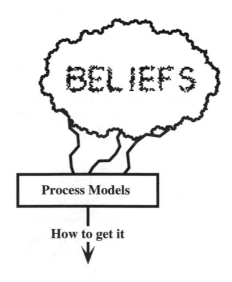

Figure 11-8.        Once we know what we want, we need a process model to know how to get it.

### 11.6.3 *Processes that provide visible evidence on progress*

In order to gain visible evidence on how the process is proceeding, we use explicit testing processes, including many hardware and software testing tools, trouble-tracking systems, and human processes such as technical reviews[12] applied to visible work products like analysis and design documents.[13]

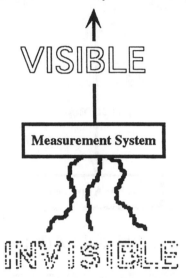

Figure 11-9.     A measurement system that makes the product visible.

### 11.6.4 *Systems to provide stability for meaningful measurements*

In order to obtain sufficient stability to make meaningful measurements, we use tools and systems for controlling changes and for keeping track of versions and releases of the same product along with all its accompanying information.[14]

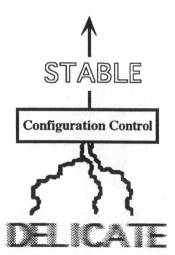

Figure 11-10     Configuration control is needed to make a potentially delicate product stable enough to measure.

### 11.6.5 *Tools and techniques to maintain design integrity*

In order to reduce complexity to dimensions we can actually control with a feedback process, we use design tools and techniques. Although there is no agreement on one best approach (nor is there ever likely to be), many outstanding books on design are available.[15]

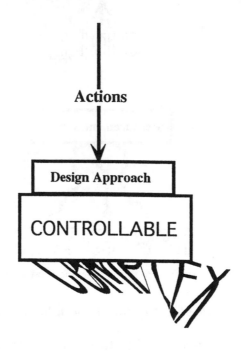

Figure 11-11.    An effective design approach is needed to make the product simple enough to be controllable.

## 11.7 Action Failures

Learning through our troubles, we have made much progress toward becoming a true engineering discipline. Like the steam boiler engineers, however, our aspirations sometimes expand faster than our competence. Our capacity to build high-quality systems has grown, but that very growth has encouraged us to attempt to build ever more difficult systems. That's why it sometimes seems as if we're going backward, even though we are learning, learning, learning.

In the end, though, knowing what to do is not enough. It is the character and personality failures of management that are the biggest cause of software failure, and these all-too-human failures limit what we can do through organizational changes. Because of the positional power of managers in hierarchical organizations, even small blunders by managers can undo our best efforts to change a culture. Managers need to act congruently, or the consequences can be catastrophic.[16] Consider this tale by Dan Starr:

> What about corporate feedback—those institutionalized processes by which the company attempts to reward and reinforce what it views as desirable behavior? Somehow, these programs seldom seem to communicate the message that the company genuinely values its people. Often, they seem geared more to the needs of the people giving the recognition than to the wants and values of those receiving it.
>
> For example, a corporate organization gave an "architecture award" to one of its department heads—a big, framed piece of paper and a glass sculpture. Each person in that department head's organization got a smaller framed piece of paper, with the department head's name in big letters and the engineer's name typed in much smaller letters. A few people still have these things on display, but not for the reasons the department head passed them out.

In the following chapters, we'll be paying special attention to this kind of feedback—information that tells workers how management views their culture—and trying to teach managers how to communicate what they really mean. Of course, if they really mean what these awards seem to imply, then there's no help for them or their organizations. But if it's a matter of style, rather than intent, such managers can readily improve the way they steer their organizations.

## 11.8 Helpful Hints and Suggestions

1.  Just because these components are fundamental, don't think improving them will be easy. In many organizations, attempts to examine software processes with an eye to improvement will meet strong political opposition. The more arbitrary the power structure, the greater the threat from an explicit study of the organization:

    > Process commentary undermines arbitrary authority structure. Industrial organizational development consultants have long known that if a social structure openly investigates its own structure and process, power equalization takes place. High power individuals are not only more technically informed but also possess organizational information which permits them to influence and manipulate. They not only have skills which allowed them to obtain a position of power but, once there, have such a central place in the flow of information that they are able to reinforce their position. The greater the authority structure of an institution, the more stringent are the precautions against open process commentary (viz., military, church). If an indi-

vidual wishes to maintain a position of arbitrary authority, then it behooves him to inhibit the development of any rules permitting reciprocal process observation and commentary.[17]

2.    Payson Hall warns that Boehm studied only projects that finished, so his sample is biased toward lower overall costs. If your organization is not competent in some cost driver area, costs can grow without bound—and often do—until the project is canceled.

3.    Jim Highsmith is typical of a number of reviewers who say they're a little put off by the constant reference to poor management:

> I wonder things like, Are software managers in general worse than other managers? When I see things like Boehm's 64 to 1 ratio, I wonder if it is because software management is so bad, or if it is because software management is so "hard." Is there something about software that makes it inherently harder to manage? I think the answer is, Yes. I think much of the content of *QSM* speaks to the fact that software is a very difficult management undertaking. I know from my own consulting work, it is very easy to attribute many of the problems to poor management, and it certainly is the case in many instances, but I try to take the position that software management is really hard and we therefore need to constantly work on it since it has such a large impact on success.

Software *is* harder to manage than most other human activities, and, moreover, the consequences of poor management are growing all the time. So, as Jim says, if you don't work on your management skills constantly, sooner or later you'll be one of those poor managers. Perhaps you'll feel better knowing you manage so poorly because software management is such a difficult job, but I doubt it. So keep working!

## 11.9 Summary

✔    Although software engineering is in many ways the same as any other kind of engineering, it also has unique properties arising from the nature of software.

✔    According to Boehm, software costs are affected by the size and complexity of the system, by people factors, by the tools that are used, and especially by poor management.

✔    Software projects fail most often when control information is missing, distorted, irrelevant, or just plain wrong, or when managers are unable to function congruently when taking actions as controllers.

✔   Control information failures take several common forms, such as

   •   not knowing what product is wanted
   •   not understanding the nature of the processes of software develop-ment
   •   having no visible evidence on how the process is proceeding
   •   lacking sufficient stability to make meaningful measurements
   •   lacking or losing design integrity

✔   Over time, software engineers are evolving solutions to information fail-ures, such as

   •   requirements processes to identify what product is wanted
   •   process models to explain the nature of software maintenance and development
   •   processes that provide visible evidence on how the project is pro-ceeding
   •   systems to provide stability by controlling changes
   •   tools and techniques to maintain design integrity

✔   In the end, though, it is the character and personality failures—the incon-gruence—of management that are the biggest cause of software failures, and these must be worked on through ongoing personal development.

## 11.10  Practice

1.   Reading about problems may set a negative tone to this chapter. To coun-teract this tone, draw a diagram of effects that shows what's needed for software success, rather than what's not needed for software failure.

2.   My colleague Barbara Purchia, a process specialist, points out another kind of information failure, one that is involved with outside informa-tion—the same kind of failure we saw when discussing strategic plan-ning. Although this might be a case of not knowing what product is wanted, it's probably a good idea to consider it separately. For example, a product might be developed from scratch that could have been purchased off the shelf, or built largely from off-the-shelf components. Generate a list of failures to get information from outside the organization itself.

3.   Phil Fuhrer points out: A boiler design that doesn't make it into produc-tion does not count as a failure. How many false starts or bad boiler designs never make it to the market? How does this compare with soft-ware false starts or bad designs? What biases in measurement are intro-

duced when we fail to consider false starts or bad designs that never make it to market?

4.   Phil Fuhrer adds:  What about software projects that were successful by accident?  Can you provide an example from your own experience?  How did that bias the organization's conclusions about good software management practices?

# 12
# Process Principles

*Here it is 1974, and the controversies about how best to manage the programming function are as intense as were the debates on this subject ten and fifteen years ago.*[1]
— R.E. Canning

Here it is, a few decades later. . . . We're still arguing.

When an argument is this intense for this many decades, perhaps we're not arguing about the right things. Or perhaps the argument is vacuous. Or our models are so different that there's no place where we can engage sufficiently to settle the argument. Or we just love arguing.

Each of these explanations is possible, but there's yet another possibility. Each time a new process model arrives on the scene, it acquires champions. Championing a process model—be it waterfall, spiral, Möbius strip, rapid prototyping, or especially one of the name brands—is a way to make a living, and a pretty good one at that. Thus, for these champions, there's a bias in the argument: If you lose, you're out of work.

Myself, I'm not one of these model champions. I've seen many models succeed, and every model fail. So perhaps I am sufficiently neutral to elevate the discussion to a higher plane. Instead of merely presenting models and arguing about them, I'm going to present some principles that I believe *any* effective process model must follow. These principles will then act as guides when I explore the strengths and weaknesses of different models. More important, they will act as guides for managers who are trying to implement one or more process models. Therefore, I will emphasize

- each principle and why it's a principle
- how to notice violations
- what to do about violations, and how to achieve conformity

## 12.1 The Millionaire Test

One of my favorite toys is called the Millionaire Machine. It's a miniature lottery machine, a scale model of the machines "used in all the state lotteries." The manufacturer advertises that by using the Millionaire, you are personally using "the exact same process for picking numbers as the large lotteries." Therefore, the claim goes, you will get the "same results."

The claim for the Millionaire reminds me of the software engineering managers who put boxes on their organization chart for all the functions on the SEI list. Then they sit back and wait to win the lottery (Figure 12-1).

Figure 12-1.     Achieving a more advanced software engineering culture is not like winning the lottery, even if you follow "the exact same process" that other organizations followed.

Perhaps you think that the Millionaire produces a random process, and so gives a random result.  That's true, but what's so terrible about random?  A random process is *not* always the worst process.  Is there a worse process for playing the lottery?  Sure.  You could lose your tickets, which is like software organizations that don't practice effective configuration management.

Even if you know you're not doing worse than random, can you show that you are doing *better*?  Random provides a powerful process test, *The Millionaire Test:*

**If you can't show that your process is better than random, don't use it.**

Curious as it may seem, you will find the Millionaire Test extremely practical.  It puts the burden of proof on anyone proposing a new process, encouraging the advocate to develop a measurable process.

Why is this test so important?  Strange as it may seem, many processes are in operation today that are demonstrably worse than random, had anyone attempted a demonstration:

- Many organizations have processes for choosing the order in which failures are serviced.  For instance, some service the failures of the loudest blamers first.  This process teaches customers to be loud blamers, a less-than-optimum situation and one that random servicing would not create.
- In organizations with a high fault feedback ratio—a high rate of putting in faults while trying to remove other faults—the process of randomly not attempting to fix faults would lead to a higher rate of success than they currently experience.[2]
- I have worked with more than a dozen organizations in which the management made exceptions to mandatory technical reviews "if a module was running behind schedule."  Of course, the *reason* they were running behind schedule was that the programmers were having difficulty reaching stability with their code.  This difficult code was written sloppily, or was overly complex, or was poorly designed.  Consequently, it was easy to show that this process was worse than the process of choosing the same number of modules at random to skip their reviews.

The point of the Millionaire Test is not to advocate random processes (though they shouldn't be ruled out willy-nilly), but to awaken organizations to the idiocy of some of their processes.  Once they open their eyes, they may begin to realize the importance of some of the other process principles, such as stability, visibility, and measurability.

## 12.2 The Stability Principle

Figure 12-2 is another view of the Cybernetic Control Model introduced in Chapter 11. Feedback works on continuity:

- The pieces in the model cannot be too large (or response will be slow).
- The pieces in the model must be stable (or response will not be predictable).

*The Stability Principle* summarizes these two requirements:

**Every part of a process must be a controlled system.**

Any acceptable process model is built out of stable parts, and each stable part looks like Figure 12-2. It contains a prerequisites part, a construction part, a measurement part, and a feedback part.

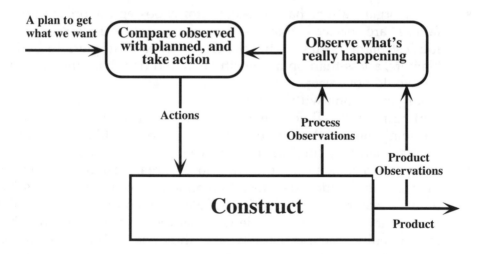

Figure 12-2.     The cybernetic model of a control system contains a measurement process whose results are fed back into the construction process. In an acceptable process for an Anticipating (Pattern 4) organization, every part of the process must be a controlled system.

Imagine building a house by bringing all the parts to the lot, then having everybody run to the foundation and put their part in place, after which people walk around and see if the lights work or the floor collapses. There is no house test in house building to compare with the system test in system building. There are, instead, many incremental, intensive tests all throughout, especially when something is added that

- other people depend on
- will be invisible (like wires and pipes in walls)

At every stage, the house must be stable. When it may not be, scaffolding is added so that the system of partially completed house plus scaffolding is stable. When the house becomes stable on its own, the scaffolding is taken away. Examples of scaffolding include concrete forms, extra framing, power brought to the site, and portable toilets.

Using the Stability Principle, we see that testing is not a *stage,* but part of a control process embedded in *every* stage. What is often called system test is not a test at all, but another part of system construction, perhaps better named "system integration." People are reworking errors in previous parts, and building the system as they do.

### 12.2.1 Phrases to listen for

The following phrases warn a manager that the process of building while using stable phases has been or is about to be violated:

- Just wait till it's all done, then you'll be surprised.
- We'll clean that up in system test.
- The testers will fix that.
- Of course we don't have what we need, but get started anyway.
- They can clean up the design when they write the code.
- Ship it. The customers will tell us if anything is wrong.

### 12.2.2 Actions to take

DO NOT allow tests to be skipped, or postponed to later stages. *Whatever is pushed to the end of the cycle will be sacrificed to the schedule.*

DO be aware that tests take many forms. Testing by running code on a machine is only one form with many variations. Other forms include testing by construction (as in Cleanroom development[3]), testing by purchasing (using pretested components), and testing by review[4] (including walkthroughs, inspections, and other forms).

Figure 12-3 looks inside the "Construct" box of Figure 12-2, suggesting that the overall process of construction is decomposed into smaller processes, each of which is stable. This decomposition can be carried down to the smallest act that transforms something from one state to another. DO NOT routinely manage to the level of "pound one nail" or even "strike one blow with the hammer." If "pound one nail" is a trustable unit of work, then it can be beneath management scrutiny.

DO NOT believe those people who claim that statistical process control cannot be applied to software work. What they're missing is the correct level for applying these controls, and the right kind of action to take. For instance, they may measure faults in code, but use the information to blame and badger individuals who fall below designated thresholds.

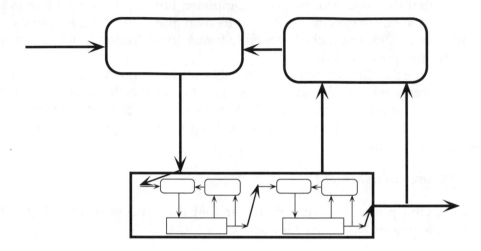

Figure 12-3.     The overall process of construction is decomposed into smaller processes, each of which is stable, and some of which can be run in parallel.

DO exercise statistical control over measurements to ensure that each unit is a trustable unit. If it proves to be non-trustable, DO open it up for inspection and process improvement, not for blaming and badgering its developers. For instance, if your organization cannot reliably create a fifty-line module of code, then DO institute some process improvement action focused on coding practice. The necessity for doing this from time to time leads to the Visibility Principle.

## 12.3  The Visibility Principle

Software that is being built or maintained is an asset. This includes all software in the broadest definition with all its scaffolding: code, process designs, data designs, requirements, internal documentation, user documentation, test cases, databases, test plans, project plans, and training materials, as well as the history of each of these things. This software asset belongs to the organization that is paying for it, just as the pieces of a house belong to the person paying for the house, not to the workers who build the house.

This ownership principle may seem obvious in house building, but for some strange reason, it isn't widely accepted by builders in the software industry. Many programmers seem to confuse pride in workmanship with pride in ownership. They balk whenever management (or anyone else, for that matter) wishes to exercise some control over the product of their work. Indeed, they balk at the suggestion that anyone should even *see* the product of their work.

Interestingly, many managers actively support this view. James Robertson tells the following tale involving his wife and consulting partner, Suzanne Robertson:

> Suzanne was urging, at my invitation, a group of managers to go and look at the work of a design class I was conducting. One manager said he felt uncomfortable looking at a subordinate's work. Another manager said, "It's just the same as being in bed with someone—you don't point and you don't laugh."

Obviously, from what we know about controlling a project, and from what we know about the natural imperfections of human beings, this concept of ownership cannot be part of *any* process model. Instead, every process model must conform to *The Visibility Principle* (Figure 12-4):

**Everything in the project must be visible at all times.**[5]

Figure 12-4.     Everything in the project must be visible at all times: code, plans, requirements, designs, test plans, test results, progress, all paper documents . . . everything.

Moreover, since nothing is real unless it has passed review and since invisible things cannot be reviewed, a corollary of the Visibility Principle is *The Reality Principle:*

**Nothing is real until it has passed independent review.**

### 12.3.1 Phrases to listen for

Violations of the Visibility Principle are easy for managers to catch if they keep their ears open for the following expressions:

- He's a very sensitive programmer. He'll quit if we review his work.
- We don't want to upset anybody by questioning their work.
- My program, your program, her program, his program, their program (or any other phrase implying private ownership) . . .
- We don't have source code for that.
- The source code for that isn't current.
- The documentation for that isn't current.
- The customers won't understand that this is only a prototype (so let's keep it hidden from them).
- He has it all in his head.
- There's only one copy of that, so we can't let you have it.
- We didn't write it *all* down, but we know what they want.
- We don't like to write things down. Don't you trust us?
- (or simply) Don't you trust us?

The "Don't you trust us?" is the killer phrase for many managers, sending them instantly into placating. The proper answer is, "Yes, I trust your honesty, but I don't trust your infallibility. I don't trust *anyone's* infallibility." If programmers respond by claiming infallibility ("But I tested it *thoroughly.*"), send them to the Vatican where a better job awaits them. Infallible programmers will kill a project every time.

If you'd rather appeal to authority, say, "Deming says that variation is part of any process." Deming happens to be right, even for software. *Especially* for software.

### 12.3.2 Actions to take

DO NOT ever allow anything to become invisible—not requirements, not designs, not code, and especially not tests. Prevention is much easier than cure.

DO stop everything and take action to correct the situation *the moment* you find out about any piece of work that's not available to be seen, or "cannot be inspected." There's no surer way for a manager to spot technical trouble, and it requires no technical knowledge whatsoever.

DO NOT accept the argument that "things will get better." Without your action, things will only get less visible over time.

DO insist on complete visibility from the start of any project, right through to the end.

DO get rid of any person who is indispensable for such reasons as "Jim's the only one who knows what's inside there." Before getting rid of Jim, offer him the aid of someone else to get things documented. If he refuses, then get rid of him. And do it now, not after things settle down. Invisible things *never* settle down.

DO trust people at a level of loss you can accept. The Visibility Principle is not a ticket for managers or anyone else to stand over people's shoulders while they're working. For example, a piece of code in progress can be invisible for a week *if you can afford to throw away a week's work* when it does become visible and you discover that it's worthless. If it's scheduled to be in progress for a week, and at the end of the week, the programmer says, "Oh, I'm running a little behind, so it's not quite ready to show anybody," then you say, "Well, in that case, bring out what you have and we'll review it right now." Then put a review together, and prepare yourself psychologically to get it built by a back-up programmer if the review shows it to need rebuilding.

DO NOT attempt to correct all invisibility problems at once. Remember the Satir Change Model, and use it to design a step-by-step process of making the invisible visible. DO start with a group that is ready and eager to become visible.

## 12.4 The Measurability Principle

It's the easiest thing in the world for people to draw boxes and arrows showing a process of constructing something. They can even show so-called tests at the end of the process. Such process diagrams are meaningless and dangerous, however, if they don't describe the *measurements* that will tell you if the work of each box has actually been accomplished. *The Measurability Principle* says,

**Anything you don't measure will be out of your control.**

Notice that the principle doesn't say "out of control," but "out of *your* control." Things may be controlled, but not by you, and not necessarily to meet your objectives. So, if you are the manager and you are not measuring, you may be lucky, but you're not doing what you're paid for—managing.

Also be warned about the common logical fallacy of inverting the Measurability Principle. When a restaurant menu says, "Good food takes time," it doesn't mean that if the service is slow, the food must be good. Similarly, the Measurability Principle says, "Good management takes measurement," but that doesn't mean that if you measure lots of things, you must be in control.

### 12.4.1  *Phrases to listen for*

Again, you don't need to know anything about technology to detect violations of the Measurability Principle.  Listen for the following phrases:

- That can't be measured.
- We can't tell you how far we've come.
- I'll let you know when I've finished.
- I'm *xx* percent complete.
- That can't be tested.
- It's an iterative process that never *really* ends.
- There aren't any deliverables.
- We can print reports, but they're not reviewable because design is a fluid, dynamic process.
- Measurement costs too much.
- Some things are just intangible.
- Just two more instructions to change.
- I'm fixing the last bug.
- We *know* that's not important.
- Don't you trust us?

The "Don't you trust us?" can be handled in the same way as with visibility problems.  (How can it be measurable if it's invisible?)   "We *know* that's not important" is a superreasonable phrase that traps some managers.  In fact, the things you *know* are not important (without even measuring them) are precisely the things that get you into the most hot water.  So, if you could only measure one thing, I'd suggest you measure that one thing that people most strongly argue is unmeasurable and, besides, irrelevant.  Of course, you don't have to measure just one thing.

### 12.4.2  *Actions to take*

DO NOT overburden yourself or others with measurements.  DO NOT let measuring become an end in itself.   DO NOT take measurements that you don't evaluate and act upon.  DO keep the number of measurements small, perhaps by dropping one for every new one.  DO drop any measurement that you aren't using.

DO keep the measurements simple.[6]  DO NOT tolerate vast spreadsheets full of numbers.  DO insist on high-level reports, with pictures whenever possible.

DO make measurement everyone's responsibility.  DO NOT make any measurer responsible for the success of the thing being measured.

DO insist on measurements from the beginning.  DO find *something* to measure, or replace your measurer.  DO try to choose something meaningful, but DO NOT paralyze your measurement program by trying to prove it's meaningful before you measure it. DO be prepared to change or adapt your measurement as you learn about its meaning. As one client told me,

> We started with the obvious measure of production—lines of code. We almost got trapped in arguments about why LOC weren't meaningful. It delayed us by two months, but finally we just got going. We quickly learned that there were many things wrong with LOC as a measure, but we corrected the major ones. For instance, we noticed that there were two major styles of commenting that gave different LOC counts, so we adjusted for that. Then we had to adjust for variations in included code. Finally, we realized that it made no sense to count code that wasn't of constant, known, quality. This last adjustment was the trigger that made us realize we had to get serious about reviewing *all* code—and that was probably the biggest single benefit of trying to measure LOC.

DO look at results *regularly and often*. Change in a measurement is significant, even when the significance of the measurement itself isn't obvious.

DO use the measurements as *indicators* of something requiring your attention. DO NOT take action based on measurements without first confirming their meaning by deeper investigation. DO NOT use measurements on individuals, but on processes.

DO assign at least one whole person for measurement. Two people are better, because they can support each other when everyone (probably including you) tries to discredit the message they're bringing.

DO budget for measurement, both time and resources. If measurement isn't budgeted, it won't happen.

DO use primary measurement rather than interpreted measurement. Each level of interpretation of the meaning uses another model, and may introduce mistakes.

## 12.5 The Product Principle

The final principle concerns requirements. *The Zeroth Law of Software Engineering* says,

**If you don't have to meet requirements, management is no problem.**

This law is important enough to deserve its own chapter, but there's a special application of the law that needs to fall under the heading of general process principles. For some curious reason, the history of the information processing business has been plagued by a focus on software and programming. What we call "software engineering" would more properly be called "information engineering," but an entire industry seems to have taken the part for the whole, so we probably have to learn to live with it. This substitution of part for whole could be accepted as harmless poetic license, were it not for the evil it can do in process design.

*The Product Principle* says,

**Products may be programs, but programs are not products.**

Violation of this principle leads to essential parts of information systems being omitted from process design, or even omitted from the product. Some typical examples include

- user training being "left to the trainers," who have no input until all the software has been released
- test data being discarded, or lost, between releases
- interface design being slapped together according to what is most convenient to code
- the creation, loading, validation, and security of databases is not considered until software decisions have locked out many possibilities

Ironically, programmers working with hardware organizations always complain that they have no input to hardware decisions that have strong implications for software, but they perpetrate the same wickedness on the people who build the other parts of the product. They build software that has strong one-way implications for the people who must sell the product, document it, train people in using it, and ultimately those who must use it every day.

### 12.5.1 Phrases to listen for

To discover if your processes simply do not address certain parts relating to non-software, start with a list of the complete product. Then, with this list in mind, listen for the following phrases:

- The programs are almost finished (with no mention of anything else).
- We can't start the documentation until the programs are done.
- Now that the programs are done, there's no need for documentation.
- We can't start the X (any product part) until the programs are done.
- We should cut a little code to see what this looks like.
- It's self-documenting.
- The *language* is self-documenting. (We've heard this for C, C++, various assembly languages, COBOL, FORTRAN, PL/I, Pascal, BASIC, APL, Lisp, Smalltalk, indeed, for just about any language that exists—and it's false for all of them.)

- It's self-training.
- It's self-installing.
- The *code* is secure.  (Notice the stress on *code*.)
- The *code* is reliable.

Managers tend to hear these things, know what they imply, but believe them anyway—because they *want* to believe them.  Wouldn't it be nice if all you needed for a reliable product was reliable code?

### 12.5.2  Actions to take

DO NOT allow everything to wait for the software.

DO put every part of the product (both deliverables and scaffolding) into the plan, as well as into the process descriptions from which the plan is derived.

DO start as early as possible on each part of the product, except the code. DO NOT rush the code "because everything else is waiting."  Not everything can be done before design is finished, but when you've attained an Anticipating (Pattern 4) culture, you'll never need to wait for code to complete the rest of the product.

### 12.6  Helpful Hints and Suggestions

1. If the software processes follow the principles in this chapter, all software work can be seen as maintenance: reducing the difference between desired and perceived behavior of a product.  Thus, there is no reason to make a great status differentiation between development and maintenance, and no need to have fundamentally different processes for the two.

2. Sue Petersen, who's in the plumbing business, says,

   > I have seen local building inspectors pass a portion of the plumbing/electrical after it's been covered over (so they can't see it), if they trust the installer and he assures them that it's okay, and if the house/repair job is under intense time pressure. For this to work long-term, all involved must be competent, knowledgeable, and ethical.

   They must also be infallible, which perhaps is easier in plumbing than in programming.  Perhaps you can pass some code without inspection—if it's written by someone who's competent, knowledgeable, ethical, and infallible.  There are thousands of programmers who *think* they meet these criteria, but in fact there's at most one person in the world who meets them, and he's not a programmer.

## 12.7 Summary

✔ There are a number of principles that *any* effective process model must follow. These principles act as guides when you're exploring the strengths and weaknesses of different models. They also act as guides for managers who are trying to implement one or more process models.

✔ The Millionaire Test says,

**If you can't show that your process is better than random, don't use it.**

The Millionaire Test puts the burden of proof on any people who propose a new process, encouraging them to develop a measurable process.

✔ Many processes are in operation today that are demonstrably worse than random. The point of the Millionaire Test is not to advocate random processes, but to awaken an organization to the idiocy of some of its processes.

✔ Feedback works on continuity. The pieces in the model cannot be too large (or response will be slow), and they must be stable (or response will not be predictable). The Stability Principle summarizes these two requirements:

**Every part of a process must be a controlled system.**

✔ The Stability Principle shows that testing is not a *stage,* but part of a control process embedded in *every* stage. What is often called system test is not a test at all, but another part of system construction, perhaps better named "system integration."

✔ From what we know about controlling a project, and from what we know about the natural imperfections of human beings, the concept of private ownership of work products cannot be part of any process model. Instead, every process model must conform to the Visibility Principle:

**Everything in the project must be visible at all times.**

✔ Since nothing is real unless it has passed review, and since invisible things cannot be reviewed, a corollary of the Visibility Principle is the Reality Principle:

**Nothing is real until it has passed independent review.**

✔ Process diagrams are meaningless and dangerous if they don't describe the measurements that will tell you if the work of each box has actually been accomplished. The Measurability Principle says,

**Anything you don't measure will be out of your control.**

The Measurability Principle also says "Good management takes measurement," but that doesn't mean that if you measure lots of things, you must be in control.

✔ The Zeroth Law of Software Engineering says,

**If you don't have to meet requirements, management is no problem.**

This law is important enough to deserve its own chapter.

✔ The Product Principle says,

**Products may be programs, but programs are not products.**

Violation of this principle leads to essential parts of information systems being omitted from process design, or even omitted from the product.

## 12.8 Practice

1. Listen for the key phrases given in this chapter and record them in a notebook. See how many you can hear in one day. Use your list to assess the cultural pattern of your organization.[7]

2. Make a list of the parts of your product that are not explicitly covered in your engineering processes. Investigate to see what process is actually used to create these parts, and what kind of quality it delivers.

3. Here's a model for process improvement that comes from Loral Space Information Systems, the first organization anywhere to be assessed at Level 5 in the SEI Capability Maturity Model:[8]

   • appropriate measures of process characteristics
   • a situation that creates dissatisfaction with the current process characteristics
   • employees who become motivated to improve the process characteristics
   • employees who are empowered to improve the process
   • process change occurs
   • timely measurements that monitor the improved process characteristics

How do the points of this model coincide with the process principles of this chapter?

4.    Naomi Karten comments: "DO get rid of any person who is indispensable for such reasons as 'Jim's the only one who knows what's inside there'" is good advice, but most people don't know how to do it. They won't do it if they fear the consequences of the resulting loss of knowledge or what the person will do when removed, but a little thought can allay that fear. Work out a plan for removing such a person, protecting against lost knowledge, lost work, and possibly destructive actions that person might take. How will knowledge of this plan actually help prevent circum-stances where someone has to be laid off?

5.    Can you identify one or more processes in your organization that are worse than random—that is, that would fail the Millionaire Test? What prevents you from immediately substituting random processes for them?

# 13
## Culture and Process

*In the long run, a society's strength depends on the way that ordinary people voluntarily behave. Ordinary people matter because there are so many of them. Voluntary behavior matters because it's too hard to supervise everyone all the time. . . . This voluntary behavior is what I mean by "culture."[1]*
— J. Fallows

While the subject of improving software cultures was on my mind, I happened upon this item from a popular computer magazine—an item that illustrates precisely what is meant by culture:

> System X (a popular software product from XXX, Inc.) began erasing his hard disk. One part of the program uses a list of files which it assumes contains at least one file. In his obscure situation, there were no files in the list, and the random contents of memory determined the target volume.[2]

I found it curious that the situation in which a list was empty would be considered "obscure" by an otherwise sophisticated columnist. When Herb Leeds and I published our very first book, back in 1961, this was a well-known situation and one that we warned beginners about.[3] For more than thirty-five years, programming authors have kept up the reminder, as in the classic *Elements of Programming Style.*[4] Apparently, the prevention of this situation has not become part of software engineering culture. At least at XXX, Inc., preventing aberrant behavior when passed an empty list is not "the way that ordinary people voluntarily behave."

This chapter considers three questions that all managers must understand if they would change their organization:

- What determines the way that ordinary people behave in an organization?
- How do those behaviors affect the organization's formal processes?
- How are ordinary people affected by those processes?

## 13.1 The Culture/Process Principle

Software engineering processes are a lot simpler when you can depend upon ordinary developers not to make simple mistakes that were well understood years before they were born. This illustrates the trade-off between culture and process:

**Whatever you can safely assume in the culture,
you don't have to specify in your process description.**

We see dozens of examples of this *Culture/Process Principle* every day. When I picked up a can of Barbasol™ shaving cream this morning, I read, "Shake well before using." It didn't tell me *what* to shake, and I smiled as I imagined someone thinking it means "shake your body" and dancing a jig every morning.

Even for those of us who know it means shake *the can*, we realize it didn't say *how well* to shake it. On a bottle of Pepto-Bismal™, I found the same instructions, word for word, but it didn't say how well to shake it either. Still, I think both process descriptions were reasonable, because culturally I *know* how well to shake a can of shaving cream, and I know how well to shake a bottle of medicine, and I know that the two are quite different processes. If I didn't know these things, the text needed to describe the process wouldn't fit on the container.

The Culture/Process Principle warns us that the same process description means different actions in different cultures. Therefore, before plunging into a delirium of process building, we need to understand the culture for which we are building those processes.

The Culture/Process Principle applies to all sorts of cultures, and particularly to software engineering cultures as described in *Volume 1* of this series.[5] If we don't understand the Culture/Process Principle, we'll commit bloopers like these:

- One organization—as part of their ISO-9000 certification—developed a process for showing new employees where the bathrooms were. The process description was three pages long. (At least they didn't have a process for showing them how to use the bathroom.)
- Another organization had a process for "spontaneous recognition" of coworkers. Every person in the organization was to give at least five "thank you's" each day.
- Back in the days when people wrote programs on paper, one of my clients required that all code be written on special forms. That was normal enough, but for this client, the paper had to be a specific shade of light green, with dark green lines. This client believed other colors were more error-provoking.

### 13.2  Examples of the Interaction of Culture and Process

Figure 13-1 is adapted from *Volume 1* to show how the level of quality culture is "forced" by either customer demands or problem demands. This does not mean that in the short run, culture is determined by these two parameters. In the long run, however, organizations that don't develop an appropriate cultural pattern will be forced to change or die.

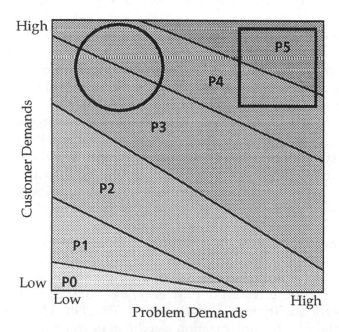

Figure 13-1.  An organization can be pressed to move to a different pattern by changing customer demands, changing problem demands, or both. The circled area (high customer demand, moderate problem demand) probably contains the pharmaceutical organization described by Stuart Scott in the text. (Adapted from *Volume 1*, Figure 3-1.)

### 13.2.1 Don't kill anyone and don't go to jail

The consistency of an organization's cultural pattern is striking, and requires no sophisticated measurements to detect. Here's how Stuart Scott describes the experience of encountering a quality-oriented culture, probably a Steering (Pattern 3) or Anticipating (Pattern 4) culture in the area circled in Figure 13-1:

> I make my living consulting with organizations that want to improve their system development processes. Two years ago, I began working with the research and development arm of a large pharmaceutical company that had an interest in information engineering. From the minute I first walked in the door, I knew I was dealing with a very different kind of IS organization. Everyone I spoke with, from the top manager to the newest rookie, took it for granted that they had a well-defined process for developing computer systems. That's unusual, in my experience. What's more, they could all describe their process to me in clear and unambiguous language, which is even more unusual. Most impressive of all, their stories matched.[6]

This consistency of spontaneous process descriptions defines a culture. In this case, the culture stems from the FDA requirement that all work connected with the use and testing of drugs be done under strict process controls so that you don't kill anyone with the drugs. If you don't follow these process controls, you go to jail.

I often use a culture-picture test based on the consistency of culture. When I start working with a new team, I ask each team member to draw a large picture of their process, be it development, maintenance, test development, documentation, or whatever. They work independently, then post their pictures and talk about them. The pictures may differ widely, but they always contain certain consistent themes, such as quality, speed, accountability, fear of managers, responsiveness to customers, professionalism, teamwork, individualism, or frenzy. These consistent themes are elements of the culture.

In this thirty-minute exercise, I can capture the important process issues that would emerge from a $75,000 formal assessment. Of course, any manager can perform the same test, without hiring a consultant even for thirty minutes.

### 13.2.2 Bring 'em back alive

Another example of a quality culture is the Houston Space Shuttle Onboard Software Project (formerly part of IBM, and now Loral Corporation), winner of many awards for quality and identified as the first Level 5 (in SEI's CMM system) organization.[7] This organization is a direct descendant of an organization that Jim Turnock, Iz Krongold, and I started for Project Mercury within IBM in 1958. I would be happy to take credit for this exemplary organization, but I'm sure that I wouldn't recognize much in the way of process details after four decades of evolution.

What I *would* recognize is the commitment to quality—a consistent under-standing of everyone in the organization that human lives are riding on the flawlessness of their software. It's this vision—bring 'em back alive—leading with consistent strength over a period of forty years, that has placed this orga-nization somewhere within the square of Figure 13-1. It was so forty years ago, and it is so today: Each proposed change is tested in the fire of a single question: "How will this enhance our mission—to bring 'em back alive?"

### 13.2.3 Quick results

The demand for quality is not the only aspect of culture that trickles down from top management. An informative contrast to the Houston Space Center and the pharmaceutical companies is the software organization that is waiting to be bought or to go public. The principal objective of these firms is not to produce life-critical systems, but to create an attractive company for the auc-tion block.

I'm a slow learner, and it took me three examples of this sort to figure out what was going on. In the first case, I was called in to help with "process improvement," but when I tried to create improvement plans, I felt that I was embedded in molasses. Any plan that took more than two months to produce results was vetoed by upper management.

Time horizon is often an important part of culture, so I should have recog-nized this pattern sooner. Sure enough, after four months of struggling to make some impact in the short run, the company was purchased by a software marketing firm, the process improvement effort was put to rest, and the top executives became multimillionaires. Although the buyout was a well-kept secret, somehow everyone in the organization knew that long-term plans (any-thing longer than two months) would not be tolerated. Such is the power of top management to communicate deep cultural themes.

### 13.2.4 Don't make a wrong decision

Not all the themes communicated by management can be considered inten-tional. A common theme in software organizations these days is *the inability to make decisions and stick to them*. This theme is communicated not by what man-agement *does*, but mostly by what management *doesn't* do. Here are three examples, drawn from one such organization:

- A task force is assembled to decide on a standard platform for all future development. After seven months of work, the task force rec-ommends platform A, with platform B as a second choice. Two top managers from the task force go to a week-long golf and technology seminar sponsored by the vendor of platform C, after which they come back and throw out the task force's recommendations. They convene another task force to make a platform recommendation.

- A measurement group is created. After three months, the group recommends four key measurements to management—system size, project effort, system reliability, and planned versus actual delivery. Ten months later, management still hasn't decided whether to implement these four measurements.

- Management recognizes the need for project management discipline. Before putting anything in place, the managers bring in project management training from firm X. After sixteen months, 90 percent of the project managers are trained, but management decides that X's approach is not the right one. Management brings in firm Y to teach their approach. After three years, neither X nor Y's approach is being used to manage projects, and management is considering the approach of Z, which seems to be, in management's words, "better."

Do you see the pattern? Do you think the employees see it? Without doubt, everyone soon gets the cultural message that the important thing is not to stick with important decisions. That way, you'll never be caught in a "mistake."

### 13.2.5 Number of customers

Another good example of the influence of culture on process is the effect of the number of customers on design and debugging. This effect is quite general, and Henry Petroski enunciated it for engineering of all types:

> There is a difference in the design and development of things that are produced by the millions and those that are unique, and it is generally the case that the mass-produced mechanical or electronic object undergoes some of its debugging and evolution after it is offered to the consumer.[8]

I recently witnessed a culture clash over this very effect when I arranged some cross-visits between a PC software company (with millions of customers) and the MIS organization of a financial company (with generally one customer for each system). The MIS managers were appalled at what they considered "cynicism" at the PC software company, whose managers coolly estimated the volume of failures and planned their revision strategy even before shipping the first release. The software company managers, on the other hand, simply could not fathom the elaborate acceptance testing constructed by the MIS organization, and considered it "pandering to the user."[9]

Understanding the Culture/Process Principle makes it easier to understand the story about the empty-list bug at XXX, Inc. They, like most PC software companies, probably don't consider such rare bugs a problem—which is one of the reasons they still call them "bugs" in the PC software industry. When you're out fishing for customers, a few mosquitoes now and then are nothing but a minor annoyance. Thus, we don't expect the processes at most PC software companies to be steeped in the tradition of fault-free delivery. We do, however, expect them to have a culture of quickly fixing such bugs, which they did in this case.

The potential power of the Culture/Process Principle is illustrated by the reaction of Payson Hall when he reviewed the preceding paragraphs in a draft version of this volume:

> Having lost substantial time this week wrestling with [PC software] failures on a bit of time-critical high-stakes analysis (five failures leading to a net productivity loss of about fifteen hours), I must take exception to your (in my view) tacit acceptance of "ship-and-fix." Is this really what you mean to imply? [10]

Payson's problem is that he *expected* a different culture behind his software, so he was surprised, or at least disappointed. He was perfectly reasonable in *desiring* a different culture, but in view of the Culture/Process Principle, he was unreasonable to *expect* it. I don't imply that this "ship-and-fix" culture is good for every customer, but I do mean to imply that it's understandable why a company making PC software would have such a culture. It's possible to understand something and detest it at the same time.

## 13.3 Three Meanings of Process

Many authors on management have identified three distinct levels of management in hierarchical organizations: top management, middle management, and supervisory management. There is only one layer of top management, and one layer of supervisory management. Everyone else is middle management, with managers above and below them. Figure 13-2 shows how these three layers are embedded in the cybernetic control process we saw earlier.

Because of their positions in the regulatory process, each of these levels tends to have a different conception of the word "process," and these differences tend to interfere with process improvement efforts. Top management is responsible for the future of the business, which will not be prosperous unless present and future customers are satisfied. Thus, they are concerned with *what could be*, the process *vision*. As we have seen, this vision is passed down to middle management, whether by intention or inattention.

Middle management is concerned with *what should be*, the process *model* that translates the vision into specific action steps. These process models are passed down to supervisory management.

Supervisory management is concerned with *what is*, the only thing that can truly be called the *process*, as opposed to the process vision or process model. Models and visions are process *descriptions*, which may or may not be followed in the actual process. Supervisory managers translate the models into actions, actions that may or may not reflect the original process vision descending from on high.

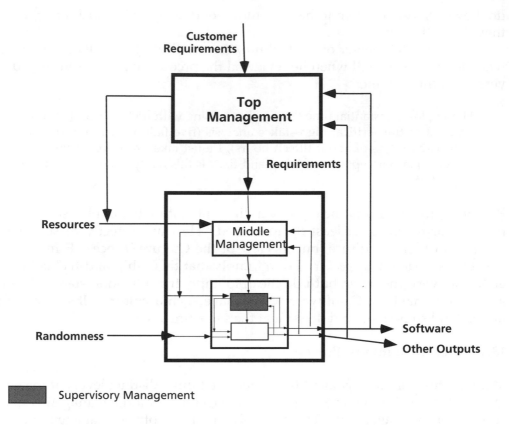

Figure 13-2.     In a cybernetic model, each level of management embeds the level below, providing an environment in which that level operates. Management regulates the flow of productive resources, without generally making direct use of most of those resources.

### 13.3.1  Supervisory level:  Making the product

At the supervisory level, "process" means literally "what is actually done to get the product," not "what was supposed to be done."  At this level, an improved process always means an improved product, for that is how supervisory managers are measured.

Out in our little Colorado mountain town, Mort the chef slings breakfast and lunch in the local diner, then supervises the preparation of dinners at the local gourmet restaurant.  Same cook, different process—and somebody must remember that you don't serve hot dogs with truffles.  What keeps it all straight is that Mort and the rest of the kitchen crew know whether it's night or day; they can directly relate the process vision to the process.

Like Mort, the people in the Houston Space Center and in the pharmaceutical companies know night from day.  Because lives are at stake, they have a consistent vision of what they're trying to accomplish, and they can relate that vision to their everyday actions.

This is quite different from the situation faced by supervisory managers in many software organizations, where there is no consistency of vision supporting their processes. They may be lacking a vision from upper management, or they may be lacking effective process models from middle management, models that translate the vision into the process. Or they may have nine layers of management whose differing visions must be reconciled. In any case, the process that results from these situations is unpredictable.

### 13.3.2 *Middle management level: Creating process models*

Middle managers, when doing their job properly, aren't concerned with *what* is done, but with *how* it's done. That is, they are concerned with the ideal models behind what is actually done.

Instead of requirements, middle managers are concerned with the process of requiring: discovering people's perceptions of what they have now and their desires for what they'd like to have when the process is finished.

To them, specification is not a document, but a process of negotiating to determine what the customer specifically wants and is willing to pay.

Design consists of a number of processes combined to discover ways of getting what the customer wants. Exploring determines if it already exists. Revising is considered a way of creating a solution from a previous solution. Innovating examines ways of creating it from scratch, or at least from simpler components.

Construction is the process of translating designs into another format, level of detail, or modality. Middle managers are not generally concerned with this level of process, except in Variable (Pattern 1) software cultures.

Testing is a process of reviewing and executing to determine if the translation produced what was specified.

Middle managers have ideal models for each of these things that should be done, and these ideals are what they mean by "process." You'll save yourself and your organization a great deal of grief if you consistently call these things process models, not processes.

### 13.3.3 *Top management level: Creating a culture*

Although it sounds good as a title or a vision, we cannot truly say that top management creates the culture. Culture is too pervasive to be created by management fiat, but the overall demands of the business need to be communicated down through the organization in some way. If they are not, then the organization molds itself to an inconsistent vision.

Stuart Scott's pharmaceutical example provides a most interesting example of the effects of consistent vision. When I showed this example to my colleague David Robinson, he confirmed he'd seen a similar culture in another pharmaceutical organization. He added, however, that those operations not subject to FDA regulation were "just more sloppy old software organizations." I then showed David's remarks to Stuart, who replied:

> In my experience, David is right. We found the boundaries between the regulated IS groups and their unregulated counterparts were virtually impermeable. The groups shared almost nothing with one another. I remember one morning we interviewed some extremely frustrated developers in an unregulated group and got quite an earful. Then we walked ten yards up the hallway and spent a couple of hours with some calm, almost complacent developers in the regulated area. When we left that evening, my colleague remarked that just walking those ten yards up the hallway was enough to give him "psychological whiplash."[11]

This example shows that somehow the top management lets the organization know what it values. We don't have enough information to know if it's good business strategy to have two cultures in a pharmaceutical software organization, but it could be. We cannot automatically assume that every organization or department needs Anticipating (Pattern 4) or Congruent (Pattern 5) work on their information systems, though my own bias suggests that we cannot automatically assume that they *don't*.

Such a split culture may be the ideal solution when the organization feels it cannot afford a truly professional development group, perhaps because it cannot attain a critical size to support technical specialists. The organization retains its own requirements process (which may be of a very advanced cultural pattern) because it is unique to the business. Simple development jobs such as generating reports from the operational database will be performed in-house, perhaps in a Variable (Pattern 1) or Routine (Pattern 2) mode. More complex tasks, such as revising the operational system and network development, will be outsourced to professional software organizations. This split culture should come as no surprise; most companies use buildings and cars, but very few companies build their own buildings or produce their own cars.

If we carry the splitting further, the companies will look for pre-built units, rather than custom outsourcing, just as most companies do when buying trucks. Thus, there will be at least four software subcultures: the requirements people, the builders of simple systems, the contractors for custom systems, and the purchasers of pre-built systems. There's no reason to believe that these four cultures will be similar.

I think this splitting of cultures will ultimately be good for the profession of software engineering, though it will mean that many people will move from in-house software organizations to larger, professional software organizations. Only those organizations with strong, unique customer demands at the core of their business will retain software development organizations above Routine (Pattern 2). The others will do Pattern 2 work themselves and farm out the rest.

## 13.4 What Creates the Culture?

If visions and process models don't create an organization's culture, what does? It's easy to be fooled by this question because many of the activities that appear to be directed at changing the culture are, in fact, attempts to conserve the culture. Perhaps the most obvious of these is sending people away to courses to improve leadership:

> Deep down, many organizations do not want more leaders. They prefer managers—and for a simple reason: they take initiative, they challenge the status quo, they encourage followings. For many companies, this is a frightening prospect. A five-day outside leadership program is a safe alternative to cultivating leadership from within. An organization can show an interest in leadership without taking a deeper responsibility for its successful realization.[12]

As someone who makes his living offering "five-day outside leadership programs," I wholeheartedly agree with this assessment. The quality of leadership is part of the culture, perhaps the part that is most dangerous to the Old Status Quo. If leadership improves, then the culture must improve, but courses *alone* will never accomplish this. An *external* event like a leadership course can provide a foreign element, or supply a transforming idea, or be an arena in which to practice new ideas; but it can never substitute for all the *internal* work that has to be done to travel through the entire change process.

Max DePree, a unique chief executive, understands this process very well:

> An institution's future is fragile. What ensures it? A number of things, each of them fragile—every promotion, every decision related to changes in leadership, the degree to which leaders balance the forces of change and continuity. Annual plans or strategic initiatives do not guarantee an institution's future; they may even betray it by blinding the organization to other goals. Every key job assignment, every missed opportunity for development, every person inspired by a true leader—these are the things that actually shape the future. I'm talking about the quality of relationships and the enabling of other people.[13]

The entire culture is created—or destroyed—one action, or inaction, or interaction, at a time. Think about this next time you attend an off-site "visioning" session. Think about it next time you compose or modify a process document. Think about it next time you come back from a leadership course brimming with ideas about how you're going to change everyone else. Most of all, think about it every time you look in the mirror.

## 13.5 Helpful Hints and Suggestions

1. Dress codes are a curious cultural measure, communicated by mysterious means. Here are a few cultural patterns concerning appropriate attire I've seen in software engineering organizations:

- There is a strict code, which nobody dares challenge. Usually, these codes are different for men than for women. Since these codes are usually made by men, the codes for women don't make any sense.
- There is an anti-code sentiment. Any hint of uniformity in dress is considered inappropriate, and met with scorn. Of course, an anti-code is actually a code of conforming nonconformism.
- Dress is irrelevant, and nobody notices or comments on what people wear.
- Dress is relevant, but only as appropriate to context. For instance, if you are meeting customers, you dress one way; but if you are working with your group, you dress another way.
- Dress is congruent, fitting the Self, Other, and Context. Nobody considers it appropriate to comment on another person's style of dressing.

I think it is informative to characterize a culture by the amount of attention paid to dress compared with the amount of attention paid to improving the software process.

2. Naomi Karten comments: Casual day on Fridays is really funny in some companies, with some people incapable of dressing down or the boss's view of casual being decidedly more upscale than the troops'. Not only is the dress code a curious cultural measure, but so, too, is a change in the dress code.

3. Dress and other physical signs provide one window on a system's culture. My colleague Jean McLendon teaches a more behavior-oriented method in our Organizational Change Shop—a method she calls "The Five P's": To understand how an organization really works, and how it will respond to change, look for Patterns of

- Pain/Pleasure (to learn what motivates them)
- Process (to learn how routine things get done, or not done)
- Problems (to learn how nonroutine things get done—how they understand the dynamics of their system, what they pay attention to, and how they cope)
- Possibilities (to learn how they envision the outside world and their own future)

4. Phil Fuhrer offers: "An acid test I use for the culture of an organization is their productivity when confronted by a different kind of problem. For example, how will a switching system development organization approach a non-real-time critical system? You can discover a lot by asking them how they would handle some new situation, then noticing what processes they provide for learning."

5.  Sue Petersen points out: If a shop can't get above Routine (Pattern 2) internally, they are still going to have to learn how to recognize good work (higher Patterns) when they see it externally, in potential vendors. This in itself is a nudge in the direction of Steering (Pattern 3), because you need to know many of the same things to steer an internal or an external organization.

6.  Concerning the culture-picture test, Naomi Karten suggests that the opposite situation can be equally informative—comparing views of how the culture *responds:*

> Have people from a given department talk in small groups about an issue such as one I often start with: "How would you characterize how well you respond to customers' needs?" They often discover very quickly that they have very different views both about how well they respond and how they assess that level of response. (They also often realize they don't know the real answer because they've never gotten any feedback from their customers.)

## 13.6 Summary

✔  This chapter considers three questions that all managers must understand if they would change their organization:

   •  What determines the way that ordinary people behave in an organization?
   •  How do those behaviors affect the organization's formal processes?
   •  How are ordinary people affected by those processes?

✔  The Culture/Process Principle illustrates the trade-off between culture and process:

**Whatever you can safely assume in the culture,
you don't have to specify in your process description.**

✔  The Culture/Process Principle warns us that the same process description will mean different actions in different cultures. Therefore, before plunging into a grand farrago of process building, we need to understand the culture for which we are building those processes.

✔  The level of quality culture is forced by either customer demands or problem demands. This doesn't mean that in the short run, culture is determined by these two parameters. In the long run, however, organizations that don't develop an appropriate cultural pattern will be forced to change or die.

✔   The consistency of an organization's cultural pattern is striking, and requires no sophisticated measurements to detect. In a culture stemming from the FDA requirement that all work connected with the use and testing of drugs be done under strict process controls, software will be done under strict process controls. If you don't follow them, you go to jail.

✔   In the culture producing space flight software, there is a consistent understanding of everyone in the organization that human lives are riding on the flawlessness of their software. It's this vision—bring 'em back alive—leading with consistent strength over a period of forty years, that has placed this organization in a very advanced software cultural pattern.

✔   In a software organization that is waiting to be bought or go public, the principal objective is not to produce life-critical systems, but to create an attractive company for the auction block. A short time horizon is often an important part of such a culture, and long-range (or even medium-range) planning is not acceptable, though it may be acceptable to put up a sham of planning to make the firm more attractive to potential buyers.

✔   Not all the themes communicated by management can be considered intentional. A common theme in software organizations these days is *the inability to make decisions and stick to them*. This theme is communicated not by what management *does*, but mostly by what it *doesn't* do: make decisions and follow through on them. The cultural message in such an environment is not to stick with important decisions. That way, you'll never be caught in a "mistake."

✔   The number of customers influences an organization's approach to design and debugging. With millions of customers, PC software companies simply don't consider shipping rare bugs a life-and-death problem. Instead, they concentrate their energies on creating a culture of quickly fixing bugs.

✔   Because of their positions in the regulatory process, each level of management tends to have a different conception of the word "process," and these differences tend to interfere with process improvement efforts.

•   Top management is responsible for the future of the business, which will not be prosperous unless present and future customers are satisfied. Thus, they are concerned with what could be, the process vision.

•   Middle management is concerned with what should be, the process model that translates the vision into specific action steps.

•   Supervisory management is concerned with what is, the only thing that can truly be called the process as opposed to the process vision or process model. Models and visions are process descriptions, which may or may not be followed in the actual process. Supervisory managers translate the models into actions, actions that may or may not reflect the original process vision descending from on high.

✔ The quality of leadership is part of the culture, perhaps the part that is most dangerous to the Old Status Quo. If leadership improves, then the culture *must* improve.

## 13.7 Practice

1.  Here's a survey for you to use to show the differences between the various meanings of process:

    -   Have you ever heard of Brooks's Law?[14]
    -   What is it?
    -   What is the dynamic underlying Brooks's Law?
    -   What would you do if you were managing a project and it was late?

    Conduct this survey in your organization and notice how the answers vary with the level of the person responding. Discuss the results.

2.  Two weeks after carrying the story about the bug in System X, the same magazine carried a story reporting that XXX, Inc., was being purchased by another company. Discuss whether that's vindication or condemnation of their cultural approach to bugs. What additional information would you need to make this decision?

3.  Janice Wormington suggests: Answer the three questions from the beginning of this chapter, for your specific organization:

    -   What determines the way that ordinary people behave in your organization?
    -   How do those behaviors affect the organization's formal processes?
    -   How are ordinary people affected by those processes?

4.  When I wrote in Section 13.4 that Max DePree was a unique chief executive, perhaps it wasn't clear what I meant. Here's one of his stories that may clarify my characterization:

    > I arrived at the local tennis club just after a group of high school students had vacated the locker room. Like chickens, they had not bothered to pick up after themselves. Without thinking too much about it, I gathered all their towels and put them in a hamper. A friend of mine quietly watched me do this and then asked me a question that I've pondered many times over the years. "Do you pick up the towels because you're the president of a company, or are you the president of a company because you pick up the towels?"[15]

What is your answer to this question? What is DePree's process model for picking up towels? Where do you think it's written down? What is the vision behind this process model? What does it have to do with establishing the culture of DePree's company?

5.   Contrast DePree's towel story with the following story posted on the CompuServe Guildnet in May 1993:

> The CEO (of a large aerospace company) got on the elevator to go from his office to the first floor. At a lower floor a mere mortal boarded the elevator and, recognizing the CEO, engaged him in a little small talk until the elevator reached the ground floor.
>
> Evidently the CEO was upset at having to relate to a common worker. The following day:
>
> 1.   a memo was issued to all personnel titled "How to conduct yourself in the presence of the CEO"
>
> 2.   one of the elevators was declared off limits to everyone except the CEO during certain hours each day, those being the times he was most likely to use it
>
> Oh, by the way, this company recognizes that they have the most serious morale problem in their history, and they have a task force looking at ways to improve it.

What is this CEO's process model for riding elevators? Where do you think it's written down? What is the vision behind this process model? What does it have to do with the serious morale problem of this large aerospace company?

6.   Sue Petersen asks: Can any manager really perform the culture-picture test of Section 13.2.1? This question can be used as another test of your culture. Think about performing it and ask these questions: Is there some reason in this organization that I couldn't do it? Is there some reason I couldn't do it well? Is there some reason I couldn't do it as effectively as someone brought in from outside?

7.   Phil Fuhrer notes: When the personal computer culture says "Old rules no longer apply with new tools and systems," we should not be surprised that developers fail to look for empty lists. "Old rules no longer apply" is a *meta-rule*, a rule about cultural rules. What cultural meta-rules can you identify in your organization that restrict attempts to change the culture (as by learning from outsiders)? What meta-rules *enable* cultural change?

# 14

# Improving Process

*Do what you can,
with what you have,
where you are.*
— Theodore Roosevelt

Organizational development consultant John F. Horne, III, described to me a pivotal moment in his professional life:

> A number of years ago, I visited the factory of a nationally recognized chainsaw manufacturer in Virginia. I toured the plant with one of the managers who extolled the high-tech nature of the manufacturing process as a model of efficiency and organization. In one corner of an amazingly clean work floor were three employees with a large roll of chicken wire. They were cutting it up into one-foot squares.
>
> I asked the plant manager what they were doing, and he replied, "Don't know. Doesn't seem to be a big problem." He continued with his commentary of the automated manufacturing process.
>
> I went over to the three employees and asked them what they were doing. They explained that the standard drying racks for the painted outer cover of the chainsaw did not hold the drying pieces—and so they fell to the

floor, which meant that they had to be repainted. These employees solved the problem by buying a large roll of chicken wire with their own money several times each month and cut it up to fashion drying racks.

I asked them (of course) if they had told management about the problem. They said, "Yeah, but they [management] just said we were not using the standard racks carefully enough."

When I reported the heart of this conversation to the manager, his response was the equivalent of "That's nice," and he moved on to point out further high-tech equipment.[1]

Many software organizations have difficulty in improving their process because they mistake the process *models* and process *visions* for actual processes. Managers who are unaware of the chicken-wire factor will never do an adequate job of developing process models, because all of the most common models focus entirely on activities involving direct work on the product, which the managers don't really see. Moreover, because these models concentrate on direct work, they omit most of the areas in which process improvement is possible. Obviously, management activities, such as looking at what's actually going on with the chicken wire, must be changed if processes are to be improved.

## 14.1 Three Levels of Process Improvement

There are three distinct types of process improvement, corresponding to the three meanings of process. Figure 14-1 suggests that the three types have very different scales. Cultural changes have much greater potential impact than process changes because one cultural change—such as driving fear out of the workplace—can affect hundreds of process changes.

Paradoxically, most change efforts take place on the process level, where the potential return is the least. Managers install measurement programs that measure only at this level; consequently, only this level of information is available for process improvement feedback. The middle managers' process models are taken for granted, and the culture is invisible, so improvement is severely limited. In order for substantial improvement to take place, the managers' levels must be open to investigation and change.

## 14.2 An Example of Process Improvement

In order to understand better how the three levels interact, let's look at a case of process improvement in some detail. The Gargantuan Gorgonzola Grocery Company (GGG) had many short software development projects. They tended to come in bunches, and they needed to be done quickly. In reaction to this customer demand, GGG developed a culture based on the extensive use of contract programmers. Although this policy smoothed the demands on the regular employees, the company experienced large variations in schedule performance.

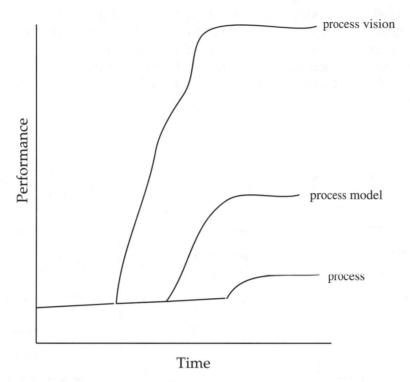

Figure 14-1. The three types of process improvement have scales that differ by orders of magnitude.

Management decided to form an improvement team to take a look at the development process to see if the variations could be reduced. The team was to follow a process improvement strategy consisting of four steps:

1. Document the actual process.

2. Discover the root cause of the problem.

3. Modify the process to reduce variation.

4. Test the process improvements.

As we follow the team members through these four steps, we'll notice how they work and why they don't work as well as logic would predict.

### 14.2.1 Document the actual process

The first step in the improvement process was to document the real process—the chicken wire—as opposed to the process model or process vision. When the team interviewed people from a dozen projects, they discovered that there were a number of instances when things being done were not part of the process model. The most notable were the activities connected with a contractor leaving in the middle of a project, as shown in Figure 14-2. These extra steps invariably turned up in the projects that were furthest behind schedule. Whenever they occurred, these steps would add three or four weeks to the schedule.

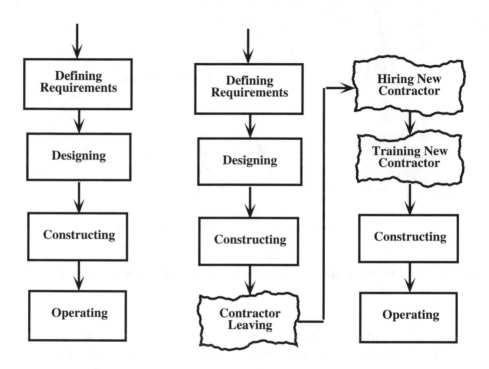

Figure 14-2.     Several process steps were not on GGG's process model (left side), but turned up regularly in the process on delayed projects (right side).

### 14.2.2 Discover the root cause of the problem

The improvement team then developed several ideas for improving the process. With respect to delays from departing contractors, for example, the team suggested the following possible approaches:

- Work with different contracting firms.
- Create a process of preselecting contractors.
- Put a penalty clause in the contracting firm's contract, as punishment if a contractor leaves before project completion.
- Stop using contractors.
- Use fewer contractors, and try to stick with those individuals who have been on GGG projects previously.

The team members then realized that they were addressing a symptom without really knowing the root cause behind the contractors leaving. They interviewed the project managers and discovered that these contractors had been fired because they didn't have the promised background in languages and operating systems. They were trying to learn on the job, and it took three to four weeks to discover that they weren't really doing anything. The contracting firms had compensated GGG by refunding their money, but there was no way they could refund the lost weeks in the schedule.

### 14.2.3 *Modify the process to reduce variation*

Once they understood the root cause of the departing contractors, the team members were able to choose among solution ideas and modify their process model by including a contractor selection step, as shown in Figure 14-3.

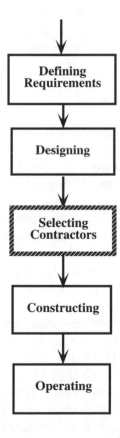

Figure 14-3.      By placing an explicit contractor selection process in the project, GGG was able to remove the problem of unqualified contractors.

Of course, there had always been some process of selecting the contractors, but this selection process was not directly associated with the product and was the responsibility of the middle managers, who didn't model their *own* processes in any way. Therefore, the selection process had remained implicit, and not subject to systematic improvement. Before it could be improved, it had to be incorporated into the process model, rather than just being a hidden part of the process.

The improvement team also proposed a cultural change that was needed to make this new process efficient. In the past, GGG had trusted the contracting firms to send only people with the specified skills. Because GGG had no explicit process for verifying the qualifications of the candidates, the firms became lax in observing GGG's requests. Generally, they sent whatever contractors they happened to have around that day.

If most of the candidates were unqualified, GGG's new contractor selection process was going to take some time before it found a suitable candidate. Rather than just receiving random candidates from the contracting firms, the team suggested that upper management start working more closely with these vendors to ensure that a high percentage of the candidates were likely to be qualified. Again, this hadn't been done before because nobody had explicitly modeled what upper management did.

### 14.2.4 Test the process improvements

Over the next few months, the improvement team monitored the effects of the improved process. The team members kept track of the number of contractor candidates interviewed, the number accepted, and the number rejected. They also kept track of how many stayed through the entire project, and the schedule variations of all the projects.

They discovered that schedule variation had been reduced, as had contractor turnover, but not as much as they had anticipated. They were puzzled as to why their improvements hadn't been more successful, so they returned to interview the two project managers whose projects hadn't shown improvement. In both cases, they were told that in spite of the selection procedure, the contractors simply weren't qualified.

They studied the contractors' resumes, and they interviewed the people who had interviewed them. All evidence pointed to the fact that they were actually quite well qualified. The team decided to interview the two individual contractors, but both refused, so they interviewed the managers of the two contracting firms that had supplied them. These managers told them that both contractors had worked successfully with other firms on numerous projects.

Somehow, the actual process was deviating from the process model, and they didn't know why.

## 14.3 Seeing the Invisible

At this point, the GGG team members were stumped. Their process improvement effort had worked, but not as well as they expected. They were concerned that the hidden source of this variation might grow out of control, because they didn't understand it.

Being desperate, they called a consultant. Having seen more of these situations, the consultant suspected something that wasn't being talked about. He conducted interviews with a number of employees who had been members of the two projects and uncovered some facts that the team had not known:

- In project A, the project manager (Peter) had dated the contractor (Tori) for two weeks before he fired her from the project. Peter confirmed that he had dated Tori, but said that his personal relationship with her had nothing to do with the firing. She was, he claimed, simply not competent to do the things that she had been hired to do.
- In project B, the project manager (Quentin) was heard acting abusively toward the contractor (Ernie) on a number of occasions. Quentin said that he acted toward Ernie no differently than he did toward any other member of the project, and had fired him simply because he wasn't competent.

The consultant pursued both these cases with GGG management and the Human Resources Department. It turned out that Peter had dated at least three other contractors on previous projects and fired each of them. He said he had done nothing wrong in dating them because "they were not employees." He stuck to his claim that they had been fired for incompetence, but this was refuted when it was discovered that two of them had subsequently worked on other GGG projects using the same technology. They had not been fired, and had, in fact, been commended for their work. Peter was removed from further management responsibilities, put on notice, and given training on the subject of sexual harassment.

Quentin turned out to be right when he claimed that he acted the same toward Ernie as he had toward other employees—abusively. The only difference was that Ernie didn't placate him like his employees did, and so was fired for his impertinence. Firing contractors was lots easier than firing employees and could be done without any investigation. In effect, the project manager held feudal lordship over contractors on the project.

Further study showed that many employees avoided getting on projects that Quentin headed, leaving him with a crew who could tolerate his abuse, or who couldn't tolerate it but didn't do anything about it. Quentin was removed from management responsibility and decided to leave GGG. Once he was gone, other project managers said that they knew about Quentin's abusiveness, but didn't feel it was their place to say anything about it, as he was their colleague. They had, however, been quite happy to receive many good employees who had opted out of Quentin's projects.

## 14.4 Preventing Future Occurrences

The removal of Peter and Quentin from their project management positions had the desired effect of greatly reducing the schedule variation due to contractor problems—which were really management problems. In many organizations, this would have been the end of the story, but for GGG, it wasn't over. The process improvement team then approached management and said that these two incongruent managers indicated a weakness in GGG's culture. What was there, they asked, to prevent such situations in the future?

The upper managers took up the challenge and instituted a number of policy changes:

- They tightened the process for dismissing contractors, so that no project manager could do this without oversight.
- They directed the process improvement team to modify the review process so that contractors would be included on review teams. This exposed their technical competence to other members of the technical staff, so that claims of incompetence would not have to be decided on one person's opinion.
- They modified the policy on employee harassment to include contractors. They met with managers to inform them of this policy and the consequences of violating it. This was probably overkill, because their actions with Peter and Quentin provided two examples to show the managers that GGG was serious about this policy.
- They directed Human Resources to improve training in the meaning of harassment, to make it clear that they were not simply interested in avoiding lawsuits, but in creating a blame-free environment. This new training was tested and given to all managers as well as any employees who wished to take it.

## 14.5 Lessons

From this example, the improvement team and GGG management learned these valuable lessons about process improvement:

- Process improvement must involve all levels of the organization. You don't know, when you embark on an improvement process, what you will have to change: the process, the process models, or the culture. In general, you can assume that all three will need some adjustment.

- Individual issues often underlie the toughest improvement situations. Short-term solutions to individual issues are necessary, but the way they are handled will set cultural precedents, so act with care. Also, unless the culture changes, the same kinds of personal issues will keep recurring, so changes beyond the single process will be required.

- Cultural changes will involve upper managers. Without their support and active participation, it's possible to make process improvements, but they will keep being undone by the same culture that created the process issues in the first place.

- You can change the logical process first, but consider this a test to see if the problem is entirely logical. To the extent that logical process improvements don't correct the problem, the problem isn't logical, but emotional.

- To address emotional problems, you'll need to get under the surface to the layers of information protected by the cultural rules governing what's not okay to talk about.

- Be careful that changes are not made in a blaming way. As the culture becomes less blaming, it becomes open to more kinds of information, so it becomes easier to improve processes—regardless of the source of the problem.

- A policy of not blaming does not mean a policy of placating. If managers are acting abusively, you can choose the way they are stopped, but they must be stopped. If upper managers wish to blame someone, they can blame themselves for creating a culture in which people turned their eyes from such behavior.

## 14.6 Sure, But We're Different

Some people reading the GGG story will say, "Yes, that's very nice, but our company is different." True, the details always differ, but the principles are the same and the results are similar. It helps to know that real companies can improve their software processes and produce the kinds of change they want.

For example, in an unpublished report, Barbara Purchia describes how Applicon, then a subsidiary of Schlumberger Technologies, totally altered its schedule culture in two years.[2] The specific things that Applicon did were almost totally different from the specific things that GGG did, but the spirit was the same, and the principles were the same. The quotations cited in the list below are drawn from Barbara's report, except as noted.

✔ *Process improvement must involve all levels of the organization.* Applicon's Vice President of Engineering stated, "We suffer from lack of long-range planning. We have to change plans because we are too focused on the short-term."

✔ *Individual issues often underlie the toughest improvement situations.* Applicon discovered that committees didn't always work as well as the company had hoped: ". . . the pace of their efforts has been too slow. This is because committee members have other primary responsibilities which typically are given higher priority than committee activities."

✔ *Unless the culture changes, the same kinds of personal issues will keep recurring, so changes beyond the single process will be required.* "While committee activities are considered during individual performance appraisals, they impact the appraisal far less than the primary job responsibilities." If this pattern of committee work were to change, there would first have to be a change in the performance appraisal system. Rather than tackle that issue immediately, the process improvement relied more on full-time individuals.

✔ *Cultural changes will involve upper management.* Two years into the process, long-range planning was in effect, and the Engineering Vice President said, "The strength of the process is the focus it gives us up front in planning and specification, and the stability that results from it."

✔ *You can change the logical process first, but consider this a test to see if the problem is entirely logical.* Because of these same cultural rules, written case studies about process improvement seldom address this principle directly. If you want to learn about such examples, you have to speak to their authors privately and confidentially. Rest assured that you will discover examples.

✔ *To address emotional problems, you'll need to get under the surface to the layers of information protected by the cultural rules governing what's not okay to talk about.* Barbara communicated to me the following information that was not in the paper:

> It was NOT okay to surprise the VP in a public forum (review meetings). It was NOT okay to change dates in a public forum (review meetings). It was NOT okay not to have communicated or coordinated efforts prior to presenting at a public forum. Whining and finger-pointing were NOT allowed at a public forum and at staff meetings.[3]

✔ *Be careful that changes are not made in a blaming way.* Technical reviews were a major tool used at Applicon to open their process to more kinds of information. In addition to the explicit goals of increasing the quality of the delivered product, the Applicon team recognized several implicit benefits that may have had even greater effects:

- "Inspections ensure traceability. They tie all pieces together including parent documents or code and applicable standards and guidelines."
- They improve "teamwork and communication."
- They also serve "as an educational mechanism for the project team."

✔ *A policy of not blaming does not mean a policy of placating.* Another essential element of the efforts at Applicon was "an insistence on setting measurable process improvement objectives and quantifiable quality objectives. The emphasis on concrete, measurable objectives for quality and productivity has provided managers with incentives for participating in many (of our) efforts to evaluate or deploy new methods and tools. . . . each development manager is required to describe, commit to, and provide progress toward quality objectives for their projects at senior engineering project review meetings." In other words, managers were not told how they had to accomplish their goals, but they were not placated by allowing them to pretend they were succeeding when they weren't.

Overall, the results of this effort were impressive:

> In 1990, 53% of all products were released on schedule, 31% were one quarter late, and 16% were two quarters late. In 1991, 89% of all products were released on schedule with the remaining products one quarter late. In 1992, 95% of all products were released on schedule with the remaining 5% one quarter late.[4]

The Moral: Don't take "Sure, but we're different" for an answer.

## 14.7 But It Costs Too Much

For a prevention effort to be successful and not sacrificed to short-term expediency, you have to have an image of what's possible, and what that's worth. Of course, that depends on where you are now, and so differs for each organization. Here's an example of our experience at one organization:

When we arrived at this organization, they were a few days away from shutting down because of lawsuits from several of their major customers. They showed all the symptoms of an organization in the terminal stages of a quality crisis. We instituted emergency measures to turn around the crisis, then implemented a comprehensive process improvement plan to prevent future crises. Here are some of the results, comparing productivity measures at initiation with those taken two years later:

- *Productivity.* Initially, one person could produce about 600 lines of code per year. Two years later, this was approximately 2,100 lines of code per person per year. Put differently, the burdened labor cost of a line of code went from $133 to $38. For their $8 million budget originally they were getting about 60,000 lines of finished code per year. Two years later, their budget was 20 percent less, but they were getting about 170,000 line of code per year.

- *Quality.* Of course, the lines of code delivered in the two instances were not strictly comparable, because the error rates were radically different. Initially, we could anticipate about one error in every 75 lines delivered. After two years, they were delivering less than one error in 500 lines.

- *Cost of Quality.* Initially, one error delivered to the field cost about $7,000 to fix, not counting costs to customers or the field service organization. After two years, this cost was reduced to about $3,500. This meant that the error-cost built into the average line of code was reduced from about $93 to $7. We did not study the cost of handling errors in the field organization, but we can assume this was much greater, if only because it was multiplied by the number of customers.

- *Visibility.* When we first arrived, we measured visibility by testing to see how long it took to find out what the completion status was on any given module in a system under development. This was greater than 500 minutes, but we didn't know how much greater because some of the searches were never completed. Two years later, this time had been reduced to less than ten minutes—the major factor being whether you had to power up your personal computer first. Similar figures were obtained on the time to track the status of a trouble report, or to get a current source listing of a known module.

- *Development Time.* Initially, we tried to measure how well managed development was by comparing actual to scheduled development time. Because of lack of project documentation, we had difficulty determining what the schedules were. Moreover, because of difficulty getting clean releases, we had difficulty knowing what the development time was. But using our best guesses, we came up with a ratio for the typical deliverable project of over 3.0. That meant that if a project was scheduled for one year, your best guess was that you'd get it in three years—if you got it at all, which was not that likely. After the change effort, the ratio of actual to scheduled time was down to 1.1, and no scheduled project had been abandoned in more than a year.

- *Control.* Initially, the observed chance of any scheduled component missing its schedule was over 80 percent. For whole systems, of course, it was much worse. After two years, the probability of a component missing schedule was less than 20 percent, and about 40 percent of systems were delivered on time. That still wasn't very good, but the probability of delivering within 10 percent of scheduled time was over 80 percent.  We concluded that there was still work to be done on placating during the estimating phase.

You can be encouraged to learn that organizations like this can be turned around by process improvement efforts.  Don't be too encouraged, however, because it's not cheap.  A turnaround program for an organization that is locked in a quality/overload crisis can raise the development budget by 20 percent for perhaps two years before showing a profit.  On the other hand, if management is unwilling to devote such resources, the problem isn't going to go away until the whole organization collapses.

Perhaps you'll be tempted not to tell your upper management the true cost of process improvement.  Perhaps your organization's culture is one of "incremental truth":  Start with an underestimate, then nickel-and-dime them to death.  Don't make that mistake.  It's better to start with a realistic idea of the commitment in time and resources than to be undermined later when executives are surprised.  Instead, start them with a picture of benefits, which will surely justify the true improvement costs.

## 14.8  Helpful Hints and Suggestions

1.  The idea that "we're different" effectively cuts off one of your most important sources of information for process improvement:

> We have seen that the easiest lessons to be learned from foreign militaries concern technology and technique—gadgets that can be plugged into one's usual way of doing business.  The most valuable lessons, however, may come from a study of other organizations and how they operate.  Yet these are the most difficult lessons to cull, because they are the least tangible.[5]

Read articles, but beware of their attention to gadgets.  The most important things cannot be written in articles, so try to visit people, or join a group (like an on-line forum or study group) that allows you to share in experiences from different organizations.

2.  Rich Cohen recently supplied me with one of his favorite quotes:

> We trained hard, but it seemed that every time we were beginning to form up into teams, we would be reorganized.  I was to learn later in life that we tend to meet any new situation by reorganizing; and a wonderful method it can be for creating the illusion of progress while producing confusion, inefficiency, and demoralization.
> — Petronius Arbiter, 210 B.C.

Apparently, this is not an easy lesson, because we haven't learned it in two millennia.  As you learn about process improvement, don't get so carried away that you keep the organization in the Red Zone we saw in Chapter 3. If you're already in a Red Zone culture, this may be the first problem you have to attack.

## 14.9 Summary

✔ Many software organizations have difficulty in improving their process because they mistake the process models and process visions for actual processes. Because these models concentrate on direct work, they omit most of the areas in which process improvement is possible: the management activities.

✔ There are three distinct types of process improvement, corresponding to the three meanings of process. Cultural changes have much greater potential impact than process changes because one cultural change can affect hundreds of process changes. In order for substantial improvement to take place, the managers' levels must be open to investigation and change.

✔ One classic process improvement strategy consists of four steps:

1.  Document the actual process.

2.  Discover the root cause of the problem.

3.  Modify the process to reduce variation.

4.  Test the process improvements.

If this model is applied at all levels, substantial improvement is possible.

✔ When you examine the real process, you will discover a number of places where things being done were not part of the process model—called the chicken-wire factor.

✔ Improvement teams often try to address a symptom without really knowing the root cause behind it. Only after understanding the root cause will the teams be able to choose among solution ideas and modify their process model to include previously implicit steps.

✔ Such process model improvements may not be possible without cultural changes to support them. Such changes will not be possible without explicit modeling of the actions of upper management.

✔ Monitoring the effects of the improved process is always necessary because real organizational changes never follow simple logical plans; the actual process always deviates from the process model in unexpected ways.

✔ Monitoring and interviewing may be essential to uncovering the invisible factors that are behind the deviations. These factors are often human factors that are not ordinarily discussable in the culture. Once these factors have been uncovered and handled, it's often necessary to institute cultural changes to prevent repetition of the same pattern in the future.

✔ Process improvement must involve all levels of the organization. You don't know, when you embark on an improvement process, what you will have to change: the process, the process models, or the culture. In general, you can assume that all three will need some adjustment.

✔ When you study many process improvement situations, you begin to see a pattern of principles:

- Individual issues often underlie the toughest improvement situations.
- The way that short-term solutions are handled will set cultural precedents.
- Unless the culture changes, the same kinds of personal issues will keep recurring.
- Cultural changes will involve upper management; otherwise, process improvements will keep being undone by the same culture that created the process issues in the first place.
- You can change the logical process first, but consider this a test to see if the problem is entirely logical.
- To address emotional problems, you'll need to get under the surface to the layers of information protected by the cultural rules governing what's not okay to talk about.
- Be careful that changes are not made in a blaming way.
- A policy of not blaming does not mean a policy of placating.

✔ A common way to avoid learning process principles is to say, "Yes, that's very nice, but our company is different." True, the details always differ, but the principles are the same and the results are similar.

✔ Another common way to avoid process improvement is to say, "Yes, but it costs too much." The answer to that excuse is that properly done process improvement does cost a lot, but it also pays a great deal more. If it doesn't pay big dividends, then it's not been properly done.

✔ Don't be tempted to hide the true cost of process improvement from upper management. It's better to start with a realistic idea of the commitment in time and resources than to be undermined later when executives are surprised. Be sure to offer a detailed picture of benefits, which will surely justify the true improvement costs.

### 14.10 Practice

1.  Can you think of three chicken-wire examples from your own organization? Does management know about them? What is their reaction? How does their reaction influence the workers?

2.  Choose an example of an attempted process change in your organization. Which process principles were applied, which were ignored, and which were violated? What was the result?

3.  How would you apply the principles of process improvement to something you'd like to improve in your own organization?

# 15

# Requirements Principles and Processes

*What did "getting it right" mean in practice? To the classically trained architect it meant, first of all, pleasing the client or, in a broader sense, the user of the building (not always the same person). This unassuming, and to most persons obvious, requirement needs emphasizing in a period when architectural design has become a self-expressive pastime. The great Chef Carême said, "In matters of cookery there are not a number of principles, there is only one and that is to satisfy the person you are serving." If I were to quote his advice to my students, they would find it a hopelessly old-fashioned and intolerable imposition.* [1]
— Witold Rybczynski

Software engineering is in the business of building, running, and maintaining things for some customer or customers. Requirements are only part of the process of connecting with your customers and responding to them, but they are usually the most important part. This chapter explores some of the principles underlying an Anticipating (Pattern 4) requirements process, in preparation for the following chapter, which shows how to implement such a process.

## 15.1 The Assumption of Fixed Requirements

Until recently, the computing industry seems to have avoided the subject of requirements the way a debutante might avoid the subject of indigestion. We knew such things existed, but if we didn't think about them, perhaps they would simply take care of themselves.

Many of the classic papers in software engineering were based on this position:

**This is how we would design and build software
(if we had unchanging requirements).**

For instance, many of the early papers on structured programming were based on the Eight Queens problem, a problem of fixed definition with no input whatsoever. Many papers on recursive programming were based on the Towers of Hanoi problem, another problem of fixed definition with no input whatsoever. The more recent Cleanroom methodology has the same basis: "The starting point for Cleanroom development is a document that states the user requirements."[2] The following quotation from Parnas and Clements shows how deeply this assumption runs, even in the most sophisticated process designers.

> Usually, a requirements document is produced before coding starts and is never used again. However, that has not been the case for [the software requirements for the A-7E Aircraft]. The currently operational version of the software, which satisfies the requirements document, is still undergoing revision. The organization that has to test the software uses our document extensively to choose the tests that they do. When new changes are needed, the requirements document is used in describing what must be changed and what cannot be changed. Here we see that a document produced at the start of the ideal process is still in use many years after the software went into service. The clear message is that if documentation is produced with care, it will be useful for a long time. Conversely, if it is going to be extensively used, it is worth doing right.[3]

Parnas and Clements describe the benefits of returning after design to create a requirements document *as if* it had been present from the beginning.

In the light of all this literature, it's easy to understand why so many software engineering managers have made the mistake of believing that they *should* have unchanging requirements before starting any project. This model or belief is what I call *The Assumption of Fixed Requirements*, an assumption that is a misreading of these classical works. These classics were not addressing the entire process of software engineering, but only selected parts of that process. What they are teaching us is *how to translate requirements into code, once we have reliable requirements*.

Translating requirements into code is an essential part of software engineering, and it is the part that has received the most research attention over the past four decades. Because of that attention, however, it is no longer the most difficult part of the process. Many organizations know how to do this part quite well, but the quality of their products does not adequately reflect their coding prowess.

In recent internal studies of serious quality problems, three different clients of mine arrived at quite similar conclusions. They divided the sources of the most serious problems into a number of categories, which I have lumped into the table of Table 15-1. (Logistics includes all problems connected with the physical handling of the product—for example, using the wrong version of a module, failing to update the acceptance test database, or using improperly trained operators.)

Table 15-1.
The Percentage of Serious Quality Problems Stemming from
Various Processes in Three Different Organizations.

| Client | Total Faults | Coding (%) | Design (%) | Requirements (%) | Logistics (%) |
|--------|--------------|------------|------------|------------------|---------------|
| A | 4,319 | 8 | 22 | 51 | 19 |
| B | 488 | 3 | 19 | 66 | 12 |
| C | 1,292 | 7 | 11 | 57 | 25 |

Notice that in all cases, coding contributed least to quality problems, and my clients would perhaps do better to work on the less glamorous job of improving their logistics processes. Perhaps these rather advanced organizations are not typical of all software engineering organizations. They still have a lot to learn about coding and especially design, but in each case, the majority of their serious problems stem from requirements.

Software engineers and their customers perceive quality differently, and this table accounts in large part for that discrepancy in perception. Over the past decade, the engineers have seen coding faults drop dramatically as a result of their quality improvement efforts. The customers, however, have not seen a comparable decrease in the number of requirements problems, and so do not perceive the same increase in quality as the engineers, who are paying attention to their own priorities—which don't happen to coincide with their customers' priorities. The engineers need to learn that they will never become an Anticipating (Pattern 4) organization by getting better and better at coding—even though that was the improvement process that brought them as far as they've come.

## 15.2 The Zeroth Law of Software Quality

If these organizations had fixed requirements, like the Eight Queens problem, their improvement efforts would have borne tastier fruit. Alas, their requirements situations are all entirely different from that assumed in that classic research, and they are faced with another important principle of software engineering. This principle appears in various forms,[4] depending on the type of requirement being discussed:

- *The Zeroth Law of Quality:*

  **If you don't care about quality, you can meet any other requirement.**

- *The Zeroth Law of Software:*

  **If the software doesn't have to work, you can meet any other requirement.**

For the purposes of a discussion of software engineering management, the same thing can be stated another way, which we've already seen:

- *The Zeroth Law of Software Engineering Management:*

  **If you don't have to meet requirements, management is no problem.**

Extending the Zeroth Law, we have this corollary:

- **The less closely you have to meet requirements and the more your requirements approximate the Assumption of Fixed Requirements, the easier it will be for you to manage.**

### 15.2.1 Phrases to listen for

Problems arise, however, when people in your organization start trying to pretend that requirements are fixed, or that they don't matter, with comments like

- Some things just can't be specified.
- It's *almost* what they want.
- It's actually *better* than what they asked for.
- They don't know what they really want (but *we* do).
- The customers will like it however we build it. What do they know, and besides, what choice will they have?
- If we specify everything, they won't buy it. Better to add requirements a bit at a time, so they never realize the full cost.
- The customer is too busy to work on requirements with us.

- We'll fill in the requirements after we build the system and see what the customer wants.
- The market is too volatile to specify in advance.
- We're building it object-oriented, so it will meet any requirements, regardless of what they turn out to be.

## 15.2.2 *Actions to take*

DO NOT allow design or construction to proceed without verified requirements unless you have a staged process. In that case, DO NOT let any stage begin without verified requirements *for that stage.*

DO NOT permit small "improvements" to slip into conversions. Convert first, verify the conversion, then improve. If it has "improvements," then it's not a conversion, so don't estimate it that way.

DO involve the customer—or customer surrogate, such as Marketing—in requirements, from the beginning and throughout. If the customers say they're "too busy," DO NOT proceed, because you don't really have any customers. Instead, DO concentrate on letting the customers know that you're ready and available to speak with them and that the system is waiting for the interaction. DO spend the time on activities that raise the capability of your staff, such as training and practice. That way, when the customer is ready to get involved, you *may* be able to move faster and make up some time.

DO make the test plan part of the requirements. The test plan answers the question, "How will I know it works?" DO insist that the test plan be able to answer this question *for you,* so you will be able to understand if your project has actually done what you are committed to do.

DO make the user documentation part of the requirements. The user documentation answers the question, "How do I use it?"

DO keep emphasizing both the cost and the value of things people desire. That's part of the management job in any requirements process.

## 15.3 Process Models of Requirements

For an organization to survive, its process models must be at least somewhat "successful"—in the same sense that the Old Status Quo is "successful." Changing to another cultural pattern requires a transforming idea that enables people to let go of their familiar, comfortable models, such as the Assumption of Fixed Requirements. In all cases I've witnessed, an organization must revise its Old Status Quo requirements process model if it's to have any chance of changing its cultural pattern.

People in Oblivious (Pattern 0) organizations tend to be oblivious to process models of any kind, let alone requirements models. The linear process models of Variable (Pattern 1) cultures represent a step up in thinking, even though linear process models have no feedback at all, but simply follow a sequence of one thing after another. That applies to the requirements process as well, as beautifully illustrated by Figure 15-1, which I lifted from a presentation by the divisional manager of a Variable (Pattern 1) organization.

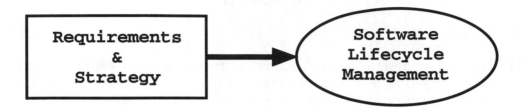

Figure 15-1.        A linear process model:  First we do requirements, then we do the software life cycle.

Routine (Pattern 2) organizations may acknowledge the nonlinearity of the requirements process, but tend to view this as something evil, rather than something natural. The exceptions to the linear process are allowed only to keep the process as linear as possible (Figure 15-2).

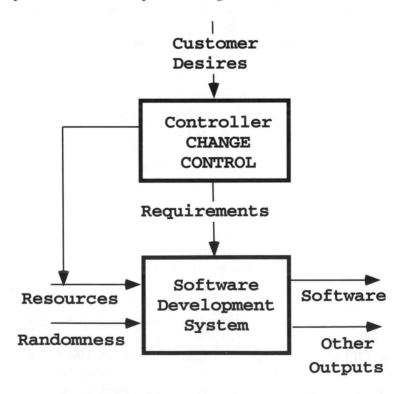

Figure 15-2.        The Routine (Pattern 2) requirements process tends to be linear *with exceptions*. The principal job of Change Control is to filter as many requirements changes as possible, to keep the process linear.

There are situations in which this Pattern 2 model works reasonably well, and thus Routine organizations can perform reasonably well. In these situations, requirements change very little from the start to the end of development, perhaps because

- projects are small, so development takes place over a small time span
- the underlying business process is very stable
- customer expectations from information systems are low, and decisions are left in the hands of developers

Much of the time, however, software work involves a constant dialogue between the product's customers and the software developers. Indeed, in all software cultures, a requirements development process *always* runs in parallel with the software development process (Figure 15-3), though the patterns differ in *where* that requirements process takes place:

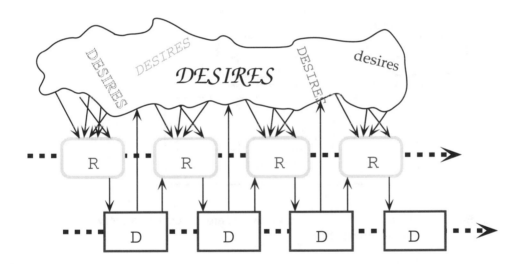

Figure 15-3.     The software development process (D) is in constant dialogue between the product's customers and the software developers. Desires change requirements (R), requirements change development, development changes the product, and the experience with the product changes desires.

- In Oblivious (Pattern 0) cultures, the requirements process runs inside the head of the same person who's doing development.

- In Variable (Pattern 1) cultures, the requirements process generally runs back and forth between one customer and one team or individual developer.

- In Routine (Pattern 2) cultures, the requirements process runs alongside development, although the developers do their darnedest to keep it from happening. When projects are small and successful, they are also of such short duration that the people involved don't notice this parallel process. When they do notice, it's time to start moving to a rather different view of the role of requirements in software engineering.

## 15.4 The Twin Processes

When they pay extra attention to the role of the requirements document and the process of developing and maintaining it, Parnas and Clements introduce a different view of the role of requirements.[5] The key idea here is that there are really *two* processes: one to develop a requirements product and one to develop a software product (Figure 15-4).

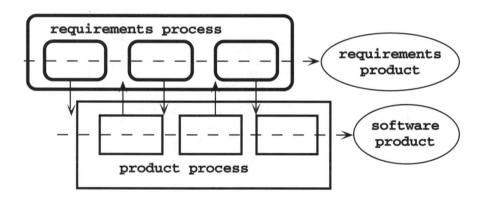

Figure 15-4.     The two processes produce two different products: a software product and a requirements product.

In this view, the software process and the requirements process are mutually controlling twin processes (Figure 15-5). They may run at different rates at different times in the life cycle, but each is always present, exercising feedback control over the other.

In mutually controlling processes, the purpose of each requirements stage is to narrow the discrepancy between what is wanted and what is documented, not to eliminate all discrepancy. Zero discrepancy is impossible, because

- the target is moving
- we are not perfect
- discrepancy gives information needed for control

Prototyping, of course, is an explicit way of making the requirements development process and the system development process mutually controlling, but effective prototyping is not by any means trivial. Too wide a gap produces an unstable requirements process in which small, quick corrections are insufficient to get back on track. Too narrow a gap may mean that customers don't know their real requirements, and are simply agreeing to whatever they see that looks "nice" on a screen.

If you adopt prototyping in order to avoid facing process issues, you are in for a series of nasty surprises. As one comedian at one of my clients said about a "rapid prototyping" development that had failed to converge after four years, "We've adopted the method called 'slow prototyping.'" Nobody laughed.

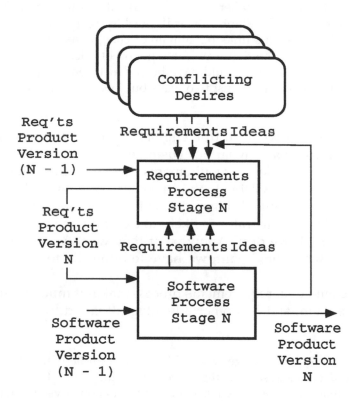

Figure 15-5.     The requirements development process and the software development process are mutually controlling processes.

## 15.5 Upward Flow of Requirements

Notice that the model in Figure 15-5 shows requirements ideas emerging from the development process and flowing upward into the requirements process, not just directly into the code without being filtered by an explicit process.

Sometimes, developers get bored when they are underutilized (or think that they are), and so they expand the problem (or the solution) to stretch their capabilities. At other times, they simply believe (often correctly) that they know something that the customers want, even though it's not in the requirements. A correspondent of mine named Brian Richter described this phenomenon to me very nicely:

> This is one of those things that I didn't know anyone else did. I suppose the way I often do it is to work towards a "better" solution. Some people seem to think that to solve a given problem takes X amount of time, and it's not so. If you give me a week to write a certain piece of code, I may be able to come up with something that works. If you give me a month to do the same thing, I'll come up with a solution that's more general or more maintainable or better in some other way. The difficulty is that the differences between the two ways are not outwardly visible right away. The differences are visible when it's time to maintain or change that code. And after too many things done the first way, some period of "cleanup" is needed to fix up things the way they would have been had I done them the second way. Actually, there are not just two ways but lots of degrees of goodness in-between. . . .[6]

What Brian describes is what all true engineers can do, but as engineers, we must orient our solutions to what our customers want. That's why we need good requirements to guide us, requirements that show the value of what we are doing that may not be visible to the customer. Do they really want a solid gold bridge? Do they want a bridge that can have a second level added at low cost, because we know that traffic is likely to expand just because of the presence of the bridge? If we don't know what they want, we have to guess. If they don't know what they want, we have to either lie to them, or educate them.

A separate but equal requirements process makes it much more likely that we can educate them, and has other advantages that address Brian's further remarks:

> Sometimes, I'll get to a stage where I'll think of an "enhancement" that could be added to a system without too much difficulty. If I understand something about how the system is to be used, I'll know myself whether the enhancement could possibly be useful or not. If I don't understand the use of the system so well, I can sometimes ask the customer directly, or ask leading questions to get a feel for where they might stand if I were to ask them directly.
>
> The approach of asking the customer doesn't work if I don't understand how the system is going to be used and also if I don't have a direct link with the customer. In a big system, some managers want to tell you what your job is rather than how what you're doing fits into the system. This leads to a situation where you know what you're being told to do, but don't have any idea what constitutes a "good" way of doing it.

The existence of this process authorizes the participation of developers in the requirements development process, focuses their efforts and makes them visible, yet keeps them under some sort of control. Without this focus, developers have difficulty making the very real contributions only they can make.

## 15.6 Management's Attitude Toward the Requirements Process

A Steering (Pattern 3) or Anticipating (Pattern 4) requirements process is a controlled feedback process in its own right, with its own products that are equal in importance to the software products. Without this equal importance, it will be impossible for the organizations in Table 15-1 to make major improvements in their quality.

The managers in these organizations, however, were sending messages that suggested that the requirements process was less important than the software development process. Figure 15-6 excerpts the eighty-page project plan template that was to be used for all projects in Company A. As you can see, the plan elevates the development of the shipping carton for this software product to the same level as writing the product requirements—a level below developing the software. Although the work process breakdown may not be intended to show priority, this was the only process document the company used, so it was a common misinterpretation to assume these levels implied priority.

In the course of my consulting, I heard one of Company B's managers give a less subtle but more common message. "This is a crisis," he shouted. "Forget the #@%*!&# requirements!" Hearing this directive, everyone knew that quality was a joke.

```
Project Plan
- 1.
- 1.1  ...
-
- 2.   ...
- 2.1  Write Product Requirements
...
... 3.   Develop Software
-
...
... 7.6  Develop Shipping Carton Design and Test
-
```

Figure 15-6.      Two equal headings from one organization's process document.

In Company C, one of the managers *ordered* the developers *never* to speak to their customers. The reasons he gave were both ridiculous and demeaning, and showed his total ignorance of how real requirements processes must be designed to produce systems of real quality.

If the organization's process model says that the requirements process isn't serious, then

- nothing will be planned
- resources will not be committed
- nobody will take full-time responsibility for anything
- requirements training will seem frivolous
- tools will seem superfluous
- development will be uncontrolled

Getting the requirements right is the most important part of product development. If it's not the right product, who cares if it works? or, if the other processes work? As we say in the process business,

**Anything not worth doing is not worth doing right.**

Chapter 16 will delve into what's required by management to change to a serious, effective requirements process.

### 15.7  Helpful Hints and Suggestions

1. Redoing a system that has already been specified is substantially cheaper and easier than doing one from scratch. This is done, for example, when using the double coding method of achieving reliability at low additional cost. In such projects, the added cost of coding twice is no more than 20 percent of the total project cost, because most of the cost is in obtaining the requirements, either directly or indirectly. For the same reason, conversion projects are often done for one to two percent of the original development cost.

2. In ambitious software projects, success—if it is obtained at all—is often obtained by scrutinizing and carefully pruning the definition of success. The basic management skill needed here is the ability to settle for less than you hoped for, but no less than you actually need. If, however, the pruning is done in a haphazard fashion, without interaction with the users of the system, then the result is what we call a WYGIWYGG, or "wiggywig," system—for the in-your-face slogan, "what you got is what you're gonna' get."

3.  To my statement that changing to another cultural pattern requires a transformation that lets go of previously successful models, Payson Hall comments: "Don't underestimate the difficulty of our letting go of models that we believe have served us well in the past—and that we may have championed in the first place because they improved on *their* predecessors." Ignoring the history and potential investment people have in the status quo is a rookie mistake that both Payson and I have made more than once.

## 15.8  Summary

✔  Software engineering is in the business of building, running, and maintaining things for some customer or customers. Requirements are only part of the process of connecting with your customers and responding to them, but they are an important part.

✔  Until recently, the computing industry seems to have avoided the subject of requirements. In the light of the classic literature, it's easy to understand why so many software engineering managers have made the mistake of believing that they *should* have unchanging requirements before starting any project—the Assumption of Fixed Requirements.

✔  Translating requirements into code is an essential part of software engineering, and it is the part that has received the most research attention over the past four decades. But because of that attention, it is no longer the most difficult part of the process, nor is it the process that will yield the most benefit to process improvement efforts.

✔  The Zeroth Law of Software Quality concerns requirements, and appears in various forms:

    •  The Zeroth Law of Quality:

       **If you don't care about quality, you can meet any other requirement.**

    •  The Zeroth Law of Software:

       **If the software doesn't have to work, you can meet any other requirement.**

    •  The Zeroth Law of Software Engineering Management:

       **If you don't have to meet requirements, management is no problem.**

- **The less closely you have to meet requirements and the more your requirements approximate the Assumption of Fixed Requirements, the easier it will be for you to manage.**

✔ Changing to another cultural pattern requires a transformation so that people let go of previously successful models, such as the Assumption of Fixed Requirements. For an organization to improve its cultural pattern, requirements process models need to be revised.

- People in Oblivious (Pattern 0) cultures tend to be oblivious to process models of any kind, let alone requirements models.
- The linear process models of Variable (Pattern 1) cultures represent a step up in thinking, even though linear process models have no feedback at all.
- Routine (Pattern 2) organizations may acknowledge the nonlinearity of the requirements process, but still try to keep exceptions to the linear process as linear as possible. The principal job of Change Control is to filter as many requirements changes as possible, to keep the process linear.

✔ The Routine (Pattern 2) requirements model works reasonably well when

- projects are small, so development takes place over a small time span
- the underlying business process is very stable
- customer expectations from information systems are low, and decisions are left in the hands of developers

✔ Much of the time, software work involves a constant dialogue between the product's customers and the software developers.

- In Oblivious (Pattern 0) cultures, the requirements process runs inside the head of the same person who's doing development.
- In Variable (Pattern 1) cultures, the requirements process generally runs back and forth between one customer and one team or individual developer.
- In Routine (Pattern 2) cultures, the requirements process runs alongside development, although the developers do their darnedest to keep it from happening.

✔ The key process idea in moving to a Steering (Pattern 3) culture and beyond is that there are really two processes: one to develop a requirements product and one to develop a software product. In this view, the software development process and the requirements development process are mutually controlling twin processes, each exercising feedback control over the other.

✔ In mutually controlling processes, the purpose of each requirements stage is to narrow the discrepancy between what is wanted and what is documented, not to eliminate all discrepancy.

✔ Prototyping, of course, is an explicit way of making the requirements development process and the system development process mutually controlling, but effective prototyping is by no means trivial. If you adopt prototyping in order to avoid facing process issues, you are in for a series of nasty surprises.

✔ Requirements ideas often emerge from the system development process and flow upward into the requirements process. A good requirements process authorizes the participation of developers, focuses their efforts and makes them visible, yet keeps them under some sort of control. Without this focus, developers have difficulty making the very real contributions only they can make.

✔ A Steering (Pattern 3) or Anticipating (Pattern 4) requirements process is a controlled feedback process in its own right. Such a process model is more in keeping with the vision that says getting the requirements right is the most important part of product development.

## 15.9 Practice

1.  Draw a graph showing various software process models—such as the Waterfall Model and the Rapid Prototyping Model—and how they narrow requirements discrepancies over time.

2.  Recall a project in which some of these requirements principles were violated. What were the effects? How did the project try to compensate for these effects?

3.  Phil Fuhrer suggests: Describe what happens when a prototyping process does not have convergent feedback that keeps narrowing requirements discrepancies. If possible, give an example from your own experience. What could have been done to the process to make the development convergent?

4.  Payson Hall adds: Describe an experience you've had when someone tried to introduce something new without adequately considering and honoring the history of the old thing it was to replace. How did you feel at the time? How did you act? Did you ever commit this kind of rookie error yourself? What was the reaction of other people?

# 16

## Changing the Requirements Process

*If those guys were women,*
*they'd all be pregnant.*
*They can't say no to anything.*[1]
— Pat Schroeder

For many software organizations, the principal barrier to higher quality is an inadequate requirements process. Such an organization typically can't say no to anything, so requirements grow out of control and projects are in a state of perpetual pregnancy, never quite giving birth. To move such an organization to a controlled requirements process, managers need to plan and execute four major steps:

1. Measure the true cost and value of requirements.

2. Gain control of the requirements inputs.

3. Gain control of the requirements outputs.

4. Gain control of the requirements process itself.

These steps are the subject of this chapter.

## 16.1 Measure the True Cost and Value of Requirements

With a long history of ignoring or assuming the requirements process, most software engineering organizations are well into the Old Status Quo stage on requirements. They need a strong foreign element to trigger a change, an element that you can provide by sponsoring research into the true costs and loss of benefits of the current requirements process.[2]

An improved requirements process pays for itself in a number of ways:

- faults caught early or not created at all
- redundant work eliminated
- better reception by customers
- faster, more manageable development
- improved maintenance

Figure 16-1 shows how these five factors affect the "iron triangle" of product quality, development economy, and delivery speed, and thus move the organization closer to the curve of best practice.

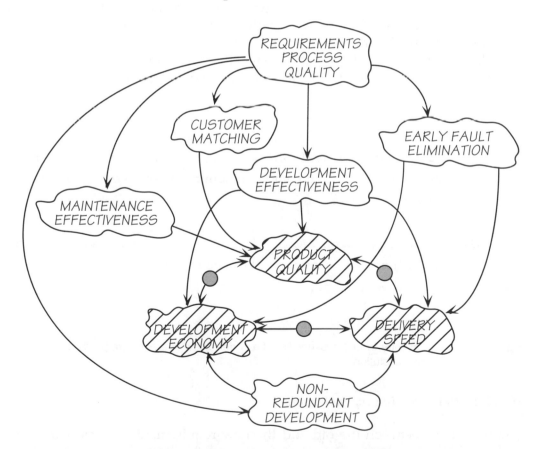

Figure 16-1.    All three corners of the iron triangle (product quality, development economy, delivery speed) can be improved by a more effective requirements process, thus moving the organization closer to the curve of best practice.

### 16.1.1 Faults caught early or not created at all

A New York financial company estimated an average cost of $2,000 to repair each requirements fault that escaped the requirements stage in their Waterfall Model. These faults included missing, wrong, conflicting, excessive, and extra requirements. On a pilot project, they established a separate team of requirements specialists with full responsibility for the requirements product. This new requirements process reduced faults from an average of 12/KLOC to 3/KLOC.

On the basis of the pilot, they decided to use the same process (with some improvements) on a 120 KLOC project, projecting 1,080 faults prevented. At their estimated cost per fault, this came to 1,080 x $2,000 = $2,160,000 projected savings, more than enough to motivate the move and cover any start-up costs.

### 16.1.2 Redundant work eliminated

A software company inaugurated a program of analyzing the source of issues turning up in code reviews (which they conducted after unit testing, a practice that's not ideal). Figure 16-2 shows a typical requirements fault discovered in the analysis. The result of the investigation showed this fault led to extra coding and design work for a feature that was simply not needed. For sixty lines of code that need never have been designed, coded, reviewed, or tested, the company estimated a cost of $300/line of code x 60 = $18,000.

```
6. (perf) Line 1838-1867 and 1860-1889 dealt with dotted line
and hairline that are available in MAC only.  Investigate how
to convert a MAC file with such properties and see if we need
these 2 blocks of code.

Result of investigation: All this code is inoperative and can
be removed since we convert all these cases to the normal
border.
```

Figure 16-2.      An entry from the issues list of a code review of a software product, along with the resolution.

### 16.1.3 Better reception by customers

The difference between the old and the new requirements process can be so striking that precise measurements are not needed to provide the motivation to proceed with revising the process. Here's a testimonial in a letter from a customer vice president in a sporting goods company to the head of Information Systems. He is talking about a pilot of a separate requirements team, and the letter was written three weeks into a fourteen-month purchasing system project.

> I don't know what you've done, but three of my employees have taken the time to tell me how effective your new team is. Apparently, they showed us that some of the features we were asking for would cost much more than they were worth, and that there was a much more cost-effective way to get the information we need. They also suggested some information we didn't dream we could get.
>
> Again, I don't know what you're doing differently, but keep it up!

What they were doing differently was using a team of requirements specialists who had just completed two weeks of special training to kick off their new roles and build their team.

### 16.1.4  Faster, more manageable, development

By the time it was finished, this "fourteen-month purchasing system project" had taken only ten months, a unique event in the history of this IS department. The time savings came from reduced rework and much less testing time, plus simply not producing parts of the system that were of no real value. In the example of Figure 16-2, we don't need elaborate measurements to tell us that it takes more time to design, code, and test sixty lines than to do nothing.

Even more important to managers is the *reduction in project variance,* which makes anticipatory management possible. Every additional requirement is like a purchase order against the project's budget, creating uncontrollable future costs and time. Try to imagine what would happen to your project's budget if every developer could personally authorize unlimited purchases of hardware and software. Isn't it silly, then, to grant unlimited requirements purchasing power to people who are not even authorized to spend $49 for a PC software tool?

### 16.1.5  Improved maintenance

Actually, a well-done requirements document frequently lives long after the software whose purpose it describes. When a system has to be reimplemented on different hardware, such a document is worth its weight in diamonds. More than one small software company has gone out of business because its staff lacked the foundation for converting their product to follow the latest hardware fashions. They had "working code," but collapsed trying to reverse engineer that code.

Of course, you don't have to wait for the demise of the system to show the value of the requirements asset. The typical information system is said to cost three times as much in continuing development during its operational life than it did during its prenatal days. Recall the quotation from the previous chapter on the impact of a well-done requirements document on this postnatal work.

> The organization that has to test the software uses our document extensively to choose the tests that they do. When new changes are needed, the requirements document is used in describing what must be changed and what cannot be changed.[3]

Compare this description with what has to be done when the requirements information is hopelessly out of date, or cannot even be found.

### 16.2  Gain Control of the Requirements Inputs

To gain control over the requirements process, the second of the four steps is to get control over the inputs. Requirements come from many places, some of which are official. Many other requirements simply leak into the process. To get control of the inputs, you need to perform two actions:

- Identify and plug all leaks.
- Replace leaks with explicit negotiation.

### 16.2.1  *Identify and plug all leaks*

Even when requirements are taken seriously, there may be leakage that destroys the process. Many managers I've talked to about leaks simply cannot believe that they happen to any great extent in their own organizations. The only way I've found to convince them is to conduct a leakage study with a team to uncover every source of every requirement, no matter how subtle.

Perhaps you will be convinced by looking at one company's leakage study. About half of this company's software is embedded in their hardware. The other half consists of stand-alone support software. Here's a list of sources of existing requirements the team discovered, ranging from perfectly legitimate to totally off-the-wall (in no particular order):

✔ program plans (business plans)

✔ priority enhancements requested by marketing

✔ "long experience in the industry"

✔ looking at what's produced by more sophisticated software organizations

✔ enhancements mentioned by distributors who were overheard by programmers who were attending a sales meeting to support a product
demonstration

✔ enhancements requested by specific customers, who are usually from
large organizations

✔ enhancements requested by system integrators

✔ enhancements requested by management

✔ enhancements inserted by programmers with "careful consideration of
what would be good for the customer"

✔ enhancements inserted by programmers as quick fixes

✔ enhancements inserted by contract programmers, who then left, leaving
no documentation

✔ mistakes that are made and shipped, and then have to be supported

✔ features that hardware engineers couldn't implement

✔ features that hardware engineers wouldn't implement

✔ corrections to hardware faults

✔ change of scope in reaction to what competitors did

✔ change of scope in reaction to what competitors were expected to do, but
didn't do

✔ change of scope in reaction to features provided by third-party software
houses

✔ anomaly reports from testing

✔ anomaly reports from customer change requests

✔ enhancements deriving from pricing negotiations, in which customers
were promised something extra in order to maintain the price

✔ phone requests from unrecorded sources

✔ things found in the code, but no one has any idea where they came from

✔ things present in reused code that now have to be supported because customers discovered them and started using them

✔ a mistake that was made in copying system drawings and is now touted as a "feature"

✔ changes needed because of the company's standards (product compatibility)

✔ changes needed because of industry standards

✔ changes needed because of international standards

✔ changes needed because of specific country standards

✔ changes needed to accommodate organizational changes, for example, other projects moved into a development group by upper management fiat

✔ "Easter eggs," or stuff hidden in the code by programmers for their own amusement and activated only by secret and unlikely input combinations

An estimate created as a by-product of another leakage study indicated that roughly half of the requirements (as measured by function points required to implement them) originated from unofficial sources. Under such circumstances, how could *anyone* control

- development schedules?
- development costs?
- product functionality?
- product performance?

In other words, unless and until this kind of random requirements input is under control, nothing else can possibly be under control.

### 16.2.2  *Replace leaks with explicit negotiation*

To gain control of this requirements chaos, you must

- recognize that requirements come from many sources, and know what those sources are
- accept these multiple interests as legitimate, but not necessarily guaranteed to have their way with the requirements
- create an explicit negotiation process that will consider anybody's requirements ideas

- develop a process—a funnel, if you like—which *guarantees* that all requirements come through a single channel

The negotiation process takes place among the many people who may have interest in the output, but the ultimate decision is with the customer (or sponsor), the one who ultimately pays the bills. Unless you go to a high enough management level, however, projects that serve several customers have many definitions, because there are different interests involved. In these situations, problem defining is fully political, and the most political act is deciding *who gets to define the problem.*

In all these situations, the purely rational approach is seen by many political players as naive, and possibly dangerous to their positions—unless they can get control over the people who get to define "rational." That's why, in most hierarchies, you need to get the blessing of the highest possible executive. If the other participants cannot agree amongst themselves in a reasonable time, this executive steps in and makes a decision in favor of a single problem statement. Generally speaking, just the threat of this intervention is enough to keep the parties negotiating in good faith. When there are several companies involved and no single person has jurisdiction over everybody else, you can be in serious trouble if you don't get up-front agreement on a "chief justice" to decide controversial cases.

Requirements conflicts happen, and if not resolved any other way, they are resolved by the customer. Such customer resolution is not the best way to resolve requirements conflicts, but is needed to back up the system when negotiation fails. By using skilled facilitators who have no conflict of interest, you can reduce the probability of such failures.

The person who facilitates the negotiations must be congruent:

- not blaming people for asking for what they want
- not placating people who are difficult to deal with by automatically giving them what they demand
- paying attention to people who tend to placate by not asking for something they think you won't be able to do, or that someone else opposes

Most often, such facilitation is part of the job of the requirements manager, who is responsible to the customer.

Figure 16-3 shows a simple process—managed by a requirements manager—that prevents leakage and converts it into an explicit requirements capture process. To understand how this process works, notice that there is a *single path* for a requirements *idea* to be converted to a *requirement.* The requirements manager, by controlling this single path, prevents leakage.

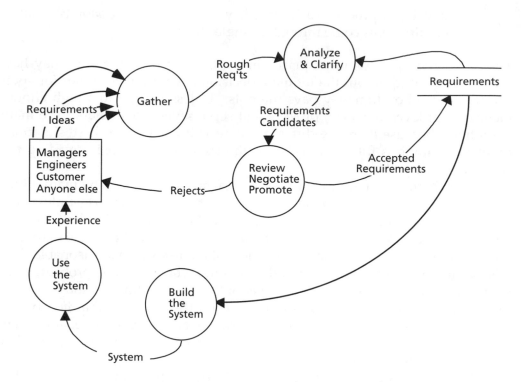

Figure 16-3.     A data flow diagram of a requirements process that is open to ideas, but closed to leakage.

The bubble called "Gather," through which all requirements ideas must be funneled, is the pivotal point in converting to such a controlled process. Anyone with a requirements idea—managers, engineers, customers, or anyone else— must understand that there is no other path by which this idea has a chance of becoming a requirement. The requirements manager does not attempt to prevent ideas from entering the system. Indeed, the system requires that all ideas be encouraged, but the proponents of these ideas must clearly understand that their submissions are simply *requirements ideas,* not requirements, until they pass through this process.

Once requirements are gathered, they are considered *rough requirements* until they have passed through a smoothing process of analysis and clarification. If they pass this step, they are considered to be in reviewable condition, and are called *requirements candidates.* Only the review process (for correctness) and the negotiation process (for compatibility and priority) can promote candidates into *accepted requirements* that are placed in the database, or into rejected requirements ideas. Rejected ideas are turned back to their originators, who may then modify and resubmit them.

The requirements database is used for building the system, and is also needed when new rough requirements are considered. That's because new requirements candidates must not only be clear and correct in themselves, but must be consistent with existing requirements. This one step allows you to spot inconsistencies, but of course the analysis must decide which of an inconsistent pair needs to be changed.

It isn't easy changing from the old backdoor way to this new process of explicit clarification, review, and negotiation. You can be sure that more than one person will challenge the system and try to return to the Old Status Quo condition. They won't always be as tough as in the following tale, but you'd better be prepared with all the congruence you can muster. The speaker is a young man in a custom machine tool company who was made requirements manager on a project that would assist in the production of proposals and bids:

> Three days after I got my new position, I was hit by the hardest situation I ever had to face. In a code review, it was discovered that Arthur, the coder, had inserted a completely undocumented spell check function. This was completely redundant, as the customer used a commercial spell checker on these documents, so I told Arthur to take it out.
>
> He protested that his spell checker was "better" than any of the commercial ones. I tried to point out that his was undocumented, untested, would be unmaintained, and since it used the dictionary of the commercial product, we would still ethically have to pay for that product. Then he literally threw a tantrum, right in my office with the door open. Lucky for me I have five kids, so I knew how to handle it.
>
> When he calmed down, I suggested that he didn't have to take my word on this, and that I would be glad to go with him to discuss it with our customer. I knew I was taking a risk that he might throw another tantrum, but I tried to frame it to the customer that this programmer had an idea that might help him. The customer listened politely and said he'd think about it. When I got back to my office, there was a phone message from the customer telling me to drop the idea.
>
> Then Arthur wrote a long letter to our president. That cost me a lot of time explaining, but in the end, the code had to be taken out. Arthur refused to do it, so the project manager took that module away from him. A couple of weeks later, Arthur quit.
>
> I was afraid this was going to damage our new requirements process, so I called a meeting of all the developers and discussed the case with them. I told them that we welcome requirements ideas arising from their knowledge of design and coding, but they would have to go through the same negotiation process as any other requirements ideas. I said that if they thought this was just bureaucratic BS, then they should try me out. Fortunately, by this time several had already had ideas accepted into requirements, so it was easier to prove what I was saying wasn't BS.
>
> Now, it works fine, even though not all ideas get accepted. The programmers know better than to waste time trying to sneak through some idea wrapped in code, and all that's left of the incident is a new piece of slang. When someone develops a piece of code that can't be clearly related to the requirements, someone else always asks, "What is this, a spell checker?"

## 16.3  Gain Control of the Requirements Outputs

A requirements document is much like a software product.  Like software, it is an *information* product, so

- it must be made visible
- it must be made stable
- it must be made controllable

### 16.3.1  Visibility

In a poorly managed situation, requirements are even less visible than code. At least people in a project *think* about code, whereas they often forget about requirements.  Probably the most common type of requirements fault is that *nobody in the project thought about some area of requirements.*  Common examples of forgotten requirements are performance, operability, maintainability, security, conversion of existing data, integration with existing systems, and cutover to production.  For instance, three years into one development effort planned for eighteen months, the only performance requirement is "Must meet acceptable time frames."  Since nothing is quantified, the real performance requirement is effectively invisible.

Moreover, requirements processes often fail to consider the needs of whole classes of users, so that certain functions simply don't exist except in the minds of users—minds that will not become actively involved in the requirements process until the product is delivered to them.

Undoubtedly, the most effective way for a manager to ensure that requirements are not forgotten is to make them visible by making requirements development into a real project, just like software development.  This may sound extreme, perhaps because we have so often fallen prey to certain myths about how requirements can be kept automatically.  Payson Hall explains two of the most common myths:

> A couple of huge disaster projects I've worked on made the rookie mistake of believing that a CASE tool could keep and organize all of the system requirements.  Things were botched badly and it's not clear whether or not the CASE tool had the theoretical capability to keep those requirements— but in practical terms, they were lost.
>
> One of the problems that has emerged in the Rapid Application Development work I've seen is a myth that suggests "the requirements are the prototype"—which is another way of focusing on the code to the exclusion of its larger context.

Good tools can help, but there is no silver requirements bullet.  To be in control, you must have a real requirements project.  There must be a full-time requirements manager, a planning process, and a staff of specially trained people supported by processes and tools appropriate to the requirements task. The project should follow all the process principles, and since all other parts of a software project are based on the requirements, it should have visibility as one of its major goals.

### 16.3.2 Stability

Because requirements leak in from so many sources, not all of which are legitimate, you will also need strict physical control of the requirements. In Arthur's case, his spell checker would never have come to light without code reviews and strict configuration control of the code. Indeed, in other products, Arthur had inserted Easter eggs *after* code reviews, because the configuration control system was not tied to the inspection of the code that went into it. Under the new system, code was placed in the database, then reviewed, then elevated to official status only after passing review. This process catches requirements that have leaked into code without passing through the requirements process.

Figure 16-4 shows a schematic data flow of how requirements ideas become translated into tested code.

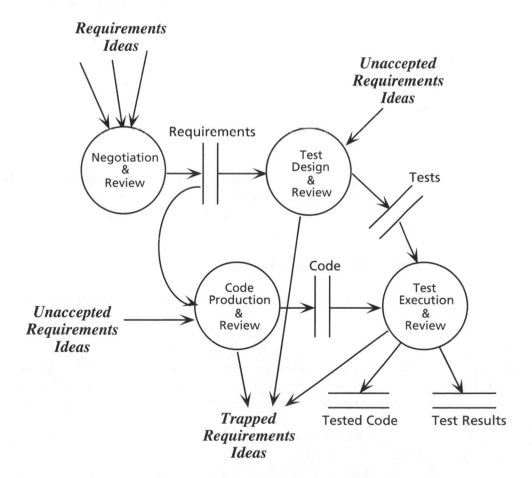

Figure 16-4.    To ensure the stability of requirements against leaks of all sorts, you must have a process of negotiation of all proposed requirements ideas, plus configuration control of requirements, tests, code, and test results.

The expanded "Negotiation & Review" bubble could look like the upper part of Figure 16-3, which controls the entry of requirements into the requirements database. But it's not sufficient to channel all requirements ideas through the negotiation and review process, because uncontrolled changes to any of the databases can also be leaks. Arthur wrote code that didn't originate in the requirements database at all, thus bypassing all the negotiation and review.

To trap this type of leakage, you must control the configuration of both code and requirements, plus other parts of the product such as tests and test results. In addition, you must also review the inside of each of these intermediate products, because leaked requirements can easily be hidden from black-box testing.

### 16.3.3 Controllability

A requirements document carries only a small part of the requirements communication load. In practice, most of the load is carried by

- individuals who understand the requirements and help other people understand
- teams that work effectively, so that they can communicate internally and externally about requirements

To have the kind of understanding that keeps requirements simple, people must learn from participation in the requirements process. One of the main purposes of a requirements process is to build the team that will build the product. But participation won't be sufficient unless information is coordinated, open, available, and of known quality.

To have the kind of teamwork needed to clarify requirements, people must be committed to the project, have a chance to participate in it, and be trained as effective teamworkers. And again, information must be coordinated, open, available, and of known quality.

### 16.4  Gain Control of the Requirements Process Itself

If you have a full-time requirements manager with a staff of trained, committed people using appropriate tools and high-quality information, you can make the requirements task into a real project, not something you just do if you happen to remember. The requirements project must be justified like any other project, planned like any other project, and pay for itself. This full-time requirements manager must be equal in competence and stature with a software development manager, and must report to the ultimate customer (or sponsor).

This separate requirements group can take several forms, as appropriate to the overall development process:

- Perhaps the most familiar form is the team of specialists that conducts requirements projects and throws the result over the wall to a build team. This is an improvement on the classical Waterfall Model in that the people who do the requirements work are motivated requirements specialists, rather than reluctant coders conscripted for the job.
- Over-the-wall teams, however, are inappropriate in most larger projects, so in these cases, the team of skilled requirements professionals coexists with the team of developers throughout the project, though they are on separate teams with distinct responsibilities. Their workload may be large toward the beginning and diminish toward the end as the requirements converge, but they are present throughout the entire project and continue on into its operational phase.

### 16.4.1 Resource support

The requirements project must be given an adequate staff of trained, committed people. The type of people you want on this team are relatively scarce in software engineering organizations. Certainly those researchers who like to assume requirements are fixed as given don't *want* to do requirements work. The same will be true of most (not all) of the computer science graduates in your shop. The people you want will be trained as facilitators, teamworkers, documenters, and business specialists, and will love all this training.

The requirements process will also be better controlled if supported with appropriate tools, such as

- configuration control of all the relevant databases
- an active requirements database that allows all interested parties to examine any part of the current requirements at any time
- network access to the database, especially if it is seamless with other network use
- electronic mail and voice mail to support person-to-person communication
- special facilities for requirements meetings

Although this may sound like a lot of work to an organization that now has a forgetful, leaky requirements process, control of the requirements process provides a stable base for the software process. If you truly understand the role of the requirements product, you'll have no trouble justifying the time and money required to establish a real, equal requirements process.

### 16.4.2 Process support

Ultimately, though, no tools will make a requirements process run itself. Management is ultimately responsible for defining what problems the organization is to solve internally, and for its customers. These managers must have the authority to establish and control the processes that make it possible for them to control this definition. Managers who do not establish a process appropriate to their situation will see their control over requirements slip out of their grasp.

For instance, systems that are produced in a series of versions—as in prototyping or regularly scheduled updates—are vulnerable to another subtle type of requirements leakage. In such systems, a single requirements database is insufficient to control the desire of various advocates to get their requirements met in the earliest possible version. Figure 16-5 shows a process that controls the allocation of requirements to specific versions. At the end of the classification process, the elements of the requirements database are sorted into N releases, plus a set of future requirements not allocated to any currently active release plan.

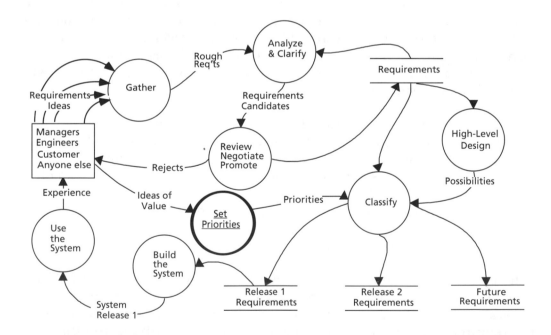

Figure 16-5.    A classification process must be added to keep legitimate requirements from leaking into the wrong release. At the end of the classification process, the elements of the requirements database are sorted into N releases, plus a set of future requirements not allocated to any currently active release plan.

*Priorities* are the value side of the equation: what it's worth to implement a particular requirement in a particular release. In this diagram, "Set Priorities" is shown as a single process bubble, but the details inside that bubble contain the key to linking the requirements to true business needs.[4] The important part of this level of analysis is that setting priorities becomes an open, explicit process, not a test of who is best able to sneak their favorite requirement into the current release without exploring the trade-offs.

*Possibilities* are the cost side of the equation: what it will cost in time, money, and other resources to implement a particular requirement in a particular release. *Possibilities* come from some kind of engineering analysis, which may be a kind of rough, high-level design, or may require some rather detailed design work, though this kind of effort should be minimized.

The decision to classify a requirement into a particular release is a management decision, aided by these inputs, but not determined by any one of them. For example, conflict between engineering and marketing is essential to good requirements decisions, but if either party should defeat the other, the project will be the loser. Your job as manager is to ensure that all of the contributing parties play fair, for example, not biasing their information so as to force your decision into something they prefer.

Another insidious form of loss of control arises when the software product is supposed to serve a number—possibly a very large number—of customers. Here, instead of the leaks occurring at the back end (coding), they occur at the front end (gathering). Because the number of customers is so large, not all customers can be interviewed, nor can all their desires be satisfied.

In such cases, somebody—a manager, a marketer, a programmer, or perhaps a representative from one large customer organization—will step forward and claim to represent the "true" customer wishes. If you accept this claim at face value, such a person can leak any requirements at all into the system. To protect against this situation, you must provide in your requirements process a more reliable way of modeling customer requirements. Figure 16-6 shows how such a modeling process should be broken out as open, explicit steps, subject to management control.

In the end, of course, marketing is somewhat of a voodoo science, and no process can guarantee that you'll be able to predict the future with certainty, but visibility and participation certainly won't hurt. For instance, participation enhances the engineers' motivation and productivity, because they're not endlessly questioning whether the requirements make sense.

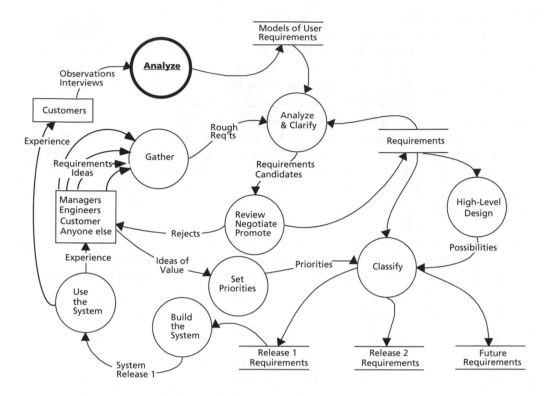

Figure 16-6.    When the number of customers is large, the process of modeling customer
                wishes should be broken out and placed under explicit management control.
                In this diagram, the processes that do that are lumped in the "Analyze" bubble.

## 16.5 Helpful Hints and Suggestions

1.  When reading *Volume 1*, Tom Watson of the Washington DPMA Study
    Group especially noted the principle that the first customers of a system
    aren't like the later ones, so the later customers' requirements are often a
    source of forgotten requirements.  He goes on to say,

    > This is particularly true when determining the requirements for a sys-
    > tem that has a geographically disparate user community.  For exam-
    > ple, when developing systems for national clients, the latest trends
    > suggest that we should employ the JAD methodology or develop pro-
    > totypes for selected subsets of the entire user community.  When used
    > incorrectly, these concepts generally promote essential requirements
    > definition errors that always result in severe design flaws.[5]

    If you use a requirements gathering exercise that is very responsive to the
    requirements of the people who happen to be in the room, you may
    become very *unresponsive* to people who don't happen to be in the room.

2.   One of the things that stands in the way of a quality requirements process is that people always think changes (repairs) cost too much. You think this when you take your car or your VCR in for repairs. Americans, at least, believe that quality things shouldn't need repairing, so that any repair is too expensive. And most of the expense is not the money but the annoyance of having to pay attention to it, to wait for it, and then not to get it exactly right. This hassle is what people are complaining about when they don't want to invest their time participating in a requirements process; they think you should *know* what they want changed, without being told. ("If you loved me, you'd *know* what I want without my having to tell you.") Therefore, when you start getting it right the first time, they'll be happy to participate. Of course, until they participate, you'll never get it exactly right.

3.   Payson Hall notes: Good requirements work at the outset also influences the quality of design. In theory, all designs are infinitely robust and extensible. In practice, when the initial requirements are well specified, potential changes in cost/benefit can be considered in the light of the architecture, which consequently is much more likely to be robust and extensible. Engineers would prefer to design a bridge to sustain the target load from the outset, rather than start with a rope footbridge and enhance it to support railroad traffic.

4.   Each requirement must be refined, but to how much detail? The answer depends on *risk* and *trust*. Just as in PLASTIC planning (**P**lan to the **L**evel of **A**cceptable **S**table **T**alent **I**n **C**ompleting Projects, Chapter 9), you refine requirements until they reach the level at which you trust that they can be implemented by the people who must implement them and tested by the people who must test them. This means that Anticipating (Pattern 4) organizations can get by with less requirements work, less filling in of details up front, because they know what they can trust and what they cannot.

## 16.6  Summary

✔   For many software organizations, an inadequate requirements process is the principal impediment to higher quality. To move such an organization to a controlled requirements process, managers need to plan and execute four major steps:

1.   Measure the true cost and value of requirements.

2.   Gain control of the requirements inputs.

3.   Gain control of the requirements outputs.

4.   Gain control of the requirements process itself.

✔ An improved requirements process pays for itself in a number of ways:

- faults caught early or not created at all
- redundant work eliminated
- better reception by customers
- faster, more manageable development
- improved maintenance

✔ Requirements come from many places, some of which are official, but many of which simply leak into the process. To gain control, management must create a process to

- identify and plug all leaks
- replace leaks with explicit negotiation

✔ When half of the requirements come from unofficial sources, you cannot possibly control software development. To gain control of this requirements chaos, you must

- recognize that requirements come from many sources
- accept these multiple interests as legitimate, but not necessarily guaranteed to have their way with the requirements
- create an explicit negotiation process that will consider anybody's requirements ideas
- survey the sources of all leaks and close them *tight* so they *must* come through a single channel

✔ Requirements conflicts happen, and if not resolved any other way, they are resolved by the customer. Such customer resolution is not the best way to resolve requirements conflicts, but is needed to back up the system when negotiations fail.

✔ To prevent leakage and convert it into an explicit requirements capture process, there must be a single path for a requirements idea to be converted to a requirement. Anyone with a requirements idea—managers, engineers, customers, or anyone else—must understand that there is no other path by which this *idea* has a chance of becoming a requirement.

✔ Proponents of requirements ideas must clearly understand that their submissions are simply *requirements ideas*, not requirements, until they pass through the process. Once requirements are gathered, they are considered *rough requirements* until they have passed through a smoothing process of analysis and clarification. If they pass this step, they are considered to be in reviewable condition, and are called *requirements candidates*. Only this review process can promote candidates into requirements that are placed in the database. Rejected ideas are turned back to their originators, who may then modify and resubmit them.

✔  The requirements database is used for building the system, and is also needed when new rough requirements are considered. That is because requirements must not only be clear and correct in themselves, but must be consistent with existing requirements.

✔  It isn't easy changing from the old backdoor way to this new process of explicit negotiation. You can be sure that more than one person will challenge the system and try to return to the Old Status Quo situation.

✔  A requirements document is much like a software product. Like software, it is an *information* product, so

- it must be made visible
- it must be made stable
- it must be made controllable

✔  A requirements document carries only a small part of the requirements communication load. In practice, most of the load is carried by

- individuals who understand the requirements and help other people understand
- teams that work effectively, so that they can communicate with one another about requirements

✔  To have the kind of understanding that keeps requirements simple, people must learn from participation in the requirements process. Participation alone won't be sufficient unless information is coordinated, open, available, and of known quality.

✔  If you have a full-time requirements manager with a staff of trained, committed people using appropriate tools and high-quality information, you can make the requirements task into a real project.

✔  The requirements process will also be better controlled if supported with appropriate tools, such as

- configuration control of all the relevant databases
- an active requirements database that allows all interested parties to examine any part of the current requirements at any time
- network access to the database, especially if it is seamless with other network use

- electronic mail and voice mail to support person-to-person communication
- special facilities for requirements meetings

✔ Management is ultimately responsible for defining what problems the organization is to solve internally, and for its customers. These managers must have the authority to establish and control the processes that make it possible for them to control this definition.

## 16.7 Practice

1. Explain why requirements control will be incomplete if test data and results are not part of configuration control.

2. James Robertson asks: What sort of people do you think should staff the requirements project team? What personality types? With what education? What job experience? What other attributes?

3. Each stage of the requirements process is a negotiation in which trade-offs have to be made. The requirements specialist needs tools to express these trade-offs. Learn and practice with each of the following trade-off curves:[6]

   - What's It Worth?: expected return versus functionality (quality)
   - What's the Chance?: probability of delivering sufficient quality versus targeted functionality
   - Expected Value: expected profit versus functionality

4. James Robertson notes: In Figure 16-5, the "Set Priorities" bubble is given without detail. Draw a context diagram for that bubble. Draw a data flow diagram of how that process ought to be done in your organization. Draw another diagram of how it is actually done.

5. James Robertson adds: In Figure 16-6, the "Analyze" bubble is given without detail. Draw a context diagram for that bubble, and then draw a data flow diagram of how that process ought to be done. Draw another diagram of how it is actually done in your organization.

# 17

# Starting Projects Correctly

*It was also becoming painfully evident that estimating the cost of technologically state-of-the-art projects was an inexact science. The experts, in spite of their mountains of numbers, seemingly used an approach descended from the technique widely used to weigh hogs in Texas. It is alleged that in this process, after catching the hog and tying it to one end of a teeter-totter arrangement, everyone searches for a stone which, when placed on the other end of the apparatus, exactly balances the weight of the hog. When such a stone is eventually found, everyone gathers around and tries to guess the weight of the stone. Such is the science of cost estimating.[1]*
— N.R. Augustine

I've studied dozens of unsuccessful projects, trying to find the earliest point at which failure could have been predicted and then prevented by management action. Most of these projects were under pressure from the moment they started—actually even *before* the moment that their process models said they started. Indeed, the primary reason for the pressure was that there were no explicit models of what happens before a project officially starts. By the time a project manager was put in charge, external decisions had put so many constraints on the project that failure was highly probable.

## 17.1 Project Prerequisites

Preceding every project is a series of high-level negotiations that lead to the decisions that constrain the project. If these negotiations are not both *informed* and *congruent*, the project is doomed before it starts.

When a project is in the fuzzy early stages, before official initiation, the first question is, of course, what *benefits* the organization expects from the successful completion of the project. This is the "What's it worth?" calculation.[2] Assuming that benefits have been projected correctly (which is frequently not the case, however), consider the next question, which is about risk.

### 17.1.1   Risk analysis

Infinite *potential* benefits will have zero value if the project isn't completed. When project benefits are large, however, it's difficult to make a congruent decision about risk. There are a number of relatively formal systems of risk analysis that can aid in making this decision, and any software engineering manager should be steeped in at least one.[3] Nevertheless, keep risk analysis as simple as possible, because complex processes

- are easy to rig in favor of any decision you ardently desire
- are costly, and your sunk cost may make you reluctant to kill a project that needs euthanasia

Boehm gives a checklist of the top ten risk factors in software, and I have found that an early, brief, and rough consideration of these ten factors generally improves the chances for project success by at least a factor of two:

1.  personnel shortfalls
2.  unrealistic schedules and budgets
3.  developing the wrong software functions
4.  developing the wrong user interface
5.  gold plating
6.  continuing stream of requirements changes
7.  shortfalls in externally furnished components
8.  shortfalls in externally performed tasks
9.  real-time performance shortfalls
10.  straining computer science capabilities

At the earliest stages, it's relatively easy to determine if several of these are potential problems and to take some action to diminish the risk. However, Boehm, like many other writers on risk analysis, never really discusses what is always the biggest risk of all: The management team isn't up to the job of performing a congruent risk analysis, let alone leading the project, as the following example illustrates.

### 17.1.2 *Congruence and risk analysis*

I had just helped a hardware company complete a successful rescue of Asteroid, a software project that had been labeled as "hopeless." The company was now proposing that I help apply the same planning methods to Comet, a project that had been bogged down for many months. While I was considering this proposal, I got the following note from Lex, the Comet project manager:

> Anyone using comparisons with Asteroid to show what plans can do to Comet is being deeply unjust. Asteroid secured some ten people from the start. Clear customer demands and agreements were defined, and these protected their goals. Technical issues were visible from the start, and quite modest in complexity and demands, well limited, and isolated. Quite a comfortable setup! I congratulated those who were assigned, because success was assured in advance. But Comet as a project is ridiculous!

Poor Lex! Like so many software managers who are unfamiliar with the role of tactical planning, he couldn't see the real message in his own note. Of course Comet was ridiculous, since it was without planning that would have

- noted the risks
- made plans to reduce these risks to an acceptable level

Two years earlier, at the start of its planning process, Asteroid had been in exactly the same state. The planning *process*, not the *plan*, was what transformed a ridiculous fantasy into a real project, whose "success was assured in advance." That's what tactical planning is all about.

Lex was operating from a placating position: He felt he had to conform to whatever fantasies upper management tossed in the hopper. He didn't see that the planning process was an opportunity to stop placating and uncover the real issues with the Comet fantasy. Not that I should have expected anything different: Lex had seen only one non-placating planning process, and that from the outside. Previously, "planning" in this company had meant hammering down anyone who raised issues of risk, until everyone was "committed" to the previously established "plan." Where blame is so intense and universal, placating will always flourish.

### 17.1.3 *Win/win negotiation*

For a project to succeed, these early negotiations must produce a congruent agreement—one that balances the Self, Other, and Context. Without that balance, the project will tear itself apart like a crooked wheel spinning at high velocity.

Many software organizations become so enmeshed with their customers that they can't negotiate well. Some are prevented from negotiating by general management. A bigger problem is that they don't know they are negotiating, or they think "negotiate" is a dirty word. Consequently, they negotiate implicitly and don't even like to call what they do "negotiating." If you don't negotiate explicitly, you won't negotiate well; you won't record your agreements; you won't honor your agreements; you won't know what your agreements are; and you often won't even be aware that you've even *made* agreements. How, then, can you measure the single most important measure of any development project: *Did we fulfill our agreement?*

One essential for making projects comparable is to be sure they start on the same basis, which implies that all negotiations must be done explicitly, must be done well, and must have the agreements recorded. Stephen Covey lists the following five elements for a win/win agreement:[4]

- *Desired results* (not methods) identify what is to be done, and when.
- *Guidelines* specify the parameters (principles, policies, and such) within which results are to be accomplished.
- *Resources* identify the human, financial, technical, or organizational support available to help accomplish the results.
- *Accountability* sets up the standards of performance and the time of evaluation.
- *Consequences* specify—good and bad, natural and logical—what does and will happen as a result of the evaluation.

The following sections examine each of these points in some detail to see why this is a good checklist for project or subproject prerequisites.

## 17.2  Desired Results

Consider two projects, A and B. They are as similar as two projects can be, each with requirements, resources, methods, tools, and schedule. Project A is completed on time, within budget. Project B runs 25 percent late and 30 percent over budget. What can we conclude about the way each project was managed?

We can, of course, make no conclusions at all unless we know how the two projects defined "completed." If their definitions were the same, we reach one conclusion. But what if Project A dropped a few requirements to meet the schedule? Does that matter? Only if their original agreement was clear on what had to be done, but in the end they didn't do it.

Judah Mogilensky describes how lack of clear initial agreement on results becomes locked into the customer/developer culture:

> The problem often lies in organizational fear of clarity. Documenting clear requirements would force the customer to accept responsibility for initiating changes if a system meeting the documented requirements does not meet the real needs. . . . Documenting clear requirements would force the developer to accept accountability for satisfying them, and could expose the developer to risk if the cost and schedule estimates turn out to be inaccurate.

Thus, even though they are operating from opposite motivations, customer and developer can covertly conspire together to keep the requirements management practices of the Capability Maturity Model from being carried out. Each side thinks they are operating to protect themselves, and strengthen their bargaining position, but in reality each side is setting themselves up for future disappointments and disputes.[5]

The culture creates this problem of such covert collusion to violate good requirements processes—it becomes a culture of fear. As such, the problem cannot be solved without changes at the top management level, a conclusion supported by numerous studies of project failures.[6]

### 17.2.1 Phrases to listen for

Here are some of the things you'll hear when fear creates a situation in which the interested parties will not negotiate cleanly on results:

- (Any of the phrases in Section 15.2.1 suggesting that fixed requirements don't matter, or that they are fixed when they are not.)
- I hope they won't hold us to the wall on that one.
- Well, I didn't understand it exactly, but what could I do but agree.
- I had no choice.
- You *will* do this. It's nonnegotiable. (Listen carefully: This may be coming out of *your* mouth.)
- If you were any good at this, you could do it. (Again, who's talking?)
- Schedule/resources will be really tight, but we can negotiate relief from requirements later. (Why not now?)

### 17.2.2 Actions to take

DO NOT allow design or construction to proceed without verified requirements, unless you have a staged process. In that case, DO NOT let any stage begin without verified requirements *for that stage*. DO NOT be sucked in by assurances that "prototyping is different." Prototyping is a staged process, and each stage needs to define its requirements, even though they are not requirements for the completed system.

As a final step in the negotiation process, DO hold a closing meeting with customers and developers to in effect sign their agreement. DO question all parties to the agreement to ascertain if there is true emotional sign-on. DO look for hesitations, reservations, or uncertainties, and DO NOT allow agreement to proceed unless and until these are cleared up.

DO establish policies that reward projects for truly satisfying customers, not beating them in some legalistic game.

DO establish policies that reward customers for cooperating in the effort to define what they want. The best reward is to show that you are listening to them, and not just rejecting their needs out of hand.

DO NOT browbeat, bribe, or manipulate your employees into "agreements" or "commitments" or "signing up."

### 17.3 Guidelines

The power of guidelines is the way they can remind us not to do foolish things when under pressure. For instance, though we know that time, resources, and function are sometimes interchangeable, they are not linearly interchangeable. In the heat of a project, we are likely to be tempted to make such interchanges and cause great trouble.

There are so many possible guidelines that we could not cover them all here,[7] so a few examples will have to suffice:

- *Brooks's Law:* Adding X percent to the staff will not generally speed the schedule by X percent.
- *The Square Law of Computation:* Adding X percent to the schedule will not accommodate X percent increase in functionality.
- *Jones's Law:* Those parts of the product that don't go through the entire development process will cause 90 percent of your problems.

Guidelines are a way to establish triggers while you are relatively sane, so they will keep you from doing foolish things when the project is driving you insane.

#### 17.3.1 Phrases to listen for

- We just want to make one simple change.
- I'll give you two new people so that you can take on that added function.
- We'll take out one function and add one function, so nothing is changed.
- We can save time for testing by cutting out reviews.
- We can save time for coding by cutting out design. We'll design as we code.
- We can save time for design by cutting down on the elaborate requirements process.

#### 17.3.2 Actions to take

DO NOT decree schedules. Schedules derived from plans should always be possible. Plans derived by working backward from schedules are often impossible, at least under the constraints given. If schedule is really a critical issue (rather than simply a way to show who's in charge), then plan in order to determine what you must spend to attain that schedule, and be prepared to spend a bundle or accept that some things simply cannot be done.

DO NOT put time pressure on projects that have reliability problems.

DO NOT add features to a project without renegotiating schedules.

DO NOT play games on blackboards or spreadsheets that cannot be supported by measurable facts.

DO learn to take no for an answer, if backed with facts. DO send naysayers back for facts when they come empty-handed.

DO insist on change control from the beginning, and DO NOT yield to temptations to shortcut it.

DO insist on configuration management from the beginning, and DO NOT yield to temptations to shortcut it.

DO get outside views from disinterested parties for reality checking.

## 17.4 Resources

All resources are not created equal. Human, financial, technical, or organizational resources each have their own algebra, so you cannot assume that each participant at the beginning of a project knows what the resource commitments mean.

For instance, it's easy to believe at a high level that people are interchangeable. They're not. One reason comes from the Satir Change Model: It takes time for one person to reach the level of the others. This is part of the explanation for Brooks's Law.

People are not divisible by ordinary arithmetic. Two half-time people are not the same as one full-time person.[8]

Time commitments have different meanings for different people. So does sharing any other scarce resource, such as hardware or network time.

It's easy to be ambiguous about technical qualifications. Are all C programmers created equal? Does one data administrator equal another?

Finally, money, as unambiguous as it seems, is a different resource when delivered today than when delivered next month.

### 17.4.1 Phrases to listen for

- We'll assign half (or any fraction) of a person to that.
- If we're running behind, we'll add people then, so we'll definitely meet the deadline.
- Don't worry. When the time comes, I'll give you two of my best people.
- We'll give you a replacement for X with the same background.
- You'll get the new hardware as soon as the budget is approved. Get started now so you'll have a head start, and you don't really require a machine to test anyway.
- He can absorb that into his other tasks.
- The people aren't available when it shows on the plan, but you can shuffle things around so you can use them when they are available.
- She knows Smalltalk. If not, she can learn on the job.

### 17.4.2 Actions to take

DO NOT split people's time.  DO get maximum productivity by giving every-one a single focus whenever possible (Figure 17-1).

Figure 17-1.    Do not split people's time.  One person doing four tasks is unproductive on all of them.

DO NOT add people late in a project, unless you extend the schedule at the same time.

DO create structures that allow people to control their environment, such as when to allow phone interruptions, what meetings to attend, how to create protected time, what hardware to use and how to use it, or how to arrange their space.

DO NOT borrow people or equipment across project lines.  If you must borrow (a specialist, for example), DO make explicit agreements with clear lim-its and consequences.

DO NOT accept budgets that do not have specific times when funds will be made available.

DO set policies that encourage people to stay, like guaranteed individual training budgets.  DO create an environment that makes staying a pleasure.

DO rotate jobs, so that more people are more interchangeable.  DO NOT wait until the end of long projects to do this, or you will find that key people have rotated themselves right out of the organization.  DO allow slack in your planning to accommodate the slight losses of such rotation—losses that are your insurance premium against much larger losses if you lose key people altogether.

DO invest in training, and follow up on training with both support and coaching.

DO set up independent projects with natural boundaries.

## 17.5 Accountability

The most common accountability fallacy in software projects is to mistake effort for results. Lacking any better measure, you employ a single standard of performance—the time put into the job, not the product produced. Aside from the unreasonable assumption that equal effort always produces equal results, there is the question of the accuracy of time reports.

Some time ago, I challenged the assumption that time reports were a reasonable basis for tracking project results. On a CompuServe forum, I posed two questions:

**Who has filled out time reports? Who has never faked them?**

The first result of this survey was that *everybody who reported* (twenty-three people) confessed that they had faked time reports. Nobody said "never." Faking time reports is part of the universal culture of software development. The only place developers don't fake time reports is in the places that don't *use* time reports.

Faking time reports is like rolling stops at stop signs—it's against the rules, everybody does it, and nobody talks about it. When anonymity is guaranteed, they do talk about it, and the results are illuminating. Here is a typical reply from a contractor who gets *paid* according to time reports:

> At many client sites, I ask them where they'd like to *see* my time reported and hand everything in a week early. That lets us concentrate on what they really want me to *do*, not what the artificial budget categories state.
>
> For instance, on most redevelopment projects, I spend *at least* 25 percent of every day informally educating and persuading the various leaders in an organization to come around to a reasonable position and help us. *That* never shows up on a time sheet or status report, but without it, nothing would happen.
>
> For two clients, the manager who hired me fills out the time sheets any way he wants. That lets me spend time on the project and lets him control his budget as he sees fit.

Obviously, there is no basis for using such "data" to account for what is happening in a project, let alone to estimate the next project. Yet another part of the culture is the recurrence of feeble attempts to make time reports realistic, as in this report:

> In my current project, we are trying to institute a system for reporting actual time spent for all projects; the assumption is that it is not possible to work the "mandatory" 37.50 hours a week. We are allowing an hour to an hour-and-a-half for "administrative" time; this includes project status meetings, coffee, talking with others in the hallway, etc. The aim is to get actual time spent on a project activity to check how good our estimates are without the fudge time to contend with.

Can anybody who has observed a real project believe that an hour-and-a-half for administrative time is realistic? Twenty or more hours would be more realistic, but this system will allow only an hour-and-a-half. If you have more than that, you'll be forced to fake it.

Another important part of accountability is the time at which evaluations take place. Here's another response to my survey:

> One of my big gripes is that many companies (including my wife's) require the time sheet to be submitted before the reporting period is over. When a client asks me to do this, I refuse. Instead I offer to fax them a copy immediately after the end of the period.

This is a noble and ethical stand, but when managers don't have the time sheets, *they* fake them. Their reports have to get out on time, though any rational person reading them could figure out that given the lead times, they can't possibly reflect actual hours worked.

### 17.5.1 Phrases to listen for

- We've made good progress. We put in 70 extra hours this week.
- We'll adjust the figures next month, when we have the actual data. (Whenever you hear "actual" data, get suspicious. What other kind is there?)
- The billing data show that we're 97 percent complete.
- It's not possible to create an acceptance test that really shows anything.
- I've talked to that programmer, and he assures me that he'll make up the deficit in hours next week.
- The hours have to match the plan. (Are you the one saying this?)
- We'll make up some acceptance tests when the product is finished.
- This guy is three times as productive as an ordinary programmer, so we schedule him for 120 hours a week, though he actually works only 40.

### 17.5.2 Actions to take

DO NOT use time reporting for project tracking; you are only measuring input, not output. DO measure results rather than effort. If you use time reporting for other purposes, such as billing or estimating future projects, DO NOT encourage people to lie.

DO insist that every task has an operationalized test that determines whether or not it is finished. DO be sure that time and resources consumed by this test are part of the plan from the outset. DO include a test review to be sure the test was performed as promised, with the promised results, so you're sure the task is finished and documented.

DO commission a separate group responsible for creating and managing acceptance tests. DO have this group report *above* the development manager.

DO see that planning is done in task units small enough to give control, and small enough to be thrown away if they don't work according to plan.

## 17.6 Consequences

Many in-house negotiations at the start of a project are like negotiations between King Kong and Mickey Mouse. The consequences of opposing King Kong (upper management) are so clear and so threatening that they trivialize any consequences for failing to fulfill the agreement. In these situations, Mickey Mouse (the project personnel) "agrees" to everything while simultaneously looking for ways to escape.

The same King Kong/Mickey Mouse dynamic reappears every time management swoops down to take a look at "progress." Managers seem fond of practicing management reviews at intervals during a project, but this practice is a holdover from cultures in which project completion was always problematic.[9] In those situations, the managers had to protect themselves against the consequences of a highly likely failure, so they would conduct a "review"—a ceremonial gathering of all project personnel who stand in front of management, stammer out a report supported by a stack of bogus transparencies, and then submit to a series of dominance displays by management (Figure 17-2).

Management reviews are popular in blaming cultures as a way of punishing any project that fails to provide management with a series of glowing reports. Wherever management reviews are practiced, they should definitely be part of the project plan's schedule, not an unscheduled consequence of unsatisfactory reporting. Otherwise, they merely encourage false reporting, a key indicator of project failure:

> In all cases, the project is running two sets of plans—the plans that the project sponsor and stakeholders are given and the plan that the team is actually following (covertly). We observed this pattern of failure in every one of the twenty major failed projects we reviewed.[10]

A three-day circus parade of project "progress" violates the basic principles of cybernetic management: Act early, act small, using more-or-less continuous feedback. A key question to ask about any kind of project review is

### What are the possible outcomes?

In most of these large reviews, there is *no* possibility that the project could be canceled, no matter how bad the material, because of how much has been invested already. Moreover, there is essentially no chance that *any* major change could be made. The chunk of work is too big.

In blaming cultures, a much more certain outcome is that lots of annoying nits from the managers will be passed down to the workers (to show that the managers are still in charge, and that they still "understand" these technical issues). These nits will almost certainly delay the project for more than the three days that the extravaganza has taken to present and the two weeks it has taken to prepare.

Figure 17-2.          For a typical management review, programmers put on ties and tell the lies their managers want their managers to hear.

If people would admit that these reviews are educational, then they would find a more efficient way to educate the management. Rich Cohen suggests a wonderful question to ask when someone proposes one of these management reviews:

**How come they don't already know what's going on?**[11]

Perhaps they could stay in contact with the project as it goes along. Now *that* would be educational.

### 17.6.1 Phrases to listen for

- You *will* be ready for this review. (Possibly out of *your* mouth.)
- (In a review) That's not how we used to do it in the good old days when we coded in binary.

- (In a review) Let me show you how that *should* have been done.
- (In a review) Okay, if you're not getting it done, what do you need? I don't want anyone to leave this review without full *commitment*. (Possibly out of *your* mouth.)
- Don't bother me with that now. Bring it up in next month's review.
- I don't want to hear any bad news out of that review, so be sure everything is prepared.
- I've invited our customer to the review, so be sure to put on a good show.

### 17.6.2 Actions to take

DO NOT use wholesale management reviews. DO establish more-or-less continuous monitoring for exception conditions. For example, DO use a Public Project Progress Poster to keep things from hiding under a rock.[12]

When an exception occurs, DO NOT call the entire project under review. DO focus on the areas that may need your assistance.

DO NOT look upon a management review as an opportunity to find blame and punish. DO NOT look upon a management review as an opportunity to slip back into the technical work you should have given up long ago and/or as a way of asserting your dominance. DO look upon a review as an opportunity to discover what kind of assistance staff members need that they can only obtain from management.

DO NOT conduct staged marketing events and call them "reviews."

DO be open and honest in communication with senior management. DO keep them educated and up-to-date.

### 17.6.3 The Hudson's Bay Start

There are many other ways to get information for managing projects than by conducting traditional management reviews. The Hudson's Bay Company, an eighteenth-century fur trader, displayed one of the most effective types of small, relevant, timely review, what Robert Fulghum calls a Hudson's Bay Start:

> Trading journeys were habitually begun with vigorous enthusiasm, yet the frontiersmen always camped the first night a few short miles from the company headquarters. This allowed the gear and supplies to be sorted and considered, so that if anything had been left behind in the haste to be under way, it was easy to return to the post to fetch it.[13]

I teach project managers to make a Hudson's Bay Start for their projects, especially if they are trying something new, such as a new methodology or CASE tools. I typically have a one-hour start, then a one-day start, and, for a big project, a one-week start. These are simulated projects (perhaps some small piece of the real project, but not necessarily) that allow the project team to run through the entire process not far from "company headquarters."

### 17.7  Helpful Hints and Suggestions

1.  A January 1993 U.S. Government Auditing Office report showed that
    trouble in project estimation and management is not confined to
    software.[14] In a fifteen-year period, NASA conducted twenty-nine major
    programs (some of which did involve software). Twenty-two of those
    twenty-nine exceeded NASA's cost projections, and the median excess
    cost was 77 percent of the original estimates. If my own experience with
    NASA is any guide, many of the contractors knew better before the pro-
    ject started, but knuckled under to NASA pressure, or pressure to get the
    contract, knowing that nothing would be done about it if they ran over.
    This report demonstrates that much of what passes as a software crisis
    has nothing to do with software, and everything to do with human
    behavior.

2.  Eileen Strider notes: Because they are paid explicitly based on a legal con-
    tract, software contracting firms often know more about negotiating tech-
    nical contracts than their customers. This knowledge gives them a great
    advantage over in-house software organizations that refuse to acknowl-
    edge that they are negotiating, let alone that they are being paid for per-
    formance. However, some of these firms either don't know or use what
    they know to play on a customer's ignorance or good faith, especially
    when they are dealing with customers from the business area. Therefore,
    to protect their business customers in outsourcing situations, in-house IS
    managers need to improve their negotiating skills, starting with bringing
    them to a more conscious level.

3.  Software work has a lot in common with fine cabinetmaking, which has a
    longer history than software work. You might want to consider the wis-
    dom of *The Cabinetmaking Rule of Two:*

    **When estimating your labor for a cabinetmaking job, compute the
    time it would take if everything went perfectly and multiply it by
    two.**[15]

    Is your estimating of projects consistently off by large factors? If so, ask
    yourself if it's because you typically believe, hope, or pray that this time
    everything will go perfectly. If so, try facing the real risks, making
    allowance for them (the factor of two), and planning to abate them.

4.  Payson Hall suggests: Note well that *The Cabinetmaking Rule of Two* is *not*
    the same as the common *The Software Rule of Two:*

    **When estimating your labor for a software job, make your best guess
    and multiply it by two.**

The key difference is between "compute the time it would take if every-thing went perfectly" and "make your best guess." The factor of two in cabinetmaking is what experience says you have to pay for things that don't go perfectly. The factor of two in software guesstimating is padding because the guesstimator doesn't have measurable experiences and doesn't understand the trade-offs. The basis of the cabinetmaking estimate is visible and reviewable, and therefore the figures are credible. The basis of the software guesstimate is invisible and not reviewable, and therefore the figures are unbelievable.

5. If you're tempted to schedule lots of overtime to meet an ambitious schedule, be sure to consider the evidence regarding the effect of overtime on productivity: After working eight hours per day or forty-eight hours per six-day week, a person must work about three overtime hours to produce two standard hour's worth of results. For heavy work, count on two hours' time for each hour's worth of output.[16]

6. Planning is always an exercise in trust. My colleague Mark Manduke gives the following good example for managers to follow:

> When I was supervising an eight-person software department for a small telecommunications firm, I would solicit estimates from the staff to complete assignments in accordance with our standards of quality and assuming a forty-hour work week. We would negotiate among ourselves but always arrive at mutually comfortable estimates.
> I provided two guarantees:
>
> 1. I would convince management and marketing that our estimates were reasonable to get the job done right.
>
> 2. Once the work was agreed to by the organization, no one, absolutely NO ONE (not even the CEO), would be allowed to coerce them into changing the schedule, or the requirements (without a renegotiated schedule).
>
> It was my responsibility to fight and win those battles. In return, if we couldn't meet our own estimates, we all worked unlimited free overtime until the commitments were met. I had so much loyalty that we were almost a union shop.[17]

Notice the congruence, taking into account the self, the team, the others outside the team, and the business context. The approach depends on a willingness to take the consequences of your own mistakes, but not the mistakes of others without renegotiating. It is open and honest.

7. On international or otherwise dispersed projects, the very first step is to get people together in a way that builds trust, because trust lessens the

subsequent need for communication. Such projects only highlight this need for communication, which, because of the distance, is costly and slow. Local projects have the same need, but it's not so obvious—until it's too late.

## 17.8  Summary

✔ Most unsuccessful projects were under pressure from the moment they started, actually even *before* the moment that their process models said they started. Indeed, the primary reason for the pressure was that there were no explicit models of what happens before a project officially starts.

✔ Preceding every project is a series of high-level negotiations that lead to the decisions that constrain the project. If these negotiations are not both *informed* and *congruent,* the project is finished before it starts.

✔ When a project is in the fuzzy early stages, before official initiation, the first question is, of course, what *benefits* the organization expects from the successful completion of the project. But infinite *potential* benefits will have zero value if the project isn't completed.

✔ When project benefits are large, it's difficult to make a congruent decision about risk. There are a number of relatively formal systems of risk analysis that can aid in making this decision, and any software engineering manager should be steeped in at least one.

✔ Rough consideration of Boehm's ten factors generally improves the chances for project success by at least a factor of two:

1. personnel shortfalls
2. unrealistic schedules and budgets
3. developing the wrong software functions
4. developing the wrong user interface
5. gold plating
6. continuing stream of requirements changes
7. shortfalls in externally furnished components
8. shortfalls in externally performed tasks
9. real-time performance shortfalls
10. straining computer science capabilities

✔ The biggest risk of all is that the management team isn't up to the job of performing a congruent risk analysis, let alone leading the project. The planning *process*, not the *plan*, is what transforms ridiculous fantasies into real projects.

✔ For a project to succeed, these early negotiations must produce a congruent agreement, one that balances the Self, Other, and Context. The single most important measure of any development project is, *Did we fulfill our agreement?* If you negotiate well, you'll be able to use this measure. If not, your project will probably fail.

✔ One essential for making projects comparable is to be sure they start on the same basis, which implies that all negotiations must be done explicitly, done well, and the agreements recorded, including

  • *Desired results* (not methods) identify what is to be done, and when.
  • *Guidelines* specify the parameters (principles, policies, and such) within which results are to be accomplished.
  • *Resources* identify the human, financial, technical, or organizational support available to help accomplish the results.
  • *Accountability* sets up the standards of performance and the time of evaluation.
  • *Consequences* specify—good and bad, natural and logical—what does and will happen as a result of the evaluation.

✔ A culture of fear creates covert collusion to violate good requirements processes. As such, the problem cannot be solved without top management change.

✔ Guidelines specify the principles and policies within which results are to be accomplished. Guidelines are a way to establish triggers while you are relatively sane, so they will keep you from doing foolish things when the project is driving you insane. Here are a few examples of guidelines:

  • Brooks's Law: Adding X percent to the staff will not generally speed the schedule by X percent.
  • The Square Law of Computation: Adding X percent to the schedule will not accommodate X percent increase in functionality.
  • Jones's Law: Those parts of the product that don't go through the entire development process will cause 90 percent of your problems.

✔ All resources are not created equal. Human, financial, technical, or organizational resources each have their own algebra, so you cannot assume that each party to the beginning of a project knows what the resource commitments mean.

✔   The most common accountability fallacy in software projects is to mistake effort for results. Lacking any better measure, you have a single standard of performance—the time put into the job, not the product produced.

✔   Another important part of accountability is the time at which evaluations take place. Reporting deadlines and delays often ensure that all reports will be works of fiction.

✔   When negotiations at the start of a project are made in an atmosphere of fear and intimidation, the project personnel will agree to everything while simultaneously looking for ways to escape. The same dynamic reappears every time management swoops down to take a look at progress.

✔   Management reviews are also popular in blaming cultures as a way of punishing any project that fails to provide management with a series of glowing reports. A three-day circus parade of project progress violates the basic principles of cybernetic management: Act early, act small, using more-or-less continuous feedback.

✔   In most of these large reviews, there is *no* possibility that the project could be canceled, no matter how bad the material, because of how much has been invested already. Moreover, there is essentially no chance that *any* major change could be made. The chunk of work is too big.

✔   There are many other ways to get information for managing projects than by conducting traditional management reviews. The Hudson's Bay Start (or shake-down cruise) is one of the most effective types of small, relevant, timely review.

### 17.9  Practice

1.   What parts of your project do you know are not being reported truthfully? What part of your culture prevents you or your employees from reporting them truthfully? What prevents you from discussing this subject with other members of the project?

2.   Discuss how each of the principles and tips in this chapter apply to organizational change projects as well as product development projects.

3.   Phil Fuhrer suggests: Suppose it is the practice in an organization for the managers to tell people, "I know that you are better than you think you are; therefore, I decrease your schedule and raise commitments and I stretch your goals to lead you by challenge." Under what conditions will this approach achieve its stated goals? Under what conditions will it create an environment for mistrust, skewed estimates, and inaccurate progress reporting?

# 18

# Sustaining Projects Correctly

*A plan is valid until the opponents make their first move.*
— Chess saying/Military saying

The plan you make at the beginning of a project says, "*If* we can do these things, I will get the result I now want." It *doesn't* say, "No other way will get it." It *doesn't* say, "I won't change my mind about what I want." And it *doesn't* say, "All of my assumptions about the world are valid."

Somehow, the all-too-human wish is that the plan says, "I *can* do these things, so I *will* get the result I want. And I *won't* change my mind about what I want, so I don't *need* another way to get it. And all of my assumptions are valid now and forevermore (or, I'm not making any assumptions!), so I can't be wrong, or become wrong."

Of course, you can *wish* for any sort of world you want, but this particular world doesn't run that way. When you let your wishes overrun your sense of reality, you make trouble, both for yourself and for others. In the software engineering management business, this trouble arrives in the form of idealistic models of software development that you translate into "methodologies."

315

Then you translate these methodologies into inflexible, unreasonable plans that you try to impose on your organization.

True, to create an Anticipating (Pattern 4) organization, you need models of software processes. After all, "model" is just another name for a guide to anticipating the future. To guide real projects, however, you need something that's less of a fantasy, and more of a reality.

To become an Anticipating manager, you also need to anticipate that nobody can anticipate everything. Therefore, you need to examine some of the common process models from a more practical point of view. As we've seen earlier, if you don't have a religious need to choose just one model, you can examine various models to determine under which conditions each is applicable. Then, of course, you need to know how to choose the model each situation demands.

### 18.1  The Waterfall Model

Each process and subprocess of building something can be represented as a standard task unit, with a beginning, middle, and end. This chapter will concentrate on the middle, for that seems to be where most of the process theorists concentrate. What they usually omit are the beginning (Chapter 17) and the ending (Chapter 19).

Let's start with the Waterfall Model, because it underlies all other development process models.[1]  Figure 18-1 shows a generalized Waterfall Model. The essence of all Waterfall Models is that one thing happens after another— that water doesn't run uphill. When one stage is finished, it's finished, and there's no going back. An analogy to the Waterfall Model is wood carving or sculpting out of stone. If you make even one mistake, the wood or stone is ruined, and you have to accept a less-than-perfect product or else start over again.

The output of each stage of the waterfall defines what the next stage has to do, each being a further translation of the original desires. If there's been nothing lost or added in translation, the final output is what was desired.

The Waterfall Model has come under attack as an unrealistic picture of software development. This is unfair and unfortunate, because this model occupies a very special place in the software engineering manager's tool kit of processes. It is the simplest class of processes, and to use anything else is to add complication. Therefore,

**Always use the Waterfall Model *when it applies.***

For instance, Cleanroom technology is an instance of a Waterfall Model.[2]  Each step is done once, and done exactly right, in the right order, using mathematical validation techniques, so there is no illusion of going backward. When you can successfully do Cleanroom development, it's clearly the best way you can proceed.

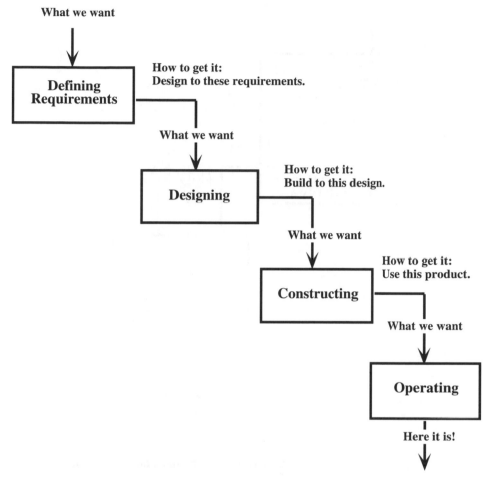

Figure 18-1.       The Waterfall Model suggests that one thing happens after another.

## 18.2 The Cascade Model

The Cascade Model is a collection of waterfalls, one after the other, or at times one beside another. For example, if you are converting a system to a new interface, using new hardware, you should attempt to use the cascade process shown in Figure 18-2. First, you convert the old application to the new hardware without changing *anything* about the interface; this is a pure conversion. Then, you change the interface to the new interface; this is a redesign.

Cascading is effective because of the Square Law of Computation. Decomposing one large problem into two smaller problems may be half the difficulty and also less risky. If you carve a statue in two parts—say, a head and a body—ruining one doesn't destroy the work on the other. DO watch for opportunities to convert large projects into cascades of smaller projects. DO NOT forget, however, that there is *always* an integration cost to cascading.

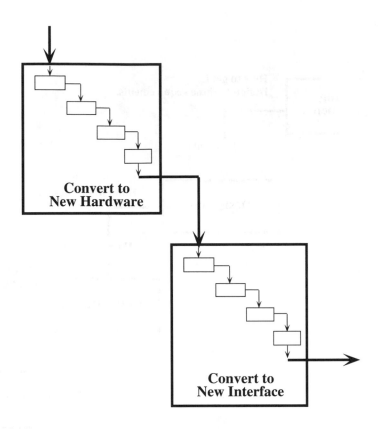

Figure 18-2.      A cascade process for obtaining a new interface on new hardware.

Many cascades are composed of parallel waterfalls. Parallel cascades are so often used to speed the building process it's easy to forget that's why we're using them. If time is of little importance, DO consider using a sequential cascade, so all the work can be done with one team and integration costs can thus be reduced. DO NOT forget to factor in the gain from lessons learned that can be applied to subsequent steps in the sequence.

Parallel cascades can also be used to reduce risk by setting up two or more waterfalls to build the same project. The best (or quickest) result can be chosen as the product, and/or the multiple products can be used as reference tests for each other. DO NOT, however, forget to consider integration risk. DO consider how you're going to handle the "losers" in this parallel race.

The popular Spiral Model is a type of cascade,[3] but drawn in a spiral to show cumulative cost (by distance from the center) and progress on each cycle (by angular displacement). Adding these extra measures is a clever bit of visual modeling, and is handy for some purposes. Perhaps the strongest feature of the Spiral Model is the way it emphasizes that development (or maintenance, for that matter) is a series of cycles, each consisting of the same kinds of processes, with the risk at each level growing successively smaller.

The Spiral Model, however, is actually more of a process *vision*, and may mislead the people who are actually carrying out the process. DO NOT forget that the Spiral Model tries to cram so much into one representation that it may not be an effective guide to implementation. DO remember that the Spiral Model relies heavily on risk management to move both developers and customers through the cycles of the spiral, so DO NOT blindly move from one cycle to the next without repeating your risk assessment and seeing reduced risk.

## 18.3 Iterative Enhancement

Iterative enhancement is software development based on an existing piece of software as a base.[4] Figure 18-3 shows two varieties of iterative enhancement, both based on the structure of the product itself. DO consider using the first case ("Change Requirements") when the requirements have changed little enough that much of the original system can be preserved.

In the second case ("Keep Requirements"), the functional requirements are preserved, but the design may change. DO consider this process to address performance problems (internal design changes) or usability problems (interface design changes). DO consider it for porting a system from one machine to another, but don't be slavish about it if the new hardware is grossly different from the old.

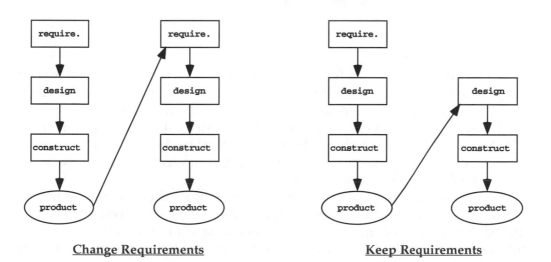

**Change Requirements**                    **Keep Requirements**

Figure 18-3.       Iterative enhancement is software development based on an existing piece of software as a base.

Figure 18-4 shows a third case: The design is preserved, but the code may change. DO consider this type of iterative enhancement to improve the maintainability of the product, so that other forms of enhancement become easier. DO NOT consider tuning performance in this way until you have found out whether or not the design is inefficient, probably through a design review. DO consider this approach for conversion to a new hardware platform, a new operating system, a new programming language, or all three.

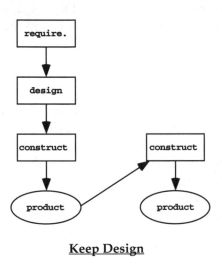

**Keep Design**

Figure 18-4.     Another form of iterative enhancement uses the same requirements and design, but changes the code.

## 18.4 Reusable Code

Iterative enhancement is a form of reuse. We may reuse requirements or design or parts of code, but some code is always changed. One of the great dreams of software development has been to reuse the code itself.

Reusable code is a great idea. Like all great ideas, it must be managed. In order for you to reuse something effectively, it must be designed for reuse, documented, cataloged, protected, disseminated, and motivated (not discouraged, as by rewarding for new code written).

Moreover, the effectiveness of the reuse strategy depends totally on the culture. If 65 percent of your development labor comes from coding and testing, then reusable code may seem like a good idea. But, if most of that 65 percent is spent fixing faults (that is, actually fixing faults *in requirements*), then reusable code will be of little value—unless you force requirements on the user according to what your reusable code does. This is an excellent example of how management can make a difference in the software process, using correct models and meaningful measurements, rather than blindly relying on the latest buzzword.

Another way to look at reuse in software development is to consider what is actually the most common method today of obtaining software: the off-the-shelf method (Figure 18-5). This is the method we use when we buy a software application. Someone else did the development, so we simply need to apply it to our needs. As more and more software is reused in this way, the software engineering organization becomes less and less of a development organization and more and more of a requirements gathering, purchasing, training, and service organization. DO be vigilant, however, so your organization does not become the first-line diagnoser of problems from careless vendors. DO NOT say you are *just* buying software, lest you forget that shopping is just as much an art as engineering.

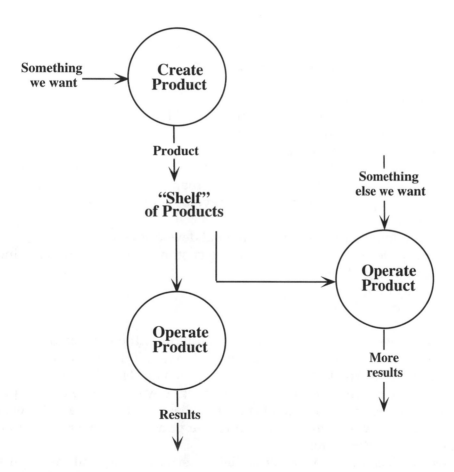

Figure 18-5.    The most common method today of obtaining software is the off-the-shelf method, using the same software for more and more situations.

It's not only purchased software that gets reused in this way. People frequently bypass all the early stages of software development and use their existing software in some new way. Some software is designed to encourage this kind of reuse, but some is not. Users don't seem to care one way or the other, because they just reuse the software with which they're most familiar. They write letters with their spreadsheet program, or use the accounts receivable program as a desk calculator.

DO NOT forget that this kind of reuse is mostly luck, and can be inefficient unless you plan and budget for it in your original design. If you didn't plan for reuse originally, you can avoid inefficiency by later budgeting extra effort on an iterative enhancement to convert a single-use program into a multiple-use product. DO estimate that this will at least triple the original cost of the program, which is a rule of thumb from my experience and that of other consultants. DO NOT forget that support will become more complex and expensive.

### 18.5 Prototyping

Prototyping is many things under a single term:

- a process to get requirements
- a process to get *something* working quickly, perhaps to
  — relieve pressure from customers or management
  — get a feel for a system
  — simulate system performance early in the development cycle
- a way to start writing code early, perhaps to smooth the workload, or perhaps just to do something developers like better than requirements work
- a disciplined process of incremental development
- a way to reduce management or customer pressure by creating a convincing illusion of progress
- a way to prove a concept
- a synonym for hacking

Figure 18-6 shows the general form for prototyping, the essence of which is "build-a-little, learn-a-little, build-some-more." We call this hacking when the amount built and learned at each stage is very small. Hacking need not be a bad process, and indeed may be the only effective way to solve certain problems. For example, one of my clients routinely has to hack software drivers for hardware devices whose manufacturers have gone out of business without leaving interface specifications.

When the increments are intermediate in size, we may call the approach "rapid prototyping," though calling it that doesn't make it rapid. Without discipline, the only thing rapid about prototyping is the rate at which it degenerates into a meandering kind of hacking, which I call "vapid prototyping."

As with iterative development, DO NOT draw the prototyping method as a loop; each stage is a different process, with different requirements and resources. DO estimate progress at each stage and use these estimates to validate assumptions and plan the number of stages. DO measure progress and replan the number of stages if assumptions change or measurements do not match the plan. DO NOT embark on this approach if either you or your customer are not willing to make your customer an integral part of the process. DO expect tremendous improvement in satisfaction if you do keep your customer involved.

Contrary to some popular impressions, there is no necessary connection between prototyping and object-oriented approaches. You can prototype with or without an object-oriented approach, and you can use an object-oriented approach with any sensible development process, and even with nonsensical ones.

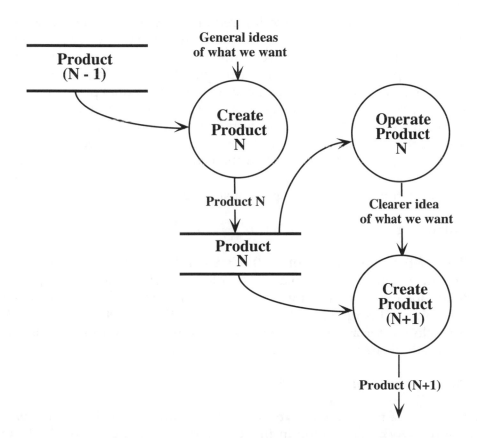

Figure 18-6.    Prototyping is a method that uses early versions of software to simulate the ultimate version in order to get feedback of information needed to complete the software. It differs from simple cascading, where we (ought to) have a clear idea of what we want before we start.

Top-down development (as opposed to top-down *design*) is one way of proto-typing. First, you build a skeleton embodying the general structure of the application. This is a working program, with "stubs" to replace unbuilt mod-ules. The stubs are simple pieces of code that match the specified interfaces, but may not do much else. As development progresses, you fill in the details by replacing the stubs with code that more and more closely resembles the desired finished product. Unlike top-down design, you don't know (or at least don't have to know) the detailed requirements when you start the process.

DO choose top-down development when the high-level requirements are well understood. DO choose top-down development when you want the over-all design of the application to be clean and stable over a long period of time. DO try to implement the stubs in the order of highest priority, because many top-down developments wind up delivering a partly finished product, and may never replace some of the last stubs. DO use top-down development when you are trying to deliver as much function as possible on an ambitious schedule.

DO NOT imagine that prototyping requires less management discipline than other forms of development; to be successful, it actually requires more. DO be aware that prototypes can raise customer expectations out of proportion to developer capabilities, because the first part looks so simple. DO NOT extrapolate linearly from early appearances to delivery of final product.

DO use prototyping on *parts* of a system where requirements are unknown or uncertain. DO plan carefully which customers will be involved giving feedback on the prototype, and how they will be involved. DO make regular assessments to determine when the prototyping has discovered those requirements you set out to find. DO set a time limit, after which a project review is mandatory and replanning is considered.

## 18.6 Replanning

Regardless of the combination of methods used, they are merely *templates* to guide you in making a project plan. The plan will elaborate the template in more detail, ideally decomposing everything to a connected network of stan-dard task units.[5] This plan then becomes the map the project is to follow. But after you follow it for a while, something happens that you didn't anticipate. What do you do then?

### 18.6.1 New information

In the middle of a project, when you reach an unanticipated situation, there is already some work done, some in process, and some planned for the future (Figure 18-7). If you have been paying attention, there is always more *informa-tion* than there was at the beginning.

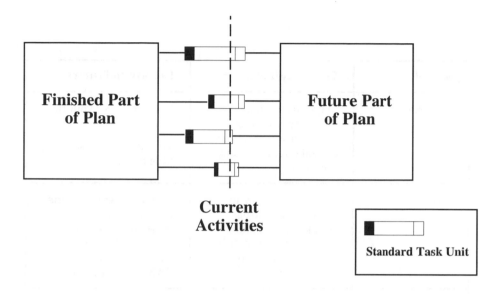

Figure 18-7.    In the middle of a project, some work is already done, some is in process, and some is simply planned for the future.

From your experience in the ongoing project, you have information about

- the quality of the work so far, which can be used to revise your predictions about future quality
- the productivity of your organization, which can be used to revise your predictions about future schedules and resource consumption
- the customer's requirements, which can be used to revise the scope of work
- which of your assumptions proved correct, and which assumptions you never noticed before
- how well the original plans have worked out, which can be used, along with all the other information, to create new plans for the unfinished part of the work

How do you know when to switch development models? Wayne Bailey suggests that each model represents a different level of capability and awareness of that capability, but the models could also describe different levels of wishful thinking, as shown in Figure 18-8. The Capability/Belief column shows the mental model that leads to the choice of a particular development model. The Fantasy Indicators are signs that you've made a choice that's no longer appropriate, and that it's time to go back to square one and reconsider.

| Model | Capability/Belief | Fantasy Indicators |
|---|---|---|
| Waterfall | I've seen and done this problem so many times that I know just what to do without making any mistakes. | You encounter your first serious mistake.<br><br>You encounter a series of little mistakes. |
| Cascade | I don't know how to solve this in one big chunk, but I do know how to solve it with $N$ "independent" chunks without error. | You discover two of the chunks aren't as independent as you thought. One of the chunks gets in "Waterfall" trouble. |
| Iterative Enhancement | I know enough to get started, and I know where I want to go. I just don't know exactly how to get there. So I do a little, see where I am, and adjust my course as I go. | Your destination changes.<br><br>You discover that one of your little chunks isn't turning out to be so little.<br><br>You've made more iterations than you predicted. |
| Prototyping (Requirements) | I know enough to get started, but I don't know exactly where I want to go. So I'll do a little, show it to my customer, and adjust my destination before I do more. | The product is diverging, growing larger with no sign of containment.<br><br>You discover that one of your little chunks isn't turning out to be so little.<br><br>You lose customer involvement. |

Figure 18-8.        Development models can represent different levels of capability and awareness, or they can represent different levels of wishful thinking.

## 18.6.2 Slack

Planning, of course, takes time and resources, so even though you get new
information every day, you don't want to make major revisions to your plan

every day. *Slack* allows you to keep replanning to a minimum. DO NOT consider "slack" a naughty word. If necessary, DO use a euphemism, such as "contingency buffers." However, if your organization understands the importance of slack, you will not need to use euphemisms.

Of course, the better your estimating, the less slack you'll need, but you can never anticipate the future perfectly. Slack can take the form of resources, time, and quality (requirements). Much of the manager's job in the middle of a project is trading one kind of slack for another, to deal with contingencies.

For example, if the project is going slower than planned, you can (with certain limitations) move slack people and/or equipment into tasks on the critical path. Or, you can relax or postpone some requirement to gain back lost time. But without slack, you have no choices and no way to get the project back on track. You have to make trade-offs all along the way and take time to make conscious choices, time that may offset the time saved by the trade-offs. Paradoxically, people abhor slack because they think it wastes time, but most projects will go faster if you allow slack.

Slack is the principal method for coping with project risks. Anticipating project managers forge all three types of slack in their plans; the amount depends on the amount of uncertainty about the future. DO NOT badger your project managers to "squeeze out the fat." DO ask them to do a risk assessment as part of their planning to determine the appropriate amount of slack. DO adjust the slack as you get new information about the project and adjust the plans.

DO NOT bury your slack in padded estimates. One padded estimate will undermine the credibility of an entire plan. DO identify slack explicitly, and DO NOT punish this practice by stealing explicit slack from the honest managers.

### 18.6.3 Mixing methodologies

As an example of using slack and mixing methodologies, consider the process of risk-based requirements management. The process starts with the question, "Which requirement presents the biggest risk?" Once that requirement is identified, the process does what is necessary to reduce that risk. Often, that means designing—or even coding—part of the system to see if it's feasible to meet the requirement. Here's an example from a financial institution that used slack in the form of a coder during the requirements phase of a Waterfall development:

> We were developing a system to run on smaller hardware in 355 branch offices. Our biggest risk was that we didn't think we could code the central loop so that it ran fast enough on this tiny hardware. For protection, I had our best coding genius code it before we got any further into the development. He found out that we needed faster CPUs. This break from our normal development cycle saved us getting 355 CPUs that we couldn't use.

Here's another example, mixing incremental development and hacking:

> Don't tell my vice president we did this, because he's on this big kick about having a "disciplined" development process. We were porting one of our products to a new operating system. In order to be ready as fast as possible, we were using a beta-test version of the operating system, and that was giving us a lot of trouble. We would report problems to the OS vendor, but their typical turnaround was two to three weeks. I set up a special team composed of two guys who weren't accepting this "disciplined" approach, but were really good hackers. Their job was to try to hack the operating system to unblock anything that was holding us up—and to do it faster than the vendor's turnaround. Without them, we would never have made the schedule this same "disciplined" vice president imposed on us.

One moral is clear: "Disciplined" doesn't mean "pig-headed." This manager traded some personnel slack for schedule time he didn't have, just as the previous one had traded for reduced financial risk. To do this, both had to deviate from a pure methodological approach, as does any manager who needs to meet objectives consistently. DO NOT be a methodology bigot. DO be a thinker.

Sometimes, you will have to operate a project with less slack than appears prudent. DO NOT forget that doing so increases the chance of total project failure. DO weigh the cost of slack and the risk of failure against the value of completing the project as planned.

## 18.7  Helpful Hints and Suggestions

1.  For those who dream the dream of reuse, consider this message from a friend who was the adult supervisor of some kids who competed in an annual event called "The Supercomputer Challenge."

    > My teams did well this year. Both teams were finalists, and one got several awards. I learned later, quite unofficially, that they were downgraded because they had modified a program they had acquired from a researcher (instead of writing one from scratch).

    Evidently, the adult judges were making sure their own prejudices against reuse would be passed on to the next generation. Don't underestimate the power of the idea that reuse of other people's work is cheating.

    Still, if we can miseducate, there's hope we can educate. Jim Highsmith responded to this story:

    > I knew a professor who went the other way. He gave the students an assignment to come up with a sort routine. He gave the highest marks to those who copied a sort routine from one of the many sources. His

comment to the class was, "Why invent something that has been around for a long time?"

2.   One part of the common fantasy of the software engineering profession is the adolescent preoccupation with newness. Why else would most models of software process have to do with the development of new systems, rather than the enhancement or correction of existing systems, where we spend at least three-fourths of our effort. But new development is a myth. We are all living with our past, and all engineering work is maintenance: removing differences between desire and perception.

3.   On the other hand, maintenance is a myth, too. Each time we enhance or correct a system, we are building something new. And each time we build a part of the software system—code, test data, project plans, user manuals, course materials, or what have you—we are building something new. So the same general development models apply to both maintenance and new development. When they are translated into specific plans, however, they will be put together in different combinations.

4.   Reuse is not easily understood by business (non-IS) management, but Eileen Strider found a dramatic and effective way to explain it:

> Our X system is an excellent example of a system designed in the early 1970's to handle one product. Over the years, products were added and new business units were added. Now it's a junked-up mess because it was never designed (nor redesigned) to be reused for other products and businesses.
>
> I found a way to "physically model" this system's history to help the business people understand how it got to be an unreliable mess by doing a "This Is Your Life" demonstration of the system. At a company meeting, I had a business person who used the system get on stage and play the role of the X system and then played out all the additions to the system to show its deterioration over time. It's an idea that ideally would be used at the beginning of a system development, rather than years later.

5.   Bent Adsersen, a Danish consultant, has been studying the differences between actual work patterns and what developers and managers *think* about their patterns.[6] He compared the measured time of one group of four developers with the time reported to the accounting system. Here are his figures:

Table 18-1.
Adsersen's Figures.

| Activity | Accounting | Measured |
|---|---|---|
| **Worker A** | | |
| Activity 1 | 5:00 | 1:41 |
| Activity 2 | 1:45 | 3:13 |
| **Worker B** | | |
| Activity 1 | 2:30 | 0:20 |
| Activity 2 | 1:00 | 0:30 |
| Activity 3 | 3:30 | 1:52 |
| **Worker C** | | |
| Activity 1 | — | 0:36 |
| Activity 2 | 3:30 | 2:17 |
| Activity 3 | 2:30 | 0:15 |
| **Worker D** | | |
| Activity 1 | 6:00 | 1:58 |
| Activity 2 | 1:00 | 4:06 |

These figures suggest that there is essentially no consistent relationship between effort reported to the accounting system and actual effort. Of course, effort isn't necessarily related to accomplishment either, so even if they were accurate, accounting figures probably shouldn't be used in project tracking or extrapolating from one project to another. If you want that kind of information, you'd better set up a separate measurement system to get it.

6.  The most important new information you have when you reevaluate a project is on how *you* are managing the project, on the *skills* of the people on the project, and on the *relationships* on the project. Each of these can be used, but as Eileen Strider says:

> Personally, I think the hardest is "information on how you are managing the project." It's hard to see yourself. It's hard to get a real picture of how you are doing. It's like looking in the mirror—you never think you are really like the image you see. It's always a projection of you,

with some distortion factor—not really you, whether it's verbal feed-back from someone else, looking at the physical results of the project, etc. You need to learn that feedback is information about you as seen through someone else's filters, and how to un-filter it.[7]

## 18.8 Summary

✔ The plan you make at the beginning of a project says, "*If* we can do these things, I will get the result I now want." It *doesn't* say, "No other way will get it," or "I won't change my mind about what I want."

✔ To become an Anticipating (Pattern 4) manager, you need to anticipate that nobody can anticipate everything. Therefore, you need to examine some of the common process models from a more practical point of view, to determine under which conditions each is applicable.

✔ The Waterfall Model underlies all other development process models. The essence of all Waterfall Models is that one thing happens after another, that water doesn't run uphill. When one stage is finished, it's finished, and there's no going back.

✔ The output of each stage of the waterfall defines what the next stage has to do, each being a further translation of the original desires. If there's been nothing lost or added in translation, the final output is what was desired. The Waterfall Model is the simplest class of processes, and to use anything else is to add complication. Therefore, you should always use the Waterfall Model *when it applies*.

✔ The Cascade Model is a collection of waterfalls, one after the other, or at times one beside another. Cascading is effective because of the Square Law of Computation. Decomposing one large problem into two smaller problems may be half the difficulty and also less risky. However, there is *always* an integration cost to cascading.

✔ Parallel cascades can be used for speed or to reduce risk by setting up two or more waterfalls to build the same project. The best (or quickest) result can be chosen as *the* product, and/or the multiple products can be used as reference tests for each other.

✔ The popular Spiral Model is a type of cascade, but drawn in a spiral to show cumulative cost (by distance from the center) and progress on each cycle (by angular displacement). Perhaps the strongest feature of the Spiral Model is the way it emphasizes that development (or maintenance, for that matter) is a series of cycles, each consisting of the same kinds of processes. The Spiral Model, however, is actually more of a process *vision*, and may mislead the people who are actually carrying out the process.

✔ Iterative enhancement is software development based on an existing piece of software as a base. There are a number of variations of iterative enhancement, as when

- the requirements have changed only incrementally, little enough that much of the original system can be preserved
- the functional requirements are preserved but the design may change
- the design is preserved, but the code may change

✔ Iterative enhancement is a form of reuse. Reusable code is a great idea. Like all great ideas, it must be managed.

✔ Another way to look at reuse in software development is to consider what is actually the most common method today of obtaining software: the off-the-shelf method. This is the method we use when we buy a software application. Someone else did the development, so we simply need to apply it to our needs.

✔ People frequently bypass all the early stages of software development and use their existing software in some new way. Some software is designed to encourage this kind of reuse, but some is not. Users don't seem to care, because they reuse the software with which they're most familiar.

✔ Prototyping is many things under a single term:

- a process to get requirements
- a process to get *something* working quickly, perhaps to
  — relieve pressure from customers or management
  — get a feel for a system
  — simulate system performance early in the development cycle
- a way to start writing code early, perhaps to smooth the workload, or perhaps just to do something developers like better than requirements work
- a disciplined process of incremental development
- a way to reduce management or customer pressure by creating a convincing illusion of progress
- a way to prove a concept or measure something
- a synonym for hacking

✔ The essence of prototyping is "build-a-little, learn-a-little, build-some-more." We call this hacking when the amount built at each stage is very small. When the increments are intermediate in size, we may call the approach "rapid" prototyping, though calling it that doesn't make it rapid.

✔ Top-down development (as opposed to top-down *design*) is one way of prototyping. First you build a skeleton embodying the general structure of the application. As development progresses, you fill in the details by replacing the stubs with code that more and more closely resembles the desired finished product. Unlike top-down design, you don't have to know the detailed requirements when you start the process.

✔ To be successful, prototyping requires more management discipline than other forms of development, not less as many people believe.

✔ Regardless of the combination of methods used, they are merely *templates* to guide you in making a project plan. The plan will elaborate the template in more detail, ideally decomposing everything to a connected network of standard task units. After you follow it for a while, something happens that you didn't anticipate. Now you have more *information* than you had at the beginning, so you *replan*, perhaps even switching development models.

✔ Slack allows you to keep replanning to a minimum. Slack can take the form of resources, time, and quality (requirements). Much of the manager's job in the middle of a project is trading one kind of slack for another, to deal with contingencies. Slack is the principal method for coping with project risks. Anticipating project managers forge all three types of slack in their plans—the amount depends on the amount of uncertainty about the future.

✔ Operating a project with less slack than appears prudent increases the chance of total project failure. Weigh the cost of slack and the risk of failure against the value of completing the project as planned.

## 18.9 Practice

1. Discuss the advantages and disadvantages of having one and only one method for all software work.

2. Information systems are the nervous system of an organization, and implementation is *surgery*. Discuss this metaphor, and its implications for designing implementation processes.

3. Give examples from your own experience of trading each of the three types of slack—resources, time, and requirements—for each of the others.

4.   Wayne Bailey suggests:  Explore your own feelings and attitudes about the various forms of "cheating" described in this chapter, such as concealing from your unsympathetic management the actual development process you're using.  What are some of the side effects of such practices?  What alternative ways can you think of to address the same problems?

5.   Barbara Purchia differentiates between two distinct forms of prototyping, exploratory and evolutionary:

> The exploratory type is [used] to determine feasibilities, compare approaches, etc., and in *no* way would the prototype become the product.  In one such case, we even prototyped in a different language from the one used in the product.

Discuss other ways to prevent the greatest danger of exploratory prototyping, that is, the use of the output as a product.  Under what circumstances would you consider violating the prohibition of using the prototype as a product?  Also, how would you prevent evolutionary prototyping from becoming evolutionary drift?

6.   Payson Hall asks:  What are the dangers in the example of hacking the beta version of the operating system to overcome poor turnaround from the vendor?  What are the dangers of concealing this practice from the boss's boss?  How would you limit these dangers and still have a chance of making an ambitious schedule?

# 19

# Terminating Projects Properly

*These projects were characteristic of Stalin's industrialization policy, one that emphasized gargantuan projects over smaller ones, output above safety, technology over human beings, rigid centralized planning over local initiative, closed decision making to the detriment of critical debate, and, above all, a madly rushed tempo.*[1]
— L.R. Graham

In well-managed projects, termination comes more or less as planned, with the delivery of the desired product or modification that meets well-defined acceptance criteria. But some projects are not managed well, which is bad enough, but perhaps excusable. It's inexcusable, however, that some of these projects are not terminated well.

Perhaps the greatest challenge and test of a good manager is the ability to terminate projects that should be terminated, when they should be terminated. Unfortunately, in many cases, the reason the project needs to be terminated abnormally is that managers haven't done an adequate job and can't face up to their failure. In those cases where success was really out of the managers' hands, they feel they have failed and cannot bring themselves to terminate the project. Failure to terminate then becomes their *real* failure.

Figure 19-1 is a slip chart of a project that went on seemingly forever, full of sound and fury but producing nothing.[2] Every time it began to approach a scheduled completion date, the date slipped away. This type of project is typical in Routine (Pattern 2) organizations, and seems to be beyond their managers' capacity to control. In Company B, such non-completing projects consumed 43 percent of the development budget.

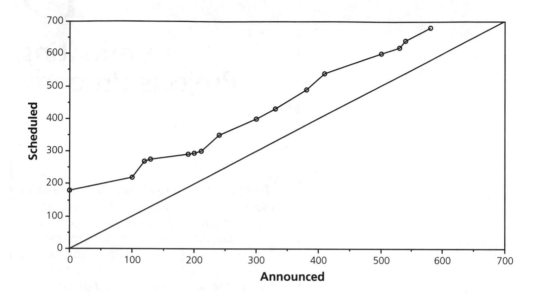

Figure 19-1.    Company B's slip chart for Project 3. Each point on the chart represents a date on which the scheduled delivery changed (slipped), with the new delivery date plotted on the Y-axis. Notice how the scheduled delivery date keeps slipping away from the actual date (straight line). Will the schedule delivery date ever arrive? Will the project ever end?

Evidently, Company B ought to spend some time on the question of terminating projects, but it is not alone. This chapter attempts to illuminate the source of Company B's problems, and many other problems besides.

## 19.1 Testing

Some readers may have noticed that testing wasn't given a separate box in any of the process diagrams in Chapter 18. That's because testing is productive, but not production. In an Anticipating (Pattern 4) organization, testing is merely part of every standard task unit in which something is built, and putting testing in a separate box may mislead people into thinking that testing is done once, at the end of the entire process. Of course, testing can be done that way, but not in an Anticipating organization. Pure after-the-fact testing always costs more, takes longer, and doesn't work as well. Why would Anticipating managers want to do it that way, unless they were misled by poor process models?

### 19.1.1 Two kinds of testing

One reason people are misled about testing is that they use the word in two different ways: process testing versus product testing. Process testing asks, "Where are we in the process?" Product testing asks, "What state is the product in?" Often, the two types of testing are related, though not identical. For instance, the process test may consist of a product test combined with a schedule test. The logic of this test might look like this:

> IF acceptance test yields 5 failures or less
>
> > THEN IF time to ship date > 1 month THEN repair and retest;
> >
> > ELSE prepare to ship.

Or a process test might not contain any product test at all, as in

> IF expenditures to date > total budget
>
> > THEN replan project.

Figure 19-2 shows a standard task unit.[3] The requirements (or prerequisites) part at the front is a process test, and so is the review at the end. In the task itself, there may or may not be product testing, but one of the things the review will examine is whatever testing has been done. Using this and other information, the review will determine whether the task of producing the product is finished.

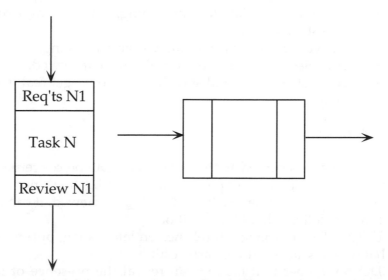

Figure 19-2.  A standard task unit has three parts. Either the vertical or horizontal form can be used. The production part of the task is sandwiched between a requirements (or prerequisites) box and a review box. The task cannot start until the requirements have been provided, after which it produces a candidate product. Only after a passed review do we have an actual product.

Most process tests take the form of asking, "Should we terminate?" or "Should we replan the task?" Product tests are different, asking, "What are the faults in this product?" Edsger Dijkstra, the Dutch computer scientist commonly credited as being the "father of structured programming," once observed that tests could reveal the presence of errors, but not their absence. Errors (or faults, as we call them) are to be exposed, not hidden, and testing is one way to expose them. Any evidence that a project is not working earnestly and effectively to expose faults is evidence for a process test that says,

> IF faults are being hidden
>
> THEN replan project

The replanning, of course, must start with a plan for finding accurate information on the state of the product and the organization.

### 19.1.2  Phrases to listen for

How do you know when a project is not working earnestly and effectively to expose faults? The airwaves will be full of revealing statements:

- This inspection really slowed down the project.
- We haven't time for inspections. We have a tight schedule.
- We haven't time for testing. We have a tight schedule.
- We don't have to review it; we tested it.
- We haven't time for test planning. We have a tight schedule.
- We don't have time for unit testing, but anything wrong will turn up in system testing.
- We were doing all right until we started testing.
- This piece of work is too complex to be reviewed.
- The testers are unrealistic. If they would get real, we could ship on time.

### 19.1.3  Actions to take

DO NOT be so concerned with deliverables; DO be concerned with "reviewables." DO NOT allow or depend on a deliverable that's not reviewable. "Not reviewable" is a review in itself. If it can't be reviewed, it can't be right, and it shouldn't be delivered. DO throw it out.

DO NOT place too much reliance on late testing, but instead DO remember that reviews are a form of early testing.

DO remember that testing can reveal the presence of faults, not their absence. DO NOT put much credence in the statement, "The test revealed that there were no faults." DO NOT buy the self-serving mind-set that "finding no faults" is equivalent to "no faults exist." DO remember, always, that you can't prove that something doesn't exist, though you can easily convince yourself, if you don't want to face reality. DO encourage people to speak more accurately: "The test revealed no faults, even if there were some." DO remember that this could be a statement about the product or a statement about the tests.

DO NOT put *any* credence in the statement that a product "passed the tests." Product tests are neither passed nor failed; they simply produce data that may be used to make process decisions. Only process tests pass or fail, and that may be partially on the basis of the data from one or more product tests.

DO NOT take any one person's word for anything—except for Edsger Dijkstra or the Pope. DO understand that some people will turn incongruent if you question their word. DO NOT placate people who are being incongruent.

DO throw away anything that "cannot be tested."

DO make plans based only on *testable* deliverables (testables or reviewables). Deliverability is a meaningless concept without testing that is based on a clearly defined standard and a process to determine concurrence. DO NOT take the *quantity* of tests as a measure of comprehensiveness of testing, unless the tests fit the standard and the results have actually been reviewed.

DO build independent verification into projects *from the start*. DO avoid later verification, which looks like witch-hunting.

## 19.2 Testing versus Hacking

Each of the process models of the previous chapter makes sense in certain situations, but one form of the iterative code-change process shown in Figure 18-4 probably represents more than half of all software effort. Most software work takes place at the level of the fix, the patch, or the update: some kind of substitution of code for code, or addition of code, done without reanalyzing the design. This code change might be intended to correct an error, to update to some modified value, or to improve performance. Most of the time, the requirement comes from operational experience, or from the construction process itself, in some subphase called testing.

The runaway project in Figure 19-1 spent most of its resources in this kind of "testing"—that is, doing construction that was not *called* construction. The testing department was blamed for the delays, but they were simply providing the message that the product wasn't finished. The resources were consumed by developers who continued to build long after the "building phase" was finished.

### 19.2.1 Loops in process diagrams: The Downfall Model

In Company B, this type of work was represented as a cascade with *loops* added, as in Figure 19-3. Although Company B called the work it was doing "testing," it was really "testing and rebuilding, or fixing." Indeed, this could also be a process diagram of the quick fix, though it's impossible to determine how quick it really is. Or, the diagram could represent a release/fix strategy. It's impossible, however, to predict how many releases there will be before the product is satisfactory. In fact, the true name for the process described in this diagram is "hacking."

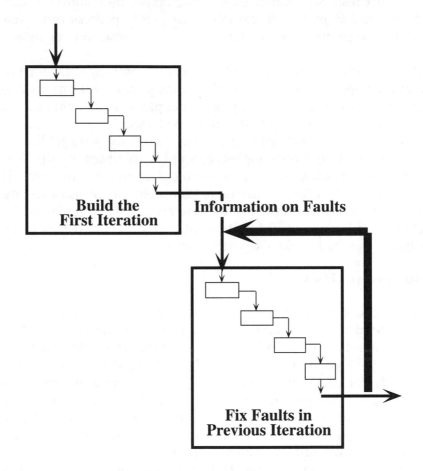

Figure 19-3.     In practice, there are many major variations to the waterfall theme. This figure represents one idea of testing, the quick-fix or release/fix strategy. In fact, it is a process diagram of hacking, and the line looping backward is an illusion, because we don't know how to go backward in time.

You never step in the same waterfall twice, so adding a line back from one stage to another does not give a true picture of the testing/quick-fix/hacking process. In Figure 19-3, the number of iterations is unknown, yet it's easy to look at this diagram and believe you're seeing a defined process. You're not. What you're seeing is an optical illusion, something more like Figure 19-4. This illusion has been the downfall of many a software engineering manager. That's why I like to call the diagram of Figure 19-3 the Downfall Model.

Figure 19-4.    The idea that your Waterfall Model can recycle is an optical illusion, like this popular clip art image after M.C. Escher's well-known drawing. The one in Figure 19-3 has cost many managers' jobs, so perhaps it ought to be called the Downfall Model.

### 19.2.2 Unrolling loops

Process loops such as shown in Figure 19-3 are one of the primary sources of overruns of project estimates. When the project manager of Company B's Project 3 (shown in the slip chart of Figure 19-1) showed me where all the time had gone, the report said that 27 percent of the time had gone into development and 73 percent (so far) had gone into testing. My own view was that 27 percent had gone into disciplined development and 73 percent had gone into hacking, just as soon as the lid of discipline was removed under the guise of testing.

How can you estimate a project schedule without knowing how many times the loop of Figure 19-3 will cycle? You can't, but you *can* estimate the number of cycles based on an estimate of the number of faults left that need fixing—after the first iteration and after each subsequent iteration. These estimates of remaining faults tend to be characteristic of each organization's culture, and are among the first measures you should obtain if you wish to stabilize your development processes.[4]

For example, suppose you are building a system that will have one hundred function points, and your organization's experience is one fault released to system testing per twenty function points. You do not wish to release the system to customers until the number of known faults is one or zero.

Your development practice is to release the internal system version 1.0, then release corrected versions, 1.1, 1.2, and so on, at one-month intervals. You also know that with each new version, your organization typically removes 90 percent of the faults discovered by system test in the previous version. Your prediction would then be that five faults would be released with this version 1.0, and that version 1.1 is likely to fix all of them, or all but one. Figure 19-5 might be a reasonable process description for this project.

This estimate also tells you exactly how to watch for trouble when you reach the first iteration. By comparing the number of faults removed to the estimate, you get an early indication that you may have more iterations (or fewer) than you'd planned.

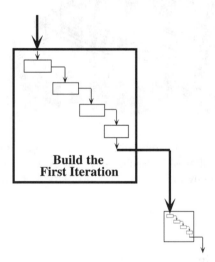

**Build the First Iteration**

Figure 19-5.    If the probability of faults is small, then the diagram given at Figure 19-3 ought to be redrawn as shown here. The estimate is for one more iteration of the process, and a small one at that.

Now suppose that with the same organization, you were building a system of ten thousand function points. If you make the optimistic assumption of linearity, the prediction would be five hundred faults delivered to system test in version 1.0. This would likely mean three iterations of fixing—to version 1.3—before reducing the number of faults to one or zero, your customer's ship criterion. Using Figure 19-5 as the process model would be a big mistake, guaranteeing in advance that estimates and schedules would never be met, unless you relaxed your quality standards.

If the ten thousand function point system is larger than the organization's typical experience, the assumption of linearity is probably optimistic, and so are the estimates of faults and fault-reduction efficiency. In that case, Figure 19-6 might be a more realistic process description on which to base your planning and estimation.

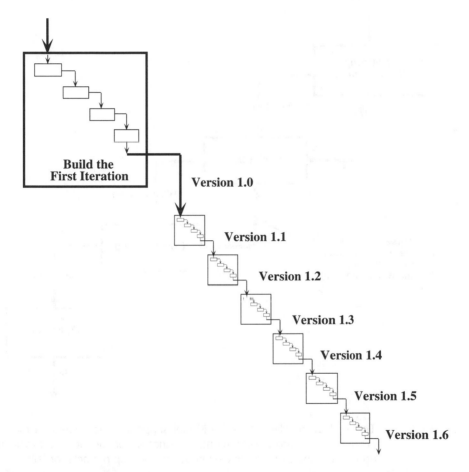

Figure 19-6.        If the probability of faults is larger, then the information depicted in Figure 19-3
                   ought to be represented this way.

### 19.2.3  No loops

The moral of this example for managers is simple:

**Never use loops in a process description.**

Except in science fiction stories, time doesn't run backward. Life has no loops. Yet process descriptions such as Figure 19-7 are often represented as if you had a time machine at your disposal.

If you want your process descriptions to be true to life, use your measurements to unroll the loops as we did in Figure 19-6. Remember, the most important use of the process description is to give everyone in the organization a reasonably accurate image of what is expected of them. Descriptions such as Figures 19-3 and 19-7 are setups for failure.

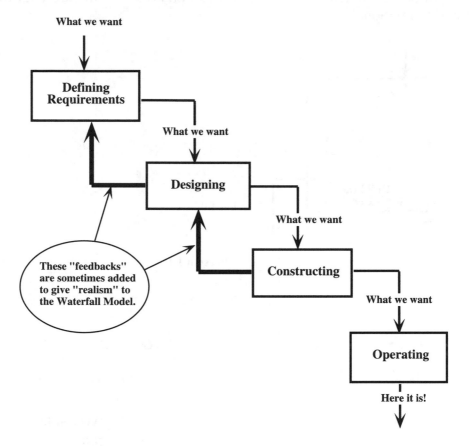

Figure 19-7.        This sort of modified Waterfall Model supposedly represents a more realistic picture of software development, but since it contains loops, it misleads managers into overly optimistic estimates and sets up projects for failure.

Of course, if you never use loops in a process description, you'll never violate an even more important rule:

**Never use loops in a plan.**

### 19.3 Ways to Know When a Project Is Failing

The first three volumes of this series demonstrate how managers without access to appropriate models and measurements tend to do exactly the wrong thing when a project is going sour. Capers Jones commented to me about this boomerang effect:

Most projects that are late appear to be on time until late coding or when testing begins, when all the shortcuts made early on slow testing to a standstill and the project crashes to a halt. Projects that controlled quality early via defect prevention or inspections zip right through testing.

Several large-scale studies at IBM and elsewhere showed that projects with the lowest volumes of customer-reported bugs (that is, those that had been most effective at preventing or removing the bugs before shipment) were also the projects with the shortest development schedules, and in particular the shortest testing schedules. Yet many managers say "we don't have time to do inspections or we'll miss our schedules."

I was part of a project audit team once, investigating a manager's decision to cancel inspections so testing could start on time. We found that the inspected modules did enter testing late, but they exited early. The non-inspected modules entered testing early, but exited late. A sample post-test inspection on one of the late modules found ten times as many bugs as testing itself because the testing was sloppy.

The audit team recommended that testing be canceled and 100% inspections be performed as the best way of achieving the delivery target and quality target concurrently. The manager's gut reaction was to do it the other way—and that would have been a failure.[5]

In short, if you're pressed for time, you need to do more testing, not less.

### 19.3.1 Phrases to listen for

Formal measurements may not help you to recognize when your project is starting to fail, because the formal measurement system may be the first thing to start failing. You need to watch and listen for signs outside that system, and STOP the project when they arise. Here are some rather robust signs:

- When the measurement system starts breaking down, STOP!
- When the insults begin, STOP!
- When people start writing notes to the file, or speaking for the record, STOP!
- When somebody says, "Thinking is a luxury we can no longer afford," STOP!
- When morale turns irreversibly bad, STOP!
- When the rats start leaving, the ship is sinking, so STOP!

### 19.3.2 Actions to take

This paragraph will be short and sweet, because the only action to take in these circumstances is STOP.

By STOP, I mean that you, the manager, should stop operating by the seat of your pants and start thinking very carefully about what's happening. You may want to terminate the project, or you may want to rebirth it, as described in Section 19.4.

### 19.3.3  The earliest sign

The earliest indicator that a project may need terminating is when you're asked to certify that a plan is achievable when it's not. This may be justified by a superior as "good for the bottom line" or perhaps simply by "I'm the boss, so you'll certify it if I say so." Perhaps you've compromised and certified a non-feasible plan at one time or another. Not me. I've been asked, but I've never compromised.

The key word for me is "certify." (Another popular term is "commit.") In answer to a request or demand to certify that the plan is achievable, I say, "Perhaps it is achievable, but I don't know how to achieve it." Upper management is in charge, so these managers can certainly go ahead with the plan, but not with my "certification." Surely, you can do the same.

It's not as hard as it sounds. You're simply talking about yourself, so it's easy to deal with objections. For instance, I've had managers tell me, "Yes, you do know how to achieve it." Then I say, "Gosh, I must have forgotten. Will you show me how? Once you remind me, I'll certainly certify the plan."

### 19.3.4  The latest sign

One of N.R. Augustine's laws says,

> **. . . the incidence of test failures is directly proportional to the square of the size of the crowd multiplied by the rank of the senior observing official.**[6]

The dynamic behind this law is simple: A large crowd of high dignitaries means that the event is planned according to external, not internal, events. Thus, "test complete" is scheduled according to when some senior manager has been promised a demonstration, not when the quality has reached a certain level.

Under this kind of pressure, managers are often asked to certify that a product is acceptable, generally when it is not. This is a sure sign that the project ought to be terminated and rebirthed with a new acceptance criterion, but that's not what your management is demanding that you do. In that case, the best you can do is similar to what you do at the beginning. You say, "Perhaps it is acceptable to somebody, but I haven't yet seen evidence that would make it acceptable to me."

Again, they can ship it, but with no certification from you. I've had managers say to me, "Of course it's acceptable. Anybody who's not a complete idiot can see that." To which I respond, "Then I guess I'm a complete idiot, because I can't see it. But I'd be very grateful if you could show me why you've come to that conclusion. If I can understand your reasoning, then of course I'll certify it."

So far, none of them has managed to show me, but if one does, I'll learn something, so I can't lose.

### 19.3.5 Morale deterioration

In the middle of a project, perhaps the most reliable indicator that a project may need terminating is a decline in morale. Morale can be thought of as the overall assessment of the project's chances by the entire staff. This makes morale a good measure of how things are going, but also makes it hard to measure directly. So, instead, it's more practical to look for the kinds of things that destroy morale:

- Attempts to force people to say things they know aren't true, as in the above examples.
- Emphasis on status, rather than achievement. For example, managers invoke "rank has its privileges" (RHIP) to get what they want, or start playing favorites and offer differential treatment to favored individuals and teams.
- Attempts to motivate by other than the professional challenge. The worst case, of course, is attempts to browbeat people into working hard, especially by higher executives brought in to display clout. For example, in one project the company president came in and gave a speech saying that all he wanted to see from now on was "butts and elbows." This was hardly flattering, depressed everyone, and certainly led to loss of productivity. But flattery can be just as depressing, especially when it is seen as flattery rather than sincere complimenting of good work. Another extremely depressing management action is to give pep talks designed to raise morale. People rather easily make the connection: "If they're giving pep talks, there must be some reason we need to be pepped up."
- Naturally, too much work over the long run will be depressing both physically and mentally. Even if you don't see signs of loss of morale, you can be sure that after several weeks of substantial overtime, people will start to burn out.
- Paradoxically, too little work is even worse. Nothing is more depressing than having to sit around with nothing useful to do—unless it's doing make-work that's to be thrown away or simply ignored. In this same category is schedule pressure that turns out to be irrelevant when the product is delivered, as when you drop everything to get a module delivered and discover that the integration team doesn't have it scheduled for inclusion in the foreseeable future.
- Interruptions that can't be controlled are awfully depressing when you're committed to a schedule. It's even worse when the interruptions are from the person who put you under schedule pressure in the first place. Perhaps the worst example is the project manager who says, "I can't get involved in details," then gets involved in details and drives you nuts over them.

- The final insult to morale generally arises when a choice has to be made between achieving quality or making the schedule. Management that has been saying, "Quality is everything," then acts as if only the schedule counts—and morale sinks to the depths of the mid-Pacific trench.

## 19.4  Rebirthing a Project

Ultimately, all these signs are mileposts along the way to the project terminating in failure, signs that your illusions are about to fail. If you don't heed them and take effective action to change the situation, you will be forced to drop the project entirely or start it over, reborn as a new project. I purposely call this process rebirthing, rather than "restarting," because too many people treat "restart" merely as a way to get the project moving again. Rebirthing is creating a new project because the old one wasn't fit to keep on living.

Although process models may be given in shorthand such as Figure 19-7, process plans must be non-looping flowcharts, with process-terminating test conditions on all branches. A plan is not a process, but a process *model* for one particular project. It is not a general process model, but an instantiation of one, since it's unlikely that we will ever have two projects with exactly the same plan, even if they follow the same process model. For example, the plan might say,

> If, after three test cycles, we haven't reached the acceptance criteria, we start a new project with a new plan.

Every plan must plan for various kinds of termination. If you want to create an Anticipating (Pattern 4) culture, remember that anticipating means *thinking of the end at the beginning*. Thus, if something happens in your plan that you didn't anticipate, the last thing you want to do is keep on pseudo-looping (hacking) as if you knew all along that this would happen.

Instead, you want to take the unanticipated need for another iteration as a signal that your plan has gone sour and you need a new plan. Since the plan is the seed of the project, what you really need is a new project. There need be no disgrace in discovering this need for a new birth, because creating new systems is always a dicey thing. The disgrace (and expense) is not in failing to track the plan, though that's a common enough mistake. The real disgrace lies in refusing to acknowledge the need for replanning, and thus continuing to waste time and money in a fruitless quest for a fantasy.

In Nature, about 30 percent of all human conceptions fail to produce live babies. Most of these are aborted spontaneously at such an early stage that the parents may not even realize that a conception took place. In software engineering, about 30 percent of all major projects fail to produce live systems, but most of these are aborted at such a late stage that they dominate the trouble and expense experienced by their organizations.[7]

Much of the software engineering effort to date has been attempting to reduce the 30 percent failure rate, but perhaps Nature has something to tell us. I believe that our profession is learning to reduce the human errors that under-lie most project failures, except for one: our boundless ambition, coupled with our boundless optimism. Because the leading edge is always moving outward, our biggest projects may always be a bit too complex for us to conceive perfect-ly. By anticipating in the planning stage that a project may be ill-conceived, or otherwise be damaged early, we can reduce the cost of these abortions to minuscule amounts, even if we still abort 30 percent of the major projects.

## 19.5 Helpful Hints and Suggestions

1. Actually, the word "testing" is used in a third way: environmental testing. Beta testing is the most easily recognized example of environmental test-ing, at least in Anticipating (Pattern 4) organizations. In less adept orga-nizations, beta testing is used as a form of product testing, to find bugs in the product by running it in large numbers of real-life situations. In an Anticipating (Pattern 4) organization, however, there are few if any faults in the prerelease product, so beta testing is used to discover ways in which the environment for the product differs from what was anticipated. The results of such beta testing are seldom used to fix the product, but instead to

    • change the product to work around specific environmental deficien-cies, such as hardware that's not fully compatible, software that vio-lates interface standards, and unanticipated user behaviors
    • warn users, when no sensible work-around is available, that certain environments will not allow the product to work as they might hope

2. Although money spent is often used as a criterion for progress, it's actual-ly much harder to estimate cost than value—unless you simply stop spending when your budgetary limit is reached. In that case, you're not actually estimating value; you're estimating *spending*. It's like going into a casino with $100 to lose. There are huge elements of randomness, so you don't know how long your bankroll will last, or how much fun you'll have, but you can precisely estimate your spending: $100.

3. One of the reasons value is easier to estimate is that we generally don't need to estimate it so precisely. If the project only has a value margin of one percent, why are we doing it, given the uncertainties in development?

4. How does a one-year project get two years behind? Fred Brooks answered, "One day at a time." I agree. The one day was the day the project managers translated their process model into a so-called plan under pressure to make it meet a schedule that had no relationship to what was required. On that day, they

- shaved a little time off each phase (which raised the fault rate)
- assumed one iteration at the end (when actually there would be more than usual because of the increased fault rate)

5.  Reviewer Leonard Medal offers an important tip about record-keeping in projects:

> You use the term "note to file" in a pejorative sense, which could easily be misinterpreted. I use notes to my file daily, not as a way to later blame people but more as a way to create a journal of what happened during a project and how I feel about it. I forget important events if I don't do this and, in forgetting, reduce opportunities for learning.
>
> My notes are public. Anyone can read them—coworkers, bosses, customers. If I can think of anyone on earth I would want to exclude from reading the note, then I know it is not ready. Actively thinking about the Helpful Model when I am writing these notes helps immeasurably.[8] Maybe you should leave the book like it is and I should call these notes "Project Journal Entries."

6.  Payson Hall has an interesting approach to helping his clients get rid of nonproductive projects:

> I ask my class to imagine a sorted list of all the projects currently under way. At the top are projects that will probably deliver what was promised, on schedule and within budget. In the middle of the list are projects that may be okay—perhaps a little late or a little over budget, but probably still marginally successful. At the bottom of the list are projects that are not really going to happen—poor-quality products that will be late (if ever) and way over budget.
>
> At this point, the class is usually smiling in a guarded way—they know a project at the bottom of the list. Now I ask, "Why are you doing this one at the bottom? Most people know it isn't going to happen—the resources being consumed are not providing value. Is it a conscious organizational decision to waste these resources? Who made that decision? Was it an informed decision?" This leads into cancellation and management communication.

The principal problem I see with Payson's method is that I've had clients who couldn't produce a list of all their ongoing projects, let alone put them in order. It's a good illustration of why you need stability to make improvements.

7.  Eileen Strider offers some ideas from her "latest project ordeal," including another one on note-taking:

- Ask yourself, "How do I know when to say STOP COMPLETELY versus take some incremental action?" I know to consider stopping completely when my incremental actions don't improve the result.

This means I have to be watching closely for the effect they have, and be able to see clearly and objectively so I can admit to myself it's not working and something more drastic is called for. I think for me it has to do not with my intentions but with the results. It means I have to question my own competence and face my ability to not be perfect.

- Pick a person to be your alter ego who will talk straight with you about what's working and what's not in a way you can hear it yet still feel supported. I think it's crucial to have someone you trust, who cares about you, who has solid management and technical skills to advise you in the role of executive.

- Have people on the project keep a diary, or at least keep one yourself. Include in the diary not only what happened, but—more important-ly—how you felt about it. The important activity associated with a diary is to *read it periodically* so you can get a sense of the emotional temperature of the project over time. This provides you with some perspective that came from you but isn't just a moment-in-time reac-tion.

- Have each person on the project draw a "life line" of the project showing the graphs of high and low emotional reactions to events.[9] This right-brain activity may surface emotional highs and lows and show you a trend over time of how the project has been going from each person's perspective. Your diary from above could help in this exercise. You might even ask people to extend the line to project how they think the rest of the project will go. This gives you an idea of their current outlook (hopes, wishes, fears, and so on) on the pro-ject. Assemble an art gallery of the team's drawings and hear what the members have to say about them. If you don't want to do this with the full team, you could just do it just for yourself.

## 19.6 Summary

✔ In well-managed projects, termination comes more or less as planned, with the delivery of the desired product or modification. Perhaps the greatest challenge and test of a good manager is the ability to terminate projects that should be terminated, when they should be terminated.

✔ Testing is productive, but not production. In an Anticipating (Pattern 4) organization, testing is merely part of every standard task unit in which something is built, and putting testing in a separate box may mislead peo-ple into thinking that testing is done once, at the end of the entire process.

✔ Process testing asks, "Where are we in the process?" Product testing asks, "What state is the product in?" The requirements or prerequisites part at the front of a standard task unit is a process test, and so is the review at the end. In the task itself, there may or may not be product testing, but one of the things the review will examine is whatever testing has been done. Using this and other information, the review will determine whether the task of producing the product is finished.

✔ Most process tests take the form of asking, "Should we terminate?" or "Should we replan the task?" Product tests are different, asking, "What are the faults in this product?" Any evidence that a project is not working earnestly and effectively to expose faults is evidence for a process test that says,

> IF faults are being hidden
>
> THEN replan project.

✔ Most software work takes place at the level of the fix, the patch, or the update in some subphase called testing—that is, doing construction that was not *called* construction. Vast resources are consumed by developers who continue to build long after the building phase is finished.

✔ Adding a line back from one stage to another does not give a true picture of the testing/quick-fix/hacking process. Since the number of iterations is unknown, this kind of shorthand easily creates a Downfall Model. Such unbounded process loops are one of the primary sources of overruns of project estimates, because hacking starts as soon as the lid of discipline is removed under the guise of testing.

✔ You can estimate the number of development cycles based on an estimate of the number of faults left that need fixing—after the first iteration and after each subsequent iteration. These estimates of remaining faults tend to be characteristic of each organization's culture, and are among the first measures you should obtain if you wish to stabilize your development processes. By comparing the number of faults removed to the estimate, you get an early indication that you may have more iterations (or fewer) than you'd planned.

✔ Never use loops in a process description. Never use loops in a plan. If you want your plans and process descriptions to be true to life, use your measurements to unroll the loops.

✔ Managers without access to appropriate models and measurements tend to do exactly the wrong thing when a project is going sour. Formal measurements may not help you to recognize when your project is starting to fail, because the formal measurement system may be the first thing to start failing. You need to watch and listen for signs outside that system, and STOP the project when they arise.

✔ The earliest indicator that a project may need terminating is when you're asked to certify that a plan is achievable when it's not. In answer to a request or demand to certify that the plan is achievable, you can say, "Perhaps it is achievable, but I don't know how to achieve it."

✔ "Test complete" is often scheduled according to when some senior manager has been promised a demonstration, not when the quality has reached a certain level. Under this kind of pressure, managers are often asked to certify that a product is acceptable, generally when it is not—a sure sign that the project ought to be terminated and rebirthed with a new acceptance criterion.

✔ In the middle of a project, perhaps the most reliable indicator that a project may need terminating is a decline in morale—the overall intuitive assessment of the project's chances by the entire staff.

✔ A plan is not a process, but a process *model* for one particular project. It is not a general process model, but an instantiation of one, since it's unlikely that we will ever have two projects with exactly the same plan, even if they follow the same process model.

✔ Every plan must plan for various kinds of termination. The unanticipated need for another iteration is a signal that your plan has gone sour, that you need a new plan. And, since the plan is the seed of the project, what you really need is a new project.

## 19.7 Practice

1. How would you go about unrolling the process description of Figure 19-7 into a plan for a real project?

2. Add your favorite phrase to the "what to listen for" lists.

3. How does the principle of non-looping apply to process improvement models, particularly continuous process improvement?

4. Much of the confusion about testing comes from our using the same word (a heteronym, like "testing") for the *many* reasons we run programs and examine results. We've already seen

   - process testing (Where are we in the process?)
   - product testing (What state is the product in?)
   - environmental testing (Will the environment really accept this?)

In addition, there are

- testing to get new ideas, such as testing human reactions to an inter-face (testing to improve, not to prove)
- acceptance testing (testing to answer legal questions, or to establish a legal position)
- process model testing (testing to get information for process improvement)

For what other reasons do we do testing? What are the advantages of combining several reasons into one set of tests? What are the disadvantages?

5.   In regard to visibility, measurement, and justifying change, Leonard Medal says the following documents had a big effect in his organization in getting to an improved requirements process. These documents can also be used within a project to compare its pattern to other projects:

> One [document] is a plot of cumulative customer time spent in requirements work during each week of a project. The chart contrasts two projects and shows a remarkable difference. It was quite an eye-opener for many people in my organization who were confused about why one project went so well and the other went so poorly.
>       The other document contrasts the requirements work in two projects with projections (only in part tongue-in-cheek) about time need-ed to conduct an effective requirements process.

Leonard also uses a software developer satisfaction chart to measure morale:

> I ask the developers the chances of a successful outcome, plot the results, and post the chart publicly and show it to the customers and management. It has had some remarkable effects on projects. It helps a lot to start it early when the results are usually not controversial. Also, if you include the customer and management on the same chart and make it public, everyone can spot the point at which reality and illusion tracks begin to diverge.

What documents does your organization use to indicate how a project is progressing? Which ones are effective? Which ones are ineffective? What's the difference? How can the ineffective ones be improved? What could happen that would sabotage the effective ones?

6.   James Robertson asks about the symptoms of morale deterioration: Do these symptoms justify terminating a project, or do they justify terminat-ing a manager? What additional information would you want in order to make that decision? Why?

# 20

# Building Faster by Building Smaller

*Speed kills!*
— Defensive driving slogan,
anti-drug slogan, and
slogan seen on the wall of more than one
software engineering organization

In an age of rapid change, our profession is one of the worst offenders. Software engineering managers who cannot cope with demands for speed soon become *former* software engineering managers. But the futile efforts to change software more quickly often mean that we change our software organizations more slowly.

The Satir Change Model suggests a number of principles concerning your response to pressure for short-term change, and these apply especially well to pressures to speed up the building process without destroying your plans for long-term improvement of your organization:

- The organization is in Chaos, so DO NOT make long-term commitments or set precedents.
- Whenever possible, DO NOT introduce new foreign elements. DO use elements of the culture that already exist.

355

- People are desperate, so DO plan for some quick successes. DO NOT seize upon the first quick success to solve everything.
- People are under stress, so the solutions they tend to grasp are those that fit their incongruent coping style: blaming, placating, superreasonable, or irrelevant. DO watch for incongruent coping behavior as warning signs about proposed solutions.

This and the following chapters will make specific suggestions about coping congruently with demands for speed that are consistent with these suggestions. There are two fundamental tactics you can use to accelerate the building process:

- increase your capacity for building
- decrease the size of what you're building

In the short-run situations, a certain amount of capacity increase is possible, but is limited by Brooks's Law in its various forms. Increasing capacity—not just numbers, but skill as well—in the long run helps achieve schedules, high performance, low costs, and just about everything else. Decreasing size, however, is something that managers can control in the short run, though many managers don't know how to do this, or cannot act congruently enough to do it. This chapter considers what managers can do, in the short run, to decrease the size of projects.

## 20.1  What Does Smaller Mean?

System size enters into many of the fundamental dynamic feedback loops of software engineering.[1] For instance, one of the fundamental dynamics of fault location is that the time to locate a specific fault grows with the size of the system (Figure 20-1). In a bigger system, there are

- more faults
- more places to look for faults
- more possibility of faults interacting, which confuses location efforts

This dynamic suggests that the system in which we are looking for faults should be as small as possible. In the short-term, of course, we have limited control over the actual size of the delivered system, but we are not without resources for reducing the *effective* size of the system we are searching.
    Up until now, I have left the meaning of "smaller" somewhat ambiguous, but now is the time to be more specific. The size I am talking about is the *mental* size of the system—the amount of mental effort required to play the game effectively. This size may correlate roughly with lines of code, but there are many ways in which programs L and B with the same number of lines may be

very different in this meaning of size.  Here are some examples (L for "little" and B for "big"):

- L's documentation may be superior to B's.
- L's initial design may be superior to B's.
- L's design may have retained its integrity better than B's.
- L may have been planned for a longer schedule than B, so it can be done with fewer people and less coordination, which makes it relatively smaller.
- L may have fewer interacting faults than B.
- L's requirements may be less extensive than B's.
- L's requirements may be less complex than B's.
- L's requirements may be less specific than B's, allowing more choice of design.
- L's customers may be less demanding of perfection than B's, and more willing to accept something reasonably good.
- L's customers may be more cooperative than B's.

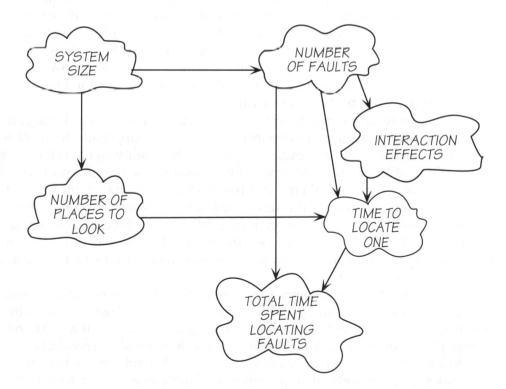

Figure 20-1.        A number of factors interact to cause the time to locate a specific fault to rise with the size of the system.

In addition, mental size is also relative to whose mentality is involved. Smarter, better-trained people working with superior tools will see a smaller system. Remember that tic-tac-toe is a pretty big game—to chickens. For example,

- L's developers may be better trained or more appropriately trained than B's.
- L's developers may be less involved with hidden agendas (such as building new tools or methodologies) than B's.
- L's developers, though committed to reasonable quality, may be less obsessed with perfection than B's.
- L's developers may be more cooperative with their customers than B's.

Changing these things is part of the longer-range approach to be described in subsequent chapters. For now, let's tackle the size of the system itself.

## 20.2 Reduce the Scope of the Specification

Systems grow in functionality when the software developers placate the customers or their surrogates, the marketers. Early in the life cycle, it may be difficult to stand up to marketing arguments about the value of increased functionality. Everyone is optimistic, and it is easier to placate the customer than to face the quality dynamics of size. After all, predictions are not *that* accurate, and nobody can reasonably insist that adding just one more function will actually affect the quality, or the delivery time.

Once you're in a schedule crisis, however, the balance of the argument shifts in the face of reality. For instance, at a crisis meeting with the marketing department of one software house, I explained the quality dynamics of size to an initially hostile, blaming audience. By the end of the presentation, the facts and figures overwhelmed them, and the marketing manager pleaded, "Can you give us *any* function on the scheduled date?" When I told him that was impossible, he begged, "Can you give us a *date* for which you can promise any function at all?" Again I told him no, and he finally said, meekly, "Well, we'd appreciate it if you could give us a list of functions and *a date when you can promise to give us a delivery date.*"

When you stop speculating and have data in hand, you have a realistic hope of reducing the actual size of the system. Now the customer who insists on getting *every* function takes a clear risk of getting nothing at all. Therefore, the first thing you ought to consider is *reducing the scope of the specification.*

When customers and developers don't understand what's needed, they start making up all sorts of requirements. That's one reason why reducing scope does not necessarily mean giving customers less. If you have an Anticipating (Pattern 4) process for gathering, analyzing, and ranking requirements, you'll know what customers want and what's most important to them. The requirements you get will be far fewer and more specific than you'll get with a more primitive process.

Unfortunately, installing such a process requires *anticipation*, and project managers are often such placaters or perfectionists that they never seriously consider a congruent requirements process until it is much too late. The placaters find it impossible to say no to any request, and the perfectionists find it impossible to say, "We didn't do as well as we thought we could do, so we want to reduce the scope." That's why upper management is in the best position to initiate scope-reduction tactics late in a project, as well as early in a project. That's a major reason why projects without an effective executive sponsor are very likely to fail. As Thomsett observes:[2]

> It is critical for senior business executives who sponsor an IT project to be actively involved, in effect, as executive project manager in the following areas:
>
> - stakeholder involvement, commitment, and conflict resolution
> - benefits planning and realization
> - quality requirements planning
> - risk management
> - project change control

Notice how strongly these factors are involved in determining the size of the requirements. If we have this kind of support, there are a number of tactics we can use when requirements must be reduced.

## 20.3 Eliminate the Worst Part

A simple nonlinear model would predict that eliminating 10 percent of the functionality might reduce the time to locate faults by 20 percent, but in practice you can do much better. Once you've actually been working with the system, you have data on which functions have shown the most faults. If you choose to get rid of the worst ones, you can have an effect that's out of proportion to size.

### 20.3.1 Error-prone modules

Many studies have verified the finding that certain modules in many systems are error-prone. Although they constitute perhaps 2 percent of the total code, they account for more than 80 percent of the total faults. Moreover, the error-prone modules reveal themselves quite clearly by their fault patterns in system test, before a system is released. In other words, error-prone modules are born error-prone and stay error-prone through the entire life of a system.

By the time you're confronted with a schedule crisis, you have the data you need to identify most of the error-prone modules. These are the modules you should first suggest eliminating from the current release. Of course, some of these functions may be truly essential to a meaningful release, but in my experience, a manager who is not a placater can negotiate away at least half of the error-prone modules if the need for speed is sufficiently pressing. The rest, of course, will have to be redone for the current release, but doing them right is always faster than doing them wrong.

Suppose you negotiate a deferral of 10 percent of the function, which includes some error-prone modules as well as some modules that are a bit behind in the testing schedule and thus are of unknown quality. Using this strategy, you may well eliminate 50 percent of the remaining faults. You've reduced the number of places to look by only 10 percent, but you've probably reduced interaction effects by at least a factor of four. Combined with halving the number of faults, the net effect could easily be a *ten times reduction in the amount of time spent locating faults.*

### 20.3.2 Effects of reduction on fault location time

Actual experiences among my clients are quite consistent with the idea of an order-of-magnitude reduction in location time from a small reduction in function. In developing one new product, a software utilities organization used fault tabulations to choose 13 potentially error-prone modules out of 73 to defer to a later release. Before the modules were pulled from the configuration, the average time spent tracking down a fault was about 7 hours. With the reduced system, the location time was less than 1.5 hours.

The developers didn't know, of course, how many faults they never had to look at. They could have checked a year later, but 6 of the 13 modules had been completely recoded, and 3 had been thrown away permanently, because of lack of customer demand—a nice bonus effect of this tactic.

You don't need fancy measurements to identify error-prone modules. Another client started searching for error-prone modules only after a system had already been released. The release was causing a crisis in the whole shop because of the number of customer calls to the developers. The manager called a meeting of the developers and asked, "If the good fairy granted you one wish, which piece would you wish wasn't in this system?" Without hesitation, they all identified the same module. They "de-released" this module simply by notifying customers that it wasn't actually in this release. Even before the crisis disappeared, the morale went up by 100 percent, which probably reduced fault-location time even further.

### 20.3.3 Eliminate what hasn't been finished

As the project passes its scheduled delivery date without completion, you have another way of predicting which are the worst modules. In fact, you don't have to predict at all, because the worst ones from the point of view of delivery are precisely those that haven't been finished. They may be stuck in testing, or they may not even have reached testing. In either case, you can make your schedule by simply dropping those modules from the release.

Of course, you will not always be able to do this, but it's always worth a try. Tell your customer, "You can have it now *without* features X, Y, and Z, or you can have it at some unknown later time, *perhaps* with X, or Y, or Z. You might even get all three, but I can't promise if or when. Which do you prefer?" Then wait for the initial reaction to cool down before you start negotiating.

An Anticipating (Pattern 4) organization will have foreseen this possibility and maintained a good, open relationship with its customer. With such a relationship, it's much more likely that this offer will not be a surprise, and not be confrontational. In that case, the customer is more likely to accept the diminished system on the spot, in which case you are finished with the first release right on schedule. All you have to do now is tackle the next release.

In some cases, you may find that the customer doesn't *ever* want X, or Y, or Z, in which case release 2.0 has a smaller system to build on a longer schedule. In other cases, you'll still have to build X as part of release 1.0, but can defer Y and Z, which, though you haven't made your schedule, is still a gain. In some cases you'll still have to produce all three in release 1.0, but at least you're no worse off than before you asked.

### 20.3.4 Eliminate the least valuable part

You could have avoided this de-releasing trouble if you had built top-down with the most important functions being built and integrated first. Then 90 percent complete would probably give 99.9 percent of value. I have seen many top-down systems that were *never* completed—in the sense of fulfilling the entire original specification—yet were happily accepted by their customers. Prototyping, of course, can have a similar effect: delivering more value for less effort by putting the more important parts first.

Even if you haven't planned your project as a top-down or prototype development, you can still get some of the benefits later, when you're in trouble. You simply present your customer with a list of unfinished functions and ask for them to be put in priority order, also showing which functions are dependent on others. From then on, you implement in that order. When each new part is integrated, you make your customer an offer to stop and take the system now, then wait to see what happens.

### 20.3.5 Deliver with faults

No software product was ever delivered fault-free, so one way to eliminate the worst part is to ship it to the customers in a way that won't bother them so much. You can present a list of known remaining faults to the customer and ask for them to be put in priority order. Categories can be like grades:

> F.   I cannot use the system with this fault.
> D.   I can use the system for a certain time with this fault, at a cost of X.
> C.   I can use the system indefinitely with this fault, at a cost of Y.
> B.   I can use the system indefinitely with this fault, at no cost.
> A.   What fault?

You can stop working immediately on the A and B faults, and put the labor you save to work on the F's. Since you now know what they're worth, you may want to offer to pay the customers for taking the system with C and D faults. You may pay in cash, or in a price reduction, or in trade. For instance, if you deduct Y from the purchase price, then the customers should be willing to accept a C fault and never complain about it. If you deduct X, they shouldn't complain for a while, anyway.

This tactic doesn't have to work for all your customers, because not everybody plans to use the system in the same way. Even if the system flunks for some of them, others may have no F's at all, or even D's. Ship to the ones who want it, and deal with the others later.

This priority approach has several unexpected advantages:

- You give the project a little taste of success, which boosts morale if presented properly.
- You give the developers greater incentive to find and fix the high-priority faults. It's much harder to fix faults if you don't truly believe they are faults.
- You may reduce the strength of the "number of users" dynamic.

### 20.3.6  Deliver with features

Reviewing the fault list with the customer sometimes reveals another category of fault:

> A++. What a great feature!

The software may not work the way they asked for, but the way it does work may actually be better, at least in some respects.[3]

For instance, one client produced an electronic mail system with a fault that crashed the system if you gave it a message longer than one screen. In reviewing the fault list, the customer said, "This would be a great way to keep down the size of memos, but I really can't afford to have people crashing the system all day long. That would cost more than the savings from shorter memos." The project manager then offered to fix the fault by simply stopping message entry when the page filled, so the system wouldn't crash. The customer bought it, and bragged about the design feature that finally did what nobody in their organization had ever been able to do before: trim the memos.

## 20.4 Eliminate As Early As Possible

Cutting down system size is a powerful intervention, and the earlier you can do it, the more powerful it is. For one thing, the earlier you reduce the size, the fewer resources you'll waste on things that don't have to be done. You'll also have more time and less pressure to get people trained to new tasks, and project managers will be able to set reasonable expectations before unreasonable ones are cast in concrete. Ideally, you would reduce the size to the minimum before planning, but lacking the benefit of hindsight, the best you can do is be on the lookout for early opportunities to reduce the size.

### 20.4.1  Prepare people for the reduction

Early reduction is also easier on the people in your organization. Overload is like cancer, and feeds on itself (Figure 20-2). Reducing the load early can boost morale and lower fatigue so that people are more productive. You must be attentive, however, to the *manner* in which you do the reduction. In a development project, programmers whose modules are cut or deferred are likely to become depressed.

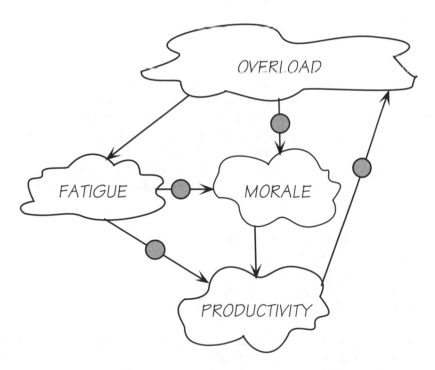

Figure 20-2.        Chronic overload is self-perpetuating, so reducing load early can have a positive snowball effect.

You can minimize such depression by *not blaming*, and by *having other work ready* for these people to do. If you cut first and then start looking for things for people to do, you imply that the objective was to get rid of bad work, which implies blame. You also have people sitting around waiting for your decision, which not only loses resources, but is the most depressing situation of powerlessness you can create.

If you have several alternative tasks for the programmers to choose—tasks that can be started immediately—you emphasize the addition, not the subtraction. In effect, you send a message that the new work is valuable, rather than that the old work was bad. Having choices reduces the feeling of powerlessness that leads to depression; by offering a choice, you give the programmers a chance for some feeling of empowerment.

But don't they need to be told that they did a poor job? How else will they learn to do better next time? Of course, they need accurate feedback about the reasons their work was cut or deferred. If you deprive them of that, you eliminate the possibility of professional growth, for them and for the organization. But you don't need to *tell* them, because they'll already know. If you simply can't resist telling them, at least wait a while, until they're out of Chaos and have rebuilt some self-esteem in the new assignment. In other words, the *way* you reduce system size is often as important as the actual size reductions. Otherwise, if you're not careful, you'll reduce your effective labor force more than you reduce the system size.

### 20.4.2 Extend the schedule

Some of the dynamic size effects are *relative* to the schedule. That is, what we perceive to be a big system to be done in two weeks could be seen as a small system if the schedule allowed two months. Trying to force a big system into a small schedule will always make the whole project take longer, so some of the effects of size reduction can be gained by slipping the schedule.

Before you negotiate a schedule slippage, however, you should study the dynamics of your system. For instance, if the schedule slips at the last possible minute (the day the system is due), you will see

- depression from feelings of failure
- elation from pressure relief
- time lost to replanning
- time lost to make up for lost personal time
- general loss of efficiency due to Chaos

As a result, you can count on losing at least two weeks any time you make a late schedule slip. This means that *extending the schedule by two weeks will buy you absolutely nothing*. If that's your best offer, DO NOT buy it. Schedule and resource slack are needed to allow for damping out, rather than amplifying,

problems. If you slip earlier, these effects are diminished. In fact, people probably won't notice a small slip if it's a couple of months before the scheduled
date.

### 20.4.3  Be realistic and be courageous

Ultimately, what helps you most is courage and realism. Knowing that
requirements can be reduced later is a useful tactic, but it can also be a trap for
the cowardly. DO NOT allow things to get into the requirements in the hopes
that you can eliminate them later. DO NOT placate early in hopes that you
will be bold enough, later on, to fight for the elimination of those parts that
aren't working out well. Even with all the data, it's always emotionally more
taxing to eliminate function later, rather than earlier.

## 20.5  Manage Late-Arriving Requirements

Even with your best efforts to cut down the size of the system, new requirements arriving late in the project make you feel like you're swimming
upstream. New requirements come from both customers and programmers, so
you must watch everywhere. Some late requirements changes are necessary in
any organization, but you must never forget that they are increasing the size of
the system. Figure 20-3 sketches some of these effects, as explained in this section.

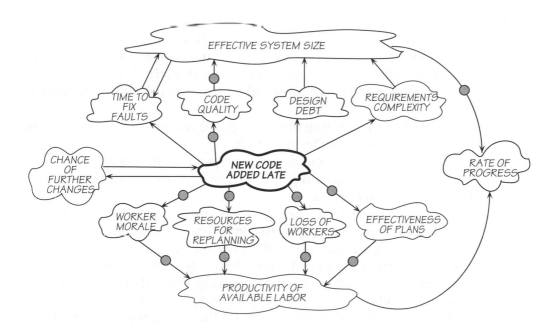

Figure 20-3.      Adding requirements late in the project slows down the rate of progress far out
of proportion to the amount of code added.

### 20.5.1 Trading time for requirements

DO NOT be tricked into easily accepting a little extra time for adding late requirements. The dynamics of system size are nonlinear, so you need to be very generous in estimating the effect of late-arriving requirements. If you go into your negotiations armed with a sense of the true costs, then you're much more likely to come out with something you can live with. If you do have to accept the late requirements, at least you will have obtained a reasonable amount of time for them.

For instance, one study showed that time to locate all faults grew by 28 percent in response to an 11 percent rise in system size. If the testing part of the project had originally scheduled 54 days for finding all the STIs (system trouble incidents), 15 more days had to be added to this effort to accommodate 10K lines of code added to the original 90K. Moreover, that increase doesn't take into account other factors, such as the following:

- Time to fix faults will also increase nonlinearly.
- The newly added code will probably cause more trouble, proportionately, because it's being developed on a compressed time scale. Good design can mitigate this effect, but never guarantee it won't happen in all cases.
- The newly added code will probably cause more trouble, proportionately, because it's not part of the original design, so it won't fit as smoothly.
- The newly added code will probably cause more trouble, proportionately, because of greater intrinsic difficulty usually found in requirements added late. If you look at why they were added late, you'll find that often they are more complex (which slowed down the requirements process) or more subtle (so they weren't recognized at first).
- When each new requirement is accepted, resources will have to be taken out of other tasks for replanning.
- Even if you take the time and resources to do it properly, the plans may be suboptimized, and thus be less effective than if you could have planned all at once.
- You may be reinforcing behavior on the part of your customers, encouraging them to make even more changes even later. Once you accept a change (especially if the customer doesn't have to pay the true cost of the disruption), your chance of further change goes up dramatically. Just the cost of considering these changes can have a substantial delaying effect on your project.
- There may be demoralizing effects on the workers as the job grows. Check your slip chart, because the workers are doing that in their heads. If their universe seems to be expanding faster than the speed

of light, they may jump off the spaceship early. Also, each time they experience this kind of expansion, they lose a little more faith in the credibility of management.

- Workers may have plans for what to do when the project ends, so that when it runs over its original estimate, you start to lose people at a great rate, and now have to add more people, which extends the time even further. I smile when I recall one desperate manager asking a developer to delay her wedding "a month or so" in order to be around for the newly scheduled end of the project. I think he really believed she might do it.

All of this adds up to a good guess that a project originally planned for two hundred working days could easily extend to two hundred fifty days or more because of a 10 percent increase in required size. If the new requirement arrives after one hundred days have already elapsed, the increase will be even bigger, because of the disruptive effects. You might reasonably estimate another one hundred days, and the customer will scream, "But you're *doubling* the delivery time for a 10 percent increase!" You're not doubling the delivery time, of course, but you are doubling the *remaining* time, which will be very hard to sell if you can't explain the nonlinear dynamics. Before you go into such negotiations, study Figure 20-3, then take it to show to your customer.

### 20.5.2 *Making a business case*

I'm not, of course, saying that you should *never* accept new requirements late in a project. For business reasons, the project may become meaningless if you don't accept them. But you have to make *your side of the business case*, too. Here's what you can do:

DO build estimating time and cost into the consideration of requirements changes. DO learn to say, "If we consider that change, we have to add X weeks and Y dollars to the delivery date, because of the people who will have to be involved in studying it." This will eliminate some of the less important pie-in-the-sky stuff right away.

Be sure you DO NOT make any estimate without a certification of the requirement through your requirements process. (This is where a lot of your resources have to be spent, which partially explains the delay.) DO tell the customer, "We'll need one week [or whatever] from the time you deliver us a full written requirement idea to conduct our reviews. We may also need time to free up the necessary people. At the end of that time, we'll know if the new requirement idea is clear enough to make an estimate, or if we'll have to get a revised requirement." Even more pie-in-the-sky will fly away.

DO check every proposed change against your models of the dynamics of your project, to discover any possible nonlinear effects. DO believe what your model says, and DO explain it to the customer when you present your estimate.

DO set priorities. Set them for yourself, and get the customer to set them, too. DO consider every new requirement a fault, because at present it is missing from the system. DO have your customer use the A–F system of ranking before you negotiate.

DO present the consequences of each change request in clear, businesslike terms. "If you want this and so, then it will cost thus and such, in time, money, and uncertainty." DO make sure that if your customer accepts the bargain, you'll be able to live with it.

DO NOT be a placater! If you've done all the above and your customer starts to pressure you, DO say, "I may have made a mistake. If you want me to recalculate, then here's how much more the project will be delayed." If they accept this offer, DO recalculate. If you haven't made any mistakes, DO NOT back down. If they threaten to replace you with someone better, that's simply part of the risk of the project management business. If they can find someone better than you, it's their right to do so, and perhaps you'll learn something.

DO tell the customer in advance that in the event that changes are requested, a specified process will be used to evaluate the request and it will take X amount of time. This is part of the educational process as well as the process of reaching agreement before starting. Late surprises produce angry customers, diminish trust, and may turn the entire relationship adversarial rather than cooperative. DO grant your customer the right to know at the outset how best to document desired changes, as well as what the evaluation process will entail. This is part of managing expectations.[4] As a result of your anticipating change in this way, some of your customers will think about their requests more fully beforehand, some may submit fewer requests, and most will accept the process much more graciously.

DO remember the Helpful Model: Most of the time, in spite of appearances, everybody is trying to be helpful. Generally, your customers simply don't understand software quality dynamics, which is your profession, not theirs. That's why they insist on pressing for new requirements late in the project, not because they're evil people trying to make you look bad.

### 20.6  Helpful Hints and Suggestions

1.  James G. Gavin, Jr., the engineer who led the lunar module project, said, "If a major project is truly innovative, you cannot possibly know its exact cost and its exact schedule at the beginning. And if in fact you do know the exact cost and the exact schedule, chances are that the technology is obsolete."[5] In other words, if you are most interested in making an ambitious schedule, try to stay away from the "bleeding edge" technologies.

2.  Error-prone modules provide one of the greatest motivations for bringing code under configuration management *before* unit test. If you have change records from unit test, you can identify the error-prone modules at the earliest possible moment.

3. Building small and fast is easier when the organization is small, and when there is trust that fosters communication. Morale is also better:

> Under Frederick II (1740-1786), when Prussia had a population of 5 million, the army was led by about 1,000 officers, all of whom were personally known to the king. Frederick William III, with his 3,000 officers, probably did not attempt to know the reserve officers among them, whose number was slowly increasing; but even so, it was no mean task to know the rest. Here we become aware of the emergence of a qualitative difference in interpersonal relations: An officer corps whose members are individually known to the king has the cohesion of an order of knights; however, if the supreme commander cannot have any personal acquaintance with the bulk of the nation's army officers, their *esprit de corps* can be only of an abstract, derivative nature.[6]

4. Another advantage to the small organization is that people know each other face-to-face, and have many opportunities to work with one another. Thus, people's reputations tend to match their demonstrated performance. Small organizations may reliably depend on performance evaluation and make better staffing decisions and estimates because of that better information.

   As they grow, however, the dynamics of reputation change. Face-to-face interactions with any one person become more rare. In this situation, an early impression may be an only impression. If Archie does something very good very early, Archie becomes known as a good guy, except perhaps to those few who work with him every day. If Doris does something very bad very early, Doris becomes known as a bad guy—an impression she can overcome quickly only in her immediate work group.

5. Payson Hall—most of whose experience is in development and systems integration for a fixed fee—points out that when you propose to cut scope in a fixed-fee contract, you have to be ready to renegotiate the whole contract. You may even have to give them some of their money back, whether they choose to throw you out, keep you, or take you to court.

   Actually, all development work would be improved if there were an explicit contract at the beginning. Then all participants would be clearer on the fact that reducing scope is always a matter of renegotiation, not some bad faith trick you're playing on your customer or sponsor. The decision should, therefore, be to everybody's advantage.

## 20.7 Summary

✔ Futile efforts to change software more quickly often mean that we change our software organizations more slowly. The Satir Change Model suggests a number of principles that show how to respond to pressures to speed up the building process without destroying your plans for long-term improvement of your organization.

✔ There are two fundamental tactics you can use to accelerate building process:

- increase your capacity for building
- decrease the size of what you're building

Increasing capacity—not just numbers, but skill as well—in the long run helps achieve schedules, high performance, low costs, and just about everything else—and so will be the subject of later chapters. Decreasing size, however, is something that managers can control in the short run.

✔ System size enters into many of the fundamental dynamic feedback loops of software engineering. For example, in a bigger system, there are

- more faults
- more places to look for faults
- more possibility of faults interacting, which confuses location efforts

This dynamic suggests that the system in which we are looking for faults should be as small as possible.

✔ The most important measure of system size is the *mental* size of the system—the amount of mental effort required to play the game effectively. This size may correlate roughly with lines of code, but there are many ways in which programs (little and big) with the same number of lines may be very different in this meaning of size.

✔ In addition, mental size is also relative to whose mentality is involved. Smarter, better-trained people working with superior tools will see a smaller system.

✔ Systems grow in functionality when the software developers placate the customers or their surrogates, the marketers.

✔ Reducing scope does not necessarily mean giving customers less. If you have an Anticipating (Pattern 4) process for gathering, analyzing, and ranking requirements, you'll know what customers want and what's most important to them.

✔ Once you've actually been working with the system, you have data on which functions have shown the most faults. If you choose to get rid of the worst ones, you can have an effect that's out of proportion to size. An order-of-magnitude reduction in location time can easily result from a small reduction in function.

✔   An Anticipating (Pattern 4) organization will have foreseen the possibility of late reduction in scope and maintained a good, open relationship with its customer.  With such a relationship, it's much more likely that this offer will not be a surprise, and not be confrontational.

✔   You can avoid de-releasing trouble if you build top-down with the most important functions being built and integrated first, because then 90 percent complete would probably give 99.9 percent of value.  As a variant, you can produce some of the new pieces in prototype form, then offer them to the customer.

✔   No software product was ever delivered fault-free, so one way to eliminate the worst part is to ask your customers to put faults in priority order:

> F.       I cannot use the system with this fault.
> D.       I can use the system for a certain time with this fault, at a cost of X.
> C.       I can use the system indefinitely with this fault, at a cost of Y.
> B.       I can use the system indefinitely with this fault, at no cost.
> A.       What fault?
> A++.     What a great feature!

✔   Cutting down system size is a powerful intervention, and the earlier you can do it, the more powerful it is:

- Fewer resources are wasted on things that don't have to be done.
- There's more time and less pressure to get people trained to new tasks.
- Project managers will be able to set reasonable expectations.
- It's easier on the people in your organization.  Overload is like cancer, and feeds on itself.

✔   Some of the dynamic size effects are *relative* to the schedule.  Therefore, some of the effects of size reduction can be gained by slipping the schedule.  Before you negotiate a schedule slippage, however, study the dynamics of your system.  Attempts to deliver a system on an impossibly short schedule will only lengthen the actual time you need to deliver.

✔   Ultimately, what helps you most in managing system size is courage and realism.

✔   Some late requirements changes are necessary in any organization, but you must never forget that they are increasing the size of the system.  The dynamics of system size are nonlinear, so you need to be very generous in estimating the effect of late-arriving requirements, and make *your side of the business case*, too.

✔ Tell your customer *in advance* that in the event that changes are requested, a specified process will be used to evaluate the request and that it will take X amount of time. Late surprises produce angry customers, diminish trust, and may turn the entire relationship adversarial rather than cooperative.

✔ Remember the Helpful Model: Most of the time, in spite of appearances, everybody is trying to be helpful. Generally, your customers simply don't understand software quality dynamics—that's *your* profession, not theirs.

## 20.8 Practice

1. Read the following comment and discuss the assumptions this speaker made in terms of system size:

> It is obvious that manual techniques can no longer keep pace with rapid application development efforts, due to the speed of application development, the tremendous volume of data generated by automated testing of graphical user interfaces, and the enormous number of errors detected.

2. Figure 20-3 represents something of a shorthand for the effects of adding code late in a project. For example, the effect of such new code is to increase design debt, but there are several paths through which that effect is created. Pick one or more of these effects and elaborate on the total dynamic by which that effect is created.

3. Janice Wormington notes: The "deliver with faults" tactic is only as good as your ability to estimate the seriousness of a particular fault. Develop a list of processes by which you can derive the estimated seriousness of a fault as close as possible to the actual seriousness.

4. Phil Fuhrer suggests: Discuss how system layering can be an effective way of reducing the apparent size of a system.

# 21
## Protecting Information Assets

*Client #1: Long ago, we established that a line of certified code cost us about $20 to produce, but we were using this figure for estimating only. It never occurred to us to use it to compute the value of the finished asset. When we eventually woke up, we realized that our code library of 20 million lines of code had cost us about $400 million to produce. That was more than our office building cost, but we were spending nothing to protect it or insure it.[1]*
*—Anonymous*

When the skywalk at the Kansas City Hyatt Regency Hotel collapsed, killing 112 people and injuring 187 others, the failure was traced to a design change that doubled the stress at the point where the walkway pulled loose. One building code official questioned after the collapse said that there is an ordinance requiring builders and designers to notify the city of structural design changes made after a building permit has been issued, but it's not enforced. Furthermore, he said it was unenforceable because of a lack of manpower, but that the city trusts architects and engineers to adhere to the code.

Even though the collapsing structure was a hotel and not an information system, this tragic story is familiar enough to software engineering managers. The dynamics in both cases are the same: misplaced trust in architects and engineers to maintain the integrity of the underpinnings of the system, leading to lack of enforcement. Management is unwilling to commit resources to the task, generally because they are unaware of the risk exposure that creates the need to monitor this information. Moreover, they may be unaware of the dynamics that lead the technical staff to take shortcuts, and certainly unaware of their own role in these dynamics.

In construction projects as in software development, changes can be introduced into translation from design to manufacturing by builders who are trying to improve the product, and problems can arise if those changes aren't subjected to the same rigorous procedure as the initial concept. The big difference between the construction industry and the software industry is that in construction, only a small percentage of such on-the-job changes produce catastrophes. Our experience in software is quite different, and typically a single unreviewed change to a large system will have less than a fifty-fifty chance of being correct. In the light of this experience, an Anticipating (Pattern 4) manager will foresee that unreviewed changes are dangerous and will take preventive action.

Information systems are assets, and it's a major part of your job as manager to protect your organization's assets. If one of your employees used a company credit card improperly for, say, a few hundred dollars, you'd probably not hesitate to dismiss him. But should that employee destroy a much more valuable asset by violating the configuration management procedures, you'd probably slap his wrist and mutter, "Boys will be boys." It's one mark of Variable (Pattern 1) and Routine (Pattern 2) cultures that software managers tend to believe the complaints of their "renegades":

> Then there are the Renegades. They know that the configuration management procedures (the "bureaucracies") are a waste of time, not to mention an affront to their individuality, creativity, and constitutional rights. They are going to do what they believe is best regardless of what you tell them. They know that what they are doing is correct and necessary, even though it violates the configuration management procedures. If they had to obey the rules, they [think they] would miss a milestone they have to meet by tomorrow.[2]

Many of the organization's assets are in the form of information, which may be why some managers find it hard to take them seriously as assets (Figure 21-1). We've already seen some of these assets, particularly the various requirements databases. Other such informational assets often available without protection to the software engineers include

- code libraries
- data dictionaries
- test libraries and histories
- designs
- standards
- project plans

- process descriptions
- process histories
- measurement libraries
- manuals and documents of all sorts

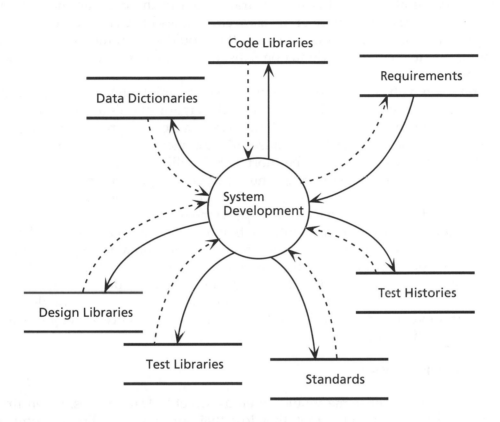

Figure 21-1.    The data environment of the software engineer includes many libraries that are totally open to access, but should only be changed through a controlled process (dotted lines) that recognizes their value as assets.

When these assets are put under control, the software engineers have an environment in which they can work with ease, without fear of destroying valuable property, or of working with damaged materials. Not only don't they become renegades, they become advocates:

> It's not surprising that software configuration management (SCM) tools are becoming more widely accepted and used in industry and the Department of Defense. What is surprising is that many people are beginning to *like* using these tools.[3]

### 21.1  Code Libraries

Code libraries—particularly object code libraries—are the asset of last resort. A change in the object code library affects the behavior of a system directly, without any further step in which to check for problems.  The immediacy and risk of change at this level is well characterized in the programmer's term "zap."  For instance, in a number of cases, embezzlers have zapped object code to create an escape hatch through which they could siphon funds to personal accounts, write checks to fictitious persons, or move charges to other people's accounts.

Yet even as bad as these criminal acts seem, unintentional damage from zapping represents a much worse threat to the organization's assets.  We've all heard these horror stories:  A last-minute patch causes a payroll system to produce 45,000 erroneous checks, or causes 450,000 incorrect disks to be cut and distributed, or causes billings to be short by $45 million.

Is it possible for a single programmer in your organization to zap object code?  If so, how can you sleep at night?  If you want to protect assets, code libraries are the first place to look for improvement.

Code is the most critical of information assets, so if you understand how to control code, control of other assets should be conceptually simple.  Control of other assets need not be as strict as code control, because there are checks and balances that follow certification of data dictionaries, designs, standards, and so forth.  Nevertheless, lax asset control tends to produce creeping deterioration, and eventually will lead to the downfall of any software engineering organization, no matter how carefully it controls code.

### 21.2  Data Dictionaries

"A rose by any other name would smell as sweet."  Data names, when first given, are arbitrary, but after that, they lose their arbitrariness.  From a compiler point of view, they are still arbitrary, but not so to anybody who has to read a program after it is first written, which may be thousands of times.  Try assigning the following name substitutions:

    rose = grxzl
    name = oetyr
    sweet = wohncriesty
    other = yugzag
    smell = iobrych

This gives the perfectly clear sentence: "A grxzl by any yugzag oetyr would iobrych as wohncriesty."

Even worse than our using arbitrary names, we could use recognizable names, but ones which are usually used for other things. For example, we could substitute

rose = cucumber
name = color
sweet = green
other = similar
smell = look

This gives, "A cucumber by any similar color would look as green." At least the arbitrary names warned us that we didn't understand. In this case, we could easily be fooled into believing we understood, and thus make a mistake.

The problem of arbitrary names grows with the size and number of systems (see Figure 21-2), so you can't imagine the true cost of arbitrary naming schemes by looking at one small example. Try, instead, to imagine a typical COBOL system under maintenance, which might have 500,000 lines of code with a vocabulary of 10,000 words (more than the average American's speaking vocabulary). Now consider the plight of a programmer transferred from another system to maintain this one, with no common data dictionary.

The data dictionary is an excellent asset with which to illustrate the costs of creeping loss of control. Many organizations operate without any explicit data dictionary and manage to blunder along, but blundering simply won't do if you want your organization to have an Anticipating (Pattern 4) culture.

Inexperienced programmers seem to have a fascination with giving names to things, like a parent naming a baby. Some seem to think that their creativity lies primarily in their ability to give data names, so they feel stifled if they have to conform to a standard naming scheme in a data dictionary. This false idea needs to be reframed: Naming things is a primitive sort of magic, but creating things from new combinations of old familiar names is truly creative. James Robertson confirmed what's possible if this reframing is done skillfully:

> I am working with one of my clients to introduce standard data names. The developers are very enthusiastic as they see the great benefits for them and for their organization. I gave them the formula; they make the names. They love it.[4]

This same fascination with naming can destroy your efforts to create an effective data dictionary process. The French Academy is reputed to have spent seventy-five years deciding whether the automobile should be feminine or masculine (*la voiture* versus *le voiture*). Committees of programmers often show the same tendency to academic debates over names, forgetting that the most important benefit of names is their *consistency*. As a manager, your job is to see that naming doesn't get out of hand, either as a debating society or somebody's power trip.

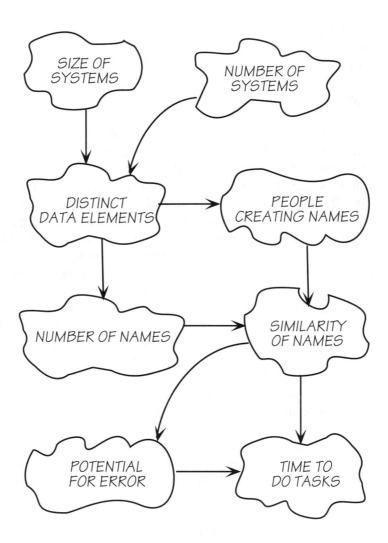

Figure 21-2.      As systems grow larger, uncontrolled naming leads to increased error and time to perform engineering tasks.

## 21.3  Standards

An organization that possesses a common language can do things faster and more reliably. An effective data dictionary helps create this cultural asset but is only one special case of standards. By standards, I don't confine my meaning to written standards such as the ISO 9000 series, but I also include any way of speaking or working that is, indeed, *standard* within the organization.

Moreover, I include whatever cultural systems serve to keep those standards standard.

The value of standards as assets is easy to miss, because usually their impact is through many small savings. Sometimes, however, the accumulated value is cashed in, like cracking the piggy bank in which you've stashed your small change for a year. One such occasion is the conversion from one hardware or software platform to another:

> Four departments in one organization converted a large number of applications from IBM mainframes under OS/360 to Macintoshes. Department A, which had achieved a high level of standardization—primarily through the use of technical reviews—had a conversion cost per line of code that was less than one-third of the cost experienced by the other departments. The accuracy of the conversion was also greater, though at the time of measurement, Departments B, C, and D were still busy paying this operational cost, so it could only be estimated—at ten times fewer conversion errors.

In the same conversion, Department C uncovered nine different routines for computing the difference between two dates, twenty-three routines for formatting dates for printing, and an unknown amount of embedded code that did things related to dates without using any of these routines. This duplication of effort was another cost of not standardizing, and illustrates how the process of standardizing can be made easier if you have good configuration control. At the same time, configurations are much easier to manage if you have standards, at the very least because there is much less code to manage.

## 21.4 Designs

Information hiding is a design principle that says that decomposition into modules is cleanest, and therefore safest, when one builder knows nothing about what is going on *inside* any other builder's modules.[5] This concept can be implemented in most modern languages, and object-oriented languages proclaim information hiding as one of their most important features. In order to enforce this concept in reality, however, we'd have to treat the builders like idiots, and even then there would be no way to prevent them from communicating. For one thing, a single builder may build two or more boxes, and could hardly be expected to forget what's inside one while building another.

A more sensible approach is to develop a culture, supported by configuration management tools, that encourages builders to play the "black box game," and act *as if* they don't know what's inside all the other black boxes. To do this, we need to manage the *design interfaces* with all the care we give to code management, for these are the only places my design changes can affect the correctness of your designs.

Design quality and configuration management quality are in a mutual feedback relationship, as sketched in the diagram of effects in Figure 21-3.

Poor design increases errors in code, which produces lots of code changes that increase the load on the code management system. Poor design also makes the code management task more complex, because it's not always clear where things are and where they're supposed to be. A good design acts as a natural index to data stored about a system, such as code, tests, and maintenance manuals. Often, complaints about the complexity of code management are actually complaints about poor design.

On the other hand, problems with code management mean that logistical errors will be more frequent, which increases the total error rate. And the more errors that must be fixed—especially in emergency mode—the more likely there will be negative impacts on design integrity.

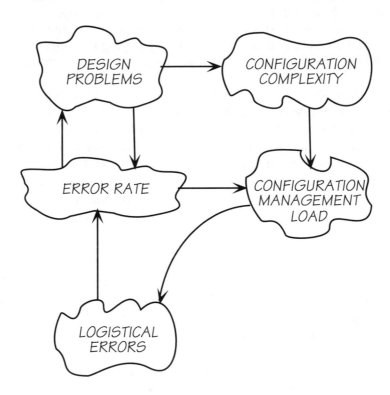

Figure 21-3.          Design influences the complexity of the configuration management job, which in turn impacts the quality of design.

## 21.5  Test Libraries and Histories

In my four decades in the software business, I've solved many mysteries, but one of them I've never yet been able to solve: Why are programmers (and their managers) so reluctant to retain the tests they have so laboriously constructed for their software? For some reason, they don't consider these tests to be assets.

Part of the problem seems to be the unsystematic way in which many organizations conduct their testing. First of all, they place heavy reliance on unit testing. When individual developers unit test their own code, they generally fail to keep accurate records, so the tests are not assets at all, and perhaps are even liabilities. Sometimes, you can improve this situation by having separate testers do the unit testing. This process tends to improve the chance of retaining tests as assets, especially if the testers are clearly informed of their responsibilities and are given tools to support test retention, as Payson Hall reminds us:

> The best software engineering firm I ever worked for had test case reviews as part of the acceptance criteria for modules. Code, test cases, unit-level design documents, unit-level specifications (interfaces and requirements), stubs, drivers, and test results were all under configuration management. The result was the best coding I've ever participated in, and regression testing was wonderful. Both the stubs and the drivers were useful during integration testing.

One problem with unit testing, even by separate testers, is that there's nothing really to prevent individual developers from doing undocumented unit testing before everything goes under control. Many developers who are quite careful when composing code go into a hacking frenzy when unit testing, destroying whatever design integrity their original version may have possessed. In the process, they also destroy valuable information about the *history* of the module, history that permits management to anticipate trouble, rather than fix it after the fact.

Years ago, Gary Okimoto and I studied the code history of OS/360 and discovered the phenomenon of *error-prone modules*. Long after the system was shipped, and even after revisions, these error-prone modules were ten to a hundred times more likely than the average module to contain problems. Thus, by noticing the early history of a module, we could predict its future and, if indicated, rebuild it. Because of the universal problem of error-prone modules, a module's history is an essential tool of maintenance, like the records of manufacturing and inspection in a nuclear plant or of an airplane.

When properly done, unit testing of modules creates a record of trouble that becomes part of a *module process history*. This history is a most valuable asset, and should contain

- the complete history of code changes
- the complete history of unit testing
- all test cases, plus expected and actual test results
- issues lists and summary reports from all technical reviews
- the schedule history (which is often an indication of error-proneness)

A generation ago, this information would have been too costly to maintain on-line, but storage costs and configuration management software have made it feasible; at the same time, the growing complexity of system maintenance has made it essential.

Paradoxically, Payson's ideal organization illustrates how difficult it may be to improve a process that is the best of its kind by introducing an entirely different process. Because this organization has such complete control over unit testing, its members have a hard time believing that unit testing adds no value and tends to disappear as organizations get very much better at software engineering: doing the code right in the first place, reviewing it before it's ever subjected to testing, and then going directly to integration testing with "untested" but almost perfect modules.[6]

## 21.6  Other Documents

As Patrick Henry said, "I know no way of judging of the future but by the past." To create an Anticipating (Pattern 4) organization, you must know the past, for there is no other way to anticipate the future. Anything that is developed on a machine can and should be archived, and the archives should be kept up-to-date and accessible. Items not already mentioned include

- project plans (as on Public Project Progress Posters[7])
- all manuals
- training materials

## 21.7  Improving Asset Protection

Moving to an improved system of protecting any form of information asset can follow a plan similar to that given for changing the requirements process:

1. Measure the true cost and value of protecting the asset.
2. Gain control of the changes (inputs) to the asset.
3. Gain control of the access (outputs) to the asset.
4. Gain control of the entire process of creating and maintaining the asset.

Let's briefly illustrate this process using code control as an example.

### 21.7.1  Measuring cost and value

As always, a study of cost and value of asset protection provides the foreign element that motivates improved code control. You can take at least three different approaches to measure cost and value: the cost of creating the asset, the asset's effects on other costs, and the risk of not protecting the asset. Client #1, quoted as an anonymous client at the opening of this chapter, characterizes the cost of creation approach. The following two client statements typify the asset's effects on the other costs approach and the risk approach.

Client #2: Our president set up a task force to determine why testing cost so much and took so much time. One of the findings showed that we often wasted enormous amounts of time testing in the wrong environment. We decided a code control system would eliminate this cost, so we implemented one. (We also found that we needed a test suite control system, and it turned out we could use the same tools, and more or less the same process.)

Client #3: We had a code control system, but it was rather lax. Several senior programmers had access that bypassed the normal controls—for use in "emergencies." Then, in one of those emergencies, a code zap introduced a side effect we didn't notice until well after it went into production. I'm not sure exactly what it cost us to clean it up—we couldn't put a value on loss of good will—but it was well over a million. We decided we could afford a lot tighter system of code control.

### 21.7.2 Controlling the inputs

Figure 21-4 shows some of the essential features needed to manage code assets.

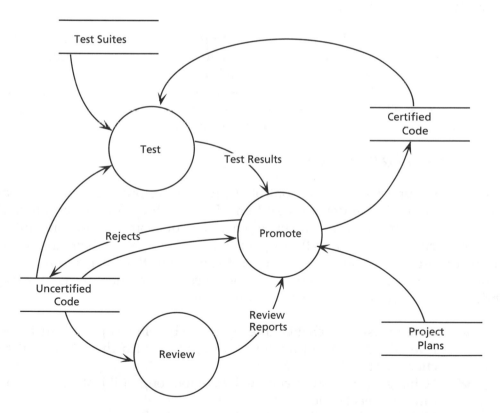

Figure 21-4.    A minimal protection of code assets requires that there be one and only one channel into the certified code database, through an explicit promotion process that considers reviews, tests, and project plans.

Promotion of code to certified code is a management responsibility, under the authority of the configuration manager. The decision is based on test and review results, coordinated with project plans. The actual placement of the code in the certified code database is best done by an administrative person who has no knowledge of coding; this practice removes the temptation to incorrectly correct changes submitted by someone else. (In the days long before photocopiers and printers, the illiterate monks who copied manuscripts by hand were far less likely to make corrections than the literate ones, and thus were much more reliable protectors of their ancient databases.)

The administrative person is the sole owner of write access to the database and inserts code only on the instruction of management. This structure absolutely prevents unauthorized zapping unless systems programmers decide to bypass database security. In the final analysis, systems programmers are potentially the most dangerous people to your organization's data assets, so any access they have to the information assets needs to be carefully monitored.

### 21.7.3 Controlling the outputs

Code control can never be made to work if programmers find it too difficult to access certified code. A common mistake is to concentrate on making it impossible to add uncertified code to the certified code database, yet ignore the work of making access effortless. With modern technology—software, hardware, and networks—there's no reason why each programmer cannot have instant read-only access to the entire certified code database.

### 21.7.4 Controlling the process

Putting code under strict asset control always annoys programmers who have heretofore operated under a lax system. Initially, they do not recognize the advantages of strict control, and even when they do, some of those advantages do not accrue to them, but to the organization as a whole. To them, this kind of control represents an inconvenience, and something that seems only to slow down their work. You can hear their annoyance in what they say as they try to induce you to bypass the system "just this once":

✔ "I can make that change directly in the baseline copy. It's just a one-line edit, so I don't have to fool around with that check-out and check-in stuff."

✔ "Changing the source code will take too long. I'll just zap this patch into the object code."

✔ "If I don't change the revision history, nobody will ever know I made a change."[8]

✔ "Since they're using this system to measure the number of changes I make, it's important that I slip a few through without recording them."

✔ "It's too cumbersome to keep track of everything."

DO NOT permit renegade behavior. DO change the reward system, both explicit and implicit, to see that renegade behavior is not rewarded and that asset-protecting behavior *is* rewarded. DO make programmers aware of the value of the code asset. DO allow time to get used to the new system, and DO allow slack in the schedules.

DO listen to what the renegade has to say. If it's about the configuration management system, DO see that the system is improved. If it's about the renegade, DO see that the renegade has a chance to improve.

DO NOT demand that people follow the system without understanding. DO see that the configuration manager takes on the job of education, and does it well.

DO make sure that there is one and only one path into the asset database. DO NOT allow changes to enter by more than one route. DO, however, provide an emergency access procedure to allow technicians to work quickly if an operational system has failed, and DO make sure that this procedure is triply protected. Lack of a solid emergency procedure will guarantee that the database integrity will eventually be violated "to save the company."

DO install change control and configuration control *from the beginning* of any project. DO NOT try to convert a project to configuration control in the middle, unless you allow for a huge chunk of effort in the project plan.

DO NOT try to convert the entire organization to any asset protection process in one fell swoop. DO convert the organization one project at a time, starting with the project most likely to succeed.

## 21.8 Helpful Hints and Suggestions

1. The importance of configuration management can be understood in terms of the theory of fractures from structural engineering. Structures fail from the propagation of cracks, and the first factor in tensile fracture is "the price in terms of energy which has to be paid to create a new crack."[9] In other words, if it's easy to create cracks, the structure is likely to collapse even under normal stress. In software, without configuration management in place, the energy cost of creating a crack is almost zero. Anyone can zap the system with a few keystrokes.

2. Norm Kerth suggests: To test your configuration management system, pick a day at random and ask for a reconstruction of the system as if there had been an earthquake that destroyed the latest version of the system. Do this first on a day that has been announced a week or more in

advance. Then, when the organization has demonstrated it can handle these early-warning earthquakes, conduct one with no warning. (Be sure to budget, though, for the effort required to handle these simulated emergencies.)

3.  It's easy to blame renegades for the destruction of assets, but you, the manager, are responsible for controlling renegades. You hired the renegades in the first place, and you reward the behavior that violates the process and puts the individual's performance above the team's. You may be deaf to reasonable feedback about the configuration management procedures and unable to communicate the reasons why these procedures are for the greatest benefit. Rather than blaming renegades, improve your management skills.

4.  For a careful case study of what a data dictionary and related tools can do for your organization, find a copy of the article "The Secrets of Software Maintenance," by David Eddy.[10] Study it.

5.  As much as some developers hate configuration management, they love new playthings. Perhaps if they understood the positive relationship between the two, they'd value configuration management as a way of supporting more and better tools. For instance, one of my clients purchased a $4,995 performance analyzer that up to 220 developers might need to use, which would have meant a cost of more than $1 million if one were bought for each developer. But a performance analyzer is infrequently used, so the company bought a single copy and put it under configuration control. Not only did this save them a heap of money for multiple copies, it put the tool in a situation where they were able to measure its usage and to use this measurement to determine that they could justify the cost of two more copies.

## 21.9 Summary

✔ In construction projects as in software development, changes can be introduced into translation from design to manufacturing by builders who are trying to improve the product, and problems can arise if those changes aren't subjected to the same rigorous procedure as the initial concept. In the light of experience with software systems, an Anticipating (Pattern 4) manager will anticipate that unreviewed changes are dangerous and will take preventive action.

✔ Information systems are assets, and a major part of your job as manager is to protect your organization's assets. Many of the organization's assets are in the form of information:

- requirements databases
- code libraries
- data dictionaries
- test libraries and histories
- designs
- standards
- project plans
- process descriptions
- process histories
- measurement libraries
- manuals and documents of all sorts

✔ Code libraries—particularly object code libraries—are the asset of last resort. A change in the object code library affects the behavior of a system directly, without any further step in which to check for problems. If you want to protect assets, code libraries are the first place to look for improvement.

✔ Control of other assets need not be as strict as code control, because there are checks and balances that follow certification of data dictionaries, designs, standards, and so forth. Nevertheless, lax asset control tends to produce creeping deterioration, and eventually will lead to the collapse of any software engineering organization, no matter how carefully it controls code.

✔ As systems grow larger, uncontrolled naming leads to increased error and time to perform engineering tasks. Many organizations operate without any explicit data dictionary and manage to blunder along, but blundering simply won't do if you want your organization to become Anticipating. The most important benefit of names is their consistency. As a manager, your job is to see that naming doesn't get out of hand.

✔ The value of standards as assets is easy to miss, because their impact is usually through many small savings. Configurations are much easier to manage if you have standards, at the very least because there is much less code to manage.

✔ A sensible approach to information hiding is to develop a culture, supported by configuration management tools, that encourages builders to play the black box game, and act as if they don't know what's inside all the other black boxes. To do this, manage the design interfaces with all the care given to code management, for these are the only places one person's design changes can affect the correctness of another person's designs.

✔ Design quality and configuration management quality are in a mutual feedback relationship:  Poor design increases errors in code, which produces lots of code changes that increase the load on the code management system.  Poor design also makes the code management task more complex, because it's not always clear where things are and where they're supposed to be.

✔ A good design acts as a natural index to data stored about a system, such as code, tests, and maintenance manuals.  Often, complaints about the complexity of code management are actually complaints about poor design.

✔ For some reason, programmers don't consider tests to be assets, perhaps because of the unsystematic way in which many organizations conduct their testing.  Sometimes, you can improve this situation by having separate testers do the unit testing.

✔ Many developers who are quite careful when composing code go into a hacking frenzy when unit testing, destroying whatever design integrity their original version may have possessed.  In the process, they also destroy valuable information about the history of the module.

✔ Error-prone modules are ten to a hundred times more likely than the average module to contain problems.  By noticing the early history of a module, you can predict its future and, if indicated, rebuild it.  Because of the universal problem of error-prone modules, a module's history is an essential tool of maintenance.

✔ Unit testing of modules should create a record of trouble that becomes part of a module process history.  This history is a most valuable asset, and should contain

  • the complete history of code changes
  • the complete history of unit testing
  • all test cases, plus expected and actual test results
  • issues lists and summary reports from all technical reviews
  • the schedule history (which is often an indication of error-proneness)

✔ To create an Anticipating (Pattern 4) organization, you must know the past, for there is no other way to anticipate the future.  Anything that is developed on a machine can and should be archived, and the archives should be kept up-to-date and accessible.

✔ Moving to an improved system of protecting any form of information assets can follow a plan similar to that given for changing the requirements process:

1. Measure the true cost and value of protecting the asset.
2. Gain control of the changes (inputs) to the asset.
3. Gain control of the access (outputs) to the asset.
4. Gain control of the entire process of creating and maintaining the asset.

## 21.10 Practice

1. Draw a diagram of effects showing how standards, configuration control, and a data dictionary work in concert to decrease mistakes and duplication of effort.

2. Jim Highsmith notes: Module configuration and history is much more complicated with client server systems. It could be located on the client, the server, the middleware, the client database, or the server database. What advantages does a distributed configuration and history database offer in return for this extra complication? Discuss what management can do to preserve the information assets while taking advantage of distributed systems.

3. Dan Starr expresses the feelings I've discovered in many people with technical backgrounds:

> I noticed I had an immediate strong reaction to the term "assets" as used to describe software. Upon some analysis, I found I agreed with the idea that software is valuable stuff and needs to be treated that way; there's just something about the term I don't like. My reaction is probably related to the management-by-fiat of "multiusable assets." I also associate the term "asset" with bureaucracy and bean-counting (corporate asset managers are the kinds of people who tell you that you can't have a modern PC because it costs too much, while ignoring the productivity cost of working on a dumb terminal). And, at least in our organization, the term "information assets" has come to replace "intellectual property" and is used in ways that carry a vaguely threatening implication that somehow your brain is the property of your employer.

How do you respond to the term "asset"? How do your coworkers respond? How does this affect the way you introduce the concept of information assets?

# 22
# Managing Design

*Bruno Bettelheim once described children's play as an activity "characterized by freedom from all but personally imposed rules (which are changed at will), by free-wheeling fantasy involvement, and by the absence of any goals outside the activity itself." This is a very good description of the designer at his drafting table. . . . Bettelheim quotes a four-year-old who asks, "Is this a fun game or a winning game?" The solitary building game [designing] is definitely a fun game—there is no opponent. . . . To say that design is fun goes a long way toward explaining the continued attraction of a profession that is characterized by relatively low pay and far from secure employment.[1]*
— Witold Rybczynski

Design *is* fun. Even software design—where the pay is higher and the employment more secure—is fun. Perhaps that's why so many managers are reluctant to keep their hands off the designers' work. Once again, this fun task is one of the things you must give up in return for a successful career in management. You may be able to satisfy your passion for design by using it to design organizations and processes, but not information systems.

This chapter is not primarily about design as fun, but about managers not fooling around with assets, because *designs are assets*. The idea of designs as assets gives you as manager the proper perspective on the kind of involvement you must have with regard to software designs, perhaps the greatest information asset of all.

## 22.1 The Life Cycle of a Design Innovation

Managers are charged with managing, which they cannot do if things become unmanageable. Therefore, although managers shouldn't be playing with designs, they must always stay involved in *reviewing* designs from the point of view that design is designed for *manageability*. Otherwise, certain designs (new or evolved) may add such a large management burden that a project based on them is not feasible. When a design is too complex, the manager must insist on simplification. If the designers insist that the complexity is necessary, the manager must have ways to validate their claim—and perhaps be ready to find new designers.

Sometimes, the excessive complexity is part of the design from the beginning, as in a monolithic CASE tool or spreadsheet engine. More often, as we have seen, repeated changes to the software increase the design debt. When the design debt grows large, management becomes well nigh impossible because management overhead increases nonlinearly as design debt increases.

The life history of many start-up software companies provides a morality play about what happens when design debt is not serviced. Typically, the Bright Young Fellas (BYF) company starts when someone has a really neat new design idea for a product. A company is formed and the product is introduced.

If the design idea is really new and the product fills a previously unfilled niche, sales increase dramatically and profits are astronomical. Eventually, BYF goes public, and the founders grant themselves hefty bundles of stock.

Possibly because of the newness of the product or the rush to market, there are lots of failures in use, which users insist must be corrected. Because people like the product, and use it, they demand new features. These demands lead to many code changes, which in turn produce a design debt—the design has begun to deteriorate.

Because BYF is so successful, it attracts not only investors, but also potential competitors. The competitors start creating copycat systems, only with improvements. Some of these competitors, profiting from the experience of BYF, base their candidates on improved designs, but in any case are initially free of design debt.

The presence of competition doesn't bother BYF's founders, for it validates their concept and increases sales. BYF's sales increase even more as their product improves and they cash in on their leading position. As a result, the stock price runs up further.

Competitors reach market with their products, some of which have used the knowledge of BYF's product to produce superior designs, inside and out. At about this time, BYF's founders cash in large chunks of their stock while urging their employees to work harder, be more innovative, and especially be committed to the company (which they can show by purchasing company stock).

In spite of all this urging, BYF's design debt doesn't allow their product to catch up with competitors while still using their old design, but the workers do keep hacking improvements. Sales growth and the stock price begin to level off.

Eventually, sales flatten and the stock price declines. BYF begins to take extreme measures to catch up. Often, professional managers are brought in to replace the founders, who are really in over their heads. Yet even in this desperate condition, BYF doesn't redesign the product.

Soon, the design crashes. It's just no longer possible to keep patching on new features and repairing the ones in the previous release. The company also crashes, but the founders are rich. The workers, however, are out of jobs and some of them hold worthless BYF stock. The product disappears, or is acquired by a multiproduct company for the product name. If so, the design is scrapped and replaced by a new design, perhaps keeping the old user interface. Then the cycle starts anew.

If, perchance, people should analyze the cause of BYF's demise, their conclusion would likely be poor design. I would agree, but not in the sense of "bad" design. To me, "poor" is used only in the sense of *pitiful:* "You *poor* design. With such inept management, you didn't stand a chance."

Designs cannot defend themselves against the slings and arrows of outrageous management. As a software engineering manager, your job is to see that designs *do* have a chance: that they're done well in the first place and are treated well throughout their life. Before you take up arms, you need to understand the diseases that designs are heir to, their effects on software, and some of their cures and preventatives.

## 22.2  Design Dynamics

The accumulation of design debt can certainly arise from "featuritis," but generally develops from excessive and/or hasty attempts to correct faults. Faults are what you create; failures are what you detect. Where you detect them isn't nearly as important as where you create them, but the common fallacy is that code is the source of most faults. As Figure 22-1 shows, most failures found in testing don't come from faults created in coding. Careless managers just think they're from coding, because *they're found immediately after coding*. Actually, they've been lurking there for a long time, but the process was not equipped to show their presence.

Here are some examples of "coding faults" that didn't originate in coding:

- code for which there was no requirement
- code for a wrong design
- code for a wrong requirement
- code not written because the coders forgot the requirement
- code that's too long because the data structure was clumsy
- code that's wrong because the interface was too complex

- code that's wrong because two parts of the design had different ideas
- code that's inconsistent with an overly complex and poorly documented design

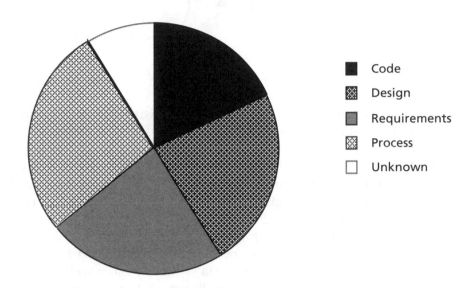

Figure 22-1.    A typical distribution, in which most faults originate before coding, though they may cause failures that are not detected until after coding.

Most faults originate in requirements and design, though process errors are also significant in poorly managed organizations. Process errors—such as duplicates, zaps, failures to update, and source code version control problems—are caused by the development process. Many of these can be addressed by an improved *process*, which is most definitely a management responsibility.

Increased design effort decreases coding effort in developing or maintaining an information system when it results in such effects as

- a better designed data structure
- modularity
- cleaner interfaces
- fewer switches and flags
- fewer global variables
- a more testable system
- reuse of constructs

The direct effect of some of these improvements is a reduction in coding effort (Figure 22-2).

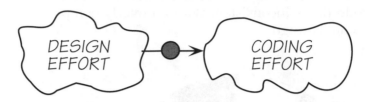

Figure 22-2.          One major reason for taking care in design is to reduce coding effort.

But less direct coding effort is not the only positive effect of good design. Another important reason for design effort is to decrease the number of large-scale errors (Figure 22-3). In one software company, a study revealed that the average design fault meant 22 lines of code were discarded and 16 lines of code were rebuilt, for a cost of roughly $10,000. The average coding fault, on the other hand, meant 3 lines of code were discarded and a single line of code was rebuilt, for a cost of roughly $1,200.

Build time consists of coding time plus design time. In this organization, the reduced coding effort because of improved design led to a reduction in overall time to build, in spite of the "extra" time to design well. This is the first answer to the objection, "We don't have that much time to devote to design."

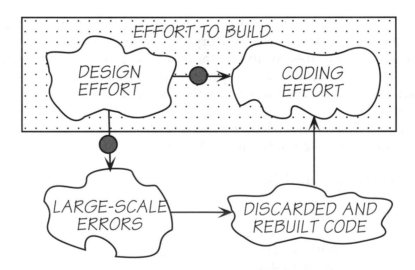

Figure 22-3.          Another important reason for design effort is to decrease the number of large-scale errors. Large-scale errors result in much discarded and rebuilt code, which further increases coding effort. Although design takes time and effort, total time and effort to build may be less if design is done well.

After introducing explicit design practices and design reviews, this organization found that the time to build is also *less variable*, making estimating and control easier for the management. The improvement of the design process also reduced the total number of faults to be repaired, which, in turn, reduced the time and effort spent in testing (Figure 22-4). This is the second answer to the objection, "We don't have that much time to devote to design."

The change to an Anticipating (Pattern 4) organization is partly a change in emphasis from coding to design, as indicated by the following aphorism:

**The goal is not to prove programs correct;**
**the goal is to write correct programs.**[2]

Although the emphasis is on preventing errors in the first place, good design makes it easier to find the few errors left behind, because good design produces code that is understandable (Figure 22-4). "It's easier to think of what might make a program right than to think of all the things that might make it wrong."[3] Understandable code is easier to maintain throughout its lifetime. It's also nonlinearly easier, because it slows the accumulation of design maintenance debt, which is the third answer to the objection, "We don't have that much time to devote to design."

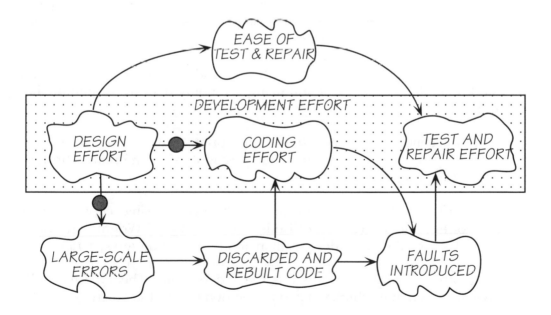

Figure 22-4.    Because design reduces the amount of coding, it also reduces the number of faults introduced by coding, and thus the testing and repair efforts. Because design makes testing and repairing easier, the effect is nonlinear.

Some managers have told me it's not *their* fault that design is rushed. They say, "The designers themselves are the ones who are in a hurry to see their product." To these managers, I offer the following comment from a great architect:

> I've often told my brightest students at Rice, "You have a disadvantage over most students. When you become architects, if you do not have the design skills to create beautiful functional buildings which radiate the aura of architecture, you will be frustrated to a point of extreme unhappiness. Some other students, who perhaps will produce buildings of lesser quality than yours, will be happy as larks, believing that their buildings are really good. They won't know the difference. Unfortunately, you will. And it is going to bug the hell out of you. You will find you now have the philosophy (you can talk architecture) but do not have the skills to create architecture. Don't put off *doing*. Make your mistakes now. . . . Put something down on that cheap yellow tracing paper. If it does not turn out right, nothing is lost, and the next sketch may be better. Think with your hands as well as your head."[4]

The fourth answer to the "not-enough-time" objection is simply that only poor designers allow themselves to be rushed by poor managers, and vice versa.

Granted that good design is essential, what are you as manager to do about it? One thing is clear: You're *not* going to try being the designer yourself. If you want to do that, get out of management and go back to the trenches. But with very little effort, you can at least help your organization prevent some of the worst design mistakes.

Thomas L. Magliozzi—cohost with his brother Ray of "Car Talk" on National Public Radio—offers the following taxonomy of design blunders that you can use as a guide:[5]

1.  Using a technology not because it's appropriate, but "because it's there." (He calls this the Sir Edmund Hillary School, after the man who first climbed Everest, "because it was there.")

2.  Being different at any cost; reinventing whenever possible; copying nothing, not even good ideas. (I call this the Frank Lloyd Wright Syndrome: caring less about making designs than about making design *history*.)

3.  Just plain stupidity. (He calls this the Ted Williams Theory, after Ted's advice, "If you don't think too good, then don't think too much.")

4.  Too many cooks.

5.  Oops! Where the hell are we going to put this?

You need not be a designer to prevent these blunders. You simply need to be the last bulkhead of sanity.

## 22.3 The Sir Edmund Hillary School

Anyone who has spent more than a month in a software engineering organization is familiar with technology-driven design. Why a month? Because that's the visitation interval hardware sellers program into their datebooks. By the end of your first month, you're sure to have heard at least one vendor advocating the design of some new system based on their latest and greatest feature set.

To be sure, there are instances when a new feature opens the gate to an essential application, like a data store an order of magnitude larger or cheaper than any previously available device. For this reason, it's important for an organization to perform some scanning for new technology; but even when something new and apparently useful does come up, it should never become a license to bypass the ordinary design process.

DO insist that every project start with a problem statement, in terms of a business need.

DO NOT let hardware or software vendors design systems for you, unless you first do requirements work and put out a request to at least three vendors. DO assess each of their development, test, and project management process approaches *before* signing anything.

DO have the organization scan for new technology. DO NOT do this job yourself, no matter how much fun it is to go to business shows. DO NOT accept gifts from vendors, in any guise.

DO be suspicious of any design involving new technology. DO NOT allow any project to use the latest, greatest technology unless you are convinced the project's designers have fully considered boring, old, time-tested technology and realistically assessed the cost of failure. DO NOT forget that *nothing* goes faster the first time you use it.

## 22.4 The Frank Lloyd Wright Syndrome

Designers who can't seem to use anything that anyone else ever thought of before are always fooling themselves. A long time ago, Goethe said, "Everything has been thought of before, but the difficulty is to think of it again." When you think you're being original, you're usually just being unaware of what went before you.

Contrary to popular lore among software engineers, most programs are not, and need not be, masterpieces of original design. DO ask, "Are we designing the Guggenheim Museum, or a country cottage?" DO NOT succumb to the temptation to achieve immortality by sponsoring the design of masterpieces, when all that's required is competent craftsmanship.

DO encourage reuse of whatever you can. DO NOT reuse things blindly. Reusability is a nice buzzword, but it takes more than buzzwords to make it reuse, rather than refuse.

DO get in the habit of asking designers whether there is something that can be reused, rather than starting from scratch. DO distinguish at least three levels of reuse:

- sharing design ideas
- sharing copies of source code, but modifying it (not maintaining the connection with the original)
- sharing object code

Sharing design ideas is the most productive of the types of sharing. Routine (Pattern 2) managers, however, think that code reuse is the best—because they think that all value comes from debugging, which makes debugged code so valuable. Most of the real value, however, comes from design, which many of them do not understand—even when they used to be designers themselves.

How much sharing is possible? One of my clients claims that 60 percent of the function in a banking system is supported by common routines. This number depends on the level you assume for your observation, since using a higher-level language makes you think that less is supported by common code. In any case, this degree of sharing was not obtained simply by management declaring that designs and code *ought* to be shared. It costs extra to make designs and code worth sharing.

DO look for opportunities to share. DO NOT assume that existing designs are quality designs. DO study how much damage one shared component can do if it's bad.

DO look carefully—using technical reviews, for example—at the quality of the common element, be it a compiler, an operating system, a subroutine, or an object class. DO compare designs to proven existing designs, and ask why they weren't used. DO prepare yourself to invest in bringing candidate designs and code up to a quality level suitable for sharing.

## 22.5 The Ted Williams Theory

You may not think you are stupid, but a sufficiently complex system can make anyone *look* stupid. Bad design destroys understandability, and anything that destroys understandability destroys design.

### 22.5.1 Do it right the first time

Doing things in a hurry reduces the quality of thinking. For example, the tendency to introduce errors while fixing code is measured by the fault feedback ratio (FFR).[6] A higher FFR means that design integrity is being destroyed at a faster rate, which in turn tends to raise future FFR, creating the collapse dynamic.

This collapse dynamic suggests the following guide: DO NOT force your people to think in the fixing mode. DO keep the pressure off, and your system will survive longer. This is one reason to take unit testing out of the hands of the coder.

### 22.5.2 Don't be greedy

N.R. Augustine's *Law of Insatiable Appetite* states,

**The last ten percent of performance generates one-third of the cost and two-thirds of the problems.**[7]

Optimization costs a bunch, so DO NOT push your people to optimize systems in any dimension, unless there is a demonstrated business need for that optimization (Figure 22-5).

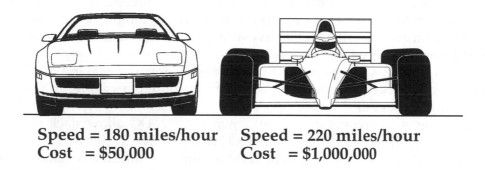

Speed = 180 miles/hour     Speed = 220 miles/hour
Cost  = $50,000            Cost  = $1,000,000

Figure 22-5.    Do not push for optimization in any dimension unless there is a demonstrated business need, because the last few percent costs disproportionately more.

DO NOT encourage micro-efficiency. DO encourage adaptability to new requirements. Besides, micro-efficiency eventually loses macro-efficiency opportunities, because micro-optimized code destroys design, and destroyed design destroys comprehension.

One kind of optimization is the quest for perfection. DO NOT consider errors as a moral issue; they are simply waste products. Manufacturers deal with waste not only by prevention, but by also paying for waste disposal. DO consider paying for errors, rather than trying to eliminate them entirely.

Errors are part of the cost of doing business. What are they worth? What do they cost? DO balance cost and value of eliminating errors. Generally, you can live with waste if it's not toxic. If it is toxic, you can pay compensation if only a few people are affected.

DO establish a refund policy, such as "No questions asked on full refunds."

DO pay certain users to do the job another way. For example, one organization simply executed a process manually for the three (out of seven hundred users) who had special requirements that would have corrupted the system design.

### 22.5.3  Create slack

> You are in a hotel. You hear someone yell fire. He runs for the fire extinguisher and pulls the alarm to call the fire department. We all get out. Extinguishing the fire does not improve the hotel.
> That is not an improvement in quality. That is putting out fires.[8]

Deming is correct about putting out fires, but this is not helpful to the manager of the hotel that's burning. While it's burning, you can't think clearly enough to improve a hotel. DO free up some time and other resources not devoted to fire fighting. DO make the first task a search for process improvements that will reduce the chances of fire. These will free up more resources for further process improvement. DO reinvest at least some of these savings in the improvement process.

This process of *preventing* fires is another form of making slack, which includes any parts of a project that aren't absolutely essential to getting the present product out the door. As we've seen, slack is always needed in complex systems to investigate the unknown future. DO allow slack in designs. DO NOT push designs to the limit. DO NOT be hasty to give away your slack. Slack is like a wild card: It can be used to improve almost any hand, but once played, it's gone.

DO allow slack in your schedules to give everyone time to think. This slack can be in the form of a specific overall contingency factor applied to all resources. DO structure some of the slack, however, if you can think of useful ways to do it. For example, a measurement function is a use of slack to see if the future is coming out as you had planned. Much of training is slack from the project point of view, though certainly not from the view of improving the overall organization's capability. Appointing a research group or encouraging play and experimentation (not in the real product, of course) is a way of being prepared for an unknown future.

DO keep the gap between desired and possible as large as possible by keeping desires small and slack large. The downfall of many software companies has been loading all sorts of features into their product, which causes them to be two years late and to lose market share.

### 22.5.4  Keep it simple

Other things being reasonably equal, DO favor simple designs over complex designs. DO NOT, however, mistake the simplistic for the simple. Teresa Home, commenting on *Volume 1* of this series, gives an excellent example of how simplicity is not always a simple matter:

> The graph on p. 219 of *Volume 1* demonstrates that a rigid rule such as no module more than 100 lines of code may not be optimal for a very large system because integration effort overwhelms the effort saved by decreasing module size.
>
> I once implemented a design for a simulation system for a tobacco company that was big on structured techniques and walkthroughs. Their rule was no more than two pages of PL/I code per module. We ended up with 205 modules. The coding went quickly, but integration was a nightmare. The average number of parameters each module required was greater than five and most of the errors were in the order or format of the parameters being passed. Integration would have been even worse had there been more than the two of us implementing this. (By the way, performance suffered because of that design also—the workhorse modules were at the bottom of deeply nested DO loops.) [9]

Simplicity in this case involved the interaction of at least three measurements: module size, complexity of communication (parameters passed), and performance. Teresa said she had learned to make these trade-offs subconsciously; but in order to teach them to others who haven't suffered this experience, you must raise them to consciousness. DO ask designers to explain how they have made their trade-offs, and what they have paid in complexity. DO remember that simple linear rules are always wrong—including this one.

DO NOT contribute to the complexity problem by issuing dispensations for violations of standards. For example, to minimize support for multiple configurations, you must design with standard interfaces, then keep those standards under control.[10] When your company is the dominant force in your industry, that's an easier rule to follow. When you are struggling to make a living, it's tempting to compromise a standard interface to win one more customer.

### 22.6  Too Many Cooks

Who actually performs the design work? The word "architect" comes from the Greek: "archi-" meaning chief or top, and "tect" meaning building or carpentry. In other words, the architect is the chief builder. In software, too, DO NOT remove the architect from the building process.

DO keep the design team involved in the building. Otherwise, the designers won't improve over time. DO NOT, however, let the design team stand over the builders and critique their work. DO have them involved in technical reviews of code.

Development progress is a race between the amount of work to be done and the resources available to do it. Reducing system size is one side of the equation. Developing human resources is the other. DO NOT, however, try to gain speed by adding people to the design team.

Finally, DO have a design *team.* If you are too small an organization to have a full-time design team, beg, borrow, or steal people (from inside or outside the organization) to get as many views as possible. At the same time, DO have a chief designer who will resolve all debates before the broth spoils.

## 22.7  Oops!

Design is supposed to be forethought; afterthoughts are an indication of failure in the design process. As an Anticipating (Pattern 4) manager, you can help prevent afterthoughts by a few simple policies.

DO insist that all designs be written down—not drawn by waving hands in air—so they can be reviewed. As Payson Hall comments,

> The bad ideas that weren't written down represent the majority of the up-front, get-in-the-way-of-getting-release-N+1-out-the-door-on-time errors I've seen. In my experience, algorithms that ALMOST deal with the complexity of data integrity, ALMOST handle data currency, and ALMOST eliminate the exposure of a design to critical failure when the "unthinkable" (like a power failure or a user hitting the big white "reset" button) occurs are a significant cause of project failure. And smart people who are true of heart can convince themselves (and you) that they have all the wrinkles ironed out. . . . without a written spec to ponder, you end up using a jack-hammer to rip up concrete and repour. . . . VERY expensive, VERY time consuming, VERY stupid.[11]

DO apply *The Rule of Three:*

**If you can't think of three circumstances in which the design might fail, you haven't thought enough about it.**

DO NOT accept designs that are described as "the only way." There are always other ways, and each way has advantages and disadvantages. DO insist that several other ways be presented to you, so you can judge how carefully the designers have done their job.

DO apply *The Paradox Rule:*

**If there is no paradox that the design must resolve, you don't understand the problem.**

In other words, there are always trade-offs, so that optimizing in one direction always hurts in some other direction. DO NOT accept designs from designers who haven't confronted the fundamental trade-offs in the problem and given you a choice of how you would like to make the trades.

Every design solves some problem, but not necessarily the problem you want solved. There are no wrong designs, only different designs. DO insist that you understand what problems the design actually addresses, by applying reverse design. Reverse design is the process of asking, "What problem is this the solution to?" Above all, DO insist on reasonableness.

## 22.8 Helpful Hints and Suggestions

1. "First, [Cleanroom engineering] develops software under statistical quality control to formal specifications. Second, it removes unit debugging from developers and replaces it by box structured design and functional verification. Third, certifiers test software for the first time and return any failures found to developers for fixing before certifying software quality. These three steps produce practically zero defect software with higher productivity than traditional development and testing. At first glance, taking unit debugging away from developers may look strange, but it moves programming to engineering in both design and test."[12]

2. Time can be budgeted among parts, depending on structure. Space can be budgeted in an additive way. But complexity budgeting is more dependent on structure than the others, and you must control it. That's where various structured programming rules and design disciplines come into play. Otherwise, it's possible for one part to push complexity onto another part. This kind of pushing creates the politics of design.

## 22.9 Summary

✔ As a manager, you may be able to satisfy your passion for design by using it to design organizations and processes, but not information systems. Because designs are assets, there is one point of view that dictates that managers must always stay involved in reviewing designs—the point of view that design is designed for *manageability*. When a design is too complex to be managed, the manager must insist on simplification.

✔ When the design debt grows large, management becomes well nigh impossible. The accumulation of design debt can certainly arise from "featuritis," but generally develops from excessive and/or hasty attempts to correct faults.

✔ The common fallacy is that code is the source of most faults, but most failures found in testing don't come from faults created in coding; they're just found immediately after coding.

✔   There are many examples of "coding faults" that didn't originate in coding:

- code for which there was no requirement
- code for a wrong design
- code for a wrong requirement
- code not written because we forgot the requirement
- code that's too long because the data structure was clumsy
- code that's wrong because the interface was too complex
- code that's wrong because two parts of the design had different ideas
- code that's inconsistent with an overly complex and poorly documented design

✔   Most faults originate in requirements and design, though process errors are also significant in poorly managed organizations.  Process errors—such as duplicates, zaps, and failures to update—are caused by the development process.  Many of them can be addressed by improved *process* design, which is definitely a management responsibility.

✔   Increased design effort decreases coding effort in developing or maintaining an information system when it results in

- a better-designed data structure
- modularity
- cleaner interfaces
- fewer switches and flags
- fewer global variables
- a more testable system
- reuse of constructs

The direct effect of some of these improvements is a reduction in coding effort.

✔   Decreasing direct coding effort is not the only positive effect of good design.  Other important reasons for design effort are

- to decrease the number of large-scale errors
- to make the time to build less variable, making estimating and control easier for management
- to reduce the total number of faults to be repaired
- to reduce the time and effort spent in testing
- to make code more understandable, and thus more easily maintained

✔ The change to an Anticipating (Pattern 4) organization is partly a change in emphasis from coding to design. Only poor designers allow themselves to be rushed by poor managers, and vice versa.

✔ As a manager, you can at least help your organization prevent some of the worst design mistakes, such as

- Using a technology not because it's appropriate, but because it's there.
- Being different at any cost; reinventing whenever possible; copying nothing, not even good ideas.
- Just plain stupidity.
- Too many cooks.
- Oops! Where the hell are we going to put this?

You need not be a designer to prevent these blunders. You simply need to be the last bulkhead of sanity.

✔ It's important for an organization to perform some scanning for new technology. But even when something new and apparently useful comes up, it should never become a license to bypass the ordinary design process.

✔ Designers who can't seem to use anything that anyone else ever thought of before are always fooling themselves. When you think you're being original, you're usually just being unaware of what went before you. Most programs are not, and need not be, masterpieces of original design.

✔ Whenever possible, watch for and exploit three levels of reuse:

- sharing design ideas, the most productive type of sharing
- sharing copies of source code, but modifying it (not maintaining the connection with the original)
- sharing object code

✔ Bad design destroys understandability, and anything that destroys understandability destroys design. Doing things in a hurry reduces the quality of thinking.

✔ Slack is always needed in complex systems to investigate the unknown future, so allow slack in designs and do not push designs to the limit.

✔ Other things being reasonably equal, favor simple designs over complex designs. Do not, however, mistake the simplistic for the simple.

✔    It's a good idea to keep the architect involved in the building process—to learn, not to stand over the builders and critique their work.

✔    Design is supposed to be forethought; afterthoughts are an indication of failure in the design process.  As an Anticipating (Pattern 4) manager, you can help prevent afterthoughts by a few simple policies:

   • Insist that all designs be written down so they can be reviewed.
   • Apply the Rule of Three.
   • Don't accept designs that are described as "the only way."
   • Apply the Paradox Rule.
   • Don't accept designs from designers who haven't confronted the fundamental trade-offs in the problem and given you a choice of how you would like to make the trades.
   • Insist that you understand what problems the design actually addresses, by applying reverse design.

### 22.10  Practice

1.    Sketch a diagram of effects of the collapse dynamic due to design deterioration from fixing.  What does the diagram suggest you can do to arrest this deterioration and various stages?  To prevent it in the first place?

2.    Sketch a diagram of effects of the process of creating a group to seek out and improve processes that will reduce fire fighting, and of putting some of the saved resources back into this same group.

3.    Sue Petersen comments:  "You can be a designer or a manager, but not both."  Are there any exceptions, such as in very small organizations?  Under what circumstances?  What are the warning signs that indicate you may have misidentified your situation?

4.    Payson Hall suggests:  Use a diagram of effects to show why management overhead increases nonlinearly as design debt increases.

# 23

# Introducing Technology

*Perfection of means and*
*confusion of goals seem*
*—in my opinion—*
*to characterize our age.*
— Albert Einstein

We techies are predisposed to believe that all we need to do to change the culture is to buy some new tools; that's why we so easily fall prey to the tool vendors. In 1992, I counted more than eight hundred offerings of software tools, by more than four hundred companies, all listed in the Zvegintzov and Jones compendium.[1] Evidently, somebody likes to build tools; but more evidently, somebody likes to buy them.

Perhaps these buyers think that changing tools is the easiest way to improve the technological culture. It isn't, but in this chapter, I want to use software tools as a symbol for technological change, a symbol that stands for the much larger set of technologies. This larger set includes

- social structures, such as formal and informal organizational relationships
- social practices, such as technical reviews and planning approaches

- standards, such as interface requirements, designs, and paper forms
- measurements, such as user satisfaction surveys and cost accounting
- technical infrastructure, such as networks, hardware, and software tools

Since tools form a simple subset of this far larger set, you can use them to study the minimum it takes to accomplish any such change. To change tool use, you need to change many elements of the culture, because a culture is a system. It takes a conscious, coordinated effort by many people to evolve a new cultural pattern for a software engineering organization. This chapter provides some theoretical and practical guides to help when you want to offer your organization a new technology or extend the use of an existing one.

## 23.1  Surveying the Tool Culture

We use tools because they help us reduce costs and increase quality. Before we can use a tool, however, we must learn to use it. The learning takes us through the Satir Change Model, increasing costs and exposing us to serious mistakes—temporarily increasing costs and reducing quality. By improving our management of the process of introducing tools (and other technologies), we can lower the costs again and reduce the mistakes that cut quality, though you can never eliminate them. The choice and use of technologies is always a balance between present and future.

Culture is conservative, and unless we do something different in the future, we'll just keep doing the same things we have done in the past. To be successful with the introduction of any new technology, we must be guided by a study of the introduction of *past* technologies. One way to do this is by conducting a *tool survey* to discover what our organization is doing with the tools we have purchased. (We can, of course, conduct a similar survey to uncover the use of any other cultural practice.) According to my observations of a number of these surveys among my clients,

- 70 percent of tools purchased by the organizations in the surveys are *never* used, other than perhaps in an initial trial. (This could be a comment on the quality of the tools they tried, or their inability to negotiate a try-before-you-buy agreement.)
- 25 percent are used by only one team or person within each organization.
- 5 percent are widely used, but not to capacity. Perhaps only 10 percent of the capacity of the tool is used.

These facts are neither good nor bad, but they influence the estimates made of the productivity impact of tools. Putting this all together into a simple model, we can see that if an organization with a hundred teams purchases a set of twenty tools that together *could* double productivity, the results would actually be

- Fourteen of the tools wouldn't be used by anybody.
- Each of four tools would be used by one group only. Assuming each group experiences a 5 percent increase in productivity, the overall organization's productivity would increase by 0.2 percent.
- One of the tools might be used with 10 percent effectiveness by everybody, perhaps increasing overall productivity by 10 percent of 5 percent, or 0.05 percent.
- Thus, the overall productivity gain is 0.25 percent, rather than the 100 percent promised if everybody used the tools fully.

No wonder we have such an unfulfilled feeling about our tools. What we need is not more tools, nor more managers believing that tools are silver bullets, but management guidance to get more benefit from the tools we do acquire. It's only in Anticipating (Pattern 4) cultures that management really steps up to the task of getting the benefits from the tools and other technologies that the organization is paying for.

## 23.2 Technology and Culture

A tool survey is one of the easiest ways to determine an organization's cultural pattern. Organizations each use (or don't use) the tools they have in ways that are characteristic of their cultural processes, and particularly their management style, which determines

- what tools they choose
- how they obtain them
- how they socialize tools
- how they use them

Notice that I did *not* say "how much money they spend on tools." Perhaps the clearest indicator of the power of culture is the way Anticipating (Pattern 4) cultures get more effectiveness out of tools while actually spending less money.

Using their tools as a microscope, let's examine the cultures that might aspire to become Anticipating as a way to see their characteristic ways of introducing new technologies, and to learn what you might have to do to change them.

### 23.2.1  *Oblivious (Pattern 0)*

As we might expect, Oblivious organizations make little use of tools. The typical Oblivious users employ only one or two tools, and only scratch the surface in their use, partly because they aren't even aware that they are tools. As a result, Pattern 0 organizations obtain very little payoff from tools.

How does this pattern acquire tools? It doesn't. Tools just happen. How do Pattern 0 users socialize tools? They don't. Most users are totally oblivious to what tools their neighbors use.

### 23.2.2 Variable (Pattern 1)

Surprisingly, Variable organizations often use tools quite well, but generally on an individual basis. Each developer uses three or four tools reasonably well, but the payoff to the organization is modest because tools spread slowly to other users.

How does Pattern 1 acquire tools? The typical pattern begins when individuals learn of some "neat" tool. The individuals then pester their managers, who cough up money for a little peace and quiet.

How do Pattern 1 users socialize tools? Typically, one person acquires a tool and tells a friend about it if it's useful. Often, the friend will avoid the managerial chain entirely by pirating a copy of the tool and learning to use it without a manual. This socialization process is sometimes effective, but it's not very dependable, is illegal or unethical, and creates tool maintenance and configuration management problems. That's why a Variable organization may have many tools, but few of them are used broadly.

In other words, Pattern 1 introduces *awareness* to the introduction process, albeit at an individual level. This pattern's members remain oblivious of their socialization process.

### 23.2.3 Routine (Pattern 2)

Routine organizations often use tools more broadly than Variable organizations, but may not use them very well. If you look on the system disk of a Pattern 2 organization developer's PC, you may find ten to fifteen tools. If, however, you observe this developer in action, you'll see that the use of these tools is both shallow and reluctant. As a result of this poor mastery, Pattern 2 organizations realize only modest payoffs from their investment in tools, even though they often point to the size of this investment as an indicator (albeit a false one) of their effectiveness.

How does Pattern 2 acquire tools? Usually, a manager appoints a study committee to find the one best tool for everybody. The committee then argues about tools for months or years, unable to come to consensus because the assigned task is nearly impossible. Sometimes, the committee overcomes the odds and finally chooses the "best" tools. The manager then buys one for everybody. Usually, the tool they choose is a compromise, and not really best for anybody.

The longer the committee deliberates, however, the more likely something else will happen.  Typically, a vendor drops in as some project is failing, and sells the manager a tool as the Big Magic that will save the project.  (It doesn't.)

How do Pattern 2 users socialize tools?  After investing a large amount of money buying copies of the tool, the manager tells everyone to use it, often in a huge kick-off meeting with vendor representatives sitting on the stage grinning like cats.  The manager usually gives a speech, the essence of which is, "Look at how much I've done for you.  Now I expect you to give me something in return."

In some Pattern 2 organizations, that's all they do.  The tool then sits on shelves and gathers dust, and the smarter managers never mention it again.  The less intelligent start looking for someone—or something—to blame for the waste of money.  They accuse many people, but, since they never look in the mirror, they never find the culprit.  Only fools blame their tools.

In more sophisticated Routine organizations, the manager gives the vendor a few tens of thousands of dollars, and all employees are paraded through tool classes (Figure 23-1).  (This process is mockingly called "sheep-dipping"— by the "sheep.")  After class, people go about business as usual.  In exceptional cases, a few people may actually find some use for the tool.

Figure 23-1.      A typical Routine (Pattern 2) approach to socialization is sheep-dipping in mass classes with no follow-up.

Some Routine (Pattern 2) organizations set up receptor groups, a concept promoted by the Software Engineering Institute as a way to identify and evaluate technological opportunities.  The receptor groups ask, "How can I take technology and apply it to how I do business?"  Since these groups understand both the technology and their organizations, they can make the match between a general technology and a specific context.

The concept is an important one, but a receptor group can't really work effectively before a Steering culture. First of all, it's seldom that one tool fits everybody, though the Routine culture believes that should always be possible. Second, there's not enough stability in the Pattern 2 organization to measure "how I do business." Even so, aspiring Pattern 2 organizations often set up receptor groups to "formalize what we do informally." These premature groups are generally the death of any remaining informal acquisition process of Pattern 1, without giving anything useful in return.

### 23.2.4  Steering (Pattern 3)

Steering cultures use tools cautiously, but rather well, on the whole. A typical Pattern 3 developer is well trained in four to eight tools, and perhaps uses five to ten others in a simple way for special situations. The organization garners a reasonable payoff from tools because of this good use and penetration.

How does a Steering organization acquire tools? Often, individuals hear about a tool that sounds useful and then justify the tool to their manager, who spends some of the tool budget. Often, though, this rather casual procedure can be improved through the use of a special receptor group.

How does Pattern 3 socialize tools? Because tools are acquired on individual initiative, it's far more likely that individuals who get tools will actually practice with them. In this culture, teamwork is effective, so if one member of a team uses a tool, it's likely the others will use it. The manager, having paid for the tool, observes the way the tool is being used, and if it proves useful, the manager plans for tool socialization. Selected volunteers are trained, the training is applied on the job, and the training and tool selection are updated according to on-the-job experience.

### 23.2.5  Anticipating (Pattern 4)

Anticipating cultures use tools vigorously, but always with a result in mind. A typical Pattern 4 developer is well trained in ten to fifteen tools, and perhaps uses ten to fifteen others in a simple way for special situations. The organization garners an outstanding payoff from tools because of this excellent use and penetration.

How does a Pattern 4 organization acquire tools? As in Pattern 3, individuals often hear about a tool that sounds useful. Pattern 4 organizations, though, almost always have a specially trained receptor group that proactively searches for useful tools, as well as for tools to address specific process problems.

How does an Anticipating culture socialize tools? Because tools are socialized by trained change artists, individuals who need tools get tools and use them well. As in Pattern 3, good teamwork increases the effectiveness of tools. Managers are less directly involved in acquisition and socialization.

Instead, they spend their efforts on determining the state of the culture and applying the Commandments (see Section 23.5) and the Laws of Technology Transfer in order to preserve and adapt the culture that makes the tool process so effective.

## 23.3  The Laws of Technology Transfer

Figure 23-2 summarizes the patterns by which different software organizations incorporate tools into their cultures. To be specific about how technology can be transferred effectively in an Anticipating (Pattern 4) organization, let's consider one area where technology is generally underused—testing—and what major forces act against successful change. These forces are summarized in two laws of technology transfer.

| Pattern | How It Obtains | How It Socializes | How It Uses |
|---|---|---|---|
| Oblivious | It is oblivious | Doesn't | Very little |
| Variable | At an individual level | It is oblivious | Quite heavy, quite variable |
| Routine | Taken over by management | By management edict | Wide but shallow, overall light |
| Steering | By management and individuals | By management encouraging team socialization | Wide and fairly deep, overall moderate |
| Anticipating | Explicit scanning of all sources, internal and external by receptor groups | By management encouraging explicit activities by change artists | Wide and deep, overall heavy, and consistent |

Figure 23-2.    The culture of a software organization is well reflected in the way it obtains, socializes, and uses tools. The same patterns show up in any technological change.

### 23.3.1  The First Law of Technology Transfer

To locate faults quickly, developers must have tools that enable them to access reliable and timely information about the systems they are working on. To reduce the time necessary to resolve faults, developers need low-overhead tools that enable them to make properly documented repairs easily. They must also be able to test their repairs quickly and reliably, so as to prevent side effects and be able to undo the repairs easily should side effects occur anyway.

There are, of course, a number of excellent software tools for test configuration control and automatic testing, so the major impediment is not a shortage of tools. The big problem is that testing is often performed in crisis mode, and there never seems to be time to set up such systems if they are not already in place. That's why it takes an Anticipating (Pattern 4) organization to beat *The First Law of Technology Transfer:*

**Long-range good tends to be sacrificed to short-range good.**

An organization needs testing tools to help it out of a quality crisis, but in a crisis, people are in Chaos and complaining, "We're so busy eradicating bugs, we don't have time or resources to introduce the tools that would help us eradicate bugs." This is the First Law of Technology Transfer.

If people weren't in the Chaos of crisis, they wouldn't have any trouble recognizing the First Law in action, because its battle cries are all too familiar:

- We don't have time to do it right.
- We can't spare him right now.
- We'll assign her one-eighth time to the task.
- We'll do it in our spare time.
- We'll do it as soon as the crisis is over.

In crisis-driven organizations, I generally find only the crudest testing tools, like the hex memory dump and the trace, which simply grow in size and difficulty as the system grows. Their lack of tools contributes to the crisis, but the crisis prevents them from introducing effective tools. This vicious feedback loop locks the organization in a situation that can only be broken by highly skilled, anticipatory management intervention.

### 23.3.2 *Temperament and the Second Law of Technology Transfer*

The obvious solution to breaking this loop would be to build or buy new testing tools, but this is a trap. Adding new tools late in a project is very much like adding new people, and Brooks's Law applies. Yet many programmers turn to tool-building or acquisition anyway.

As we've seen previously, people in crisis mode tend to react not according to the logic of the situation, but according to their temperaments.[2] The NT Visionaries (especially the ENTP Inventors) start looking for the perfect tool, for their motto is

**I would rather build software that builds software than build software.**

This illustrates *The Second Law of Technology Transfer:*

**Short-range feasibility tends to be sacrificed to long-range perfection.**

The battle cries of the Second Law are also well known:

- It's not part of the plan.
- We'll set up a task force.
- It's not the elegant way.
- We need to study the implications.

When you hear the Visionaries arguing over the perfect tool to solve your problems, step in and find something useful and specific for them to do. Don't let them evade crises by irrelevant tool-building. When the crisis is over, they can become your best tool designers.

You won't hear the SP Troubleshooters discussing tools. They'll just secretly build adequate ones. In fact, they've probably been building them all along, which is one possible source of quick relief. I believe that even the organization in Chaos has all the tools its members need, though most people don't know about them because the tools haven't been explicitly socialized.

In other words, first consider the hypothesis that your tool problem is not one of manufacturing, but of *distribution*. One of your NF Catalysts will love the job of performing the tool survey—interviewing everybody to create an inventory of what tools are now in use and what they are good for. Then he or she can work with one of your SJ Organizers to create ways of getting successful tools more widely used. Working in problem-solving teams, of course, is the simplest, cheapest, most natural, and most effective way to spread the good tools and filter out the bad.

## 23.4 From Crisis to Calm Configuration Control

To illustrate some general principles of technology transfer—even to a crisis-driven organization—let's look in some detail at one set of tools: its benefits to such an organization, a test for determining what is needed, and a case study of successful introduction of a tool set.

### 23.4.1 Benefits

Organizations in crisis-mode testing don't generally consider introducing configuration management tools. They believe that such tools are for routine operations, and don't understand the many things such a system could do for them, *especially* in crisis:

- Configuration control helps reduce the time to locate faults. This helps improve repair time, because if someone creates a fault while repairing something else, others can find it faster.
- If they do make a mistake while repairing, configuration control helps them back out the fix in a reliable manner. If programmers cannot count on doing this, they will be much too cautious in trying out fixes, thus slowing down repair time.

- "Hacking"—trying things, testing them, and changing again—is a time-honored way of making repairs, and not just in software. (If you don't like the term "hacking," call it "experimental repair," but recognize that's the way much repair work has to be done. Use it to your advantage.) With good configuration control, organizations in crisis can have an experimental repair system that is totally isolated from any production system, so that their hackers cannot hack the system to pieces.
- Configuration control helps keep people from fixing the same fault twice. Or thrice. Or from people fixing different faults in the same module, thus unfixing the fixes.
- A configuration control system ensures that people know what version they're working on. Otherwise, if they're looking in the wrong place, they'll never find a problem.
- Configuration control helps keep repairs in one place from affecting work in another, and allows people to work in parallel without disturbing one another.
- The total configuration control system is also capable of controlling the test cases, test plans, and test scripts that are a necessary part of a successful software repair effort—as well as controlling any other valuable project documents, including all versions of the project plan.
- Ideally, the system keeps design documents, pictures, view graphs, presentations, and all the other material a project produces under control. That way, nobody wastes precious time looking for them— or even worse, omits them—at the end of the project when everybody is in a rush to ship the product.

If your organization is not getting these benefits, then attention to your configuration control system could help alleviate a crisis.

### 23.4.2  A simple test of configuration control

Do this simple test of how your present configuration control system is working: Simply tell a developer, or tester, "There's a fault in this module. Get me a copy of the current source listing, on paper or on the screen."

Measure the time that passes until you get the listing. If it's less than one hour—and if the result is accurate and repeatable—you may be able to live through a crisis with your present system, especially if you do a little fine tuning. But if it's longer than an hour, you're probably in deep trouble. You won't be able to live with it, but how can you live without it?

Warren was the development manager at a software company where I had done some change artist training. As part of one of his training projects,

Warren tried this find-the-source test on three different developers, and described his results:

> One found a listing in twenty minutes, but it was for an earlier version of the module. One got a listing on the screen in thirteen hours. It was current, he said, "except for the binary patches." The third programmer simply disappeared. I had given up on her until she showed up the next week with a fresh listing. It was actually of the correct version of the correct module. By this time, I knew I had to do something about their configuration control.

What he did is an instructive tale of tool introduction for any manager whose organization is in crisis.

### 23.4.3 *An old-fashioned configuration control system*

Warren knew that the present configuration control system wasn't working. In fact, with several thousand failures to be accounted for, at one week of access time per correct source listing, the situation was untenable. He established a team of two change artists to install a modern system, but he also knew that the project couldn't just sit and wait for the team to get an automated system up, running, and universally used.

To beat the First and Second Laws of Technology Transfer, he established a dual approach. As an interim measure, he suggested setting up a paper source code. Everyone said that it would be a waste of time, and they had no time to spare. This, of course, was the standard reaction to every suggestion for getting out of the overload, so Warren ignored it. He created the library using clerical workers. Because he didn't use any developer time, nobody seriously tried to stop him. The initial library was established in two days, in an unused junk room, using furniture scavenged from hither and yon.

Warren was told by the furniture police that there would be a three-week wait for the furniture movers to be authorized to bring anything to the library.[3] He told his photocopying clerk that she was now in charge of maintaining the library, so she helped him carry in the furniture. People noticed their initiative, which several people later told him was inspirational to the moribund organization. Before the move was finished, several of the developers were also bearing chairs, tables, files, and bookshelves. Then, he said,

> I put out e-mail messages and posted signs that the library was now in operation. After the first week, I started doing spot checks by dropping into the library and seeing what people were doing there. I never found fewer than three programmers in the library using the materials. On one visit, there were eleven, and there were only five chairs. I found some new chairs—and carried them in myself.

Two months later, the teams' "automatic" configuration control system was in a workable state, but by then the crisis had been successfully passed. Warren put the paper librarian—his former copy clerk—in charge of the new system, and for several months, the two systems were operated in parallel. Eventually, the automatic system was sufficiently reliable, and he let the paper source code be gradually replaced with a library of technical books and manuals.

## 23.5 The Ten Commandments of Technology Transfer

Warren was a competent manager, saving his people by parting the waters of the First Law and surviving the desert of the Second. He was helped in his exodus by following *The Ten Commandments of Technology Transfer* (Figure 23-3).

- *Thou shalt have a plan to lead thee out of the wilderness.*
- *Thou shalt not worship thy plan.*
- *Thou shalt ask for no person in vain.*
- *Thou shalt not work seven days a week.*
- *Thou shalt honor thy users and listen to them.*
- *Thou shalt not kill support for change.*
- *Thou shalt not adulterate the work.*
- *Thou shalt not steal resources from the work.*
- *Thou shalt not bear false witness against thy plan.*
- *Thou shalt not covet thy neighbor's optimal technology.*

Figure 23-3.        The Ten Commandments of Technology Transfer.

### 23.5.1  *Thou shalt have a plan to lead thee out of the wilderness*

Without a plan, technology transfer either doesn't move at all or is vendor-driven. Fundamentally, it drifts. Unless management actively structures the situation otherwise, the First Law's short-term expediency will dominate efforts at technology transfer. The plan is the first step in providing the structure needed to resist the First Law.

Warren had a plan from the beginning. He determined where the organization was, knew where he wanted it to be, and broke the transition down into a series of reasonable steps.

### 23.5.2   *Thou shalt not worship thy plan*

A narrow plan is one that, like a single thread, breaks at its weakest point. One kind of narrow plan is the massive plan, with no incremental progress short of total religious conversion of everybody to a new technology.

The massive plan is also inflexible. An inflexible plan is one that has no replanning process built into it, or has no feedback from the progress to drive that replanning process, or has neither one. Such plans would work in a perfect, predictable world. The world of technology transfer is neither perfect nor predictable.

Warren's plan was specific, but flexible. He had alternative courses of action, and he was ready to modify actions, resources, and schedules if the original plan wasn't working well.

### 23.5.3   *Thou shalt ask for no person in vain*

This commandment says you must have the right person for each task. The first and foremost requirement for a change artist is the ability to work with people, quite often in conflict situations. All too frequently, the people assigned to technology transfer are brilliant technicians who prefer to work in a cave. If forced to work with others, they can do so, but only if the others are equally brilliant. Otherwise, they don't transfer technology, they transfer contempt.

The change artists you want are enthusiastic, resourceful, problem solvers, persistent but tactful with other people, and generally not at the top of the list of brilliant technicians—or not technicians at all. For them, moving in this technology will be considered an achievement worth doing. Brilliant technicians tend to lose interest once they see that something *can* be done by mere mortals.

When Warren chose the team investigating a tool, he picked two people trained as change artists, and made sure he got them. When he chose his photocopying clerk as librarian, he made his selection based on these change artist qualities—to the astonishment of some of his fellow managers. He also recruited others to the task by the Principle of Attraction: They saw people doing something that seemed worthwhile and stepped forward to volunteer their services. The Principle of Attraction guarantees that the participants will think that the job is worth doing.

### 23.5.4   *Thou shalt not work seven days a week*

Every change has a curve of cost versus time to make the change (Figure 23-4). If you shorten the schedule, you start to ascend a steep sloping cost curve. (The inverse curve can be drawn for probability of success.) Managers are rightly afraid of the upslope of the curve as time is extended: the Parkinson's

Law region, where work expands to fill the time allotted. But in avoiding this region, these managers tend to edict fictitious, impossible schedules, arguing, "People will respond to the challenge" and thus meet their true, but hidden, schedule. Soon everyone is playing the game of trying to guess the real schedule.

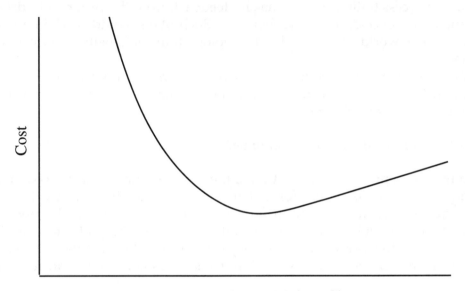

Time Taken to Make a Change

Figure 23-4.          Forcing the time for a change increases the cost nonlinearly. Taking too long may also increase the cost, though not as starkly.

Even if the managers succeed in reducing the schedule, it's a costly game. A project that was planned for one year but actually took two is far more expensive than one that was planned for two in the first place and then well managed.

Warren put no schedule pressure on the configuration management team. Indeed, his paper source code room strategy relieved them of pressure. He did motivate them by convincing them of the importance of the work.

### 23.5.5 *Thou shalt honor thy users and listen to them*

People who are the "victims" or "targets" of technology transfer attempts will always tell you what isn't working—which you need to know to adjust your plans. They may not tell you in so many words, and their attempts to give you this information are easy to label "resistance." The usual management response to resistance is to argue, blame, and push back. These tactics don't work because the status quo has enormous inertia.

People tell you what they need in order to change, sometimes in subtle and indirect ways. Once you know what they need, you can reframe the technology transfer process so it meets their needs as well as yours.

Warren heard that his developers were under a lot of pressure and wouldn't do anything that they perceived would add to their burden. By providing the library room, he gave them a chance to come forward at their own speed and test what a better configuration system could do for their immediate problems.

### 23.5.6 *Thou shalt not kill support for change*

When specialists are assigned full-time to transferring technology, they can easily discourage others from participating. To muster the full participation needed for successful transfer, people must always perceive various kinds of available opportunities. That way, any person who becomes enthusiastic at any time can buy into the process. This doesn't mean that they can do anything they happen to want, but rather that the plan must have many options available, no matter how small.

Warren was very skilled at providing many small options. Just helping to move furniture allowed people to literally and figuratively put their fingerprints on the project early. Keeping the library room completely open—with no comments like "How come it took you so long to come up here?" or "Oh, I thought *you* didn't *need* any help finding things"—had the same effect of gaining small, low-risk increments of commitment.

### 23.5.7 *Thou shalt not adulterate the work*

To overcome the power of the First Law of Technology Transfer, somebody must have a faithful, monogamous relationship with the change project. This means that at least one person (and generally two) must be assigned full-time to the project. Otherwise, part-timers will let the project slip under the press of other duties. Sometimes a transfer is effected by part-time people, but they generally are people who have voluntarily acquired the task—usually without management knowledge—and who let their assigned jobs fall by the wayside for the time being.

Although Warren's strategy was to use as many volunteers as possible, the core of his effort was three full-time people: the configuration tool team and the librarian. He made sure that they understood they were not to discourage any part-time help, but that they were the ones fully responsible for getting the job done.

### 23.5.8  Thou shalt not steal resources from the work

People aren't the only resource that needs to be assigned full-time. Technology transfer resources are often considered fair game for the first "real" need that comes along. Managers with day-to-day responsibilities consider such resources as unproductive slack—and collect them the way homeless people collect shopping carts.

Warren chose a room that nobody else wanted and equipped it with surplus furniture. Even so, once the room became attractive, others began to covet the space. Warren wasted no time disabusing them of their notions of seizing the library or any of its contents.

### 23.5.9  Thou shalt not bear false witness against thy plan

If you don't measure before and after the project, you won't know whether you're succeeding or failing. Even worse, you won't be able to withstand political criticism that says nothing is happening—nor political enthusiasm that claims the moon. The measurement need not be fancy,[4] but without measurement, it isn't engineering.

Warren used the find-the-source test to establish the current state of configuration control, and he monitored the usage of the library room to gauge the response to the intermediate system. Using the room, anyone could find a current source listing in less than twenty minutes—not very impressive when compared with an on-line tool, but stunning when compared with the previous approach.

One of the important requirements Warren set for the on-line tool was that it be capable of measuring several factors that would indicate progress in adoption, such as completeness of coverage, change activity, and usage errors.

### 23.5.10  Thou shalt not covet thy neighbor's optimal technology

The Chinese say, "The best is the enemy of the good." One reason is that asking a technical committee to find the *optimal* technology is like giving a pack of sharks a chunk of bloody flesh. The sharks rage into a feeding frenzy; the committee boils into an *optimizing* frenzy.

Contrary to the preaching of technology vendors, we seldom need optimal technology for successful technology transfer. The desire for optimal technology arises from perfectionist yearnings, which lead to the idea of massive, comprehensive projects. Successful technology transfer, on the other hand, generally proceeds in small, robust increments. Ideally, each increment

- provides some immediate benefit, however small, to users
- prepares the way for future increments
- gives management something measurable

By establishing these conditions, you establish a base of trust and an environment that makes the next increment proportionately easier. Most often, however, the first indigestible step kills somebody's appetite for anything else.

Warren was an avowed anti-optimizer, well aware of the Second Law of Technology Transfer. By choosing an unwanted room and furnishing it with old, worn chairs, tables, and files, he sent a message to the rest of the organization that he was looking for anything that worked. He gave this same message to the tool search committee, and reinforced it whenever vendors started to get carried away with their exquisite feature set.

### 23.6 The Eleventh Commandment

Although the Ten Commandments are powerful, their power is magnified a hundredfold by the addition of an *Eleventh:*

**In times of trial, always remember the Helpful Model.**

*The Helpful Model* says,

**No matter how it looks, everyone is trying to be helpful.**[5]

If you forget this commandment, you will begin to see resistance everywhere. Then you will begin to counter this resistance, which will engender real resistance—not to the technology, but to your anti-resistance efforts.

If you heed this commandment, you will be able to hear the real information present in all resistance. Then you will be able to use this information to correct your mistakes and enlist everybody's participation.

### 23.7 Helpful Hints and Suggestions

1. People vary. This simple fact is the bane of some managers' existence. When they want to get rid of variation in their products, their first idea is to get rid of people, to automate. But people must be used to implement the automation, and they often introduce more variation than existed in the first place.

   Instead of fighting this variation, use it to your advantage. Because of variation, a tool survey will reveal many useful but hidden tools and new ways of using tools. Gather them, then propagate them.

2. The length of a wrench handle is designed to protect against stripping threads, but many people think it is to help them select the right size wrench. Of course, that's right, too. In a good tool, it's difficult to identify one thing as the purpose. Don't get hung up on the *right* purpose of a tool. When getting started, take advantage of any purpose people have

for a *tool*.  Later, you can follow with change artistry to expand their usage.

3.  Izumi Kimura notes: "Hard" tools are those that everybody *must* use to gain their maximum benefit; operating systems and configuration management tools are examples.  "Soft" tools can be used fruitfully in one place and not used in some other places, and thus require less coercion to introduce.  For instance, when introducing a new soft tool, don't *allow* everyone to use it at once, but instead make a competition for which team is best qualified as first user.  In any case, don't manage as if a new tool is hard when it's actually soft.

4.  Mithridatism is a 2,000-year-old idea that can be used when introducing new hard tools.  Mithridates VI, King of Pontus (120–63 B.C.), was concerned about being poisoned, so he acquired a tolerance for the poison by intentionally taking gradually larger doses of it.  Even though a tool is hard, find ways to introduce it in small doses, until people acquire tolerance.  For example, you might keep two configuration management systems in use for a period of time, first adding tested common components to the new system.  People will use the new system to create test builds, but won't have to use it at first for their own development.  As more and more components are added, mithridatism will have its effect.

5.  The Selection Fallacy warns us not to make false projections from the ease or difficulty experienced by the first group to use a new tool.[6]  Ask members of the first team using the tool, "Was it difficult getting started?  Did you have to do anything special?"  If they say, "No, nothing special," their answers will probably give you no information.  If they had any difficulty or had to do anything special, they probably would have given up trying to adopt the tool—and so wouldn't be the first adopters.  What you have to discover is what is ordinary to them that might not be ordinary to other teams.

## 23.8  Summary

✔  The choice and use of technologies is always a balance between present and future.  We use tools because they help us reduce costs and increase quality, but before we can use a tool, we must learn to use it.  The learning takes us through the Satir Change Model, increasing costs and exposing us to serious mistakes.  By improving our management of the process of introducing tools, we can lower the costs and reduce these mistakes.

✔  To change tool use, we need to change the culture, not vice versa.  A good way to start changing tool use is to conduct a *tool survey* to discover what people are doing with the tools they have. Usually, the survey shows that what is needed is not more tools, but management guidance to get more benefit from the tools we acquired.

✔ People in an organization use the tools they have (or don't use them) in ways that are characteristic of their organization's cultural processes, and particularly its management style, which determines

- what tools they choose
- how they obtain them
- how they socialize tools
- how they use them

✔ Oblivious (Pattern 0) organizations make little use of tools. Variable (Pattern 1) organizations often use tools quite well, but generally on an individual basis. Routine (Pattern 2) organizations often use tools more broadly than Pattern 1 organizations, but the use of these tools is both shallow and reluctant.

✔ Receptor groups identify and evaluate technological opportunities. They ask, "How can I take technology and apply it to how I do business?" These groups understand both the technology and their organizations, so they make the match between a general technology and a specific context.

✔ Steering (Pattern 3) organizations use tools cautiously, but rather well, on the whole, though often without an overall plan or coordination. Anticipating (Pattern 4) organizations use tools vigorously, but always with a result in mind. They almost always have a specially trained receptor group that proactively searches for generally useful tools, as well as tools to address specific process problems. Because tools are socialized by trained change artists, individuals who need tools get tools and use them well.

✔ The First Law of Technology Transfer says that long-range good tends to be sacrificed to short-range good. The battle cries of the First Law are all too familiar:

- We don't have time to do it right.
- We can't spare him right now.
- We'll assign her one-eighth time to the task.
- We'll do it in our spare time.

✔ The Second Law of Technology Transfer says that short-range feasibility tends to be sacrificed to long-range perfection. The battle cries of the Second Law are also well known:

- It's not part of the plan.
- We'll set up a task force.
- It's not the elegant way.
- We need to study the implications.

✔ When you hear the NT Visionaries arguing over the perfect tool to solve your problems, step in and find something useful and specific for them to do. Don't let them evade crises by irrelevant tool-building, though when the crisis is over, they can become your best tool designers.

✔ Even the organization in Chaos has all the tools it needs, though most people don't know about them. Work first under the hypothesis that your tool problem is not one of manufacturing, but of distribution.

✔ Use a dual strategy to beat the two Laws of Technology Transfer: Find the long-term solution while using a short-term solution to relieve the pressure.

✔ The Ten Commandments of Technology Transfer form a useful mnemonic guide to avoiding the sins of technology transfer:

- Thou shalt have a plan to lead thee out of the wilderness.
- Thou shalt not worship thy plan.
- Thou shalt ask for no person in vain.
- Thou shalt not work seven days a week.
- Thou shalt honor thy users and listen to them.
- Thou shalt not kill support for change.
- Thou shalt not adulterate the work.
- Thou shalt not steal resources from the work.
- Thou shalt not bear false witness against thy plan.
- Thou shalt not covet thy neighbor's optimal technology.

✔ The power of the Ten Commandments is magnified if you remember the Helpful Model:

**No matter how it looks, everyone is trying to be helpful.**

If you forget this commandment, you will begin to counter so-called resistance, which will engender real resistance—not to the technology, but to your anti-resistance efforts.

✔ Listen for the real information present in all resistance, so that you can use this information to correct your mistakes and enlist everybody's participation in changing your organization.

## 23.9 Practice

1.  Paradoxically, it's generally easier to move people from one tool to a *better* tool than from no tool at all. Warren's configuration room was an example of this two-step strategy. For some tool you'd like to introduce, list a few less-powerful tools that could be used as stepping stones.

2.  Conduct a tool survey of your organization. Don't try to survey the entire organization, but use a sample. If the sample proves interesting, survey the rest of the organization.

3.  When you automate one part of a process, it changes the task mix. The nature of the work changes, and people have to learn skills that were less important before, the skills to handle things the tools won't handle. For instance, Peg Ofstead of the Washington DPMA Study Group commented to me on the impact of successful tool use on the profile of faults.[7] She observed that in a successful ICASE environment, most coding faults and many design faults were eliminated. Although this successful tool use decreased the total *number* of faults, it increased the *proportion* of requirements faults. Because requirements faults tend to be more costly than coding faults, the total cost impact of the ICASE was rather less than anticipated. Moreover, the organization now experiences a greater percentage of faults in areas where its people feel less competent, which can have a depressing effect on the organization. The wise manager will anticipate this failure-from-success effect and prepare by retraining, or otherwise changing the skill set of the staff.

    Consider one tool you're thinking of introducing, and plot the task mix before and after successful introduction. What additional training will people need to handle the greater load of nonautomated tasks?

4.  James Robertson asks: Do the lessons of this chapter apply equally well to individually built tools? What's the same, and what's different?

5.  Innovations carry risk. You can lessen the risk for the person who tries the innovation by offering insurance, as is done for farmers planting new seed varieties in India. Even if the crop fails entirely, the farmer is assured of being paid at least as much as was earned on the same land last year. Consider a tool you want to introduce. What kind of insurance can you offer the first team that takes the risk of using it?

# Part V
# Epilogue

*Every man is working out his destiny in his own way and nobody can be of help except by being kind, generous, and patient.*

— Henry Miller

Except for the first volume of this series, I've established a tradition of closing each volume with what I intend to be an inspiring epilogue. As I write a book, I raise my antennae to search for notable quotes that I might use. This time I found several, including the one above from Henry Miller, which reminds me that my readers are working out their destinies in their own ways and that I can't really help as much as I'd like simply by writing an epilogue.

Since I couldn't decide which among my chosen quotes would be best for each of you, I decided to use several. I've put them in the framework of a self-quiz you can take before embarking on your quest to change your piece of the world.

Here goes, starting with Miller's observation:

**Question 1.** (For 15 points total, score 5 points for each yes answer to a part question.)

During the past month,

a. Have you been as kind as you want to be?

b. Have you been as generous as you want to be?

c. Have you been as patient as you want to be?

**Question 2.** (Give yourself 25 points for an honest answer; no points if you cannot answer.)

> It is said that "power corrupts," but actually it's more true that power attracts the corruptible. The sane are usually attracted by other things than power. When they do act, they think of it as service, which has limits. The tyrant, though, seeks mastery, for which he is insatiable, implacable.[1]
>
> — David Brin

Why are you seeking the power to change things?

**Question 3.** (Of 20 points total, give yourself 5 points for each affirmative part answer.)

> Fear less, hope more;
> Eat less, chew more;
> Whine less, breathe more;
> Talk less, say more;
> Hate less, love more;
> And all good things will be yours.
>
> — Swedish proverb

In the past month,

a.   Have you been handling both fear and hope with moderation?

b.   Have you been taking care of your health?

c.   Have you been staying centered and taking responsibility for yourself?

d.   Have you been listening and thinking before trying to help others change?

**Question 4.** (Of 20 points total, give yourself 10 points for each part to which you can answer yes.)

> I believe that the concept of failure . . . is central to understanding engineering, for engineering design has as its first and foremost objective the obviation of failure. . . . To understand what engineering is and what engineers do is to understand how failures can happen and how they can contribute more than successes to advance technology.[2]
>
> — Henry Petroski

In the past month,

a.   Have you forgiven yourself for failures?

b.   Have you learned from them?  (Give examples.)

**Question 5.**  (For 20 points, answer yes to part *a* and no to part *b*.)

Some people cause happiness wherever they go; some whenever they go.

— Oscar Wilde

Are you causing happiness

a.   by your coming?

b.   by your going?

**Extra credit.**  (Give yourself 10 points for each yes.)

a.   Are you hating less?

b.   Are you loving more?

The answers should cover your activities over the past month, and you can take this quiz again every month for as long as you continue to be a change artist.  You might even want to plot your scores on a chart on your wall, as your first change-artist metric.

# Appendix A
# Diagram of Effects

An important skill of Steering (Pattern 3) managers is the ability to reason about nonlinear systems, and one of the favorite tools for this purpose is the *diagram of effects*.[1] In Figure A-1, the diagram of effects shows the effects of management pressure to resolve software failures (system trouble incidents or STIs). We can use this diagram as an example of the major notational conventions.

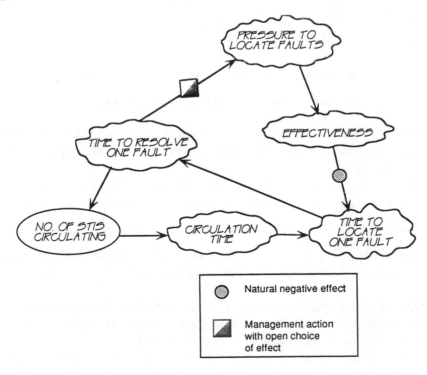

Figure A-1.        Sample diagram of effects.

A diagram of effects consists primarily of nodes connected by arrows:

1.    Each node stands for a measurable quantity, like Circulation Time, Effectiveness, Time to Locate One Fault, or Pressure to Locate Faults. I prefer using the "cloud" symbol over a circle or a rectangle as a reminder that nodes indicate measurements, not things or processes as in flow-charts, data flow diagrams, and the like.

2.    These cloud nodes may represent either actual measurements or concep- tual measurements—things that could be measured, but are not measured at present because they may be too expensive to measure, or not worth the trouble, or just not measured yet. The important thing is that they can be measured, perhaps only approximately, if we are willing to pay the price.

3.    To indicate an actual measurement currently being made, use a regular, elliptical cloud, as for No. of STIs Circulating in Figure A-1. Most of the time, however, effects diagrams are used for conceptual—rather than mathematical—analysis, so most of the clouds will be appropriately rough.

4.    An arrow from node A to node B indicates that quantity A has an effect on quantity B. We may know or deduce the effect that leads us to draw the arrow in one of three ways:

       a.    a mathematical formula for the effect, as in

             Time to Locate One Fault = Circulation Time + Other Factors

       b.    deduced from observations, for instance, when people are observed to get nervous and lose their effectiveness when under pressure from management
       c.    inferred from past experience, for instance, noticing on other projects how management changes the pressure when fault resolution time changes

5.    The general direction of the effect of A on B may be indicated by the pres- ence or absence of the large gray dot on the arrow between them.

       a.    No dot means that as A moves in one direction, B moves in the same direction. (More STIs circulating means more circulation time; fewer STIs circulating means less circulation time.)
       b.    A dot on the arrow means that as A moves in one direction, B moves in the opposite direction. (More effectiveness means less time to locate one fault; less effectiveness means more time to locate one fault.)

6.  A square on an effects line indicates that human intervention is determining the direction of the effect:

   a.  A white square means that human intervention is making the affected measurement move in the same direction as the movement of the cause (just as a plain arrow indicates a natural same direction).

   b.  A gray square means that human intervention is making the affected measurement move in the opposite direction as the movement of the cause (just as a gray dot indicates a natural opposite direction).

   c.  A half-white/half-gray square means that human intervention can make the affected measurement move in the same or the opposite direction as the movement of the cause, depending on the intervention. In the case of Figure A-1, management can react to an increase in the amount of fault resolution time by either increasing or decreasing pressure to locate faults. The square shows that this dynamic depends on the manager's choice of response.

# Appendix B
# Satir Interaction Model

The Satir Interaction Model says that everyone's internal observation process has four major parts:  Intake, Meaning, Significance, and Response, as shown in Figure B-1.  For the purpose of this explanation, I act as the observer.[1]

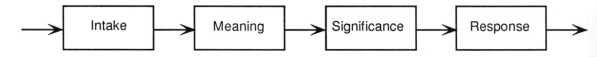

Figure B-1.　　The four basic parts of the Satir Interaction Model.

**Intake**
In the first part of the process, I take in information from the world.  Although some people may believe that intake just happens to me as a passive participant, I am actually exercising a great many choices.

**Meaning**
Next, I consider the sensory intake and give it meaning.  The meaning doesn't lie in the data; data have no meaning until I provide meaning.

**Significance**
Data may suggest certain meanings, but never the significance.  Without this step, the world I perceive would be an overwhelming flood of data patterns.  With it, I can give priority to a few patterns and largely ignore the rest.

**Response**
Observation is rarely passive, but elicits response.  I may not, and should not, respond to every observation immediately.  I am always sifting observations according to their assigned importance and storing them away to guide future actions.

# Appendix C
# Software Engineering
# Cultural Patterns

This volume makes extensive use of the idea of software cultural patterns. For ease of reference, I summarize here the various aspects of those patterns.

To my knowledge, Crosby was the first to apply the idea of cultural patterns to the study of industrial processes.[1] He discovered that the various processes making up a technology don't merely occur in random combinations, but in coherent patterns.

In their article "A Programming Process Study," Radice et al. adapted Crosby's "stratification by quality" scheme to software development.[2] Later, Watts Humphrey of the Software Engineering Institute (SEI) extended their work and identified five levels of "process maturity" through which a software development organization might grow.[3] Other software engineering observers quickly noted the usefulness of Humphrey's maturity levels. Bill Curtis proposed a "software human resource maturity model" with five levels.[4]

Each of these models represents points of view of the same phenomenon. Crosby named his five patterns based largely on the *management attitudes* to be found in each. The names used by the SEI are more related to the *types of processes* found in each pattern, rather than to the attitudes of management. Curtis made his classification on the basis of the *treatment of people* within the organization.

In my own work with software engineering organizations, I most often use the cultural view[5] combined with Crosby's original focus on management and on attitudes, but I find each view useful at various times. The following summary incorporates material from each point of view.

---

| Pattern 0 Oblivious Culture |
| :---: |

**Other names:** This pattern doesn't exist in Crosby's, Humphrey's, or Curtis's models.

**View of themselves:** "We don't even know that we're performing a process."

**Metaphor:** Walking: When we want to go somewhere, we just stand up and go.

**Management understanding and attitude:** There is no comprehension that quality is a management issue.

**Problem handling:** Problems are suffered in silence.

**Summation of quality position:** "We don't have quality problems."

**When this pattern is successful:** To succeed, individuals need three conditions or beliefs:

✔     "I'm solving my own problems."

✔     "Those problems aren't too big for what I know is technically possible."

✔     "I know what I want better than anyone else."

**Process results:** Results depend totally on the individual. No records are kept, so there are no measurements. Because the customer is the developer, delivery is always acceptable.

---

## Pattern 1  Variable Culture

**Other names:**

| | |
|---|---|
| Crosby: | Uncertainty Stage |
| Humphrey: | Initial Process |
| Curtis: | Herded |

**View of themselves:**  "We do whatever we feel like at the moment."

**Metaphor:**  Riding a horse:  When we want to go somewhere, we saddle up and ride . . . if the horse cooperates.

**Management understanding and attitude:**  There is no comprehension of quality as a management issue.

**Problem handling:**  Problems are fought with inadequate definition and no resolution (but with lots of yelling and accusations).

**Summation of quality position:**  "We don't know why we have quality problems."

**When this pattern is successful:**  To succeed, individuals (or teams) need three conditions or beliefs:

✔     "I have great rapport with my customer."

✔     "I'm a competent professional."

✔     "My customer's problem isn't too big for me."

**Process results:**  The work is generally one-on-one between customer and developer.  Quality is measured internally by its function ("It works!"), externally by the working relationship.  Emotion, personal relations, and mysticism drive everything.  There is no consistent design, randomly structured code, and errors removed by haphazard testing.  Some of the work is excellent, some is bizarre, and it all depends on the individual.

---

### Pattern 2  Routine Culture

---

**Other names:**

| | |
|---|---|
| Crosby: | Awakening Stage |
| Humphrey: | Repeatable Process |
| Curtis: | Managed |

**View of themselves:** "We follow our routines (except when we lose our nerve)."

**Metaphor:** A train: When we want to go somewhere, we find a train, which has large capacity and is very efficient . . . if we go where the tracks are. We're helpless when off the tracks.

**Management understanding and attitude:** There is a recognition that quality management may be of value, but there is no willingness to provide money or time to make it all happen.

**Problem handling:** Teams are set up to handle major problems. Long-range solutions are not solicited.

**Summation of quality position:** "Is it absolutely necessary to have problems with quality? Maybe if we just don't deal with them, the problems will go away."

**When this pattern is successful:** To succeed, people in these organizations need four conditions or beliefs:

✔     "We realize the problem is bigger than one small team can handle."

✔     "The problem is not too big for us to handle."

✔     "The developers must conform to our Routine process."

✔     "We hope we don't run into anything too exceptional."

**Process results:** The Routine organization has procedures to coordinate efforts, though its members only go through the motions of following them. Statistics on past performance are used not to change, but to prove that they are doing everything in the only reasonable way. Quality is measured internally by the numbers of errors ("bugs"). Generally, the organization uses bottom-up design and semi-structured code, with errors removed by testing and fixing. Routine organizations have many successes, but a few very large failures.

---

## Pattern 3  Steering Culture

**Other names:**

| | |
|---|---|
| Crosby: | Enlightenment Stage |
| Humphrey: | Defined Process |
| Curtis: | Tailored |

**View of themselves:** "We choose among our routines based on the results they produce."

**Metaphor:** A van: We have a large choice of destinations, but we must generally stay on mapped roads, and must be steered to stay on the road.

**Management understanding and attitude:** There is comprehension of quality as a management tool: "Through our quality program, we learn more about quality management, and become more supportive and helpful."

**Problem handling:** Problems are faced openly and resolved in an orderly way.

**Summation of quality position:** "Through commitment and quality improvement, we are identifying and resolving our problems."

**When this pattern is successful:** To succeed, people in these organizations need four conditions or beliefs:

✔      "The problem is big enough that we know a simple routine won't work."

✔      "Our managers can negotiate with the external environment."

✔      "We don't accept arbitrary schedules and constraints."

✔      "We are challenged, but not excessively."

**Process results:** They have procedures that are always well understood, but not always well defined in writing, and that are followed even in crisis.  Quality is measured by user (customer) response, but not systematically.  Some measuring is done, but everybody debates which measurements are meaningful.  Typically, they use top-down design, structured code, design and code inspections, and incremental releases.  The organization has consistent success when it commits to undertake something.

---

### Pattern 4  Anticipating Culture

---

**Other names:**

| | |
|---|---|
| Crosby: | Wisdom Stage |
| Humphrey: | Managed Process |
| Curtis: | Institutionalized |

**View of themselves:** "We establish routines based on our past experience with them."

**Metaphor:** An airplane: When going somewhere, we can travel fast, reliably, and anywhere there's a field, but going this way requires a large initial investment.

**Management understanding and attitude:** There is understanding of the absolutes of quality management, and recognition of their personal role in this continuing emphasis.

**Problem handling:** Problems are identified early in their development. All functions are open to suggestion and improvement.

**Summation of quality position:** "Defect prevention is a routine part of our operation."

**When this pattern is successful:** To succeed, individuals need three conditions or beliefs:

✔    "I'm solving my own problems.

✔    "We measure quality and cost (internally) by meaningful statistics."

✔    "We have an explicit process group to aid in the process."

**Process results:** They use sophisticated tools and techniques, including function-theoretical design, mathematical verification, and reliability measurement. They have consistent success even on ambitious projects.

---

## Pattern 5  Congruent Culture

**Other names:**

| | |
|---|---|
| Crosby: | Certainty Stage |
| Humphrey: | Optimizing Process |
| Curtis: | Optimized |

**View of themselves:** "Everyone is involved in improving everything all the time."

**Metaphor:** The Starship Enterprise: When going somewhere, we can go where no one has gone before, we can carry anything, and we can beam ourselves anywhere, but this is all science fiction.

**Management understanding and attitude:** Quality management is considered an essential part of the company system.

**Problem handling:** Except in the most unusual cases, problems are prevented.

**Summation of quality position:** "We know why we do not have quality problems."

**When this pattern is successful:** To succeed, these organizations need three conditions or beliefs:

✔    "We have procedures, which we improve continuously."

✔    "We identify and measure all key process variables automatically."

✔    "Our goal is customer satisfaction, which drives everything."

**Process results:** Here are all of the good things achievable by the other patterns, plus the willingness to spend to reach the next level of quality. Quality is measured by customer satisfaction and by the mean time to customer failure (ten to one-hundred years). Customers love the quality, and can bet their life on it. In some sense, Pattern 5 is like Pattern 0 in being totally responsive to the customer, but it is much better at what it does.

# Appendix D
# Control Models

Each software cultural pattern has its own characteristic pattern of control. The study of patterns of software control starts with the question, What is needed to control anything?  Here, I discuss two possible answers to this need.

The *Aggregate Control Model* says that if we're willing to spend enough on redundant solutions, we'll eventually get the system we want.  Sometimes, this is the most practical way, or the only way we can think of.

The *Feedback Control Model* (or cybernetic model) tries for a more efficient way of getting what we want.  A controller controls a system based on information about what the system is currently doing.  Comparing this information with what is planned for the system, the controller takes actions designed to bring the system's behavior closer to plan.

The job of engineering management is to act as the controller in engineering projects.  Failures of engineering management can be understood in terms of the Feedback Control Model.  Routine (Pattern 2) managers, for example, often lack this understanding, which can explain why they experience so many low-quality, or failed, projects.

## D.1  Aggregate Control Model

One general approach to shooting at moving targets is the technique of *aggregation*.  Aggregate control is like shooting with a shotgun or, more precisely, with shrapnel.  If we simply send more bullets flying through the sky in sufficiently random directions, we will increase our chances of hitting a target, no matter how it is moving.

In software engineering, the aggregate approach says, roughly, to be sure of getting a good product, start a large number of projects and choose the one that produces the best product.  From the viewpoint of an individual software company, aggregation may be a useful way to ensure success in special circumstances.

Aggregation is most commonly used when we are considering a software purchase. Of several products considered, we choose the best for our purposes. If our selection procedure is at all sensible, we should wind up with a better product than if we only considered one.

Sometimes, the use of aggregation is not fully intentional. Routine organizations frequently employ unintentional *serial* aggregation. When the first attempt to build a system doesn't turn out well, a second project is started. If the second does not turn out well either, the organization may actually return to the first, now accepting its poor quality as the better of a bad lot. Aggregation is a universal strategy, and no pattern is without its examples. In Pattern 3, however, there is a more conscious use of explicit manipulation of aggregation to aid in quality improvement.

## D.2 Feedback Control (Cybernetic) Model

Whereas aggregation is like shooting with a shotgun, feedback control is like shooting with a rifle. Cybernetics, the "science of aiming," is a topic that every software engineer needs to understand.[1]

### D.2.1 The system to be controlled (the focus of Patterns 0 and 1)

The cybernetic model starts with the idea of a system to be controlled (Figure D-1). A system has inputs and outputs. For a system that produces software, the outputs are Software, plus Other Outputs, which may include all sorts of things that are not the direct goal of the system, such as

- greater competence with a programming language
- software tools developed while doing the intended software
- stronger, or weaker, development teams
- stress, pregnancies, influenza, happiness
- anger toward management
- respect for management
- thousands of failure reports
- personnel appraisals

The inputs are of three principal types (the 3 R's):

- Requirements
- Resources
- Randomness

A system's behavior is governed by the formula:

**Behavior depends on both state and input.**

Thus, control depends not only on what we put in (requirements and resources) and what gets in by some other way (randomness), but also on what's going on internally (the state).

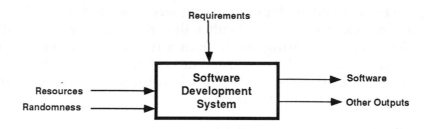

Figure D-1.        Cybernetic model of a software development system to be controlled.

Figure D-1 represents the entire model of software development as understood by Pattern 1 organizations. In effect, it says,

    a.    "Tell us what you want (and don't change your mind)."
    b.    "Give us some resources (and keep giving whenever we ask)."
    c.    "Don't bother us (that is, eliminate all randomness)."

These are the ABC's of Pattern 1 software development, and by listening for these statements, you can reliably identify a Pattern 1 organization.

If you drop the "A" (the external requirements), you get the identifying phrases for Pattern 0 organizations, which already know what they want, without help, thank you. Figure D-1 can thus be transformed to the Pattern 0 diagram by dropping off the requirements arrow, thus isolating the system from direct external control.

### D.2.2  The controller (the focus of Pattern 2)

To get more quality (value) from our software development with this Pattern 1 model, we would have to use the aggregate approach—in effect pumping more resources into the development system. One way to do this would be to initiate several such development systems and let each do whatever it does best. If we want more control of each system, however, we must connect it to some sort of *controller* (Figure D-2). The controller represents all our efforts to keep the software development on track, and is Pattern 2's addition to the problem of getting quality software.

At this level of cybernetic theory, the controller cannot access the internal state of the development system directly. So, in order to be able to control, the controller must be able to change the internal state indirectly through the inputs (the lines coming out of the controller and into the system). Examples of such attempts to change the programming staff may include

- offering training courses to make them smarter
- buying them tools to make them smarter
- hiring Harvard graduates to make them smarter (on average)
- offering cash incentives to make them more motivated
- offering more interesting assignments to make them more motivated
- firing Berkeley graduates to make them more motivated (on average)

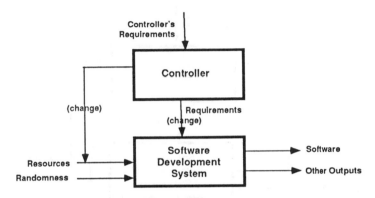

Figure D-2.    Model of a software development system controller.

The control actions are added to the system's *uncontrolled* inputs (the randomness), either by changing requirements or changing resources. Notice that no matter what the controller does to these inputs, there is still randomness coming in, which simply represents all those external things that the controller cannot totally control. The thought of these inputs is most frustrating to some Pattern 2 managers.

### D.2.3 Feedback control (the focus of Pattern 3)

An effective method of limiting losses due to flu (an uncontrolled input) would be to send people home at the first sign of symptoms. The Pattern 2 controller pictured in Figure D-2 cannot do this because it has no knowledge of what the system is actually doing. A more versatile and effective model of control is the feedback model shown in Figure D-3. In this model—which represents the Pattern 3 concept of control—the controller can make measurements of performance (the line coming out of the system and into the controller) and use them as an aid in determining its next control actions.

But feedback measurements and control actions are not enough for effective control. We know that behavior depends on both state and input. In order for the control actions to be effective, the Pattern 3 controller must possess models to connect the state and input with the behavior—models of what "depends" means for this system.

Overall, for feedback control to operate, the system of control must have

- an image of a *desired* state (D)
- the ability to observe the *actual* state (A)
- the ability to compare state A and state D for differences
- the ability to act on the system to bring A closer to D

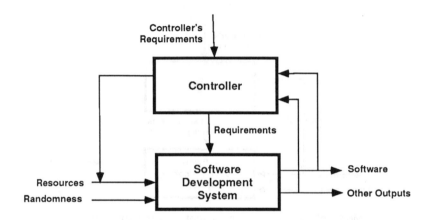

Figure D-3.      Feedback model of a software development system requires feedback of information about the system's performance, plus requirements for the controller to compare with that information. This is the model that distinguishes Pattern 3 from Patterns 0, 1, and 2. It is also used by Patterns 4 and 5.

A characteristic Pattern 2 mistake is to equate "controller" with "manager." In the Pattern 3 model, managing is essentially a controller job. To manage an engineering project by feedback control, the manager needs to

- plan what should happen
- observe what significant things are really happening
- compare the observed with the planned
- take actions needed to bring actual closer to planned

Managers who are able to do these things consistently are what we call Steering managers. Patterns 3, 4, and 5 all require Steering management, which seems to be the limiting factor for most organizations that wish to make the transition out of Pattern 0, 1, or 2 to one of these patterns. In the *Quality Software Management* series, the first three volumes are devoted to encouraging the transition to Steering management, and *Volume 4* addresses the transition to managing an Anticipating (Pattern 4) organization.

# Appendix E
# Three Observer Positions

Even when you are congruent, you may not be in the best position to observe what you need to work on in a crisis. One of the most effective interventions in a crisis is to provide information taken from a different point of view. Whenever you act as an observer, you have a choice of where to "stand" to make your observations: the self, other, or context.

**Self (Insider) Position**
Inside yourself, looking outward or inward. This position gives you the ability to realize what your own interests are, why you are behaving the way you are, and what you may be contributing to the situation. An inability to observe from this position often results in placating or superreasonable behavior. Many burnouts result from forgetting to spend time in the self position.

**Other (Empathic) Position**
As if you were inside another person, observing from his or her point of view. This position gives you the ability to understand why people react the way they do. An inability to observe from this position often results in blaming or superreasonable behavior.

**Context (Outsider) Position**
Outside, looking at yourself and at other people. This position gives you the ability to understand and place things in context. An inability to observe from this position often results in irrelevant behavior.

Nothing says you have to take any particular observer position, or any position at all. Sometimes, you become so panicked in a crisis that you are unable to take any observer position.  You ignore your own feelings, don't notice what's happening to others, and have no connection with the overall situation.

In managing, you need to be flexible, observing at times from Position 1, or Position 2, or Position 3.  If you cannot reach one or more of these observer positions, you may be stuck and behave incongruently (either blaming, placating, or acting superreasonable or irrelevant).  In this way, you have given away some of your observational power, just when you need it most.

# Appendix F
# The MBTI and Temperaments

This appendix summarizes two models of behavior explored in *Volume 3:* the Myers-Briggs Type Indicator (MBTI) and the Keirsey-Bates model of four temperaments based on the MBTI types.

### F.1 The Myers-Briggs Type Indicator

The Myers-Briggs Type Indicator describes four dimensions of a person's working style. The dimensions correspond to how a person prefers to get energy, to obtain information, to make decisions, and to take action. Managers find this system a valuable way to start understanding the people they manage and work with, which helps them manage better, be managed better, and be better team members.

A person's preference on each of the four dimensions is represented by a single letter, one of a pair for each dimension. In my case, for example, a selection of the four letters INFP abbreviate my own assessment of the four components of my working style. These letters correspond to a description of each dimension:

- Internal or External (I or E), according to how I prefer to get energy
- Sensing or iNtuitive (S or N), according to how I prefer to obtain information
- Thinking or Feeling (T or F), according to how I prefer to make decisions
- Judging or Perceiving (J or P), according to how I prefer to take action

So, my INFP is a shorthand way of saying that I *prefer* to get my energy from inside (I), find information intuitively (N), make decisions on the basis of values (F), and take action that keeps possibilities open (P). ESTJ, by contrast, means I would prefer to get my energy from others (E), obtain information through facts (S), make decisions using logic (T), and take action to have things settled (J).

Take careful note that the description INFP does not say that I cannot get energy from outside, find information through my senses, make decisions on the basis of logical thought, or take action that closes possibilities. It merely says that when simple or unconscious preference determines my choices, I'll tend to do certain things and not do other things. With that caution in mind, let's examine these four dimensions of preference.

The first dimension describes how people prefer to get the energy to do things or how they recharge their batteries. In an organization, you can see people's *Internal/External* (I/E) preference very clearly in meetings and especially at breaks. External processors tend to use breaks to socialize; Internal processors use breaks to be alone and regenerate.

The second dimension describes how people prefer to get the information they need to do things. Within an organization, you can also see the *Sensing/Intuitive* (S/N) preference in meetings, especially during presentations. Sensors want the facts, lots of facts, while Intuitives want the big picture.

The third MBTI dimension, *Thinking/Feeling* (T/F), describes how people prefer to make decisions: using logic (thinking) or values (feeling). In an organization, you can see the T/F preference in action whenever decisions are to be made. Both types want good decisions, but they differ in what attributes make a decision good. Thinkers want objectivity, logic, and impersonality; Feelers want humanity, values, and cooperation. In arriving at decisions, neither type objects to consideration of the other's attributes, but merely considers them of low priority.

The fourth MBTI dimension describes a person's preferred mode of taking action. The *Judging* (J) preference is to have things settled, while the *Perceiving* (P) preference is to keep options open on the chance that more information will affect the choice. Judging refers not to the tendency to be judgmental, but to the preference for making decisions. Perceiving refers not to the tendency to be perceptive, but to the preference for taking in information (hence the word *perceiving*). My own preference, with twenty/twenty hindsight, would have been the words *closure-seeking* (for *judging*) and *information-seeking* (for *perceiving*).

## F.2 Temperaments

The four dimensions of the MBTI model are useful to a manager in and of themselves, but when they are combined as described below, they can be even more powerful. Keirsey and Bates reduced the sixteen possible personality types represented by combinations of the four MBTI letters to four *temperaments:* the NT Visionary, the NF Catalyst, the SJ Organizer, and the SP Troubleshooter.[1] Let's look at the four temperaments in turn, along with an example of how each reacts to an out-of-control situation—a trap that tests the temperament type's presumed form of control, whether intellectual, physical, emergency, or emotional control.

### F.2.1 The NT Visionary

The Visionary (NT, or Intuitive Thinker in the Myers-Briggs system) likes working with ideas. NT Visionaries are most interested in designing, rather than implementing, things. Their strength is captured in the saying "Nothing is more dangerous than an idea whose time has come." NT Visionaries are dangerous to the established order, because they lead the rest of us out of our complacency into their brave new worlds. Without them, we'd still be shivering in caves, waiting for someone to invent fire.

You can trap an NT Visionary by saying, "Capture the essence," for the NT Visionary easily gets caught in oversimplifying complex details into a unified theory. In other words, "Nothing is more dangerous than an idea when it is the only one you have."

### F.2.2 The NF Catalyst

Catalysts (NF, or Intuitive Feeler) like working with people to help themselves grow, but they are concerned that people not suffer. NF Catalysts are needed to keep everybody working together through the rough times, and to support individuals going through tough emotional times.

You can trap an NF Catalyst by saying, "Make sure everyone agrees," for the NF Catalyst values harmony above all else. There are many circumstances when it's unnecessary for everyone to agree, but the NF Catalyst has a hard time recognizing them. I've heard more than one NF facilitator ask, "Does anyone object to our taking a bathroom break?"

This question perfectly characterizes the most common and destructive NF management mistake. If one person doesn't want a bathroom break, are all the rest of us to sit in pain and misery? NF Catalysts, in their passion for taking care of everybody, often harm a great number of people in an overly focused effort to save one.

### F.2.3 The SJ Organizer

The Organizer (SJ, or Sensory Judge) likes order and system. The important thing to an SJ Organizer is not just doing it, but doing it right. Most SJ Organizers would heartily agree with the slogan "Anything worth doing is worth doing right."

You can trap an SJ Organizer by saying, "Do it right" or "Do it on time," for they value order over everything else. They have a hard time understanding that other slogan: "Anything not worth doing is not worth doing right."

There are many occasions when things need not be in perfect order, but the SJ Organizers have a hard time recognizing them.

### F.2.4  The SP Troubleshooter

Troubleshooters (SP, or Sensing Perceiver) like getting the job done and want quick fixes, not elaborate plans. They say, "If it ain't broke, don't fix it." They also say, "If I can't fix it, it ain't broke."

The way to trap an SP Troubleshooter is to ask for, and get, a quick-and-dirty solution, for an SP values results above all else. In some circumstances, the SP's quick-and-dirty solution is more dirty than quick, if you add the clean-up time that will be required. When it comes to software, the SP's favorite word seems to be *zap*, and SP Troubleshooters often see configuration management systems as the devil's own invention.

### F.3  Typing Schemes As Tools for Understanding

The MBTI model and the Keirsey-Bates temperaments make managers more aware of some important dimensions of what they're choosing when they interact with others. I believe this added consciousness will make all of us better managers.

Whereas many other personality models arose from attempts to find out what is wrong with people, the MBTI model was designed to discover each of our special, but differing, gifts. However, the innocence of its origins doesn't prevent a tool from being abused by mean-spirited or ignorant people.

I cannot protect against the mean-spirited, but ignorance is curable. One of the dangers is that this discussion is merely the briefest introduction to the MBTI model and the temperaments, and an introduction from the point of view of one type among sixteen. My Thinking colleagues, particularly, object to the way I approach this subject, and of course they're right to object. Each of us has to approach our own personality in our own way.

For me, it took a good deal of study and experimentation even to discover my own type and to understand some of its implications. When first introduced to the MBTI system, I believed I was an ENTP (External, Intuitive, Thinking Perceiver). After a year or so of study and practice, I realized I was an ENFP, but then further understanding led me to believe I'm an INFP. That's where I've stayed for a number of years, but who knows where self-discovery might eventually lead. If I can make several mistakes about my own type, you can see that it would be easy to abuse the MBTI model. If it seems a valuable tool to you, please make the effort to study it more deeply. Here's the way an INFP would do it:

- Practice first on yourself, not on others.
- When you are ready to move out into the world, find a partner or

partners who differ from you in one or two dimensions.

- Connect with your sameness as you explore your differentness with, not on, your partner.
- Share your own gifts and let your partner teach you about gifts that are less familiar to you.
- Do all this practice with much more humor than judgment.

Let me conclude this abbreviated discussion with some advice from my colleague Dan Starr. In Dan's words, the main values of any "typing" scheme (not just the two models discussed here) are

- They remind me that people are different—in a lot of ways.
- They give me some models of the areas in which people are different.
- They invite me to ask what I prefer in a number of areas—and allow me to get a better understanding of who I prefer to be.
- They remind me, when I'm having trouble understanding some other person, that it just might be because we prefer to approach the world differently.
- They give me some models of approaches to the world other than mine, which may allow me to solve communication problems . . .
- . . . or, which may remind me of other ways in which I might approach a problem at hand.

Dan sums this all up by saying, "I try to use the temperament/type models as tools for understanding and influencing myself, not for labeling others." We would all do well to follow his example.

# Notes

## Acknowledgments

1 N. Karten, *Managing Expectations* (New York: Dorset House Publishing, 1994).
2 J. Robertson and S. Robertson, *Complete Systems Analysis* (New York: Dorset House Publishing, 1994).

## Preface

1 J. Herbsleb, A. Carleton, J. Rozum, J. Siegel, and D. Zubrow, "Benefits of CMM-Based Software Process Improvement: Initial Results," CMU/SEI-94-TR-13 (Pittsburgh: Software Engineering Institute, 1994).
2 To assist in your reading process, this book contains several appendices referring to material in *Volumes 1, 2,* and *3*.
3 Admiral H.G. Rickover, quoted in T. Rockwell, *The Rickover Effect: How One Man Made a Difference* (Washington, D.C.: Naval Institute Press, 1992).
4 C. Jones, "Risks of Software System Failure or Disaster," *American Programmer*, Vol. 8, No. 3 (1995), pp. 2–9.

## Chapter 1

1 See Appendix C for a summary of the software engineering cultural patterns.
2 See *Volume 1, Systems Thinking* for additional examples of boomerang effects.
3 See Appendix A for an explanation of a diagram of effects.

## Chapter 2

1 See, for example, V. Satir, J. Banmen, J. Gerber, and M. Gomori, *The Satir Model: Family Therapy and Beyond* (Palo Alto, Calif.: Science and Behavior Books, 1991).
2 For more on the behavior of controllers, see *Volume 1, Systems Thinking*.
3 For a summary of the various software engineering cultural patterns, including the Routine (Pattern 2) culture, see Appendix C.

## Chapter 3

1    L. Hellman, *The Autumn Garden* (New York: Little, Brown & Co., 1951).
2    Virginia Satir, personal communication.
3    Lynda McLyman, personal communication, 1990.
4    For more information on the PPPP, see especially *Volume 2, First-Order Measurement*, pp. 272–83.
5    See Appendix C for a brief description of the software engineering cultural patterns.
6    J. Stevens, "Shugyo," *Aikido Today* (December 1994), pp. 13–14.
7    See Appendix F for a brief description of the Myers-Briggs personality type indicators.

## Part II

1    F. Peavey, M. Levy, and C. Varon, *Heart Politics* (Philadelphia: New Society Publishers, 1986).

## Chapter 4

1    "A Master Class in Radical Change," *Fortune* (December 13, 1993), pp. 82–90.
2    D. Keirsey and M. Bates, *Please Understand Me: Character & Temperament Types*, 4th ed. (Del Mar, Calif.: Prometheus Nemesis Book Co., 1984). The subject of temperaments is treated extensively in *Volume 3, Congruent Action*, and is summarized here in Appendix F
3    T. DeMarco and T. Lister, *Peopleware: Productive Projects and Teams* (New York: Dorset House Publishing, 1987).
4    In addition to Weinberg & Weinberg's own Problem Solving Leadership Workshop and Congruent Leadership Change Shop, I highly recommend the following workshops to aspiring change artists: Tom Crum's Magic of Conflict; Barry and Karen Oshry's Power and Systems Laboratory; and NTL's Human Interaction Lab.
5    See G.M. Weinberg, *Becoming a Technical Leader* (New York: Dorset House Publishing, 1986).
6    In addition to this volume, see V. Satir, J. Banmen, J. Gerber, and M. Gomori, *The Satir Model: Family Therapy and Beyond* (Palo Alto, Calif.: Science and Behavior Books, 1991).
7    See G.M. Weinberg, *An Introduction to General Systems Thinking* (New York: Wiley-Interscience, 1975). Also see *Volume 1, Systems Thinking*.
8    See Satir et al., op. cit. Also see C.N. Seashore, E.W. Seashore, and G.M. Weinberg, *What Did You Say? The Art of Giving and Receiving Feedback* (Columbia, Md.: Bingham House Books, 1991); and *Volume 2, First-Order Measurement* of this series.

9    See Keirsey and Bates, op. cit.; O. Kroeger and J.M. Thuesen, *Type Talk at Work* (New York: Delacorte Press, 1992); and I.B. Myers, *Gifts Differing* (Palo Alto, Calif.: Consulting Psychologists Press, 1980).

10   G.M. Weinberg and D. Weinberg, *General Principles of Systems Design* (New York: Dorset House Publishing, 1988).

11   T.F. Crum, *The Magic of Conflict* (New York: Touchstone/Simon & Schuster, 1987).

12   E. Cross, J.H. Katz, F.A. Miller, and E.W. Seashore, eds., *The Promise of Diversity* (Burr Ridge, Ill.: Irwin Professional Publishing, 1994).

13   Lee Copeland, personal communication, 1994.

14   M. Knowles, *The Adult Learner: A Neglected Species* (New York: Gulf Publishing Co., 1973), pp. 89–91.

15   See *Fortune*, op. cit.

## Chapter 5

1    C.I. Barnard, *The Functions of the Executive* (Cambridge: Harvard University Press, 1938), pp. 4–5.

2    W.E. Deming, in the foreword to M. Walton's *The Deming Management Method* (New York: Dodd, Mead & Co., 1986).

3    See W.B. Cannon, *The Way of an Investigator* (New York: W.W. Norton & Co., 1941), p. 113. Cannon coined the terms "homeostasis" and "the wisdom of the body," which describe the elaborate systems that maintain living organisms.

4    Dan Starr, personal communication.

5    For more on controller models, see Appendix D. See also *Volume 1, Systems Thinking*.

6    Rich Cohen, personal communication, 1994.

7    C. Argyris, *Knowledge for Action: A Guide to Overcoming Barriers to Organizational Change* (San Francisco: Jossey-Bass, 1993).

8    For more on observing nonverbal reactions, see *Volume 2, First-Order Measurement*.

9    See G.M. Weinberg and D. Weinberg, *General Principles of Systems Design* (New York: Dorset House Publishing, 1988).

10   I. Wendel, *Software Maintenance News,* Vol. 9 (1991), pp. 24–25.

11   I'm grateful to Peter de Jager for inspiring this section.

12   See G.M. Weinberg, *Becoming a Technical Leader* (New York: Dorset House Publishing, 1986).

13   See, for example, Walton, op. cit.

14   See *Volume 3, Congruent Action* of this series for an extensive discussion of blaming behavior.

## Chapter 6

1   R. Fulghum, *It Was on Fire When I Lay Down on It* (New York: Villard Books, 1989), p. 6.

2   Adapted from V. Satir, *The New Peoplemaking* (Palo Alto, Calif.: Science and Behavior Books, 1988), p. 71.

## Part III

1   W.E. Deming, in the foreword to M. Walton's *The Deming Management Method* (New York: Dodd, Mead & Co., 1986).

2   See Appendix C.  Note that my cultural patterns resemble the "Maturity Levels" proposed by the Software Engineering Institute (SEI).  This is no coincidence, because both are based on Crosby's work.  The cultural patterns, however, emphasize the role of *management*—which is more or less excluded from the SEI models.

3   P.B. Crosby, *Quality Is Free* (New York: McGraw-Hill, 1979).

## Chapter 7

1   For ways of getting customer information and measuring customer satisfaction, see, for example, D.C. Gause and G.M. Weinberg, *Exploring Requirements: Quality Before Design* (New York: Dorset House Publishing, 1989). Also see W.J. Pardee, *To Satisfy & Delight Your Customer: How to Manage for Customer Value* (New York: Dorset House Publishing, 1996).

2   See C. Jones, *Applied Software Measurement: Assuring Productivity and Quality* (New York: McGraw-Hill, 1991).  Also see *Volume 2, First-Order Measurement.*

3   M. Paulk, C.V. Weber, B. Curtis, and M.B. Chrissis, eds., *The Capability Maturity Model: Guidelines for Improving the Software Process* (Reading, Mass.: Addison-Wesley, 1995).

4   W.E. Deming, *Out of the Crisis* (Cambridge, Mass.: MIT Center for Advanced Engineering Study, 1986).

5   See *Volume 2, First-Order Measurement.*

6   See *Volume 1, Systems Thinking.*

7   See *Volume 2, First-Order Measurement.*

8   The Law of Limiting Factors was formulated by Blackman, an English plant physiologist, circa 1905.

9   M. Doyle and D. Strauss, *How to Make Meetings Work: The New Interaction Method* (Chicago: Playboy Press, 1977).

10   L.J. Spencer, *Winning Through Participation* (Dubuque, Iowa: Kendall/Hunt Publishing, 1989).

11   W. Peña, *Problem Seeking: Architectural Programming Primer,* 3rd ed. (Washington, D.C.: AIA Press, 1987).

12   Gause and Weinberg, op. cit.

13    G. Laborde, *Influencing with Integrity: Management Skills for Communication and Negotiation* (Palo Alto, Calif.: Syntony Publishing, 1984).

14    C.L. Karass, *Give and Take: The Complete Guide to Negotiating Strategies and Tactics* (New York: Thomas Y. Crowell Company, 1974).

15    R. Fisher and W. Ury, *Getting to Yes: Negotiating Agreement Without Giving In* (New York: Penguin Books, 1981).

## Chapter 8

1    See D.C. Gause and G.M. Weinberg, *Are Your Lights On? How to Figure Out What the Problem Really Is* (New York: Dorset House Publishing, 1990).

2    See Appendix A for a brief description of the diagram of effects, or see *Volume 1, Systems Thinking.*

3    J.P. Scott, "Critical Periods in Behavioral Development," *Science,* Vol. 138, No. 3544 (November 30, 1962), pp. 949–57.

4    See W.S. Humphrey, *Managing the Software Process* (Reading, Mass.: Addison-Wesley, 1989).

5    For more on dealing with incongruence, see *Volume 3, Congruent Action.*

6    See V. Satir, J. Banmen, J. Gerber, and M. Gomori, *The Satir Model: Family Therapy and Beyond* (Palo Alto, Calif.: Science and Behavior Books, 1991).

7    For information on rule transformation, see Ibid. Also see G.M. Weinberg, *Becoming a Technical Leader* (New York: Dorset House Publishing, 1986).

## Chapter 9

1    J. Jacobs, *Cities and the Wealth of Nations* (New York: Random House, 1982), p. 221, as quoted in J. Fallows, *More Like Us: Putting America's Native Strengths and Traditional Values to Work to Overcome the Asian Challenge* (Boston: Houghton Mifflin, 1989), p. 55.

2    This chapter is adapted from material taught in the Weinberg, McLendon & Weinberg seminar Congruent Organizational Change Shop.

3    B.W. Boehm, "A Spiral Model of Software Development," *Computer* (May 1988), pp. 61–72.

4    For more information on congruent action, see *Volume 3, Congruent Action.*

5    For ideas on how to identify the customers and other affected people, see D.C. Gause and G.M. Weinberg, *Exploring Requirements: Quality Before Design* (New York: Dorset House Publishing, 1989), and W.J. Pardee, *To Satisfy & Delight Your Customer: How to Manage for Customer Value* (New York: Dorset House Publishing, 1996).

6    For ideas on how to define what part of the context should be preserved, see Gause and Weinberg, op. cit.

7    See Ibid., Chapter 4, "The Tried but Untrue Use of Direct Questions."

8    For information on how to change feedback loops, see *Volume 1, Systems Thinking.* For the specific example given here in Figure 9-10, see Chapter 8 in *Volume 1.*

9 For more on obtaining emotional information, see *Volume 2, First-Order Measurement.*

10 Boehm, op. cit.

## Chapter 10

1 M. DePree, *Leadership Jazz* (New York: Doubleday, 1992), pp. 27–29.

2 See especially *Volume 3, Congruent Action,* Chapter 2, "Choosing Management."

3 For this definition, see *The American Heritage Dictionary of the English Language,* ed. W. Morris (Boston: Houghton Mifflin, 1970).

4 For those readers not familiar with discussion of the Feedback Control Model as described in the earlier volumes, see Appendix D for a summary.

5 W.E. Deming, as quoted in M. Walton's *The Deming Management Method* (New York: Dodd, Mead & Co., 1986), p. 77.

6 S.R. Covey, *The 7 Habits of Highly Effective People: Restoring the Character Ethic* (New York: Fireside/Simon & Schuster, 1989), p. 39.

7 D.A. Norman, *The Psychology of Everyday Things* (New York: Basic Books, 1989), p. 112.

8 K. Tohei, *Ki in Daily Life* (Tokyo: Ki No Kenkyukai H.Q., 1978), p. 110.

9 P.B. Crosby, *Quality Is Free* (New York: McGraw-Hill, 1979).

## Chapter 11

1 S. Beer, *Cybernetics and Management* (New York: John Wiley & Sons, 1959), p. 89.

2 *Datalink* (August 11, 1986).

3 R.R. Whyte, ed., *Engineering Progress Through Trouble* (London: The Institution of Mechanical Engineers, 1975).

4 V. Bignell, G. Peters, and C. Pym, *Catastrophic Failures* (Milton Keynes, England: The Open University Press, 1977).

5 J.E. Eyers and E.G. Nisbett, "Boilers," *Engineering Progress Through Trouble,* ed. R.R. Whyte (London: The Institution of Mechanical Engineers, 1975), pp. 109–15.

6 Tom DeMarco wrote a book with this title. For answers rather different from mine, see T. DeMarco, *Why Does Software Cost So Much? And Other Puzzles of the Information Age* (New York: Dorset House Publishing, 1995).

7 B.W. Boehm, *Software Engineering Economics* (Englewood Cliffs, N.J.: Prentice-Hall, 1981).

8 Ibid., p. 486.

9 Confidential communication from a source inside the telephone industry, 1994.

10 See F.P. Brooks, Jr., "No Silver Bullet: Essence and Accidents of Software Engineering," *Information Processing '86* (North Holland: Elsevier Science Publishers B.V., 1986). Reprinted in *Computer,* Vol. 20, No. 4 (April 1987), pp. 10–19. Also reprinted in T. DeMarco and T. Lister, eds., *Software State-of-the-Art: Selected Papers* (New York: Dorset House Publishing, 1990), pp. 14–29.

11   See, for example, D.C. Gause and G.M. Weinberg, *Exploring Requirements: Quality Before Design* (New York: Dorset House Publishing, 1989), and D.J. Hatley and I.A. Pirbhai, *Strategies for Real-Time System Specification* (New York: Dorset House Publishing, 1987).

12   For the subject of testing, see, for example, W. Hetzel, *The Complete Guide to Software Testing* (Wellesley, Mass.: QED Information Sciences, 1984); or B. Beizer, *Software Testing Techniques*, 2nd ed. (New York: Van Nostrand Reinhold, 1992). For technical reviews, see, for example, D.P. Freedman and G.M. Weinberg, *Handbook of Walkthroughs, Inspections, and Technical Reviews*, 3rd ed. (New York: Dorset House Publishing, 1990); or T. Gilb and D. Graham, *Software Inspection* (Reading, Mass.: Addison-Wesley, 1993).

13   For a discussion of analysis and design documents, see J. Robertson and S. Robertson, *Complete Systems Analysis* (New York: Dorset House Publishing, 1994).

14   For the subject of configuration control, see W.A. Babich, *Software Configuration Management* (Reading, Mass.: Addison-Wesley, 1986).

15   On the subject of analysis and design, see, for example, B. Cox, *Object Oriented Programming: An Evolutionary Approach* (Reading, Mass.: Addison-Wesley, 1986); R.C. Linger, H.D. Mills, and B.I. Witt, *Structured Programming: Theory and Practice* (Reading, Mass.: Addison-Wesley, 1979); H. Mills, R. Linger, and A. Hevner, *Information Systems Analysis and Design* (Trov, Mo.: Academic Press, 1986); Gerald M. Weinberg, *Rethinking Systems Analysis and Design* (New York: Dorset House Publishing, 1988); M. Page-Jones, *The Practical Guide to Structured Systems Design*, 2nd ed. (Englewood Cliffs, N.J.: Prentice-Hall, 1988); M. Page-Jones, *What Every Programmer Should Know About Object-Oriented Design* (New York: Dorset House Publishing, 1995); S. McConnell, *Code Complete* (Redmond, Wash.: Microsoft Press, 1993); or J. Robertson and S. Robertson, *Complete Systems Analysis* (New York: Dorset House Publishing, 1994).

16   For a full discussion of congruent action, see *Volume 3, Congruent Action*.

17   I.D. Yalom, *The Theory and Practice of Group Psychotherapy* (New York: Basic Books, 1975), pp. 128–29.

## Chapter 12

1   R.E. Canning, "Issues in Programming Management," *EDP Analyzer*, Vol. 12, No. 4 (1974), p. 13.

2   For a definition and discussion of Fault Feedback Ratio, see *Volume 2, First-Order Measurement*.

3   See H.D. Mills, M. Dyer, and R.C. Linger, "Cleanroom Software Engineering," *IEEE Software* (September 1987).

4   See D.P. Freedman and G.M. Weinberg, *Handbook of Walkthroughs, Inspections, and Technical Reviews*, 3rd ed. (New York: Dorset House Publishing, 1990).

5   See, for example, S. Robertson, "Quality Time," *IEEE Software*, Vol. 12, No. 3 (July 1995), p. 95.

6   See *Volume 2, First-Order Measurement*.

7   For a reminder about software engineering cultural patterns, see Appendix C.

8   P. Koester, "The Use of Metrics in Optimizing a Software Engineering Process," *CrossTalk*, Vol. 7, No. 11 (1994), pp. 5–8.


## Chapter 13

1   J. Fallows, *More Like Us: Putting America's Native Strengths and Traditional Values to Work to Overcome the Asian Challenge* (Boston: Houghton Mifflin, 1989), p. 13.

2   Based on an August 1993 news item, this fictionalized version conveys a sadly typical event.

3   H.D. Leeds and G.M. Weinberg, *Computer Programming Fundamentals* (New York: McGraw-Hill, 1961).

4   B.W. Kernighan and P.J. Plauger, *The Elements of Programming Style* (New York: McGraw-Hill, 1974).

5   Also see Appendix C for a brief description of the software engineering cultural patterns.

6   This scenario is developed in more detail in S.M. Scott, "A Glimpse of IS Heaven," *American Programmer*, Vol. 6, No. 12 (1993), pp. 3–9.

7   See Chapter 6 in M. Paulk, C.V. Weber, B. Curtis, and M.B. Chrissis, eds., *The Capability Maturity Model: Guidelines for Improving the Software Process* (Reading, Mass.: Addison-Wesley, 1995).

8   H. Petroski, *To Engineer Is Human* (New York: St. Martin's Press, 1985), p. 26.

9   For other examples of the relationship between number of customers and culture, see *Volume 1, Systems Thinking*.

10  Payson Hall, personal communication, 1995.

11  Stuart Scott, personal communication, 1994.

12  J.A. Conger, *Learning to Lead* (San Francisco: Jossey-Bass, 1992), pp. 189–90.

13  M. DePree, *Leadership Jazz* (New York: Doubleday, 1992), pp. 44–45.

14  If your answer is no, then you ought to read F.P. Brooks, Jr., *The Mythical Man-Month* (Reading, Mass.: Addison-Wesley, 1975).

15  DePree, op. cit., pp. 218–19.


## Chapter 14

1   John F. Horne, III, personal communication, 1995.

2   B. Purchia, "Transforming the Software Environment at Applicon," unpublished report, 1993.

3   Barbara Purchia, personal communication, 1995.

4   Purchia, op. cit.

5   E.A. Cohen and J. Gooch, *Military Misfortunes* (New York: Free Press, 1990), p. 235.


## Chapter 15

1   W. Rybczynski, *The Most Beautiful House in the World* (New York: Penguin Books, 1989), p. 64.

2    R.W. Selby, V.R. Basili, and F.T. Baker, "Cleanroom Software Development: An Empirical Evaluation," *IEEE Transactions on Software Engineering*, Vol. SE-13, No. 9 (September 1987), pp. 18–23. Reprinted in T. DeMarco and T. Lister, eds., *Software State-of-the-Art: Selected Papers* (New York: Dorset House Publishing, 1990, pp. 256–76), p. 258.

3    D.L. Parnas and P.C. Clements, "A Rational Design Process: How and Why to Fake It," *IEEE Transactions on Software Engineering*, Vol. SE-12, No. 2 (February 1986), pp. 251–57. Reprinted in T. DeMarco and T. Lister, eds., *Software State-of-the-Art: Selected Papers* (New York: Dorset House Publishing, 1990, pp. 346–57), p. 356.

4    For further discussion of these various forms, see *Volume 2, First-Order Measurement*.

5    Parnas and Clements, op. cit.

6    Brian Richter, on the CompuServe Management Forum, 1994.

## Chapter 16

1    Congresswoman Pat Schroeder, on the inability of government officials to cut costs by making choices.

2    For techniques of cost and benefit estimation, see *Volume 2, First-Order Measurement*.

3    D.L. Parnas and P.C. Clements, "A Rational Design Process: How and Why to Fake It," *IEEE Transactions on Software Engineering*, Vol. SE-12, No. 2 (February 1986), pp. 251–57. Reprinted in T. DeMarco and T. Lister, eds., *Software State-of-the-Art: Selected Papers* (New York: Dorset House Publishing, 1990, pp. 346–57), p. 356.

4    For more on the linking of requirements to true business needs, see D.C. Gause and G.M. Weinberg, *Exploring Requirements: Quality Before Design* (New York: Dorset House Publishing, 1989).

5    Tom Watson, personal communication, 1994.

6    Gause and Weinberg, op. cit.

## Chapter 17

1    N.R. Augustine, *Augustine's Laws* (New York: Viking/Penguin, 1986), pp. 65–66.

2    For several ways to calculate the benefits of a project, see *Volume 2, First-Order Measurement*.

3    One that I favor is B.W. Boehm's *Tutorial: Software Risk Management* (Washington, D.C.: IEEE Computer Society Press, 1989).

4    S.R. Covey, *The 7 Habits of Highly Effective People: Restoring the Character Ethic* (New York: Fireside/Simon & Schuster, 1989), p. 223.

5    J. Mogilensky, "Key Process Area Spotlight: Requirements Management," π *Strategies*, Vol. 1, No. 1 (1993), pp. 9–13.

6    See, for example, "Software Failures," a special issue of *American Programmer*, Vol. 8, No. 7 (July 1995).

7   The references given throughout this book have been chosen with an eye to providing the reader with a number of sources of such guidelines.

8   For results on interruptions and context-switching, see T. DeMarco and T. Lister, *Peopleware: Productive Projects and Teams* (New York: Dorset House Publishing, 1987).

9   For a good exposition of management reviews at their best, plus some of the pitfalls, see M. Page-Jones, *Practical Project Management* (New York: Dorset House Publishing, 1985).

10  R. Thomsett, "Project Pathology: A Study of Project Failures," *American Programmer*, Vol. 8, No. 7 (July 1995), pp. 8–16.

11  Rich Cohen, personal communication, 1994.

12  See *Volume 2, First-Order Measurement*.

13  R. Fulghum, *Uh-Oh* (New York: Villard Books, 1991), p. 25.

14  As reported in *Technology Review* (August/September 1993), p. 62.

15  T. Parker, *Rules of Thumb* (Boston: Houghton Mifflin, 1983), p. 22.

16  Parker, op. cit., p. 109.

17  Mark Manduke, personal communication, 1994.

## Chapter 18

1   C.E. Walston and C.P. Felix, "A Method of Programming Measurement and Estimation," *IBM Systems Journal*, Vol. 16, No. 1 (1977), pp. 54–73.

2   See, for example, A. Hevner, S.A. Becker, and L.B. Pedowitz, "Integrated CASE for Cleanroom Development," *IEEE Software*, Vol. 9, No. 2 (March 1992), pp. 69–76.

3   See B.W. Boehm and P.N. Papaccio, "Understanding and Controlling Software Costs," *IEEE Transactions on Software Engineering*, Vol. 4, No. 10 (October 1988), pp. 1462–77. Reprinted in T. DeMarco and T. Lister, eds., *Software State-of-the-Art: Selected Papers* (New York: Dorset House Publishing, 1990, pp. 31–60), p. 40.

4   V.R. Basili and A.J. Turner, "Iterative Enhancement: A Practical Technique for Software Development," *IEEE Transactions on Software Engineering*, Vol. SE-1, No. 12 (December 1975), pp. 390–96.

5   For more on this planning process, see *Volume 2, First-Order Measurement*.

6   Bent Adsersen, personal communication, 1992.

7   For learning how to see yourself as others see you, through their filters, see C.N. Seashore, E.W. Seashore, and G.M. Weinberg, *What Did You Say? The Art of Giving and Receiving Feedback* (Columbia, Md.: Bingham House Books, 1991).

## Chapter 19

1   L.R. Graham, *The Ghost of the Executed Engineer: Technology and the Fall of the Soviet Union* (Cambridge: Harvard University Press, 1993), excerpted in "Red Elephants," a sidebar to L.R. Graham, "Palchinsky's Travels," *MIT's Technology Review* (November/December 1993), pp. 26–27.

2    This is a reproduction of Figure 5.8 from *Volume 2, First-Order Measurement*, p. 79.

3    Standard task units were introduced in *Volume 2, First-Order Measurement*. See especially Figure 17.1, p. 272.

4    See, for example, P. Koester and T. Peterson, "Fault Estimation and Removal from the Space Shuttle Software," *American Programmer*, Vol. 7, No. 4 (1994), pp. 13–21.

5    Capers Jones, personal communication, 1994.

6    N.R. Augustine, *Augustine's Laws* (New York: Viking/Penguin, 1986), p. 239.

7    See, for example, J. Johnson, "Creating Chaos," *American Programmer*, Vol. 8, No. 7 (1995), pp. 3–7.

8    The Helpful Model says, "No matter how it looks, everyone is trying to be helpful." For more on this model and concept, see, for example, *Volume 3, Congruent Action*, p. 208.

9    For a more detailed description of personal life lines, see G.M. Weinberg, *Becoming a Technical Leader* (New York: Dorset House Publishing, 1986).

## Chapter 20

1    See especially Chapter 9, "Why It's Always Hard to Steer," in *Volume 1, Systems Thinking.*

2    R. Thomsett, "Project Pathology: A Study of Project Failures," *American Programmer*, Vol. 8, No. 7 (1995), p. 13.

3    For more on "featuring failure," see G.M. Weinberg, *The Secrets of Consulting* (New York: Dorset House Publishing, 1985).

4    For a great deal more on this subject, see N. Karten, *Managing Expectations* (New York: Dorset House Publishing, 1994).

5    J.G. Gavin, Jr., "Fly Me to the Moon," *Technology Review* (July 1994), pp. 61–68.

6    P. Rassow, "Some Social and Cultural Consequences of the Surge of Population in the Nineteenth Century," *Population Movements in Modern European History*, ed. H. Moller (New York: Macmillan, 1964), p. 63.

## Chapter 21

1    Personal communication from an anonymous client, circa 1988.

2    W.A. Babich, *Software Configuration Management: Coordination for Team Productivity* (Reading, Mass.: Addison-Wesley, 1986), p. 94.

3    V. Mosley et al., "Software Configuration Management Tools: Getting Bigger, Better, and Bolder," *CrossTalk*, Vol. 9, No. 1 (1996), pp. 6–10.

4    James Robertson, personal communication, 1995.

5    D.L. Parnas, "On the Criteria to Be Used in Decomposing Systems into Modules," *Communications of the ACM*, Vol. 15, No. 12 (1972).

6    C. Billings, J. Clifton, B. Kolkhorst, E. Lee, and W.B. Wingert, "Journey to a Mature Software Process," *IBM Systems Journal*, Vol. 33, No. 1 (1994), pp. 46–61.

7    See *Volume 2, First-Order Measurement*.

8   These first three examples are quotes from Babich, op. cit., p. 94.
9   J.E. Gordon, *Structures: or, Why Things Don't Fall Down* (New York: Da Capo Press, 1981), p. 93.
10  D. Eddy, "The Secrets of Software Maintenance," *American Programmer*, Vol. 7, No. 3 (1994), pp. 7–11.


## Chapter 22

1   W. Rybczynski, *The Most Beautiful House in the World* (New York: Penguin Books, 1989), pp. 38–39.
2   Harlan Mills, personal communication, 1992.
3   Ibid.
4   W.W. Caudill, *Architecture by Team* (New York: Van Nostrand Reinhold, 1971), p. 167.
5   T.L. Magliozzi, "If It Ain't Broke, Don't Break It," *MIT's Technology Review*, October 1992, pp. 72–73.
6   See *Volume 2, First-Order Measurement.*
7   N.R. Augustine, *Augustine's Laws* (New York: Viking/Penguin, 1986), p. 138.
8   W.E. Deming, *Out of the Crisis* (Cambridge, Mass.: MIT Center for Advanced Engineering Study, 1986).
9   Teresa Home, personal communication, 1993.
10  For more on the subject of configuration complexity, see especially *Volume 1, Systems Thinking,* Section 11.4.
11  Payson Hall, personal communication, 1994.
12  H. Mills, as quoted in an interview in *The Dorset House Quarterly*, Vol. II, No. 2 (April 1992), p. 7.


## Chapter 23

1   N. Zvegintzov and J. Jones, eds., *Software Maintenance Technology*, Release 3.1 (Los Altos, Calif.: Software Maintenance News, 1992).
2   See Appendix F for more information on the Keirsey-Bates temperaments.
3   For more on the concept of furniture police, see T. DeMarco and T. Lister, *Peopleware: Productive Projects and Teams* (New York: Dorset House Publishing, 1987), pp. 37–41.
4   For many ideas on simple measurements, see *Volume 2, First-Order Measurement.*
5   See *Volume 1, Systems Thinking,* pp. 154–55.
6   Ibid., pp. 192ff.
7   Peg Ofstead, personal communication, 1994.


## Part V: Epilogue

1   D. Brin, *The Postman* (New York: Bantam Books, 1985), p. 267.
2   H. Petroski, *To Engineer Is Human* (New York: St. Martin's Press, 1985), p. *xiii.*

## Appendix A

1  For a more detailed description, see *Volume 1, Systems Thinking.*

## Appendix B

1  V. Satir et al., *The Satir Model: Family Therapy and Beyond* (Palo Alto, Calif.: Science and Behavior Books, 1991).

## Appendix C

1  P.B. Crosby, *Quality Is Free* (New York: McGraw-Hill, 1979), p. 43.
2  R.A. Radice, P.E. Harding, and R.W. Phillips, "A Programming Process Study," *IBM Systems Journal*, Vol. 24, No. 2 (1985), pp. 91-101.
3  W.S. Humphrey, *Managing the Software Process* (Reading, Mass.: Addison-Wesley, 1989).
4  B. Curtis, "The Human Element in Software Quality," *Proceedings of the Monterey Conference on Software Quality* (Cambridge, Mass.: Software Productivity Research, 1990).
5  See *Volume 1, Systems Thinking.*

## Appendix D

1  N. Wiener, *Cybernetics, or Control and Communication in the Animal and the Machine,* 2nd ed. (Cambridge, Mass.: MIT Press, 1961).

## Appendix F

1  If you want to fully understand why these four combinations are singled out, consult D. Keirsey and M. Bates, *Please Understand Me: Character & Temperament Types,* 4th ed. (Del Mar, Calif.: Prometheus Nemesis Book Co., 1984), p. 70.

# Listing of
# Laws, Rules, and Principles

*The Affirmation Challenge for Becoming a Change Artist:* Each and every day, give one affirmation to one person. (p. 99)

*The Assumption of Fixed Requirements:* The assumption that developers should have unchanging requirements before starting any project. (p. 262)

*Augustine's Law of Insatiable Appetite:* The last ten percent of performance generates one-third of the cost and two-thirds of the problems. (p. 399)

*Augustine's Ratio of Test Failures:* ". . . the incidence of test failures is directly proportional to the square of the size of the crowd multiplied by the rank of the senior observing official." (p. 346)

*The Basic Principles of Cybernetic Management:* Act early, act small, using more-or-less continuous feedback. (p. 307)

*Brooks's Law:* Adding X percent to the staff will not generally speed the schedule by X percent. (p. 302)

*Cannon's Principle of Structure and Function:* "structure and function are inseparably related." (p. 71)

*Copeland's Law of Discontinuity:* A discontinuity is an opportunity to stop doing old things and start doing new things. (p. 66)

*The Culture/Process Principle:* Whatever you can safely assume in the culture, you don't have to specify in your process description. (p. 230)

*Deming's Fifth Deadly Disease:* "running a company on visible figures alone." (p. 117)

*The Eleventh Commandment of Technology Transfer:* In times of trial, always remember the Helpful Model. (p. 423)

*The $50 Million Rule of Management Error:* If it's a $50 million error, then the management at the $50 million level must be responsible. (p. 189)

*The First Law of Technology Transfer:* Long-range good tends to be sacrificed to short-range good. (p. 414)

*The Helpful Model:* Most of the time, in spite of appearances, everybody is trying to be helpful. (p. 368)

*Jones's Law:* Those parts of the product that don't go through the entire development process will cause 90 percent of your problems. (p. 302)

*The Law of Limiting Factors:* When a number of conditions are necessary to a process, its rate is controlled by the least favorable of these conditions. (p. 120)

*The Loop Rule for Plans:* Never use loops in a plan. (p. 344)

*The Loop Rule for Process Descriptions:* Never use loops in a process description. (p. 343)

*The Measurability Principle:* Anything you don't measure will be out of your control. (p. 221)

*Mills's Principle of Design:* The goal is not to prove programs correct; the goal is to write correct programs. (p. 395)

*Mills's Principle of Understandable Code:* It's easier to think of what might make a program right than to think of all the things that might make it wrong. (p. 395)

*Minot's Law, Extended to Organizational Growth:* Management's efforts to raise quality by successful organization may succeed for a while, but may also produce a more complex organization, which becomes harder to organize for additional improvements. Thus, the current changes eventually become growth-rate-limiting structures for future changes. (p. 132)

*The MOI Model:* Evaluate the **M**otivation, **O**rganization, and **I**nformation resources required for implementation of a plan. (p. 167)

*The Newtonian Model Lessons, Applied to People Management:* When you push in one direction, people may move in the opposite direction. When you push harder, people may move less easily. When you push in one direction, people may move in a totally unexpected direction. When you push less, people may move more easily. When you push too fast, they may shatter—like glass when it is struck, rather than pushed. (p. 12)

*The Newtonian Model Principles:* The bigger the system you want to change, the harder you must push. The faster the change you want, the harder you must push. To change in a certain direction, you must push in that direction. Push works both ways. (p. 10)

*The Paradox Rule:* If there is no paradox that the design must resolve, you don't understand the problem. (p. 402)

*The PLASTIC Model:* **P**lan to the **L**evel of **A**cceptable **S**table **T**alent **I**n **C**ompleting Projects. (p. 165)

*The Principle of Attraction:* People will volunteer their services when they see people doing something that seems worthwhile. (p. 419)

*The Principle of Similitude, Applied to the Growing Organization:* As the organization grows, its relationship with the outside is strained as it tries to maintain its internal viability. (p. 135)

*Process Improvement Lessons:* Process improvement must involve all levels of the organization (p. 252). Individual issues often underlie the toughest improvement situations. Cultural changes will involve upper managers. You can change the logical process first, but consider this a test to see if the problem is entirely logical. To address emotional problems, you'll need to get under the surface to the layers of information protected by the cultural rules governing what's not okay to talk about. Be careful that changes are not made in a blaming way. A policy of not blaming does not mean a policy of placating. (p. 253)

*The Product Principle:* Products may be programs, but programs are not products. (p. 224)

*The Reality Principle:* Nothing is real until it has passed independent review. (p. 220)

*The Right Product Principle:* Anything not worth doing is not worth doing right. (p. 272)

*Rule of Decision Making in the Chaos Stage:* Chaos is definitely not the time to make long-term decisions. (p. 24)

*The Rule of Three:* If you can't think of three circumstances in which the design might fail, you haven't thought enough about it. (p. 402)

*Satir on Resistance to a Foreign Element:* Familiarity is always more powerful than comfort. (p. 22)

*The Second Law of Technology Transfer:* Short-range feasibility tends to be sacrificed to long-range perfection. (p. 414)

*Simple Rules for Change Artistry Management:* Don't blame. Give and receive information. Don't placate. Take no job that you don't believe in. Cut out the superreasonable slogans and exhortations. No tricks. Means *are* ends. Trust, and merit trust. Never stop training yourself in change skills. Never stop seeking improvements right around you. Remember that you were born little, just like everybody else. Just because you have a title, you haven't ceased to be a human being. Be an example of what you want others to be. (p. 81)

*The Software Rule of Two:* When estimating your labor for a software job, make your best guess and multiply it by two. (p. 310)

*The Square Law of Computation:* Adding X percent to the schedule will not accommodate X percent increase in functionality. (p. 302)

*The Stability Principle:* Every part of a process must be a controlled system. (p. 216)

*The Swiss-Style Rule of Thumb for Assigning Control Responsibilities:* a) Push every decision down to the lowest level that has the information and tools to make that decision; b) Push all tools and information to the lowest level that will take them. (p. 186)

*The System Behavior Principle:* Behavior depends on both state and input. (p. 445)

*The Ten Commandments of Technology Transfer:* Thou shalt have a plan to lead thee out of the wilderness. Thou shalt not worship thy plan. Thou shalt ask for no person in vain. Thou shalt not work seven days a week. Thou shalt honor thy users and listen to them. Thou shalt not kill support for change. Thou shalt not adulterate the work. Thou shalt not steal resources from the work. Thou shalt not bear false witness against thy plan. Thou shalt not covet thy neighbor's optimal technology. (p. 418)

*The Theory of Critical Periods of Development:* Early small decisions about the organization may have an enormous impact on the ultimate success of the organization. (p. 133)

*The Visibility Principle:* Everything in the project must be visible at all times. (p. 219)

*The Waterfall Model Rule:* Always use the Waterfall Model *when it applies.* (p. 316)

*The Zeroth Law Corollary:* The less closely you have to meet requirements and the more your requirements approximate the Assumption of Fixed Requirements, the easier it will be for you to manage. (p. 264)

*The Zeroth Law of Quality:* If you don't care about quality, you can meet any other requirement. (p. 264)

*The Zeroth Law of Software:* If the software doesn't have to work, you can meet any other requirement. (p. 264)

*The Zeroth Law of Software Engineering:* If you don't have to meet requirements, management is no problem. (p. 223)

# Author Index

# Subject Index